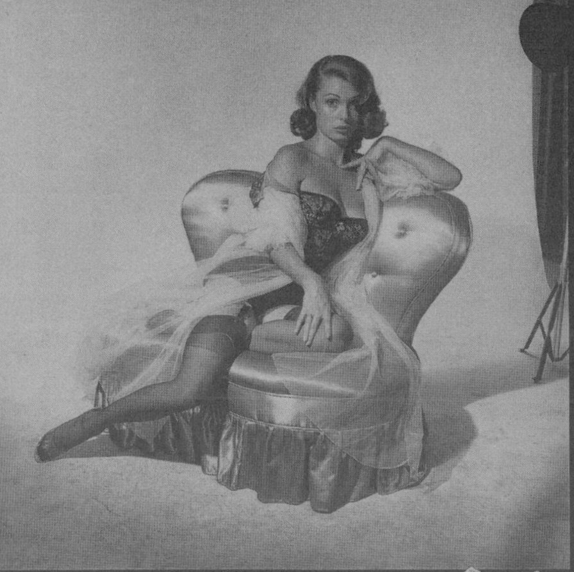
340

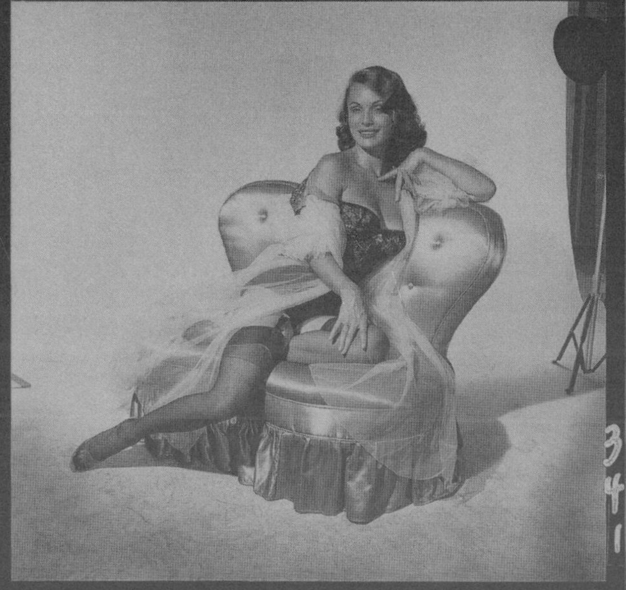
341

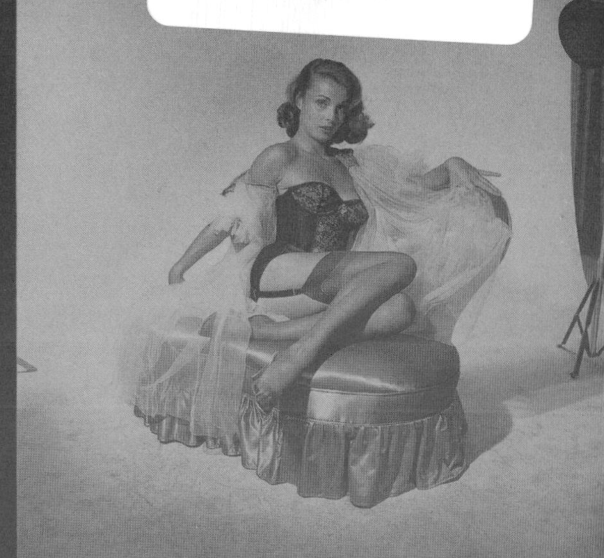
342

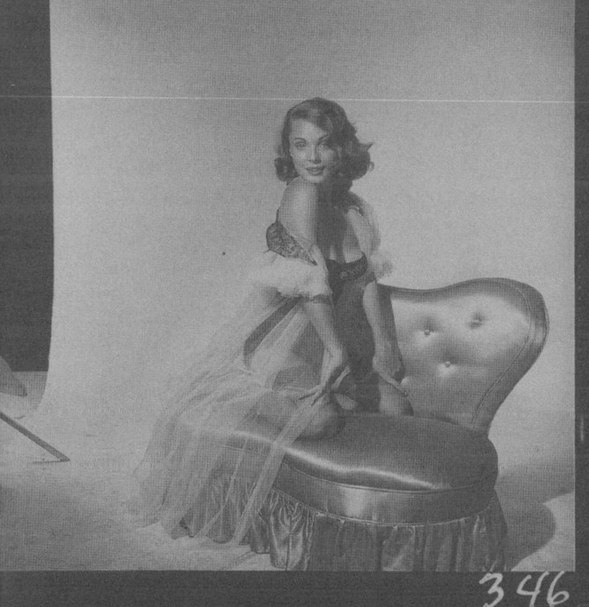
346

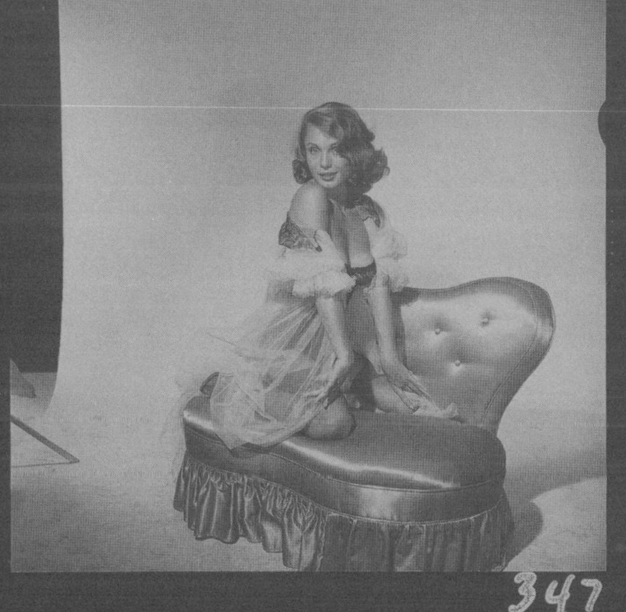
347

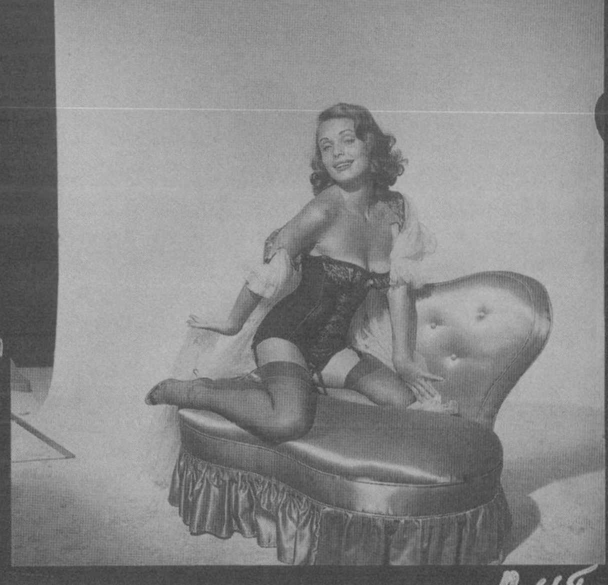
348

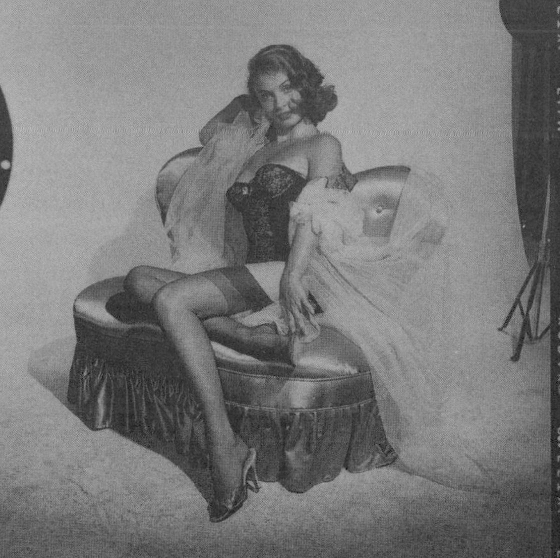
KODAK SAFETY FILM
352

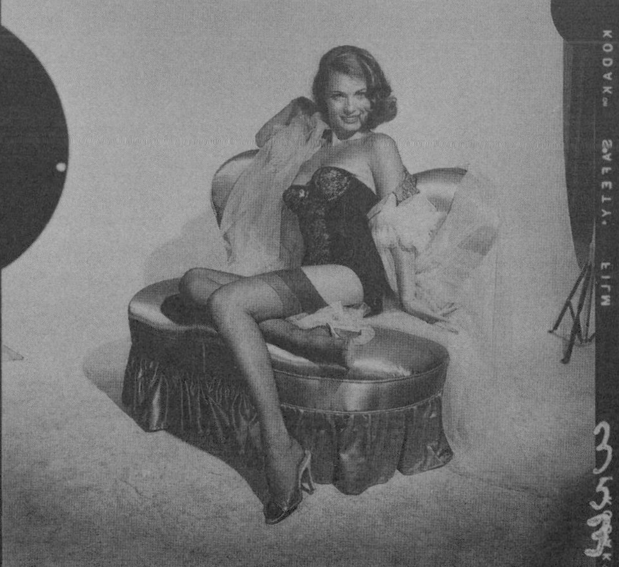
KODAK SAFETY FILM

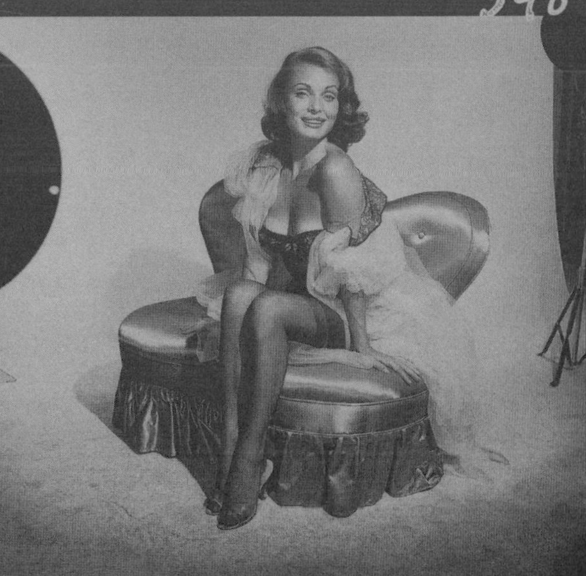
354

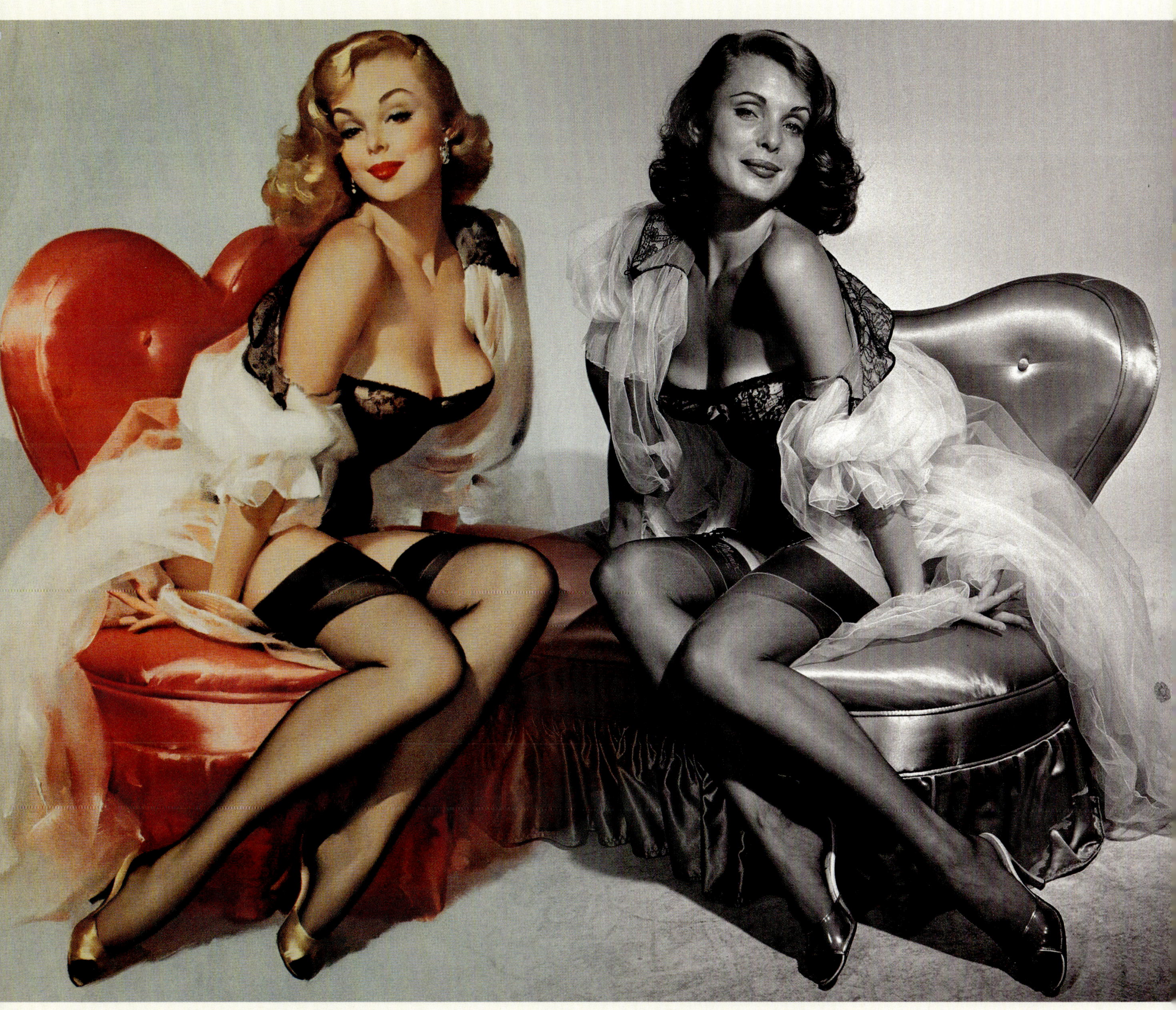

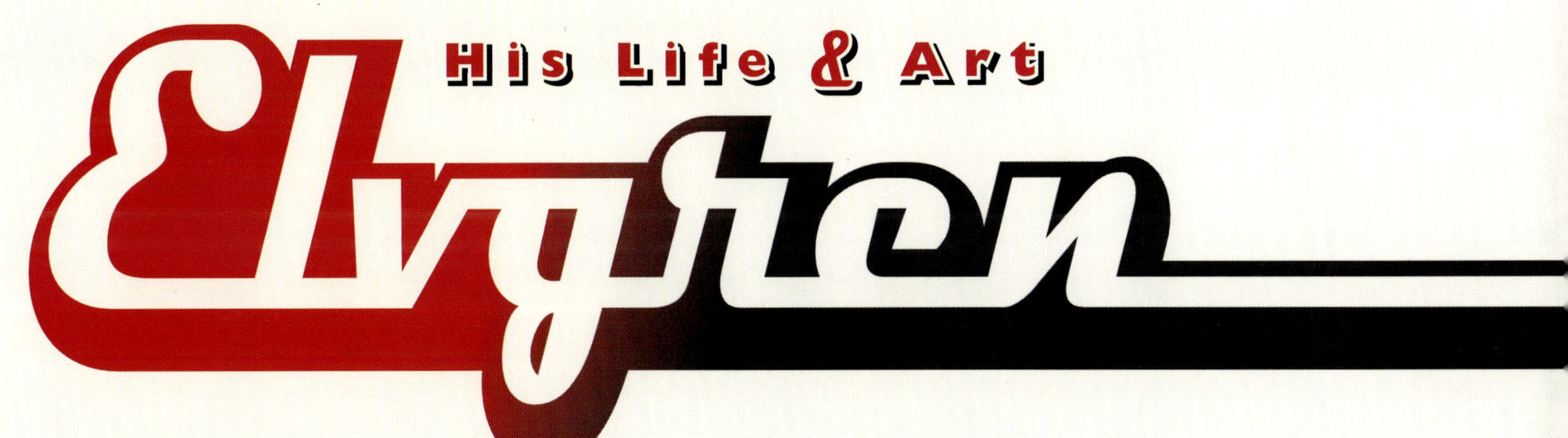

Max Allan Collins & Drake Elvgren

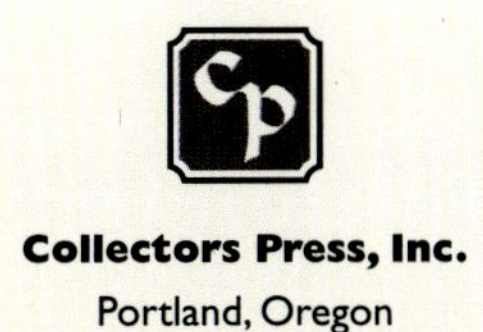

Collectors Press, Inc.
Portland, Oregon

Designed and typeset by *Principia Graphica*

Edited by *Ann Granning Bennett*

Distributed to the U.S. book trade by *Universe Publishing*, a division of Rizzoli International Publications, Inc. through St. Martin's Press, 175 Fifth Avenue, New York, New York 10010

Distributed in Canada by *McClelland & Stewart*

The publisher extends special thanks for help in assembling information to complete this book to *LeRoy Darwin, Jim Camperos, Illustration House, N.Y., Art Amsie*, and *William Klinkey*.

Author's Note:
In addition to Drake Elvgren's reminiscences, both Karen and Gillette Elvgren, Jr., shared their memories for this portrait of their father. Vintage materials, including articles in *Modern Man, Photography Handbook* and *Figure Quarterly* provided further background, as did clippings and correspondence in a family scrapbook provided by Drake; contemporary articles by Marianne Ohl Phillips and Charles G. Martignette, two acknowledged experts in the pin-up field, filled in gaps — my thanks to them both. Martignette's book *The Great American Pin-Up* (co-authored with Louis K. Meisel) was also helpful, as was *A Dream of Santa: Haddon Sundblom's Vision* published by Staples and Charles (no author listed). Co-author Collins also drew from his previously published Collectors Press "Vignettes" on Gil Elvgren, as well as his Kitchen Sink trading card set, "Painted Ladies."

Printed in China

Library of Congress Cataloging-in-Publication Data

Collins, Max Allan.
Elvgren — his life & art / Max Allan Collins & Drake Elvgren. —
1st American ed.
p. cm.
Includes bibliographical references.
ISBN 1-888054-05-0. — ISBN 1-888054-17-4 (limited ed.)
1. Elvgren, Gillette. 2. Painters — United States — Biography.
3. Women in art. 4. Pin-up art — United States. I. Elvgren, Drake,
1944– . II. Title.
ND237.E585C65 1998
759.13
[B] — DC21 97-51938
CIP

First American Edition

10 9 8 7 6 5 4 3 2

Contents

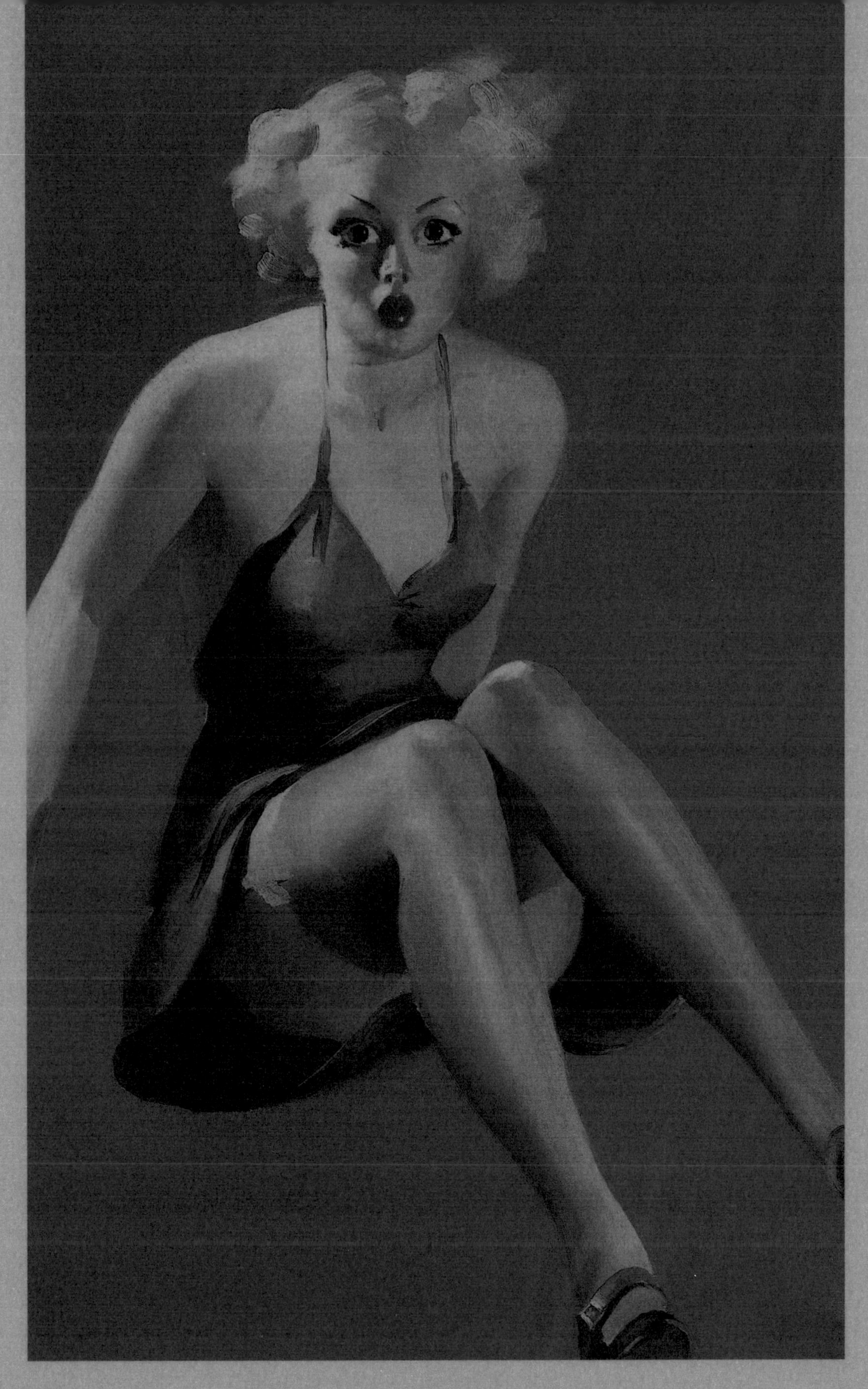

1930s Portfolio

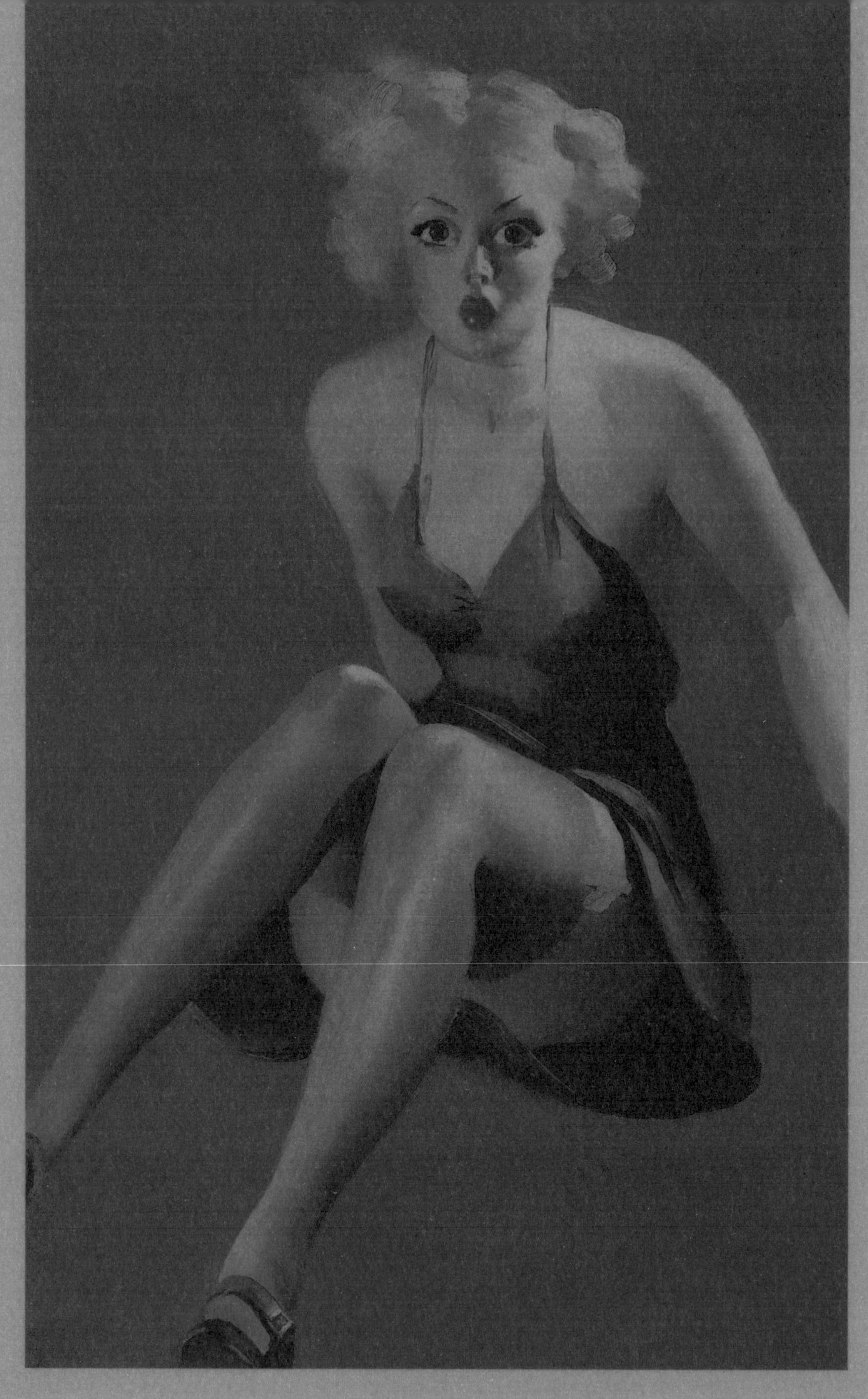

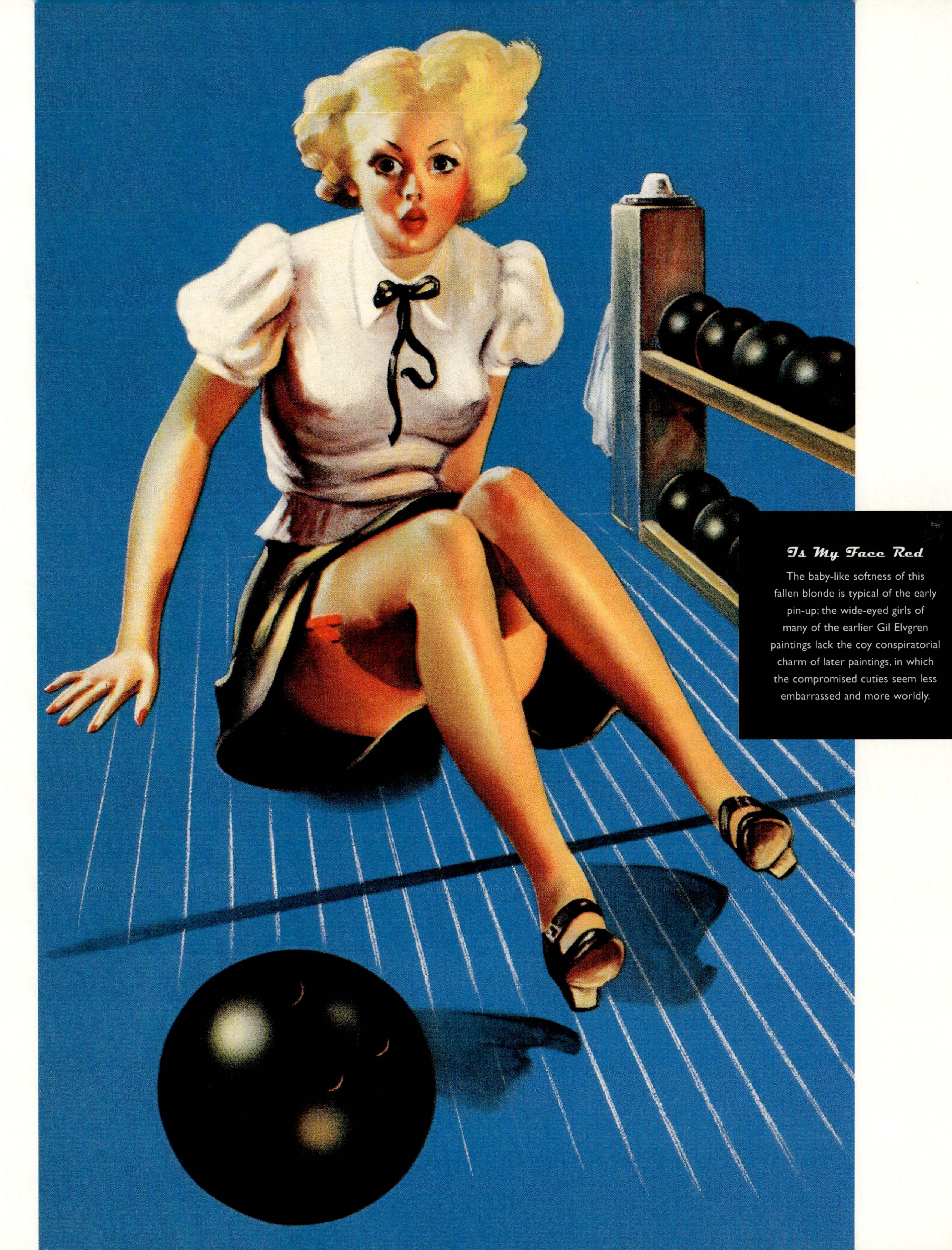

Is My Face Red

The baby-like softness of this fallen blonde is typical of the early pin-up; the wide-eyed girls of many of the earlier Gil Elvgren paintings lack the coy conspiratorial charm of later paintings, in which the compromised cuties seem less embarrassed and more worldly.

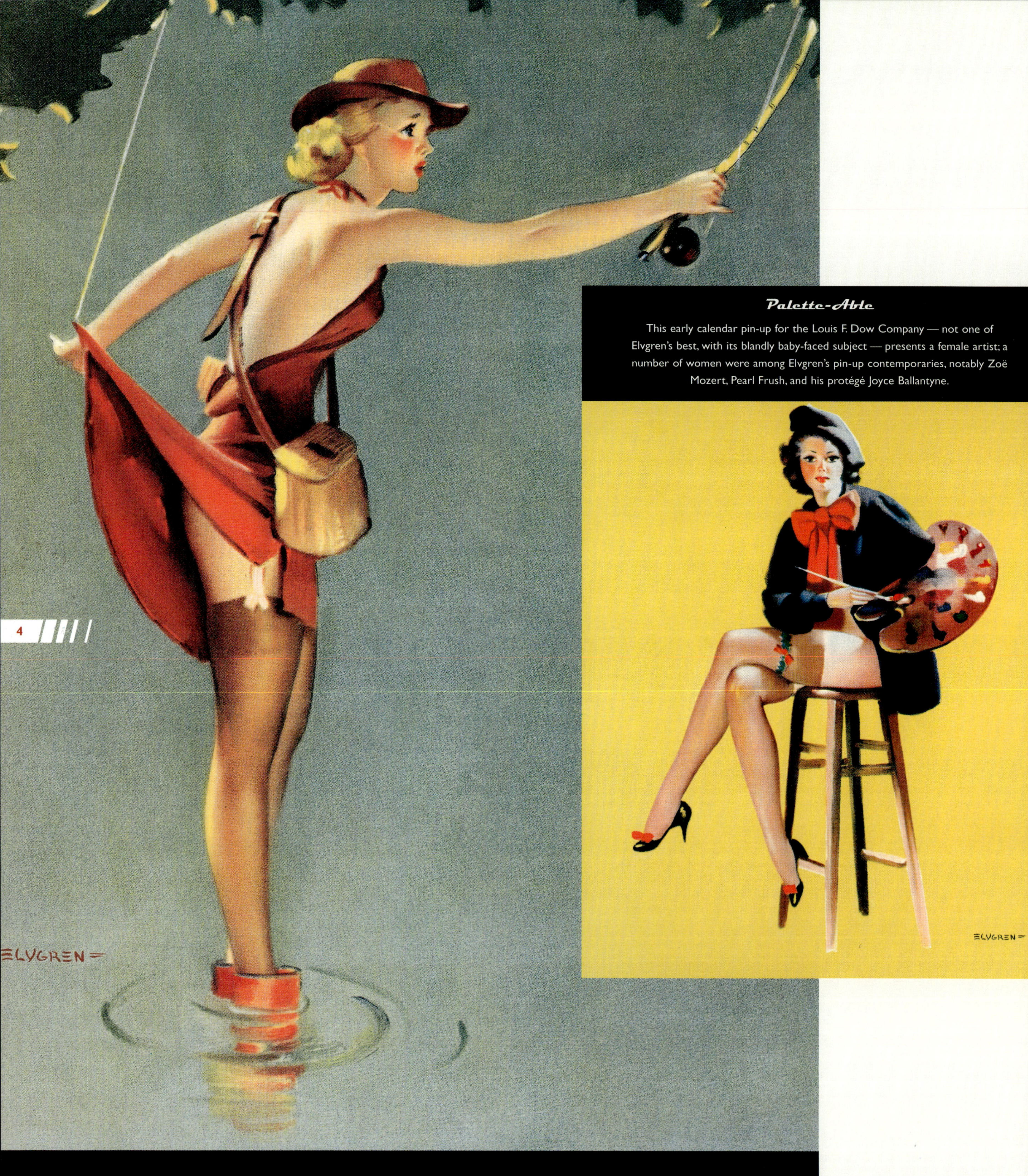

Palette-Able

This early calendar pin-up for the Louis F. Dow Company — not one of Elvgren's best, with its blandly baby-faced subject — presents a female artist; a number of women were among Elvgren's pin-up contemporaries, notably Zoë Mozert, Pearl Frush, and his protégé Joyce Ballantyne.

A Good Hook-Up

One of the better of the earliest Dow pin-ups, the subject still has that baby-faced, unformed look, but an emerging pin-up genius is revealed in the lovely rendering, the unusual and thoughtfully composed design and the comical dilemma that has not yet occurred to our blonde fisher-gal.

Out on a Limb

Early, formative, but what form! One of Elvgren's most strikingly designed art deco pin-ups.

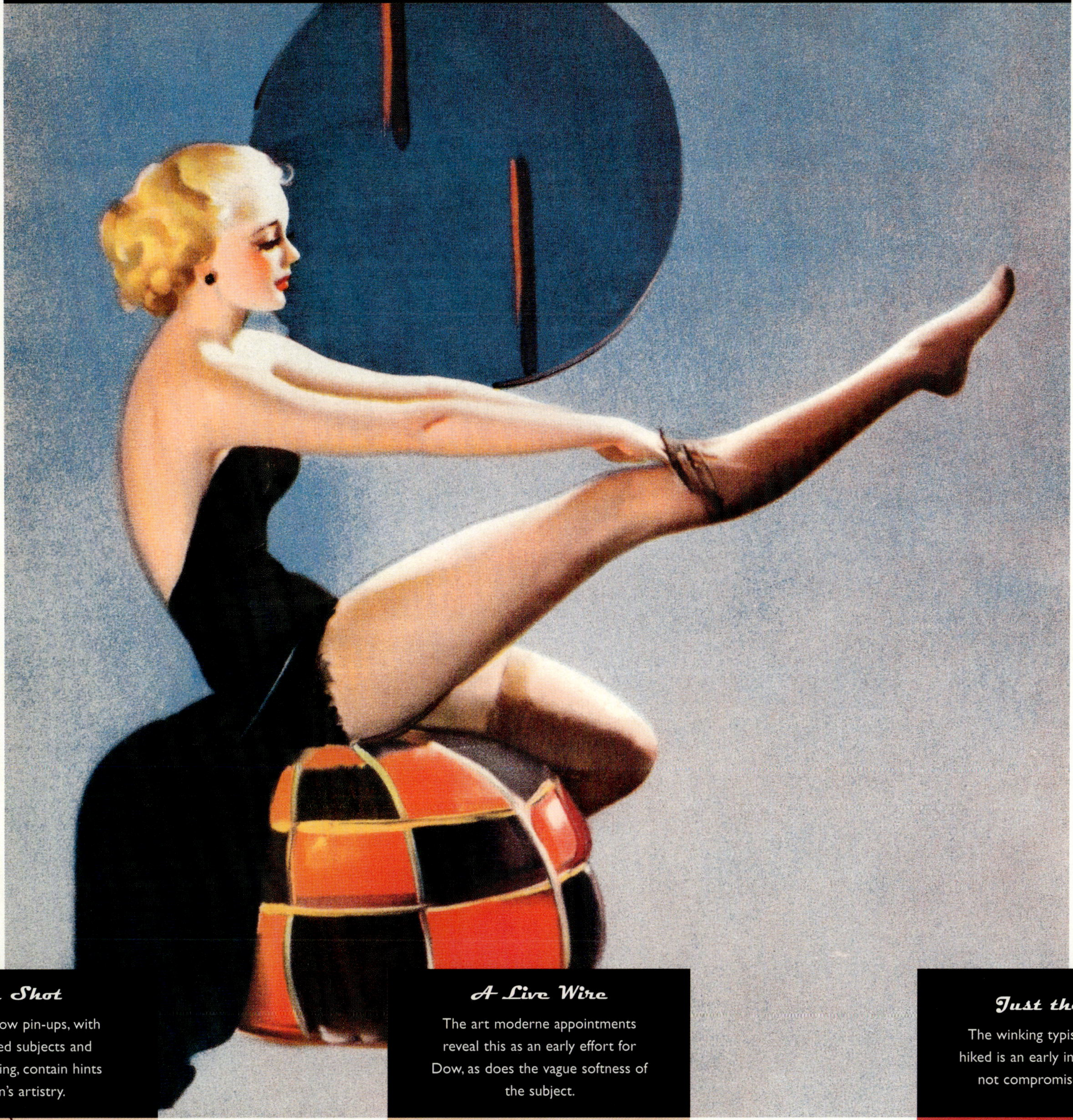

Sure Shot

The earliest Dow pin-ups, with their doll-faced subjects and absurd costuming, contain hints of Elvgren's artistry.

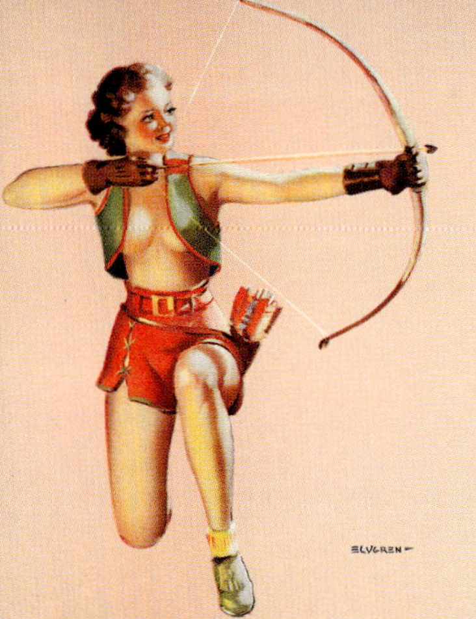

A Live Wire

The art moderne appointments reveal this as an early effort for Dow, as does the vague softness of the subject.

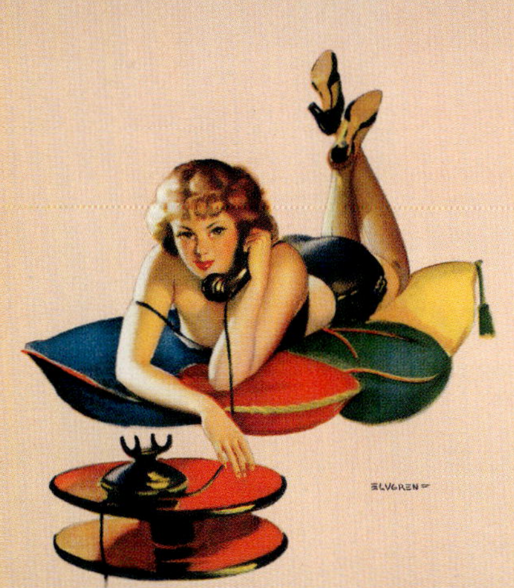

Just the Type

The winking typist with her skirt hiked is an early instance of a cutie, not compromised, but willing.

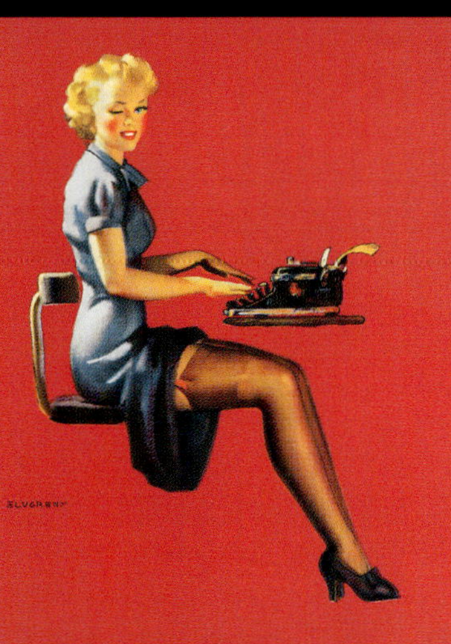

Social Security

This formless subject in an early Dow pin-up is redeemed by a strong, art moderne design.

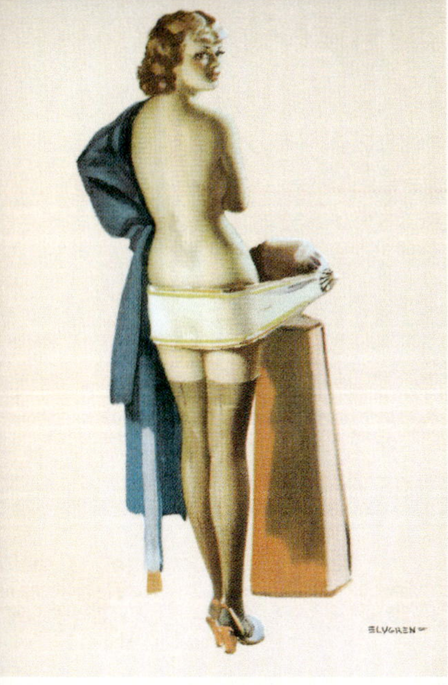

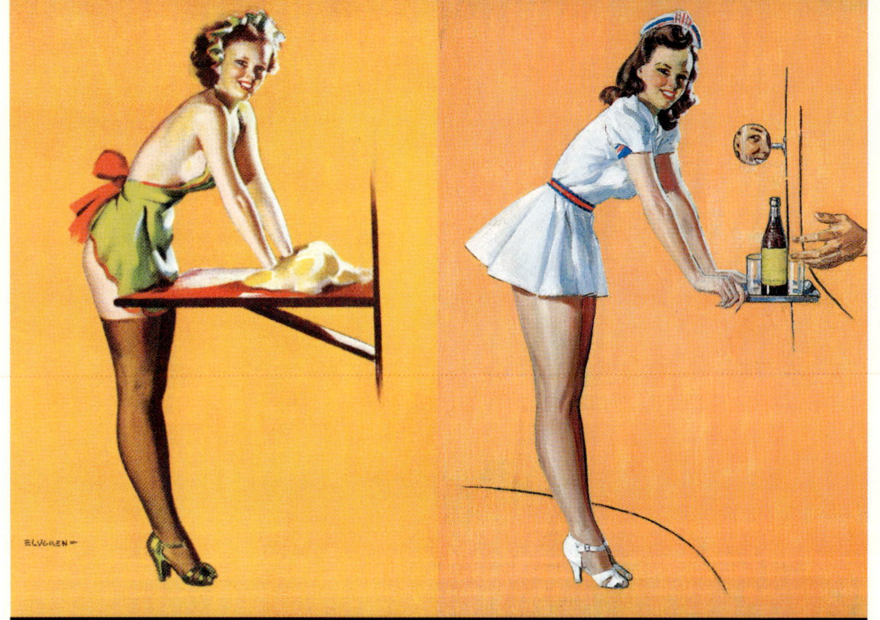

In the Dough

This is a rare instance when the overpainting, arguably, improves the original painting, as Elvgren's baby-faced, dough-kneading cutie is not one of his most inspired concepts.

Ankles Aweigh

This outstanding early pin-up reveals the emerging genius of Elvgren (and the nyloned legs of its subject, who seems to be glorying in her own beauty), as well as the artist's skillful, restrained use of props.

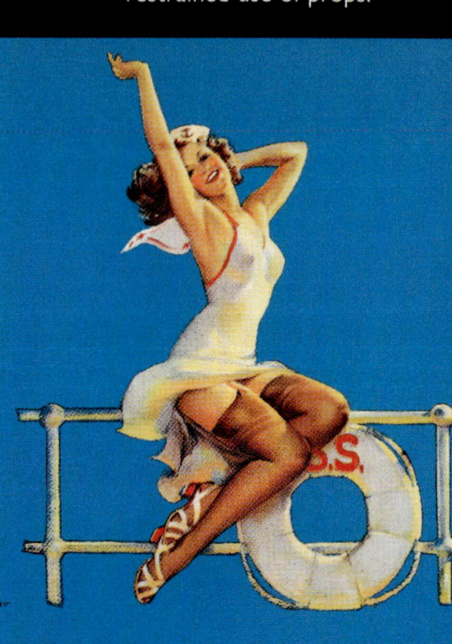

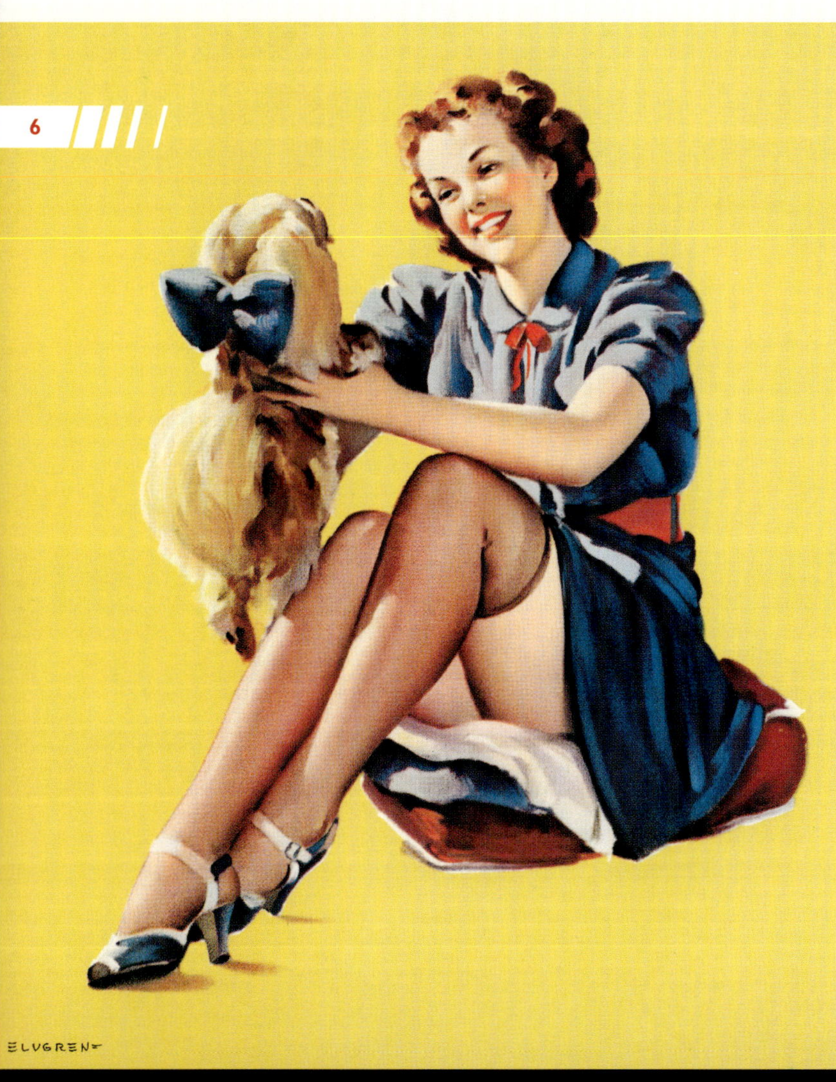

A Peek-a-Knees

This lovely, mature pin-up combines the best of the Dow images with the already delivered promise of the Brown & Bigelow masterworks to come; the model for this is very likely the luminous actress Barbara Hale.

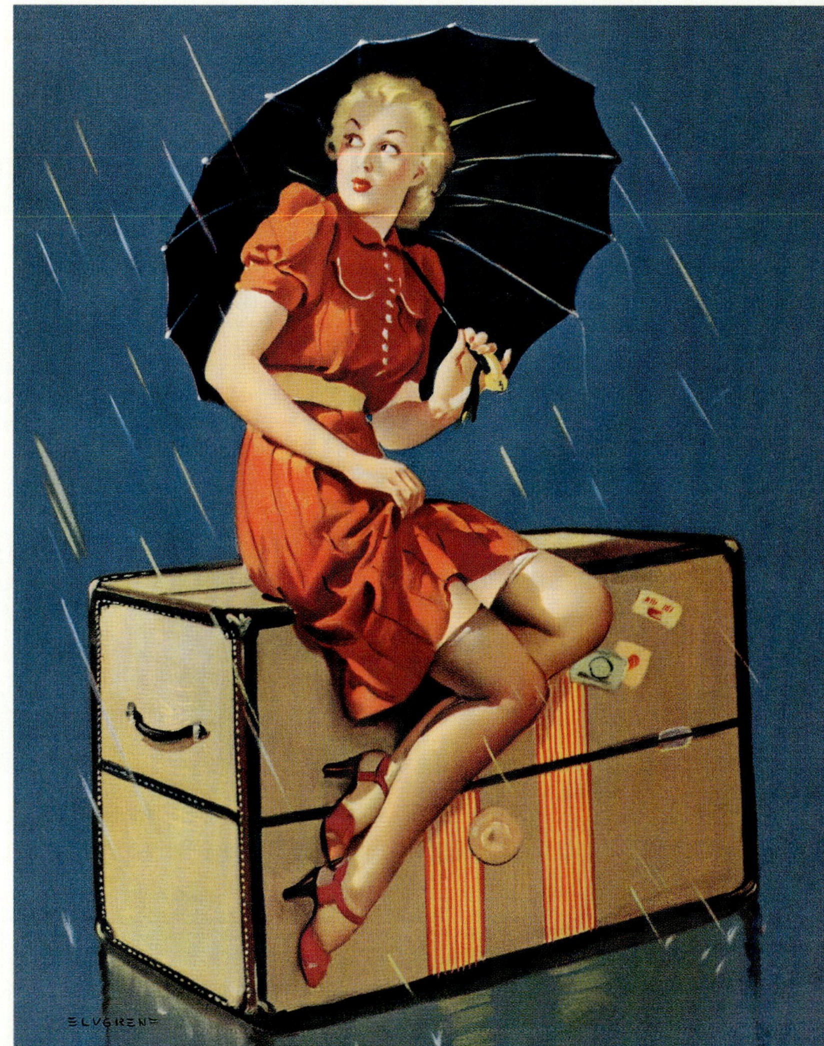

Disturbing Elements

Rain is the enemy of Elvgren's perfectly coifed cuties, but rain is the artist's friend, enhancing and fueling the situations like this one; a beautiful girl and an umbrella give his compositions a spotlight effect.

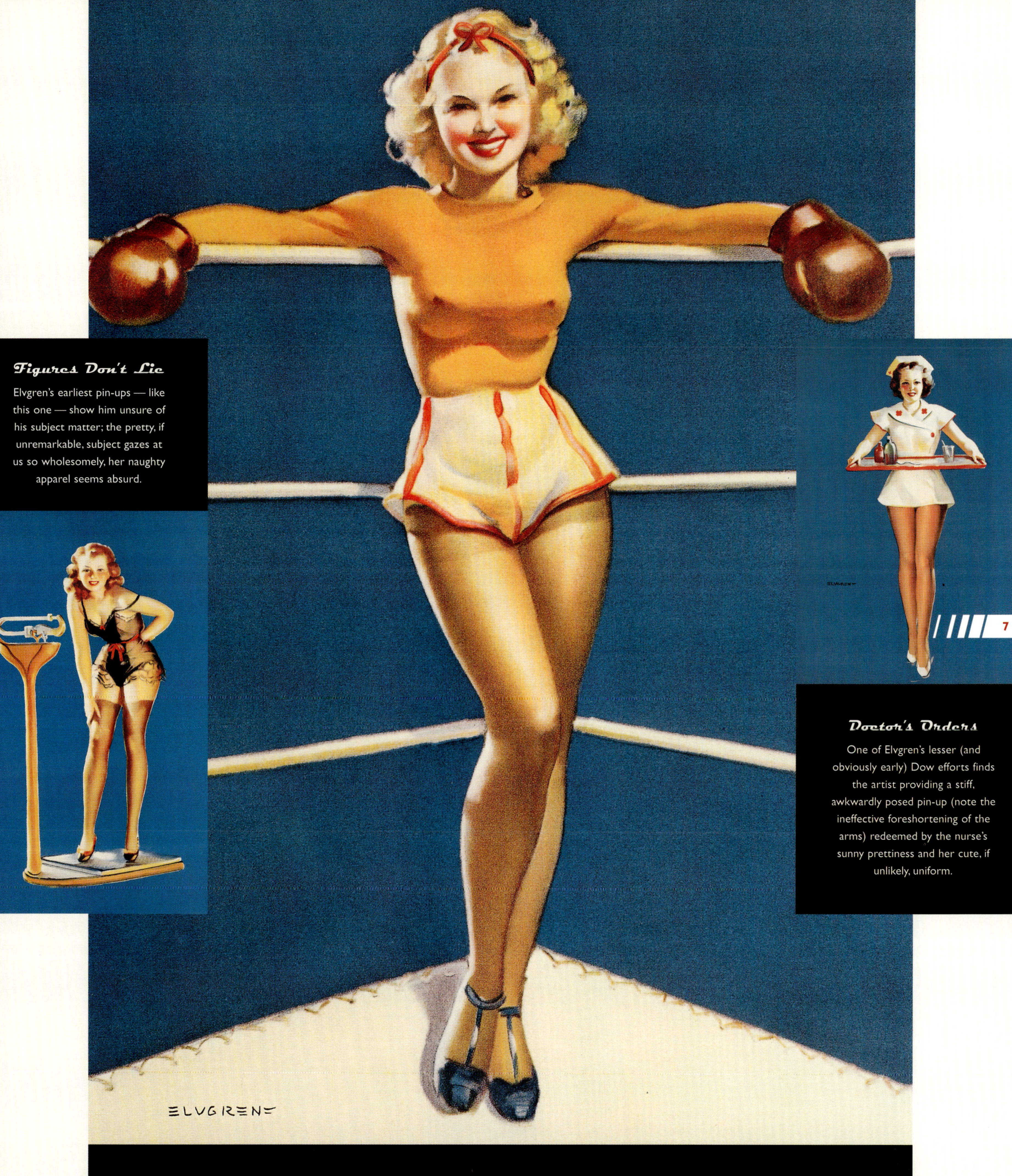

Figures Don't Lie

Elvgren's earliest pin-ups — like this one — show him unsure of his subject matter; the pretty, if unremarkable, subject gazes at us so wholesomely, her naughty apparel seems absurd.

Doctor's Orders

One of Elvgren's lesser (and obviously early) Dow efforts finds the artist providing a stiff, awkwardly posed pin-up (note the ineffective foreshortening of the arms) redeemed by the nurse's sunny prettiness and her cute, if unlikely, uniform.

A Knockout

One of the first full-fledged examples of Elvgren's radiant girls next door — heartbreakingly sexy yet beaming wholesomely.

French Dressing

The pin-up of a lovely, well-rounded dish putting on her skirt and enjoying us watching her do so is erotic in a straightforward, even wholesome manner; the baby-faced deco dolls are evolving into Elvgren's self-assured young women.

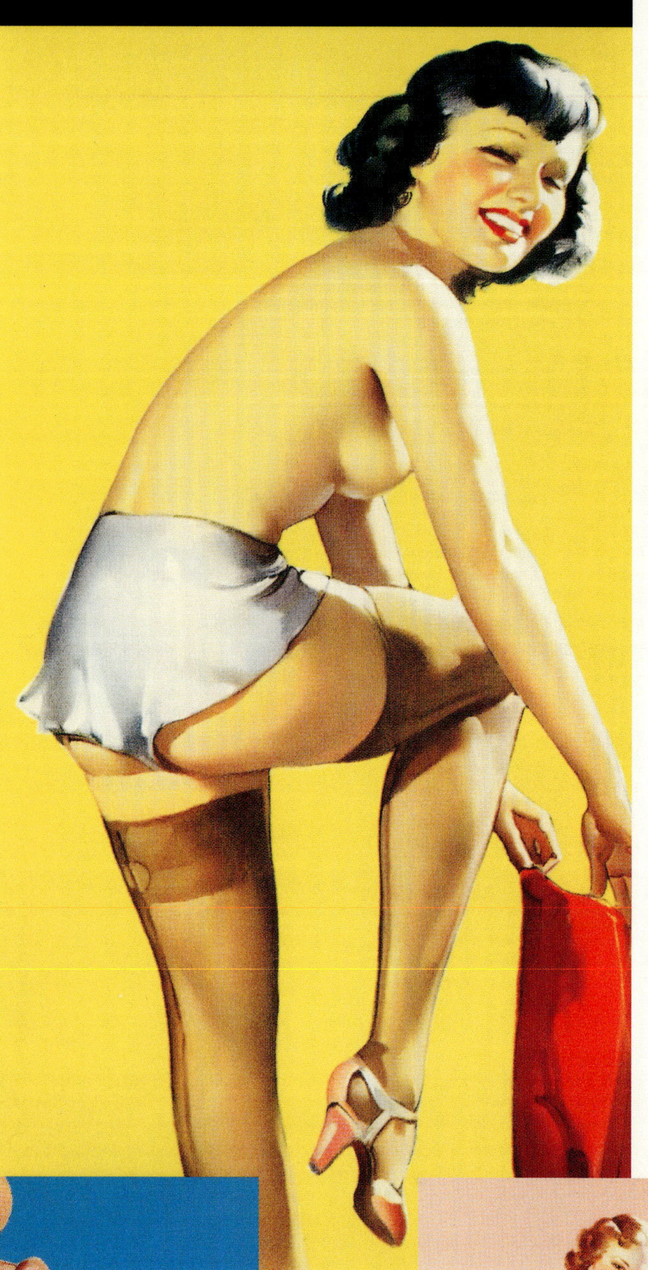

Thar She Blows!

Gil Elvgren was remarkably consistent, turning out one wonderful pin-up after another; this early pin-up for Dow, with a blonde foreshadowing Marilyn Monroe by at least ten years, reveals not just lovely nyloned limbs, but the sense of fun, the command of color, design, and brushstroke that characterize this American master.

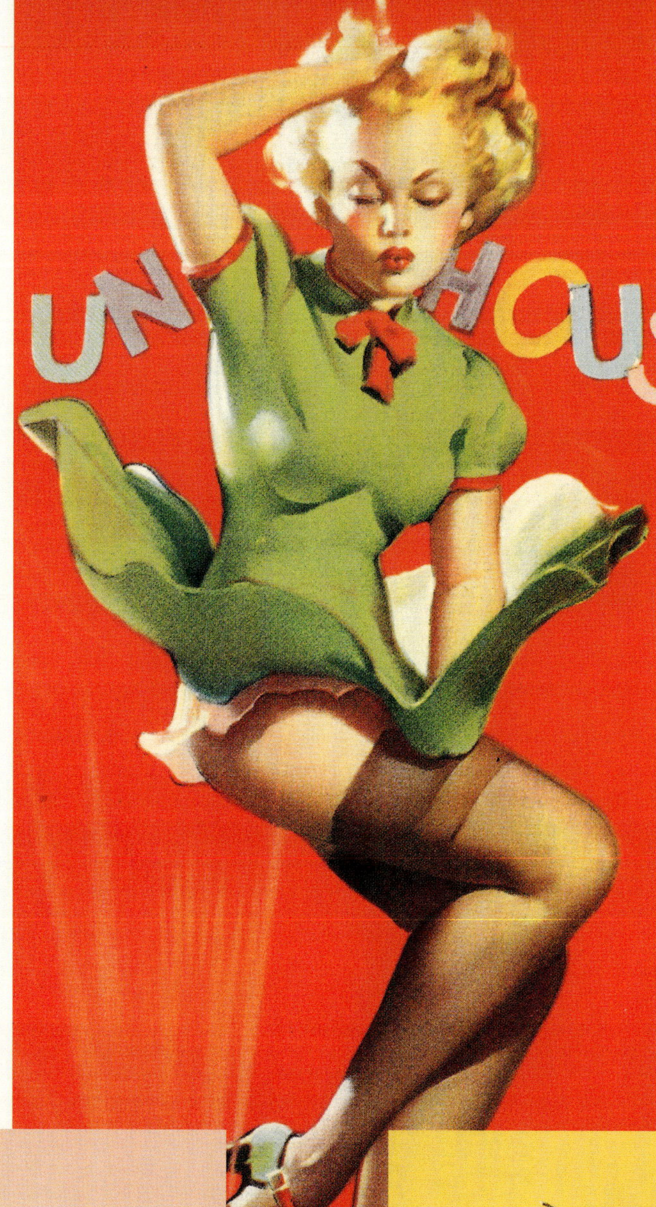

Help Wanted

A trifle stiff but charming, this pin-up shows Elvgren developing his compromised-cutie theme in a well-designed, even bold manner.

Sitting Pretty

The full-blown Elvgren girl within is struggling to emerge in this Dow pin-up, one of the more charming early examples, using a natural situation and art deco props and design.

Foil Proof

Beautifully designed and boldly free of any excuse for the model's state of dishabillé, this pin-up reflects a charming confidence on the part of both artist and subject.

*T*ouched

slightly by Elvgren's interest in flying, this Coca-Cola ad seems less influenced by fellow artist Haddon Sundblom than by J.C. Leyendecker.

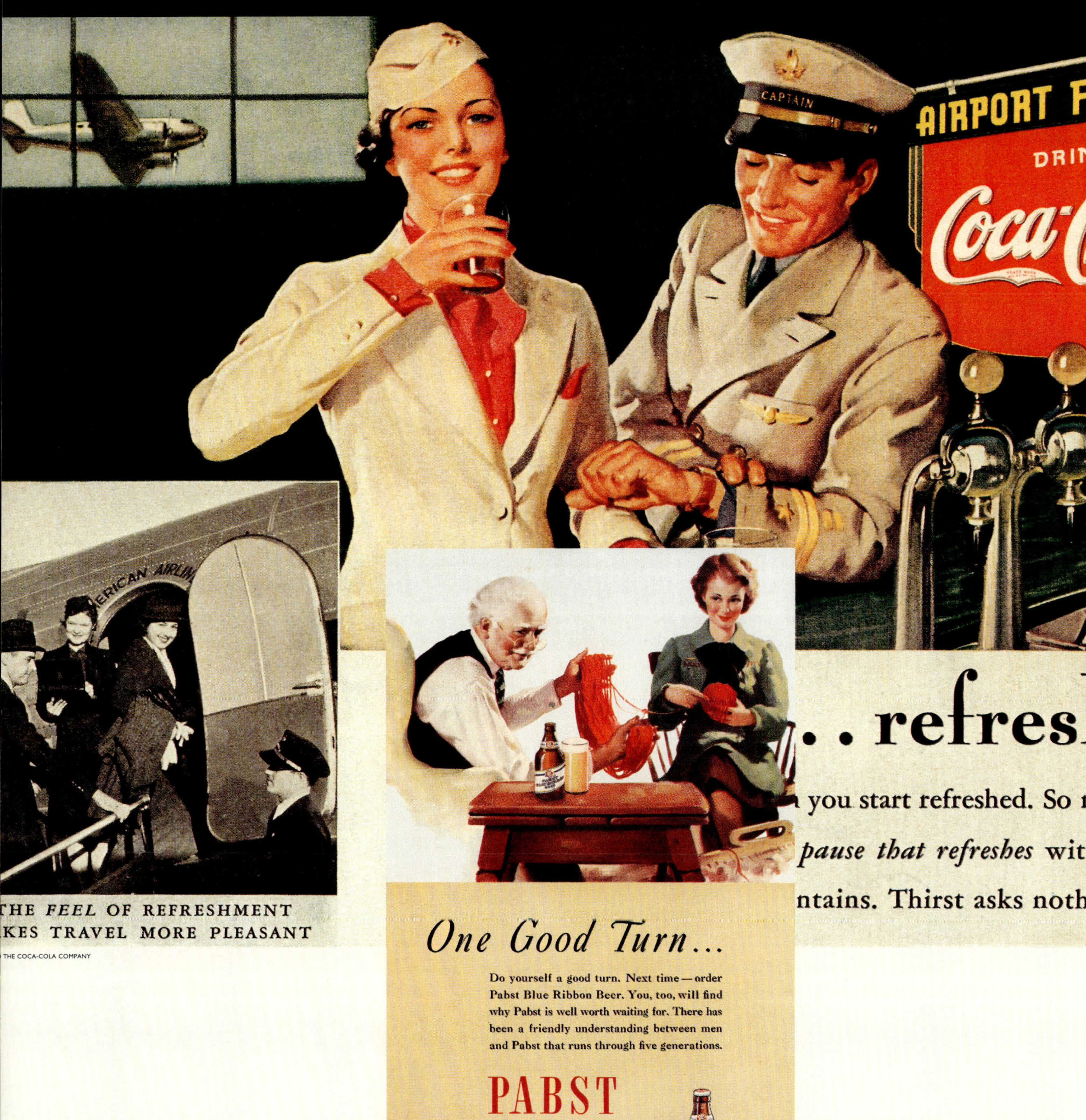

*H*ere's

an outrageous example of using Norman Rockwell-style Americana to sell beer: it's okay with Grandpa! This untypically demure Elvgren housewife still carries some sublimated sex appeal.

THE DIONNE QUINTUPLETS

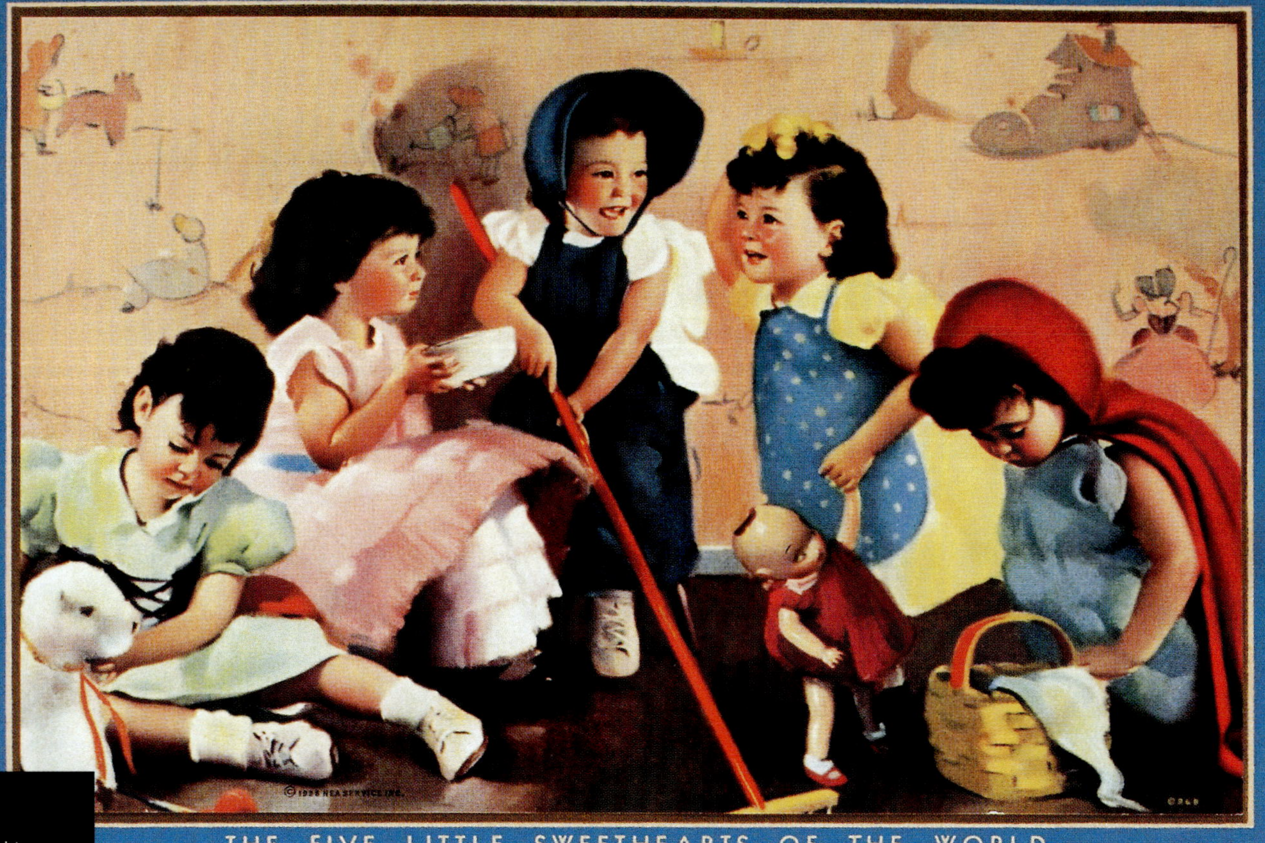

Elvgren's first professional triumph (and his introduction to calendar powerhouse Brown & Bigelow) depicts the famous Dionne quintuplets — ironic subject for a pin-up master and an artist who hated drawing kids.

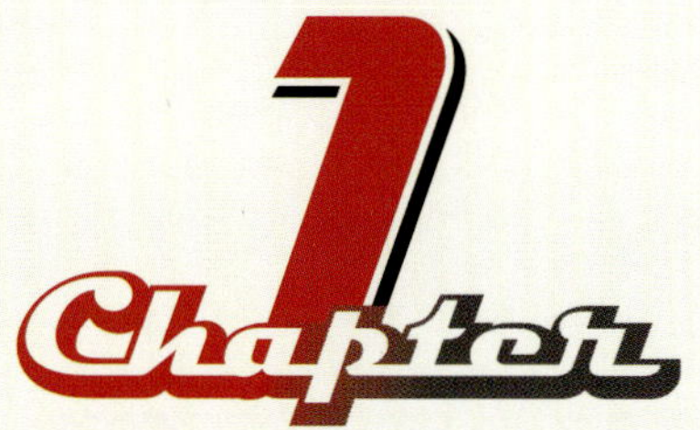

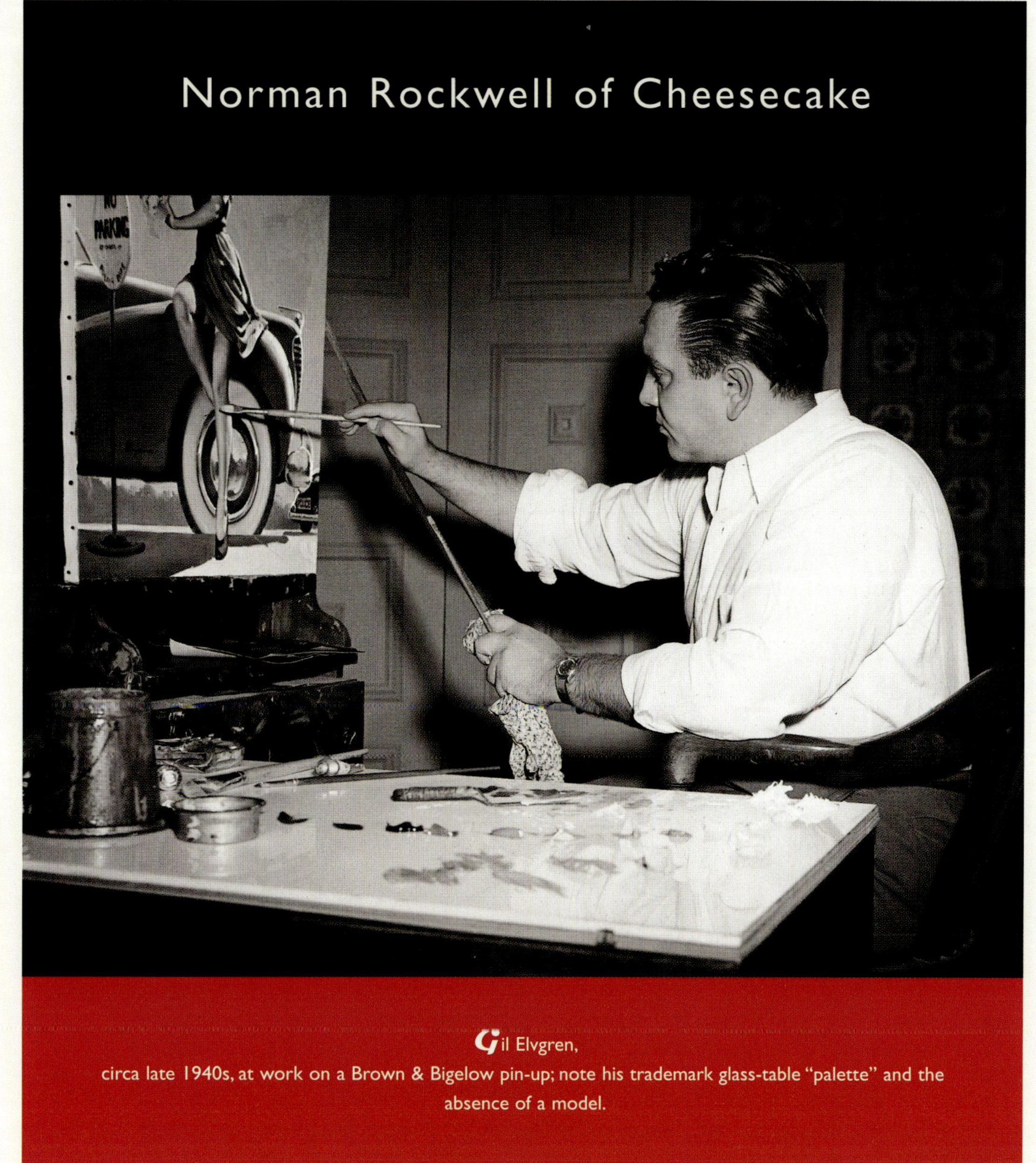

Norman Rockwell of Cheesecake

Gil Elvgren, circa late 1940s, at work on a Brown & Bigelow pin-up; note his trademark glass-table "palette" and the absence of a model.

In recent years, the late Gil Elvgren has been called "the Norman Rockwell of Cheesecake," a fitting, if vaguely patronizing, designation for one of the finest American illustrators. Had Elvgren not fallen into creating "pretty girl" calendar and advertising art, he might have earned a reputation to rival Rockwell's as a painter of idyllic *Saturday Evening Post* images of family life in the United States; or perhaps—as some of his sketches, charcoal drawings, and portraits indicate—a following in the fine arts as a latter-day Dégas, an artist he much admired. Shortly before his death, when the pin-up market had all but dried up, Gil Elvgren speculated on his career as a pin-up artist with one of his sons. Had he turned to portrait art earlier, would it have taken him further? Or perhaps to fine art? In reality, the narrowness of his subject matter—the sexy, pretty girl next door—has worked in his favor, at least posthumously. Otherwise he might have joined the ranks of hundreds of gifted American illustrators whose talents and in some cases genius did not find the household-name fame of Rockwell. Do such names as Bradshaw Crandell, Saul Tepper, Mead Schaeffer, Albert Dorne, and Robert Fawcett ring many bells? For those of you who find these names familiar, run them past your family and register the blank looks. Probably it's for the best that Elvgren's career had so limited a focus. Certainly, several generations of American men who have admired Elvgren's glowingly glamorous women—even those admirers of Elvgren's work who would not recognize the distinctive flourish that was his signature—would not regret the artist's choice of subject matter. Still, the Rockwell of Pin-ups should be a household name. Instead, that level of fame has gone to Alberto Vargas, who has even been given that same "Rockwell" designation, though there is nothing remotely *Saturday Evening Post*-like about the sleek, airbrushed, Ziegfeld-esque sophistication of the Varga girl. The Vargas name has become synonymous with pin-up girls, but in the early '40s, Peruvian Alberto Vargas (1896–1982) was just a commercial artist hired by *Esquire* magazine to imitate departed star George Petty, who bolted over pay. Vargas initially aped Petty's sleek women with their telephone posing and large-hat lounging, even down to the Petty-like cartoon touches (phones and hats drawn in with red crayon). Soon, however, Vargas' distinctive, delicate watercolor style emerged, his pin-up girls more voluptuous and individualized than his predecessors'. Nearly as unreal as Petty's, the Vargas Girl seemed more grounded in reality, an impossible dream with at least some chance of coming true. These wide-eyed, wasp-waisted wonder-women rivaled Betty Grable as the ultimate World War II pin-up girl. Vargas, who signed his *Esquire* work with the slightly less ethnic-sounding "Varga," had already achieved some notoriety for his Ziegfeld Follies and movie-poster art. But *Esquire* (and its yearly calendars) made him famous, though he was poorly paid and wretchedly over-worked. Like Petty, he eventually quit, but legal problems over ownership of his work — even his own signature, when he marketed his own calendar and playing card sets in the late '40s — plagued him for decades. Vargas found a second home at the less sophisticated *True* magazine, where his lovely pin-ups were accompanied by photos of the artist and his models (one of them, famed TV "Sheena" Irish McCalla) at work; similar layouts appeared in *Modern Man*, and Vargas never disappeared from the scene. An occasional movie poster appeared — the 1951 RKO feature, *Behave Yourself*, had Shelley Winters posing — but by the mid-'50s, Vargas was painting "legacy nudes" for his beloved wife Anna to sell after his death. In 1957, however, Vargas was given a second shot at fame and fortune by longtime fan Hugh Hefner, an ironic salvation considering Hefner's *Playboy*, with its lush photographic nudes, had largely put the purveyors of painted pin-ups out of business. Vargas' regular *Playboy* slot through the '60s and '70s elevated the artist to a pinnacle, eclipsing even Petty himself. Vargas lived to see his work achieve a fame and financial success that virtually made him the pin-up artist equivalent of Norman Rockwell. Championed by author Reid Austin, Vargas is the subject of more books than the pin-up field itself; his original paintings fetch prices outdistancing anyone in the pin-up field, yearly calendars continue to be issued, as are pricey limited-edition prints, despite the late artist's unavailability to sign them. Like George Petty, Vargas had his own quirky vision of feminine beauty; unlike Petty, Vargas could impart an individuality to his women — and perhaps that was ultimately the biggest difference between these two giants: Petty painted girls; Vargas painted women. Yet it's only been in recent years that a capricious, revisionist history has made "Varga girl" synonymous with pin-up girl, and those in the know are well aware that Alberto Vargas was a remarkably gifted replacement for that faded household name, George Petty. Robust commercial artist George Petty (1894–1975) began a series of color cartoons for *Esquire* in the early '30s, featuring gorgeous girls and their unlikely un-handsome suitors with gags provided by another of the seminal men's magazine's top cartoonists, E. Simms Campbell, himself no slouch when it came to drawing pretty girls. Soon the beauties — with their dazzling smiles and sleek-as-a-Buick curves — held solo center stage, and the "Petty Girl" was born. The classy if risqué venue of *Esquire* gave the pin-up respectability, and Petty's amazing airbrush technique put him at the forefront of commercial artists; Petty and his namesake pin-up girl became household words. He landed major advertising accounts, such as Old Gold cigarettes (which issued the first Petty pin-up calendar), Springmaid sheets, and Jantzen swimsuits, and his pin-up style rendering of Rita Hayworth even graced the cover of *Time* magazine (Nov. 10, 1941). But his *Esquire* pay rate did

Gil Elvgren
sits back to appraise his work, in this case an untypical subject: a nonpin-up girl with a dog calendar painting.

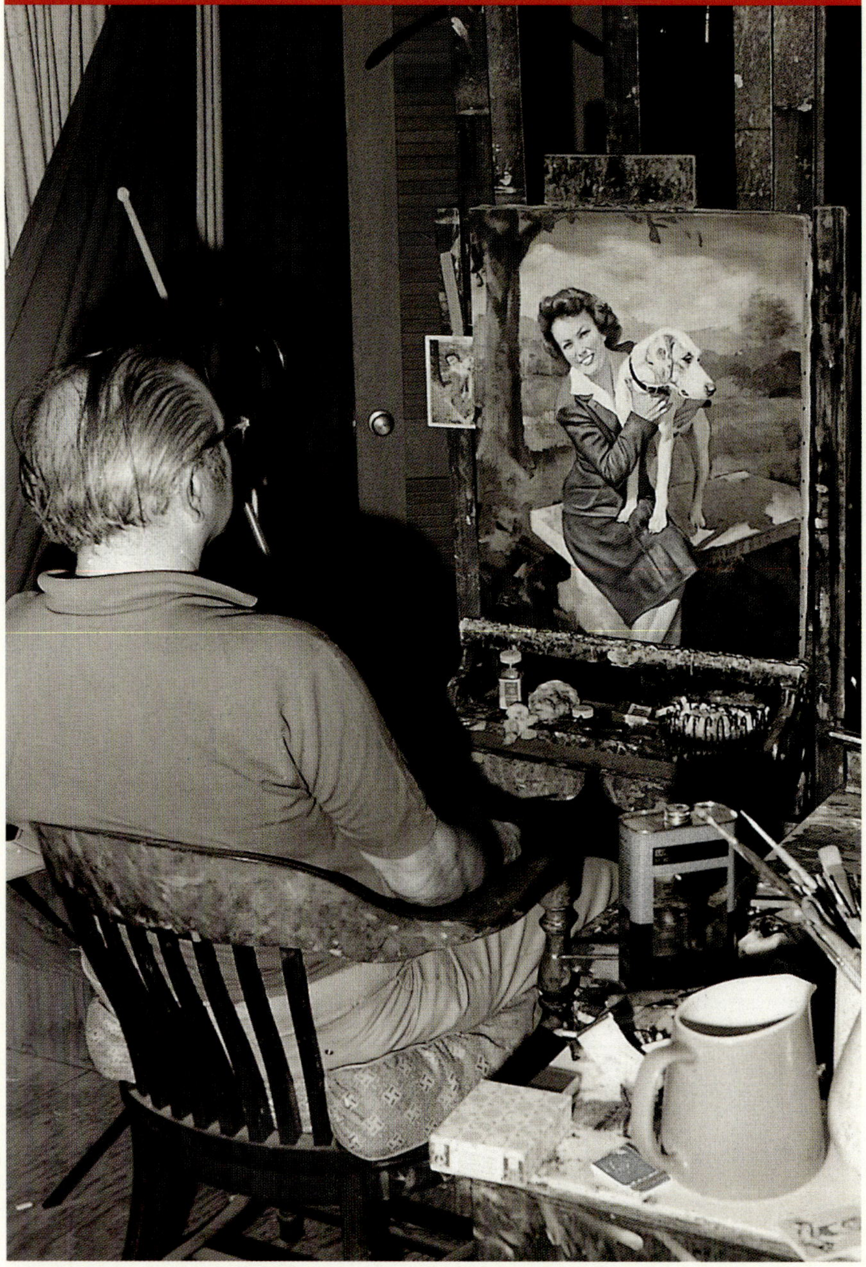

not keep pace with his popularity, and, in the early '40s, he bolted *Esquire* in a money dispute, replaced by, yes, the also underpaid Alberto Vargas. Post-*Esquire*, Petty — like Vargas — painted calendar girls for *True* magazine (1945 – 1948) and, finally, a long-running series for the evocatively named company Rigid Tools. He also did a notable series of covers for the program booklet of the traveling *Ice Capades* show. In the 1950 Hollywood film *The Petty Girl*, the rotund artist was portrayed by a slim Robert Cummings; "The Petty Girl" herself was more accurately depicted by actress Joan Caulfield, and an entire calendar was brought to life by twelve lovely models. (Earlier, Petty provided a stunning series of pin-ups for the 1946 musical, *Ziegfeld Follies*.) For many, the Petty Girl remains the ultimate pin-up, a canny combination of pseudo-realism and fantasy. Yet Petty's girls hardly embody the standards of female beauty of the various eras the artist worked in — oversize head, impossibly tilting breasts, defined musculature, heavy legs, archly positioned hands and feet (the latter, in later years, frequently ensconced in ballet slippers). But his flawless technique, its sheen as seductive as a new-car showroom, allowed him to deliver his personal vision of pulchritude in a manner so irresistible his audience never seemed to notice it didn't match their own. Petty, who studied art in Paris before World War I, lived a Hemingway-esque life style, hunting big game in Africa; his daughter Marjorie, who was his primary model, described him as a "perfectionist," who often spent ten days on a single painting. Shortly before his death, Petty buried the hatchet and drew one last Petty girl for *Esquire* — her figure unchanged, her hair turned a dignified gray, and granny-glasses perched on a pert nose. If Petty has receded in fame (and memory — though a Reid Austin book on the artist recently has been published), the true Norman Rockwell of pin-up art remains shamefully neglected. Rockwell himself paid homage to this artist in a calendar image that portrayed Grandma disapprovingly noting Grandpa approvingly gazing at a Gil Elvgren cowgirl. And a major Elvgren revival is afoot, as evidenced by this and other volumes. But, in truth, "revival" is a misnomer: Elvgren was never famous, certainly not as famous as Petty or even Vargas, though for most American males it was Elvgren's girls next door, caught in saucy compromising positions, that typified the calendar-girl genre. Snobbery is at work here. Remember, the Petty Girl and the Varga variation were published in that toniest of men's magazines, *Esquire*, right next to Hemingway fiction and Brooks Brothers fashion layouts. Petty and Varga were risqué and, reluctantly, respectable. Gil Elvgren toiled in obscurity, his lush oil paintings appearing on the walls of barbershops, barracks, saloons, filling-station garages, frat houses, firehouses, and Elks Clubs — anywhere men gathered to work or play. Elvgren was racy and, hence, less than respectable. Yet Elvgren almost certainly had a wider constituency than his more famous rivals; of the eighty million calendars a year (a mid-'40s figure), a majority were glamour art. Apparently, beautiful women showing their nyloned legs were more popular with the masses (the male masses, at least) than rural scenes, funny hobos, and puppy dogs. Calendars weren't the only place an Elvgren image could be found — blotters, notepads, playing cards, matchbook covers, drinking glasses, even a lamp, bore his playfully erotic images. And Elvgren's pioneering definition of the sexually attractive girl next door — a fantasy female who combined innocence with sexual availability, whose rosy, apple cheeks and ample, supple curves created an aura at once wholesome and provocative — proved far more influential with other pin-up artists of the day than Vargas and Petty. Where Elvgren attracted a score of imitators, only a handful (notably Merlin Enabnit) worked the sleek, airbrushed Petty/Vargas side of the street. And the Elvgren girl's presence in various advertising campaigns, her face beaming from billboards and Coca-Cola trays and NAPA ads, gave her a popular cultural presence Vargas never had. (Petty came closer with his many advertising accounts.) True, it was a nearly down-and-out Vargas who cheesecake maven Hugh Hefner invited into *Playboy*'s pages; but it was Elvgren's girl next door that influenced the Playmate. The choice of Vargas only reflected Hefner's obsessive desire to make *Playboy* his generation's *Esquire* (a goal he achieved and then some). One can only imagine that Hefner, in those early days, would have found Elvgren less than hip — even corny — a blue-collar pin-up artist, a working man's fantasy maker, not fit for swinging bachelors of the '50s and '60s. And yet this working-man mystique is at the heart of Elvgren's enduring appeal. It is what makes this virtuoso of brush and oil the true Rockwell of the pin-up and is what crowns this all-American portrayer of all-American girls as the most likely of all glamour artists to achieve lasting fame: Gil Elvgren beauties are as typically and wholesomely American as Coca-Cola, the Senior Prom, and Santa Claus.

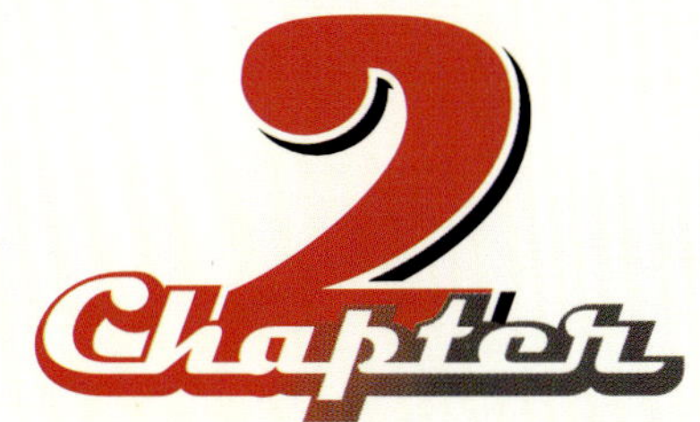

Artist's Artist, Man's Man

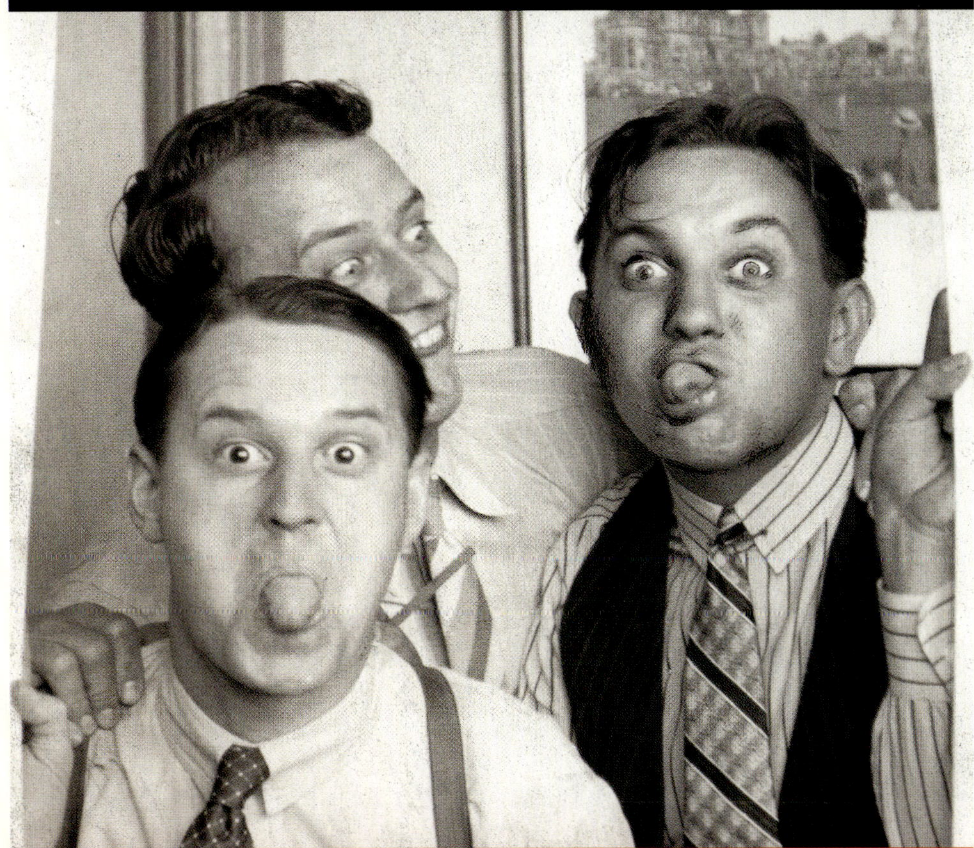

Gil Elvgren was generally low-key and quiet, though he did serve up a slice of ham now and then, particularly in social settings, as he does here with his pals.

Not surprisingly, Gil Elvgren was a product of the midwest, born in the home of the calendar girl, St. Paul, Minnesota, on March 15, 1914. His father Alex Aner Elvgren was born in a castle outside Stockholm, Sweden, in 1882. The depression of the 1880s and 1890s left Ake's father destitute, and he traveled to St. Paul in 1886. Gil Elvgren's grandfather displayed the same combination of roughhewn man's man and sensitive craftsman that later characterized his grandson, becoming a lumberjack, furniture maker, carriage maker, and artist. He sent for his family to join him only after he'd made his own way in the new land. Elvgren's father, Daddy Ake, as the family called him, was a soft-spoken, gentle soul with an appreciation for art that he passed on to his son; he ran a Benjamin Moore paint and wallpaper store (with an art supply area in the back) in St. Paul. "Dad's father sold the store," Gil Elvgren's son Drake recalls, "but since it did such strong business and had such a good reputation, the new owners asked him if they could keep the name." The store is still in business and bears a neon sign that echoes the famous signature father and son shared. Daddy Ake also passed on his love for sports and games to his boy; Ake was a renowned tennis player and a champion billiards player. Gil Elvgren's mother Goldie Alice Gillette, who was of English, Dutch, and French extraction, was born in LaCrosse, Wisconsin, in 1886 (she lived to age 106). A twin, Goldie was also artistically blessed, performing with her sister as the Gillette Sisters, entertaining at social clubs and churches, singing and dancing, and Gillette Elvgren, Jr., recalls that they were "the toast of the Twin Cities." Gil Elvgren's memories of his mother, however, were probably not of an entertainer but of a doting mother and grandmother with a reputation as a fine cook, particularly of such sweets as custard and coffeecake. If Elvgren got his lifelong love for art from his father, his

FEE COLLECTED
One Dollar

CITY OF SAINT PAUL
DEPARTMENT OF PUBLIC SAFETY—BUREAU OF HEALTH
DIVISION OF VITAL STATISTICS
CERTIFIED COPY OF BIRTH RECORD № 8

TO WHOM IT MAY CONCERN:
This is to certify that the following is a true copy from the Birth Records of this bureau:

PLACE OF BIRTH — THE STATE OF MINNESOTA, Division of Vital Statistics, RECORD OF BIRTH

1. County of RAMSEY
City of SAINT PAUL — West Side General Hospital (No. ______, St.: ______ Ward) ______ (If birth occurred in a hospital or institution, give its NAME instead of street and number)

2. FULL NAME OF CHILD: GilBette Elvgren — If child is not yet named, make supplemental report as directed.

3. Sex: Male | If plural births: 4. Twin, triplet, or other ______ 5. Number, in order of birth ______ | 6. Premature ______ Full term ______ | 7. Legitimate? Yes | 8. Date of birth: March 15 1914

FATHER		MOTHER	
9. Full name	Alex A Elvgren	16. Full maiden name	Goldie Gillette
10. Residence	576 So Robert St.,	17. Residence	576 So Robert St.,
11. Color or race	White	18. Color or race	White
12. Age at last birthday (Years)	31	19. Age at last birthday (Years)	26
13. Birthplace	Sweden	20. Birthplace	Wisconsin
Occupation: 14. Trade, profession, or particular kind of work done, as farmer, bookkeeper, etc.	Dept Manager	Occupation: 21. Trade, profession, or particular kind of work done, as housekeeper, typist, nurse, clerk, etc.	Housewife
15. Industry or business in which work was done, as factory, office, bank, etc.		22. Industry or business in which work was done, as own home, lawyer's office, factory, etc.	

23. Number of children of this mother (At time of this birth and including this child) (a) Born alive and now living 1 (b) Born alive but now dead ______ (c) Stillborn ______

24. If stillborn, period of gestation { months or weeks | 25. Cause of stillbirth { Before labor ______ During labor ______

26. Was 1% silver nitrate used to prevent infant blindness? Yes No

CERTIFICATE OF ATTENDING PHYSICIAN OR MIDWIFE*

I hereby certify that I attended the birth of this child, who was ______ (Born Alive or Born Dead) at ______ M., on the date above stated, and that the above facts as given are true to the best of my knowledge, information and belief.

*When there was no attending physician or midwife, then the father, householder, etc., must make this return.

(Signature) Jennette M McLaren, M. D., PHYSICIAN, [struck out] (Cross out words which do not apply)

Given name added from a supplemental report ______, 19___

Date ______ Address ______

(Signature) ______ REGISTRAR.

Filed Mar 17, 19 14 Address ______

Amended pursuant to authority received and filed in the Minnesota State Department of Health on ______

This Form is issued in accordance with provisions of the 1923 General Statutes of the State of Minnesota as amended by Chapter 190 of the 1925 Session Laws.

[signature] Registrar

I, Isabel Rhody, deputy registrar of vital statistics of the City of St. Paul, Minnesota, do hereby certify that I have compared the above copy of the certificate of birth with the record on file in this office, and that the same is a true and correct copy of said record and of the whole thereof.

(Dated) April 1 1952 (Signed) Isabel Rhody Deputy Registrar.

10M 8-48

The birth certificate of Gillette Elvgren; "Gillette" is his mother's maiden name.

obsession with chocolate came from his mother. (Gil was known to slather a piece of chocolate cake with chocolate ice cream and top it with chocolate sauce.) An only child, Elvgren respected his father and adored his mother. His artistic bent revealed itself at an early age in his penchant for drawing, wood carving, and model-plane building. Gil, Jr., recalls his grandmother telling of the family being "amazed at the figures young Gil would carve in soap during the inordinately long baths he would sometimes take, lost in his creative work." Those who saw the lad's sketches sometimes invoked the word "prodigy." "Dad always wanted to be creative," Drake says. "He had an innate sense of color, proportion, and a wonderful imagination." Though not particularly fond of academic pursuits, young Gil excelled at math, and throughout his life he enjoyed solving "brain teaser" math puzzles. He graduated from University High School in 1932 and promptly enrolled at the University of Minnesota, where he briefly studied architecture before giving into two loves: painting and his high-school sweetheart. In 1933, at age 19, he and Janet Cecilia Cummins eloped and moved to Chicago.

Gil's 1932 high-school graduation picture, with Janet Cummins, his wife-to-be.

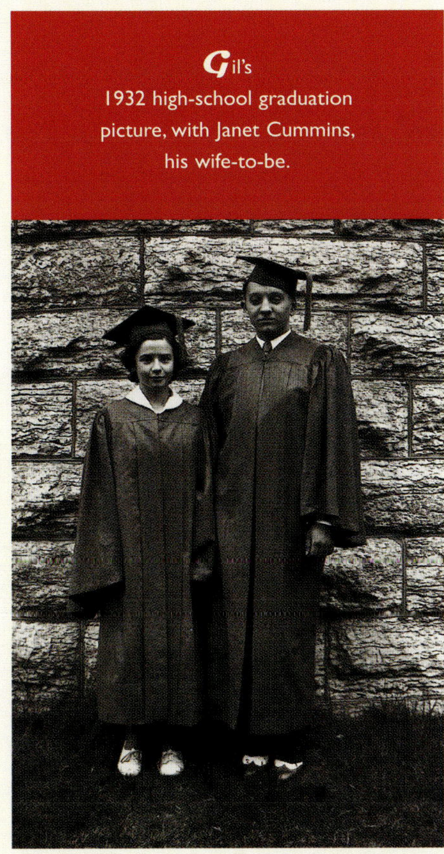

Janet was the daughter of a prominent St. Paul attorney, Carl W. Cummins, who was none too happy about his darling daughter running off with an artist. Cummins didn't dislike his daughter's new husband but did have serious misgivings about Elvgren's precarious line of work. The marriage began on an unintentionally adventurous note. Outdoorsman Elvgren took his bride on a canoeing trip in the North Woods of Minnesota, where Janet had an appendicitis attack. Elvgren had to row her five miles in a storm for help. In Chicago, on the safer shores of Lake Michigan, the budding artist enrolled at the American Academy of Art, where he studied with Bill Mosby. Elvgren excelled at the academy, graduating in the mid-'30s. "Dad is still one of their golden boys," Drake recalls of his father's American Academy of Art tenure. "They were proud to acknowledge him as one of theirs." One of Elvgren's instructors wrote on his report card, "Gil is one of whom we will say,

'We knew him when.'" And indeed, in the family scrapbook, correspondence with the Academy in the late '50s reveals the school's efforts to obtain an Elvgren Brown & Bigelow calendar image or a Coca-Cola ad of his to put on permanent display. "I remember Dad telling me," Drake continues, "that when it came time for him to graduate, the academy said he still had to complete a course in perspective. He told them that he knew perspective already and asked if he could pass the class by taking the final exam. They said, 'Sure,' knowing that perspective was one of the hardest classes, and no one passed the exam without first taking the class. Dad passed with flying colors and graduated." Instructor Mosby, in a 1956 interview, spoke highly of his dedicated student (Elvgren's paintings were used as examples in the academy catalogue), but pointed out an attribute that many pin-up artists of the first half of the twentieth century seemed to share: Gil Elvgren was a man's man. To Mosby, Elvgren—a husky five-foot-eight inches—was more like a football player than an artist, and photographs confirm that Elvgren's hands were (as Mosby put it) "huge paws." Mosby was astounded that Elvgren's thick fingers and bulky fists could produce such subtle, graceful work. In fact, Elvgren had played high school football—a first-string guard in a single-wing formation—and throughout his life remained athletic. Gil, Jr., speculates that his father would have remained "vigorous" in sports if he hadn't been burdened with recurring gout. "Just pitching the baseball," Gil, Jr., recalls, "could set his knee off." A lifelong passion for golf began in his teens, and he excelled at the sport, shooting in the high seventies when he was well into his sixties. Wife Janet was athletic, too, and joined him on the links and on the badminton court. He was an avid sports enthusiast, who would watch one college football game on TV while listening to another on the radio. Gil, Jr., remembers his father taking "great joy" in following his son's "miserable" high-school football team (first loss—85 to nothing). Games in general held a fascination for the artist. He loved Ping Pong, chess, and crossword puzzles, and he and Janet were inveterate card players—canasta, hearts, and especially bridge. "Dad was very competitive," Drake recalls, "and was not prone to let anybody win just to be nice. So if you beat Dad at anything, you could really feel good about it, because you knew he had really tried." But Gil, Jr., adds, "I remember that after I beat him continually at chess and Ping Pong, he stopped playing with me." His childhood love for wood carving followed him throughout his life, as well, from whittling to carpentry. Not surprisingly, Elvgren was good with his hands and turned out some handsome furniture with little effort. "Everything he touched with his hands came out beautiful," Drake says. "I remember one day when a friend gave him an antique dueling pistol. Dad realized that he really didn't have a proper way to display this and his other antiques, so he marched into his workroom, found some boards laying around and two hours later had this gorgeous gun cabinet. The only thing that didn't come from scrap was the felt lining and the closures." Like fellow pin-up artists George Petty, Earl MacPherson, and Rolf Armstrong, Elvgren was an outdoorsman, a dedicated hunter who prior to his relocation to Florida spent at least one month every summer in his beloved North Woods — Northern Minnesota, near Canada — fishing for lake trout, walleyes, and northern pike. Boating itself brought him great pleasure: he always had a nice boat and enjoyed taking it out for a cruise, stopping to meet friends at a favorite "bait camp" restaurant. Canoeing also appealed to him, and he often went on long canoeing expeditions with a boyhood friend. Still, as much as he loved the outdoors, his trek north was in part the effort of a chronic hay fever sufferer to avoid the summer pollen season. "Later when he had a family," Drake remembers, "Dad would pack us up in the car, drive from Winnetka where we were living, just north of Chicago, to St. Paul. We would spend a couple days visiting dad's parents and mom's and then travel on up past Grand Marais up the 'Gunflint Trail,' and rent a log cabin past the Trail's End Camp." Those summers in the North Woods are among Drake's fondest memories of his family. Drake (born March 3, 1944) was the youngest of Elvgren's three children; his sister Karen is six years older (born April 29, 1938) and his brother Gillette, Jr., two years older (born January 6, 1942). "Everybody swimming in the cold lakes, fishing for Northern and walleyed pike, and stopping on a small island and cooking our catch right then," Drake recalls fondly. "No fish ever tasted as good as those fresh caught and cooked on an open fire. Canoe trips down the rapids, living in log cabins, lying in bed at night listening for the mouse traps to go off. Catching your hair in the fly paper, getting ice cut from the lakes in winter from the log ice house, my sister feeding peanuts to the chipmunks who would climb up on her shoulder and take them out of her mouth, and the half-mile walk to the Trail's End to get a strawberry soda." Gil, Jr., recalls that his father kept a studio in the North Woods for a time, "way up on a hill." He also remembers late-night trips to a spider-infested outhouse, stepping on pine cones, and imagining bears, "which were a constant presence along with loons and porcupines." The artist also enjoyed flying, and the man from whom the Elvgrens rented their cabin in the summer, Willard Waters, had two Piper Cub pontoon planes. Waters frequently took Elvgren and his children flying "all over the North Woods." "Mr. Waters used to take us up," Drake says, "and do stunts. Dad was like a kid — he *really* enjoyed that!" Elvgren's passion for the outdoors and hunting extended to guns — he was a collector of firearms, both modern (Colts, Mausers, and Lugers) and antique, and was an expert shot. When his gout kept him out of active military service in World War II, Elvgren took a position as a civilian firearms instructor, specializing in small arms, at the Great Lakes Naval Station, near Chicago; he taught pistol shooting to members of the Civil Air Patrol, Coast Guard, and Civil Defense and later the police. Several times he almost got shot by his neophyte trainees. He also may have suffered some hearing loss from shooting, according to Gil, Jr. During his years in the Chicago area, he told one interviewer that he had "no desire to compete in matches;" but in his later life he competed in NRA Bullseye Matches and became Florida State "Expert" champion in the late 1960s. The publicity he received for his marksmanship rivaled that of his pin-up career. He tinkered with guns, as well, working to improve the accuracy and trigger pull of his weapons, and in doing so became an accomplished amateur gunsmith. When he was working on his guns, he brought the same intensity and focus he gave to his painting, often oblivious to what was going on around him. Man's man Elvgren has also been said to be a two-fisted drinker, though some sources have exaggerated this, indicating that drinking may have contributed to his relatively early death. (Elvgren died of cancer of the liver, February 29, 1980, at age 66.) Drake Elvgren discounts this, saying, "Dad smoked most of his adult life and enjoyed a drink, too. He was personable and sociable after a drink or two but basically fairly quiet and a little introverted." His political views — he was a dyed-in-the-wool, Goldwater-style conservative, a near reactionary who expressed an even then politically incorrect admiration of Senator Joseph McCarthy, with whom he shared a loathing of Communists — ruffled a fair number of feathers in the artistic circles he sometimes traveled in. Certainly Gil Elvgren — like George Petty and Rolf Armstrong — was one of that breed who seemed almost to overcompensate for succumbing to the unmanly calling of artist. As one interviewer put it, "In his spare time, Elvgren gets as far away from the sophisticated and ephemeral art world as he can." For a man whose working life was sedentary, Elvgren remained vital and active in his athletic and outdoorsman pursuits; and for an artist whose subject matter was pretty young women, he seemed a devoted family man almost to a fault.

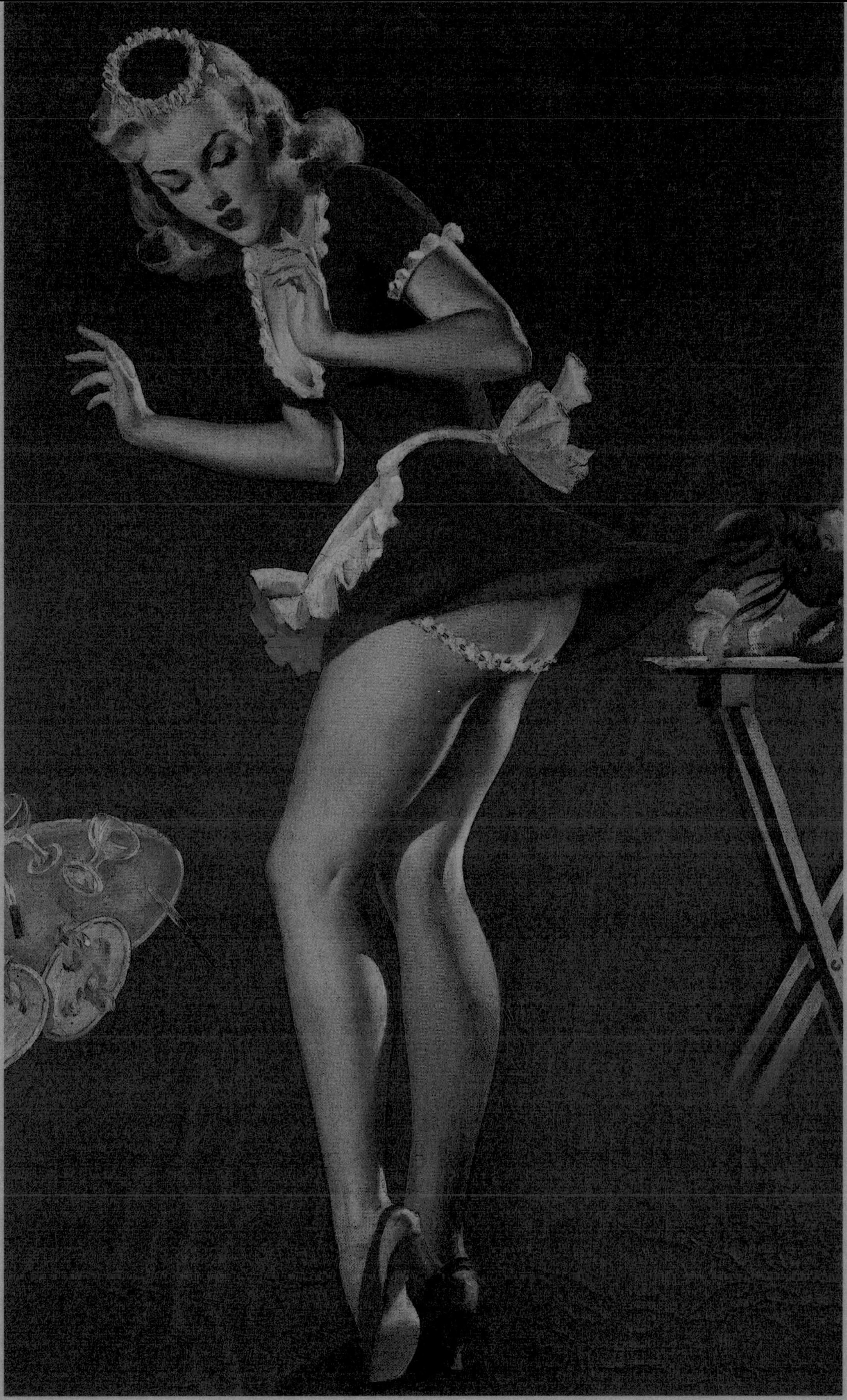

1940s Portfolio

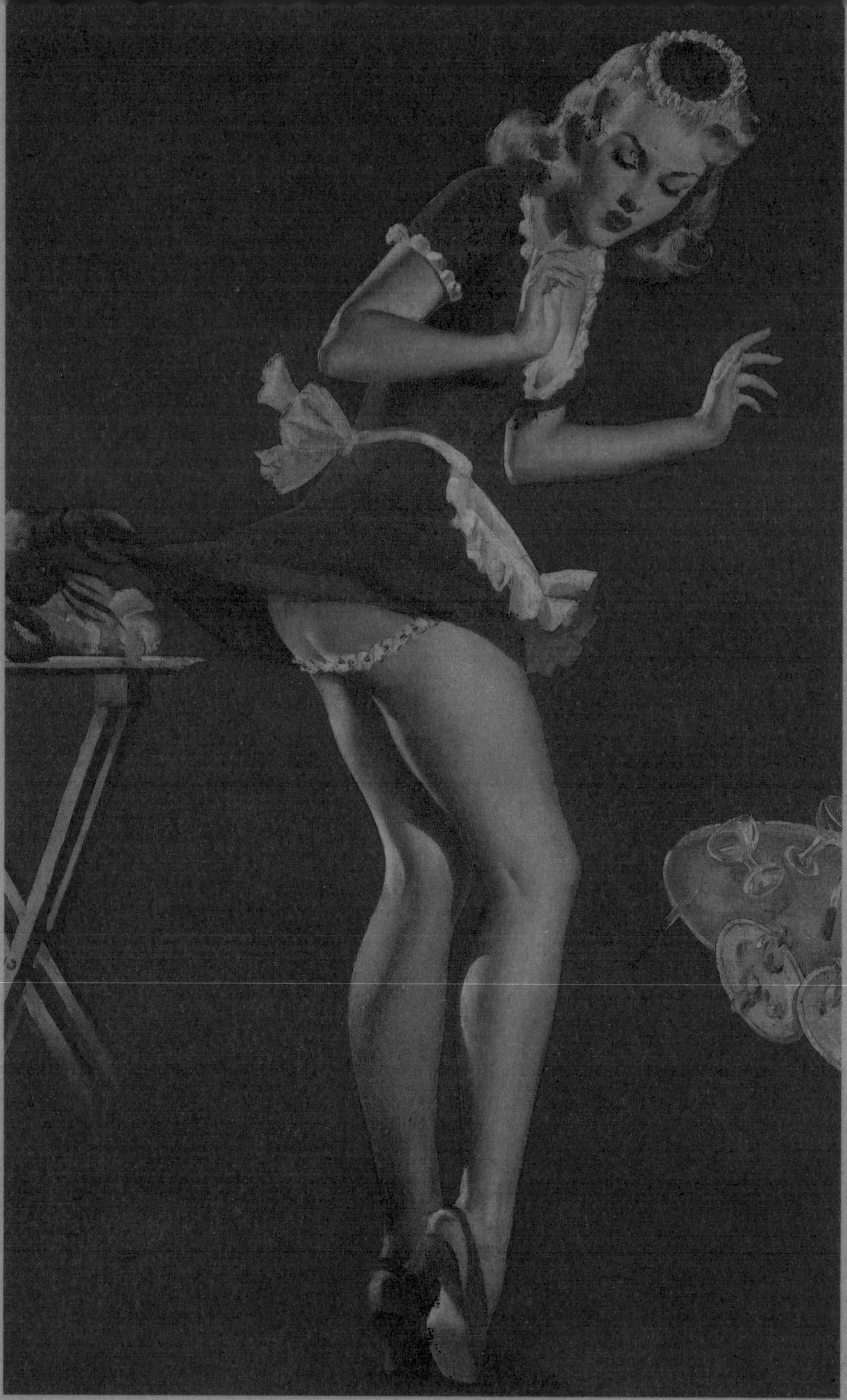

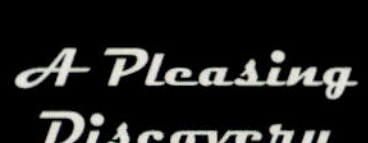

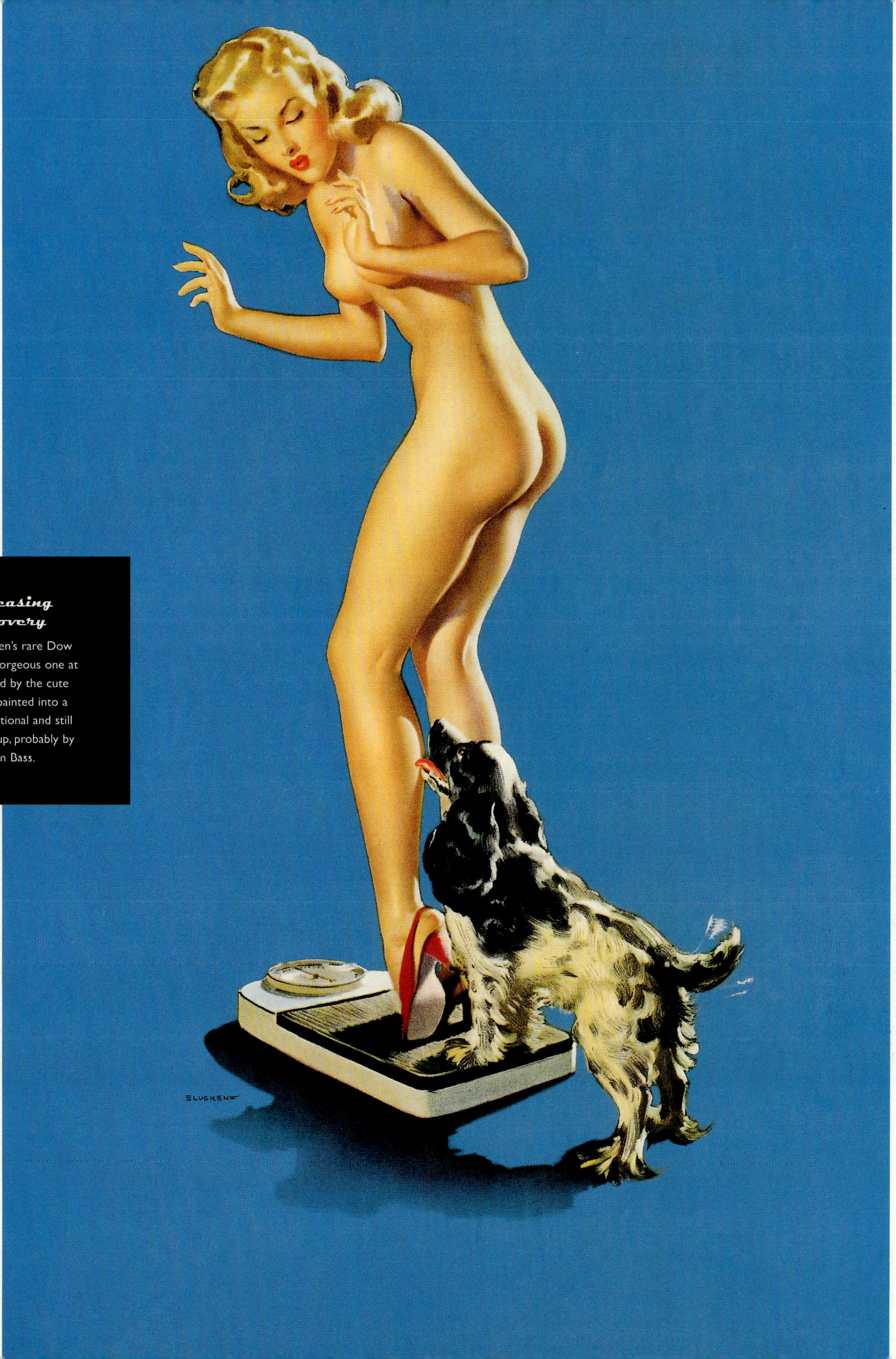

A Pleasing Discovery

One of Elvgren's rare Dow nudes, and a gorgeous one at that, softened by the cute dog, is overpainted into a more conventional and still effective pin-up, probably by Vaughn Bass.

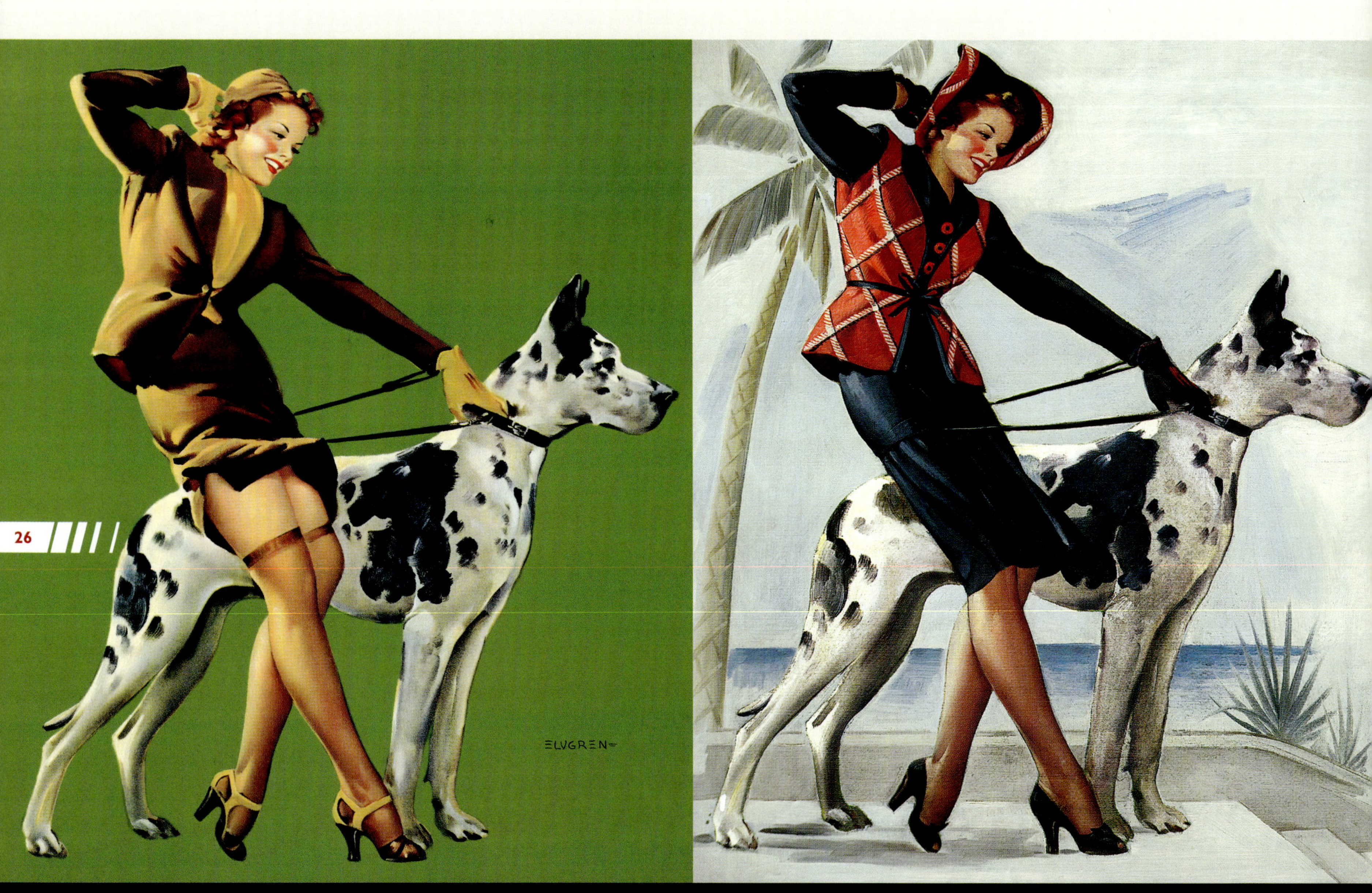

A Perfect Pair

While the modernized, overpainted version is an attractive (and recognizably Elvgren) pin-up, the original — one of the artist's earliest variations on a favorite theme — retains greater charm and shows more leg.

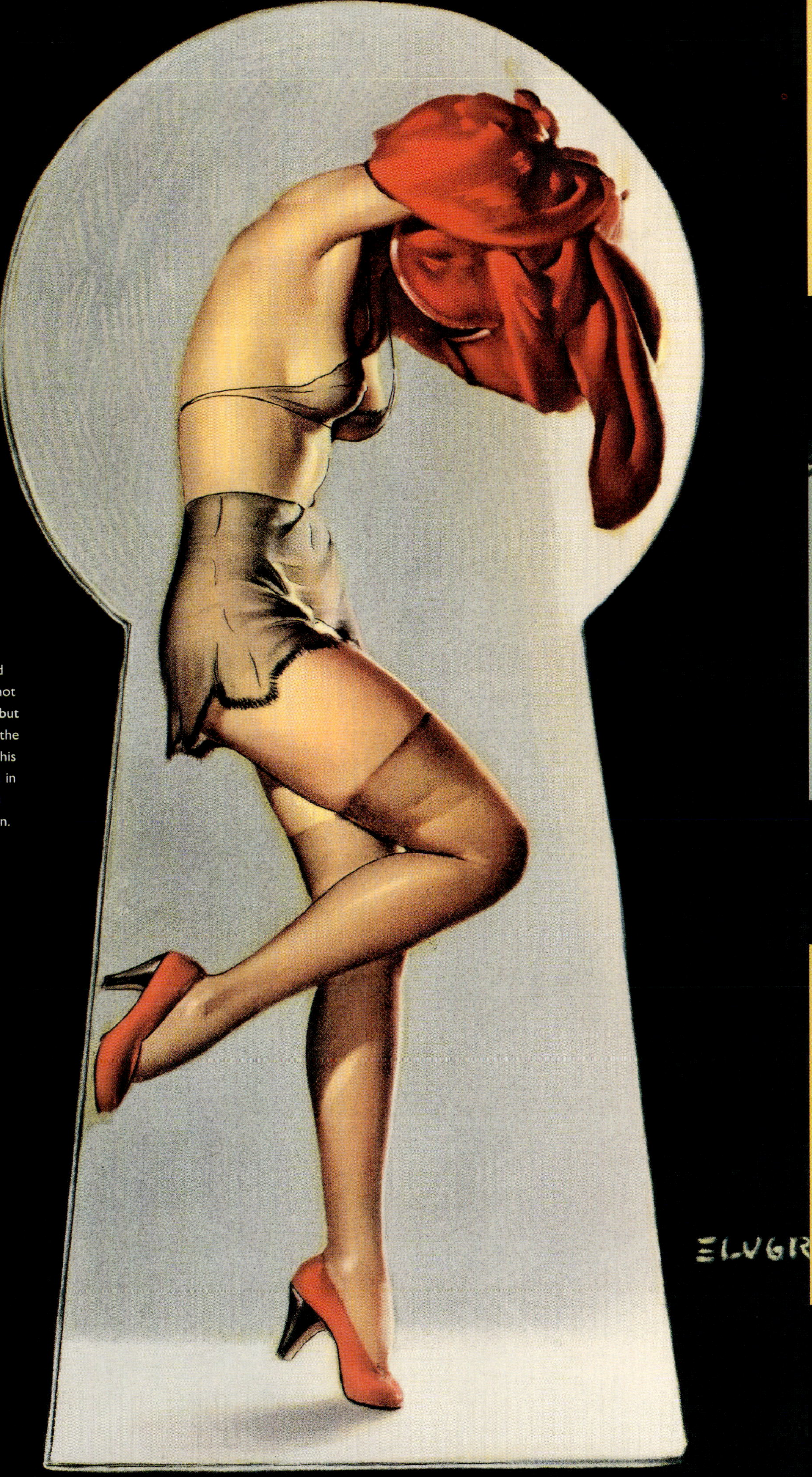

Peek-a-View

In this highly accomplished pin-up, the subject's face is not seen — an Elvgren rarity — but the lushly rendered form of the girl makes the point moot; this keyhole view was later used in many paintings by Elvgren contemporary Peter Driben.

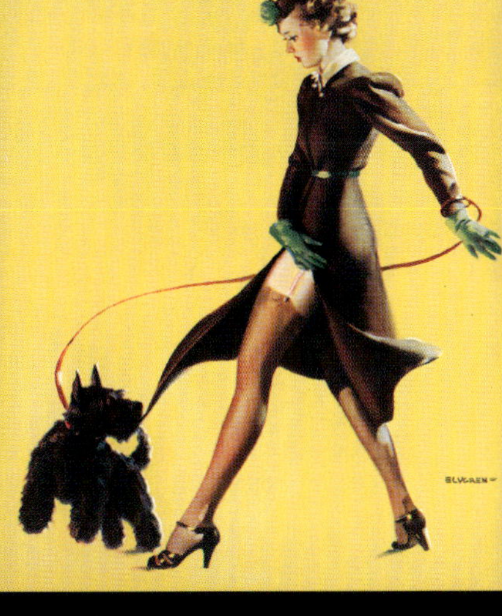

Man's Best Friend

A good early Dow example of Elvgren's experimentation with his doggie-compromising-cutie motif.

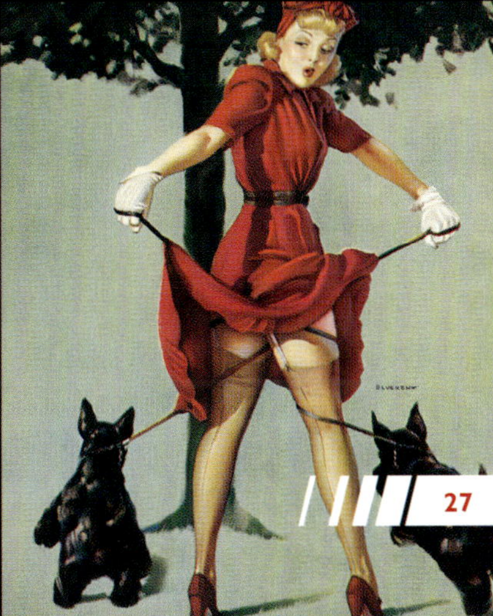

Tree for Two

A fine, later Dow pin-up finds Elvgren in near Brown & Bigelow form, with his beaming cutie compromised by two Scotties.

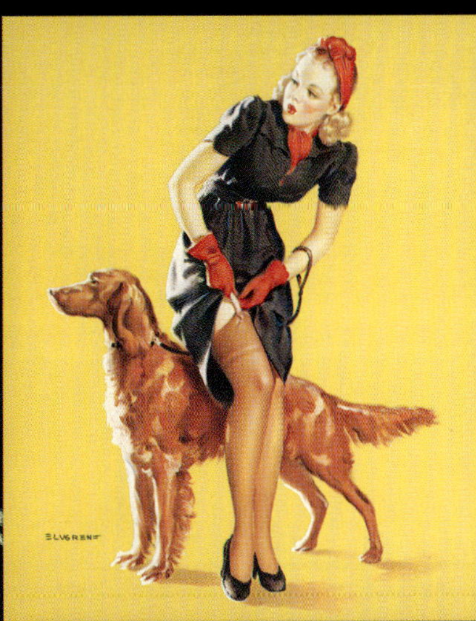

A Hitch in Time

This beautifully painted Dow pin-up allows us to innocently observe the stunning blonde's garter adjustment, while her dignified pooch stands guard (looking in the wrong direction!).

Sport Model

This mature, confident pin-up is identifiable as a Dow image only by the lack of the artist's later flourish of a signature; the self-assured, sexy woman, who knows she's letting us see her nyloned limbs, and the automobile prop are vintage Elvgren.

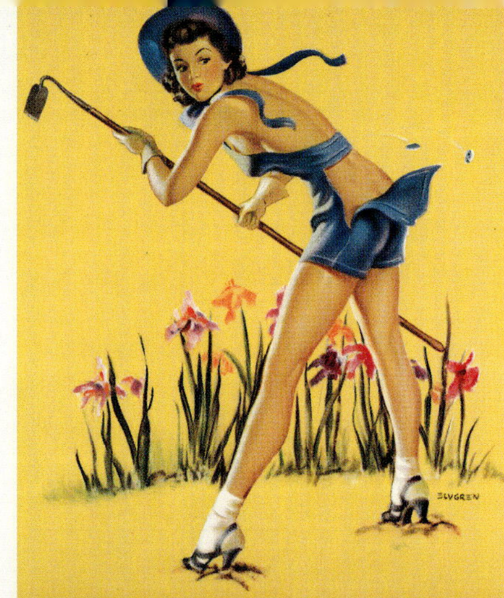

What Hoe!

This charming and well-designed pin-up — with its naughty rearview cleavage — is an early example of Elvgren's judicious use of props and setting, moving away from the isolated images of Petty and Vargas.

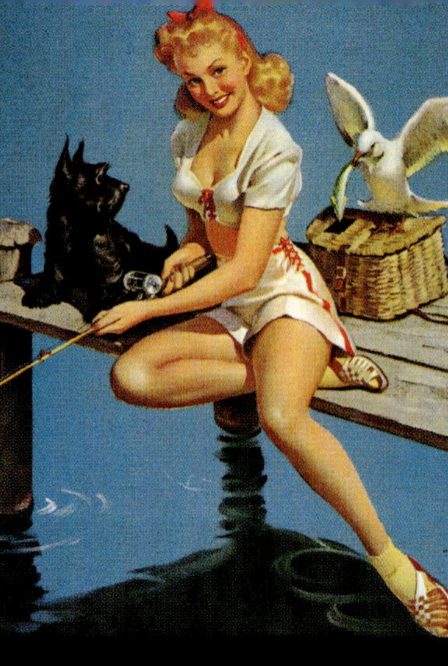

Catch On

In the 1940s, Elvgren developed a fantasy of the impossibly beautiful, wholesomely sexy girl next door, who smiled as she showed off her lovely limbs, even as winsome dogs and birds played tricks on her.

This rare, early nude makes a provocative, lyrical calendar study and indicates Elvgren's later willingness to use fully realized settings.

No Stares

One of Elvgren's earliest masterpieces, "No Stares;" shrewdly designed and beautifully lighted, it presents a lyrical beauty sweetly unashamed of her sexuality.

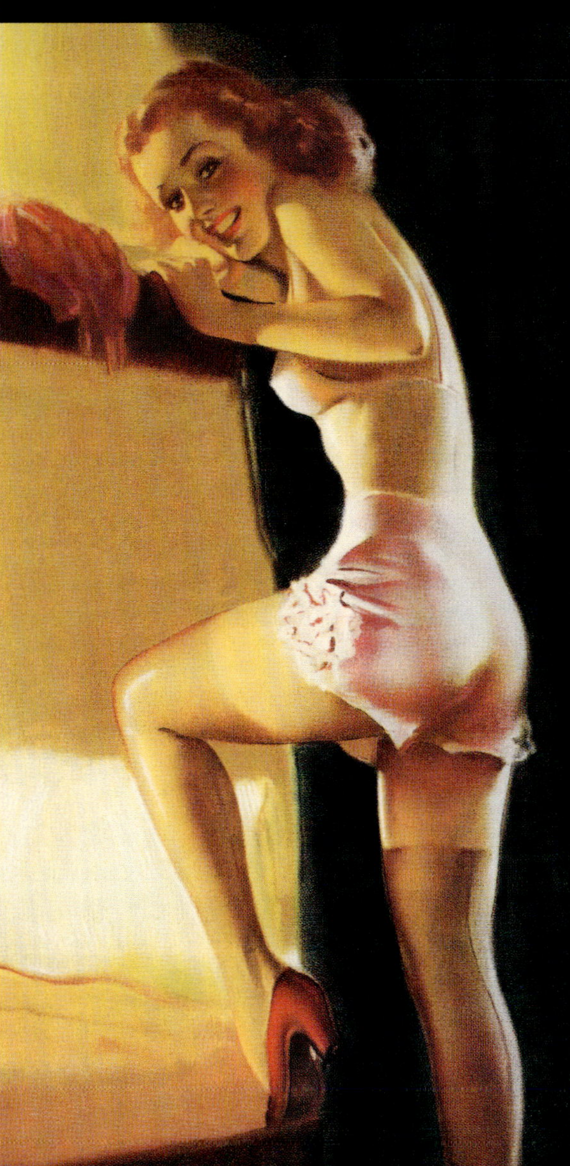

A Lad-Her Problem

Is she eloping? If so, one can only envy the husband-to-be waiting below in this exceptionally mature Dow pin-up.

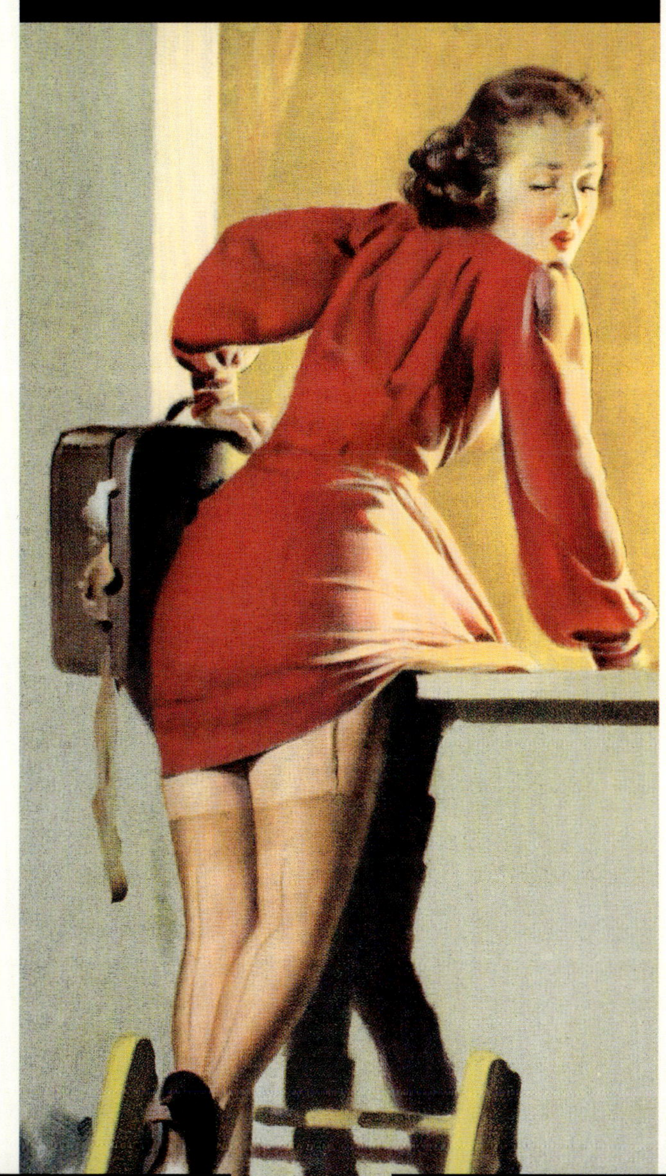

Shirt-ing Trouble

Another remarkably mature Dow pin-up is typically carefully composed (the umbrella isolating the beautiful woman's face) and nicely contrasts the furry German shepherd with sleek nyloned limbs.

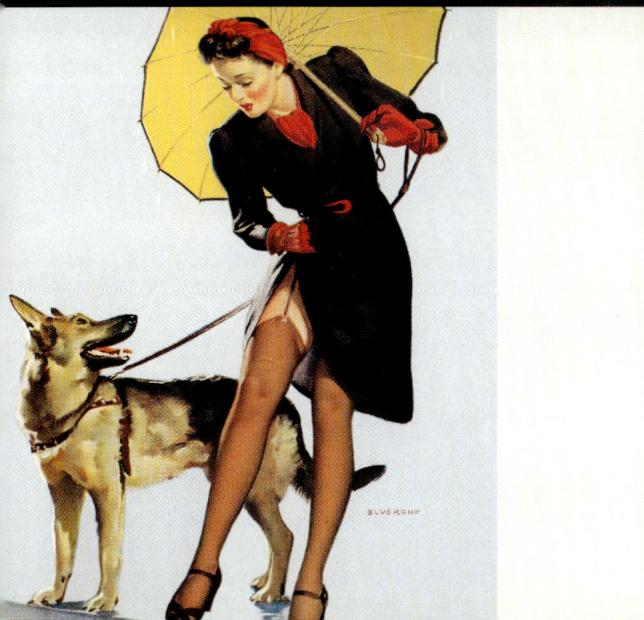

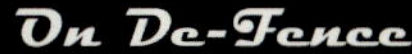

On De-Fence

An early example of a more completely realized world, this Dow pin-up is an unusual instance of an Elvgren girl not facing the camera and a reminder of the cartoon, gag-like nature at the root of the pin-up genre.

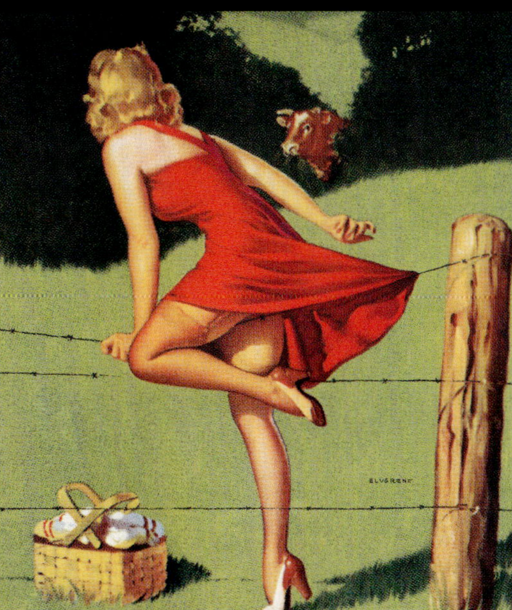

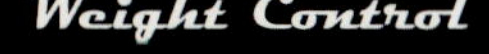

Weight Control

One of Elvgren's most overtly erotic pin-ups, "Weight Control," juxtaposes smooth, well-rounded female flesh in sheer undies and nylons against fur in a provocative pose; an early masterwork.

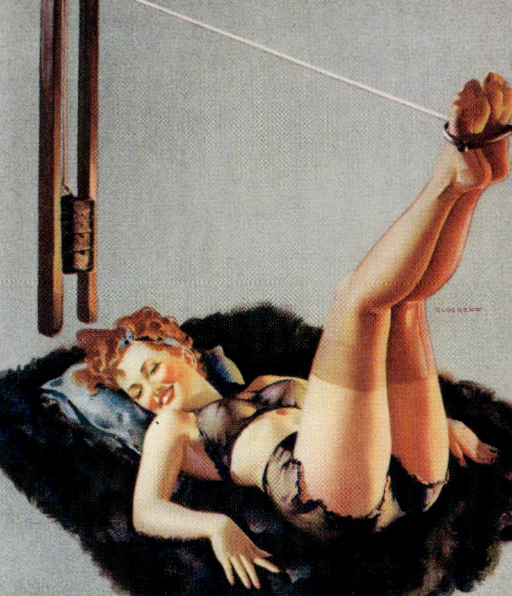

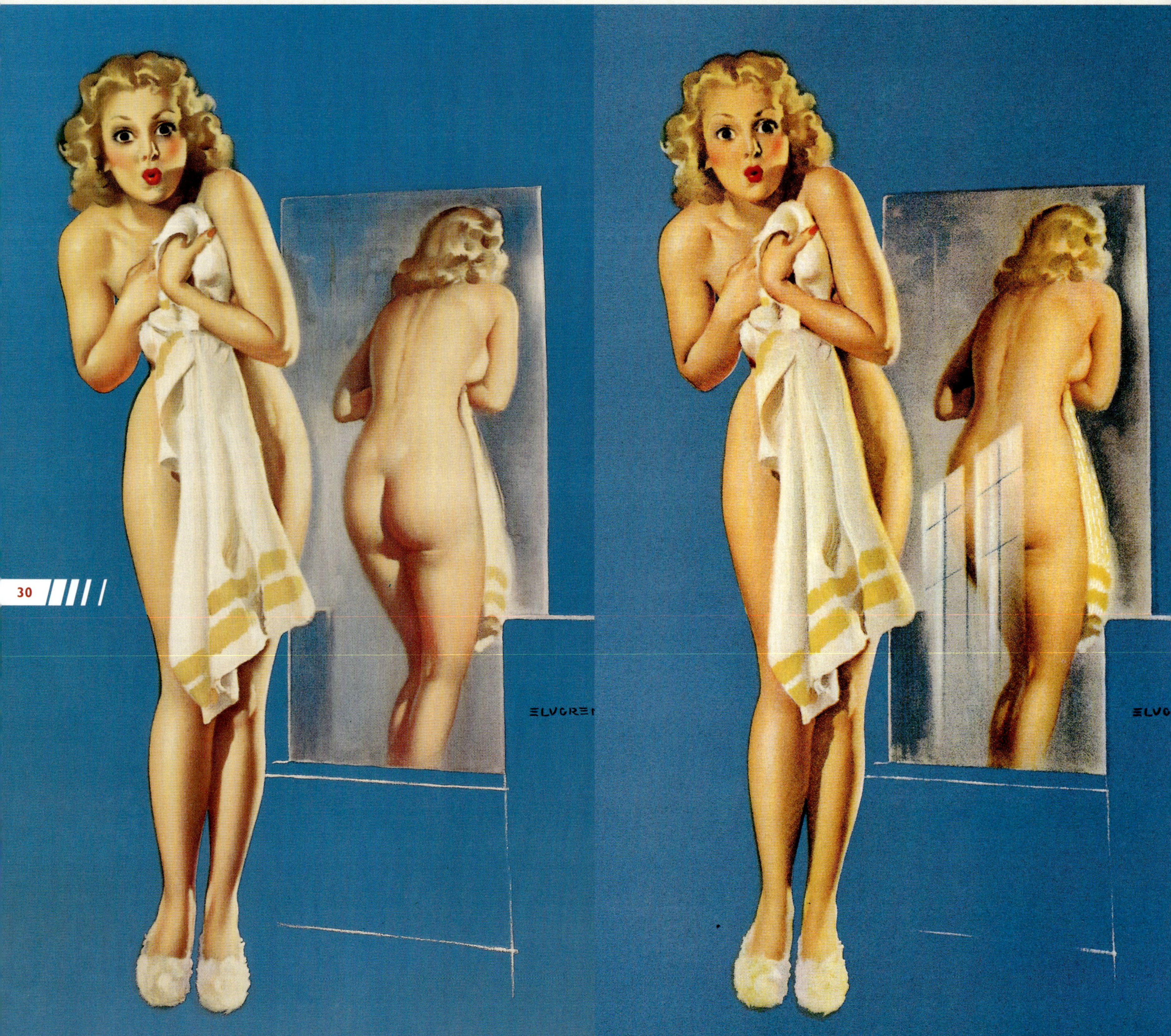

Double Exposure

Presented here in both its censored and uncensored versions, this pin-up was a frequent source for "nose cone" art on fighter planes. Our voyeuristic, secret view of the compromised cutie's backside is not typical Elvgren fare.

Belle Ringer

Elvgren came into his own in the Dow pin-ups, when he developed his compromised-cutie theme; again, a judicious use of props enhances the whimsical situation.

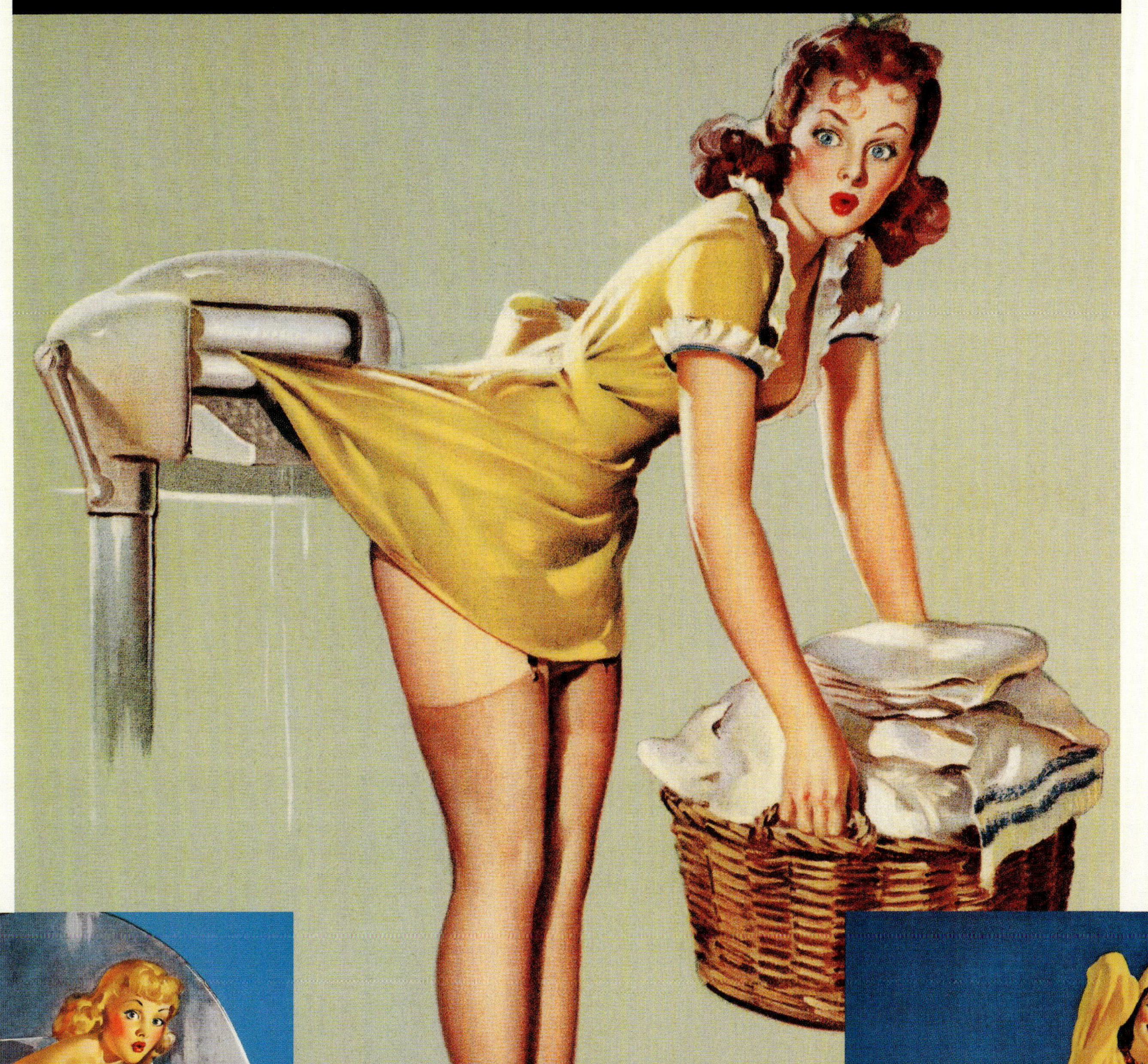

Over Exposure

Is she the same blonde from "Double Exposure?" This seems to be a sequel, and it's perhaps even better, with the subject's generous curves so perfectly rendered and her eyes just catching us watching her.

Tail Wind

Elvgren's enthusiasm for flying helps fuel this, one of the Dow pin-ups that could pass for a later, mature Brown & Bigelow work.

Slip Off Shore

Images were recycled by Dow for many years after Elvgren's prewar stint as their pin-up master.

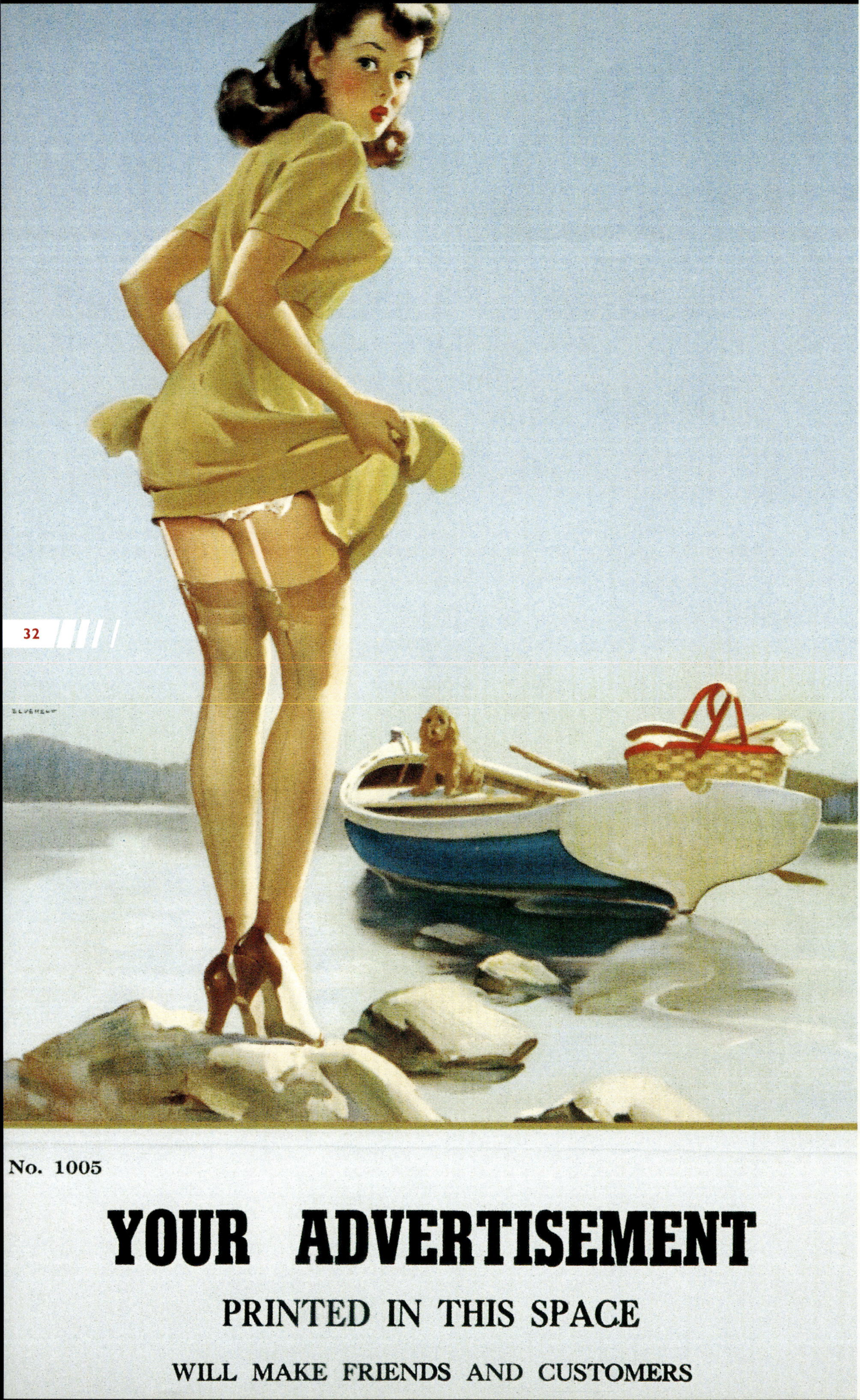

No. 1005

YOUR ADVERTISEMENT

PRINTED IN THIS SPACE

WILL MAKE FRIENDS AND CUSTOMERS

Miss-Placed Confidence

Another gag cartoon in full pin-up drag, this piece is rare in its glimpse at a barely dressed girl, who does not acknowledge our presence (or anyone's, other than the naughty dog's).

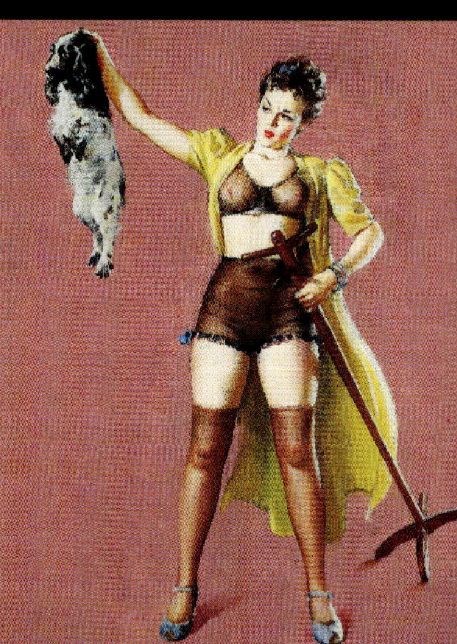

Short on Sails

Attractive as she is, this blonde on a raft has a disturbingly baby-ish softness — another early effort.

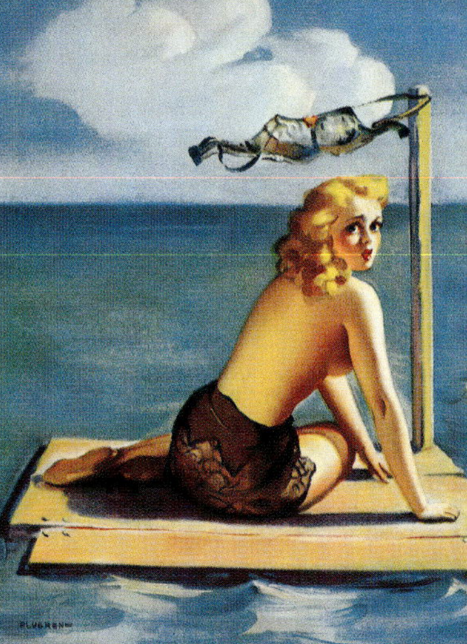

Net Results

One of the best early pin-ups, the subject is still baby-faced but the coy, compromised cutie is emerging.

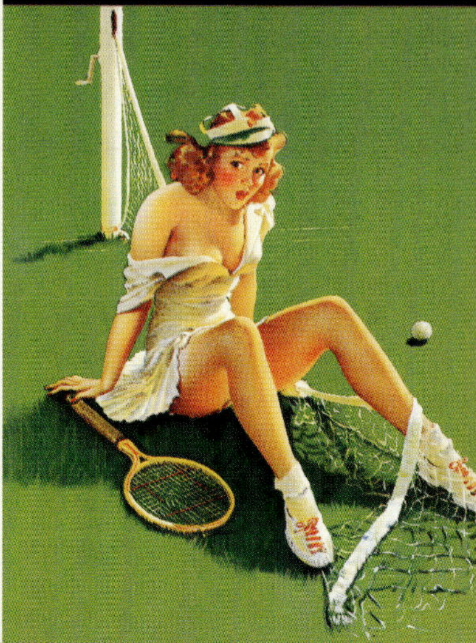

Station WOW

Another early masterpiece — a provocative pose with the pretty subject daring you to look at her; an art moderne radio in the background and floating music notes tie this to early, Petty-influenced days.

ELVG

Teeter Taught Her

The wholesomely sexy Elvgren girl comes into her own in this Dow pin-up; this image was overpainted into a girl riding a carousel horse (not pictured).

Caught in the Draft

During his short tenure with Dow, Elvgren's rapid maturity is mind-boggling; this slickly rendered, well-conceived image evidences his growth.

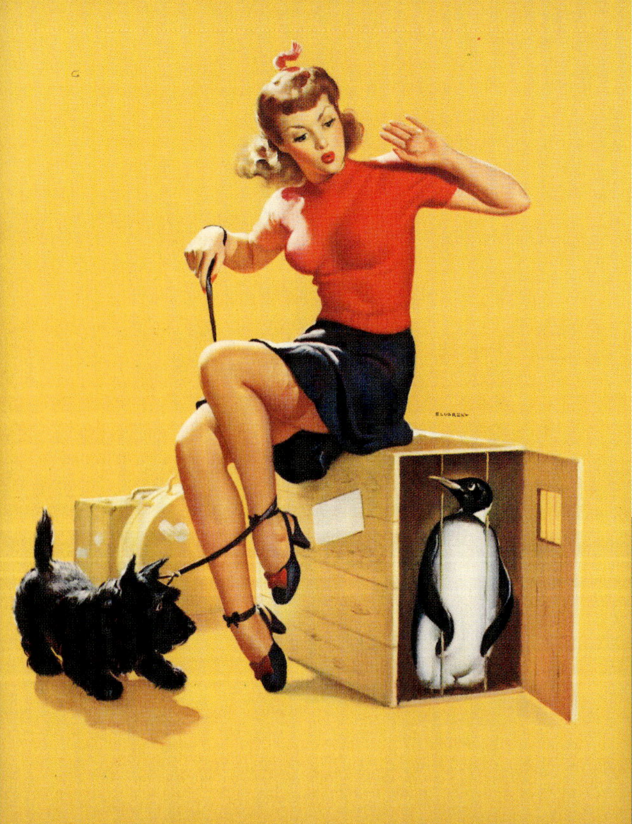

What's Cooking

The Elvgren style is in full bloom in this late Dow image, with lovely lighting effects and cute animals enhancing a stunningly beautiful subject; the shapeliness of the girl is equaled only by her supple grace.

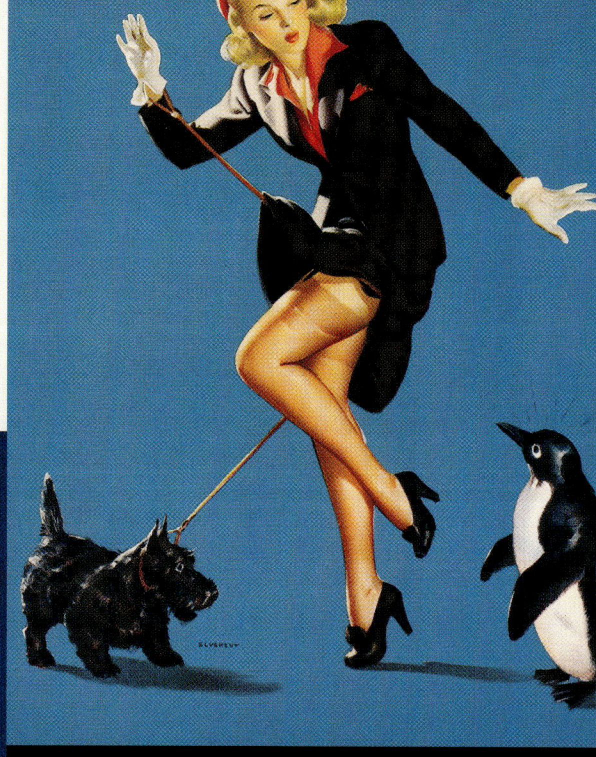

Bird's Eye View

The warm, sunny style that flourished at Brown & Bigelow is blossoming in this charming pin-up, where cute animals absurdly add to this stunning blonde's nylon-baring dilemma.

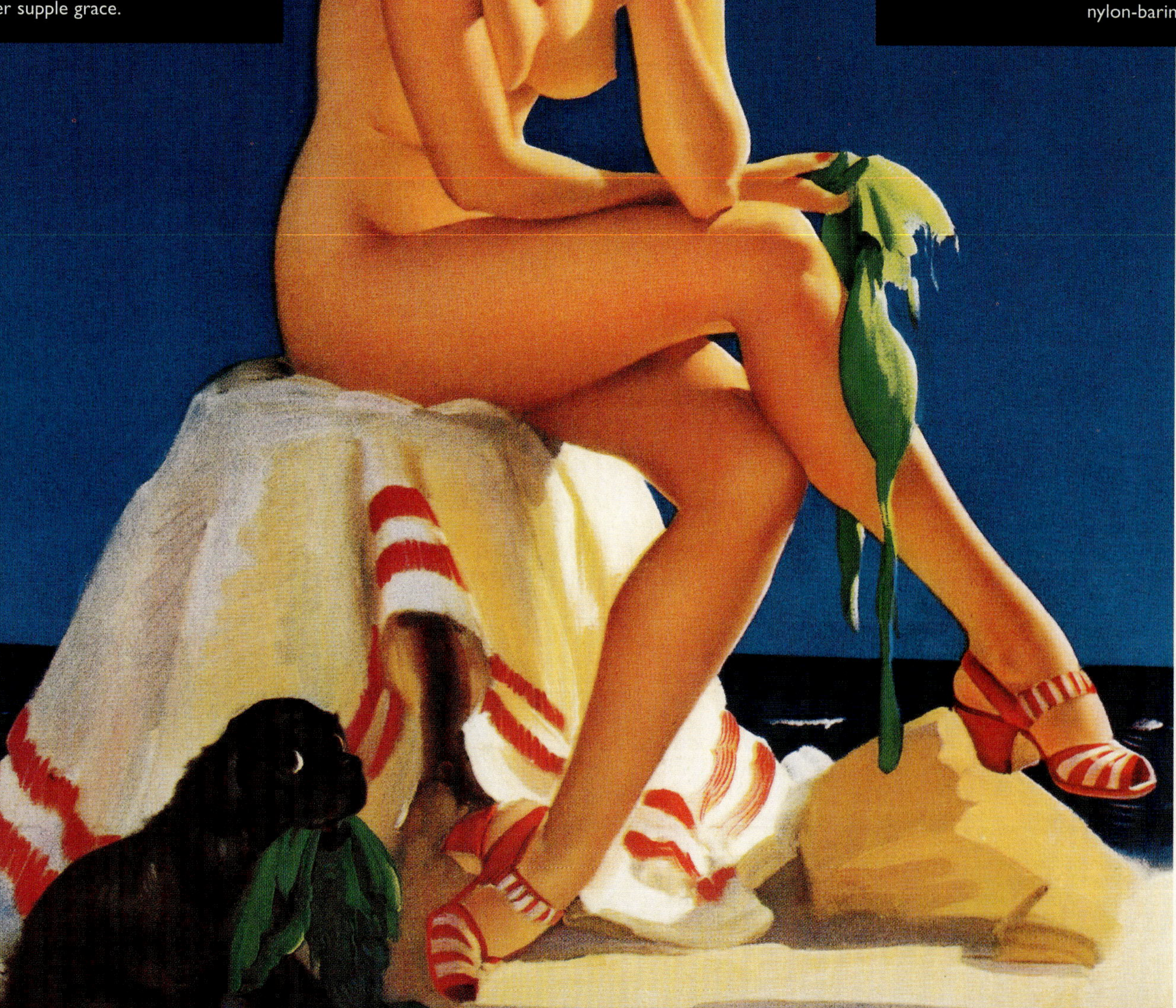

In for a Tanning

A rare combination of Elvgren's compromised cutie with it's gag-like elements and a voyeuristic glimpse of an unaware, gracefully rendered nude.

Sleepy-Time Girl

One of Elvgren's most striking art moderne Dow pin-ups — beautifully designed, with its yawning, lovely blonde perched on a stool — is overpainted competently into a more conventional (and later period) bedroom suite.

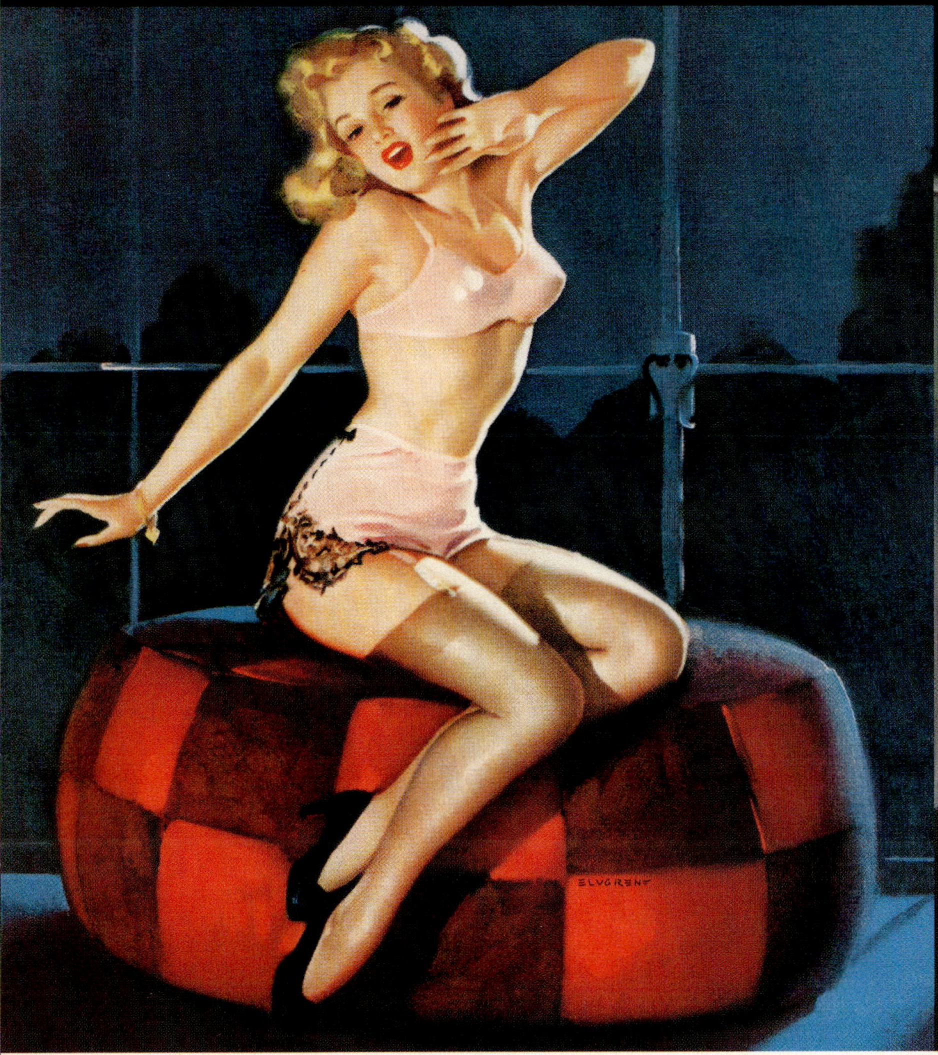

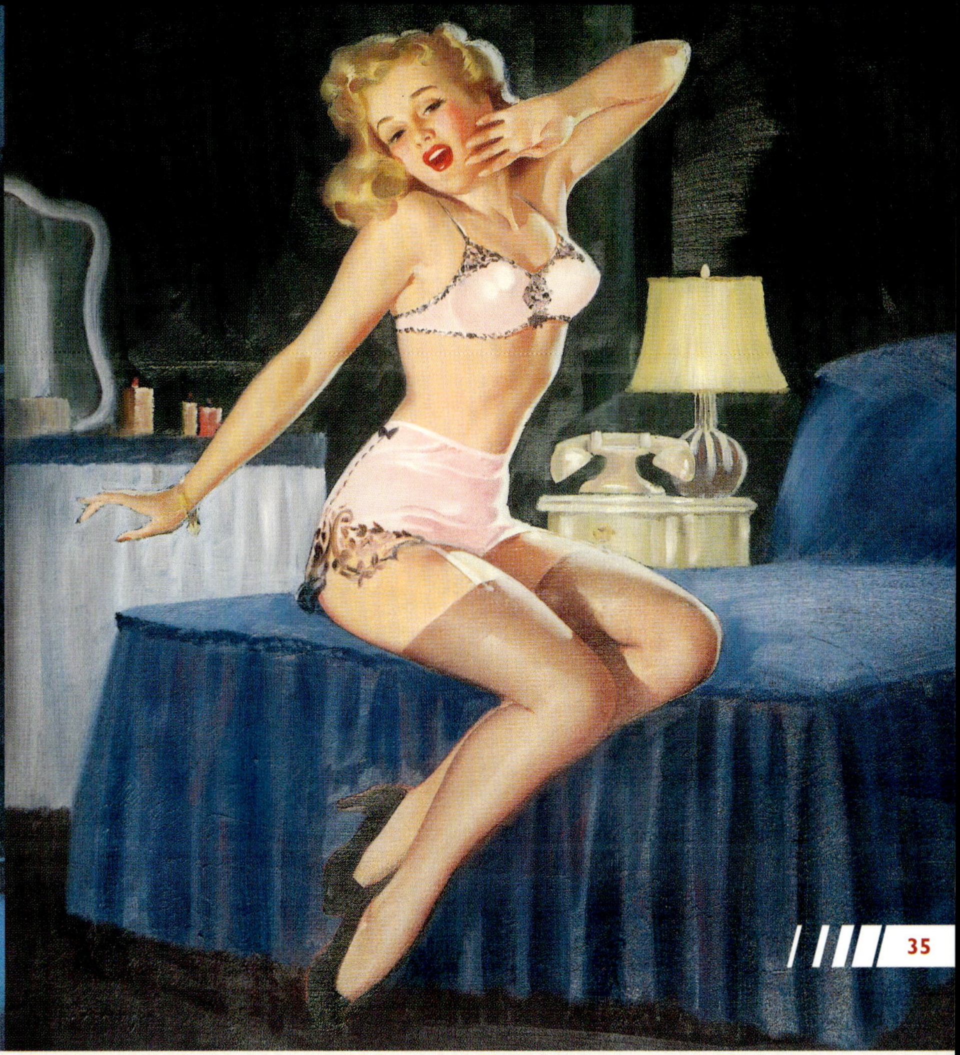

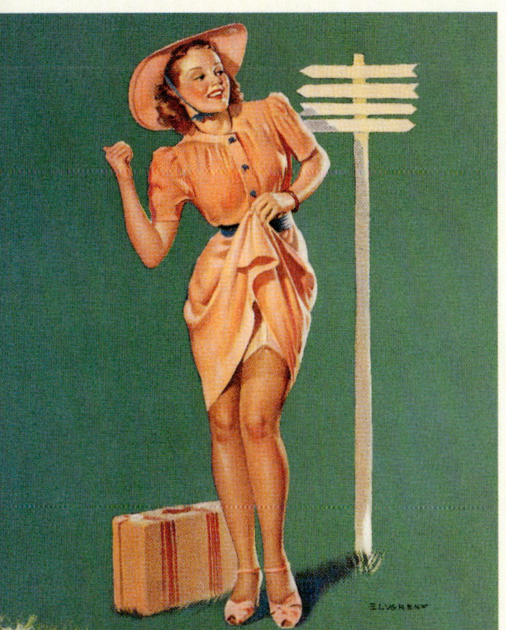

Kneeding a Lift

This pretty hitchhiker's innocence is offset by the boldness of her hitching, inspired no doubt by Claudette Colbert's silkened flash in *It Happened One Night* (1934).

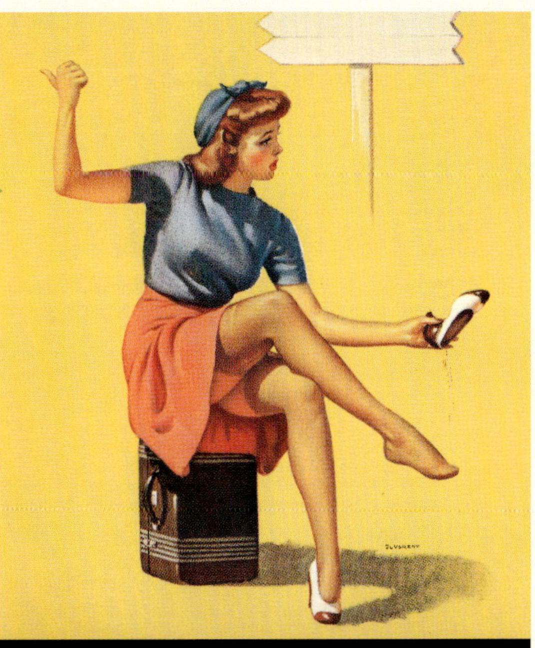

The High Sign

Beautiful hitchhikers are a recurring presence in Gil Elvgren's pin-ups, particularly the early ones. An overpaint (not pictured) transforms this hitchhiker into a customer in a shoe store.

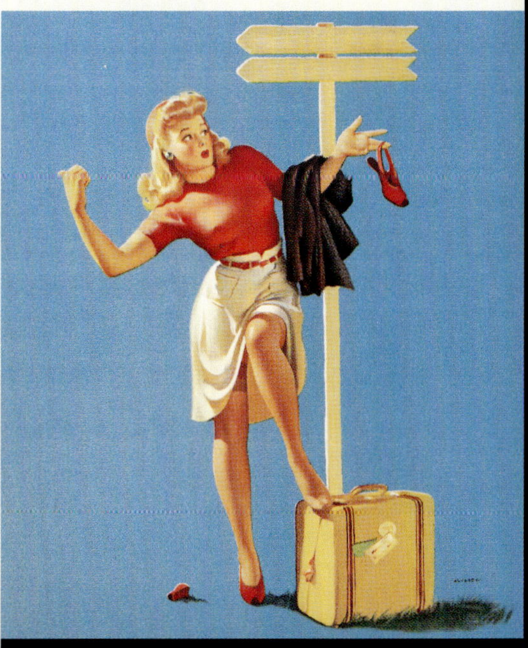

Foot-Loose

Perhaps the best of his Dow hitchhikers, this pin-up is as effectively posed as she is lovely, the props (in particular, the shoe in one hand) telling her story.

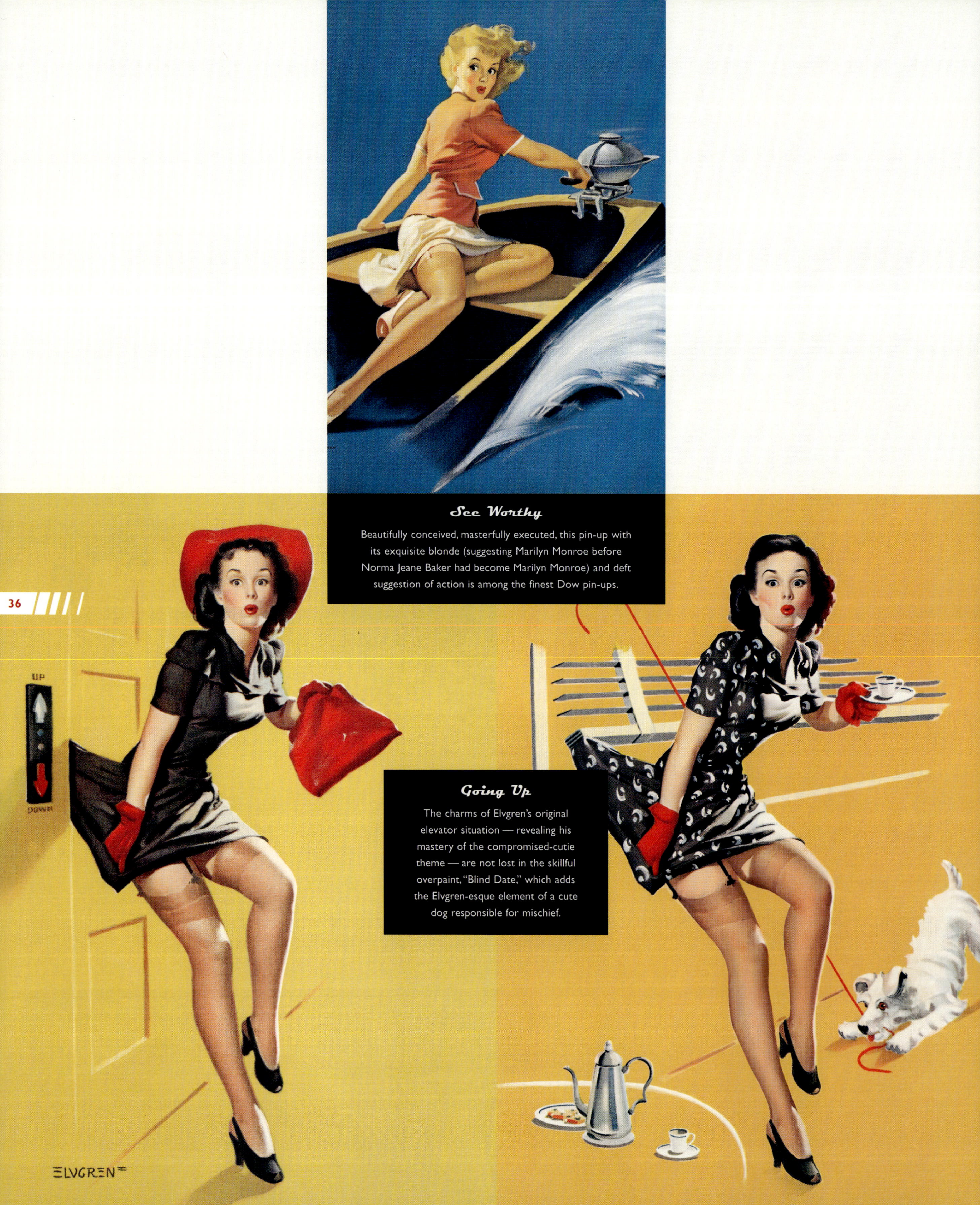

See Worthy

Beautifully conceived, masterfully executed, this pin-up with its exquisite blonde (suggesting Marilyn Monroe before Norma Jeane Baker had become Marilyn Monroe) and deft suggestion of action is among the finest Dow pin-ups.

Going Up

The charms of Elvgren's original elevator situation — revealing his mastery of the compromised-cutie theme — are not lost in the skillful overpaint, "Blind Date," which adds the Elvgren-esque element of a cute dog responsible for mischief.

Lucky Dog

Despite the somewhat silly subject matter, this show-biz pin-up is one of the Dow images that could be mistaken for a Brown & Bigelow, so mature and sure is Elvgren's work here.

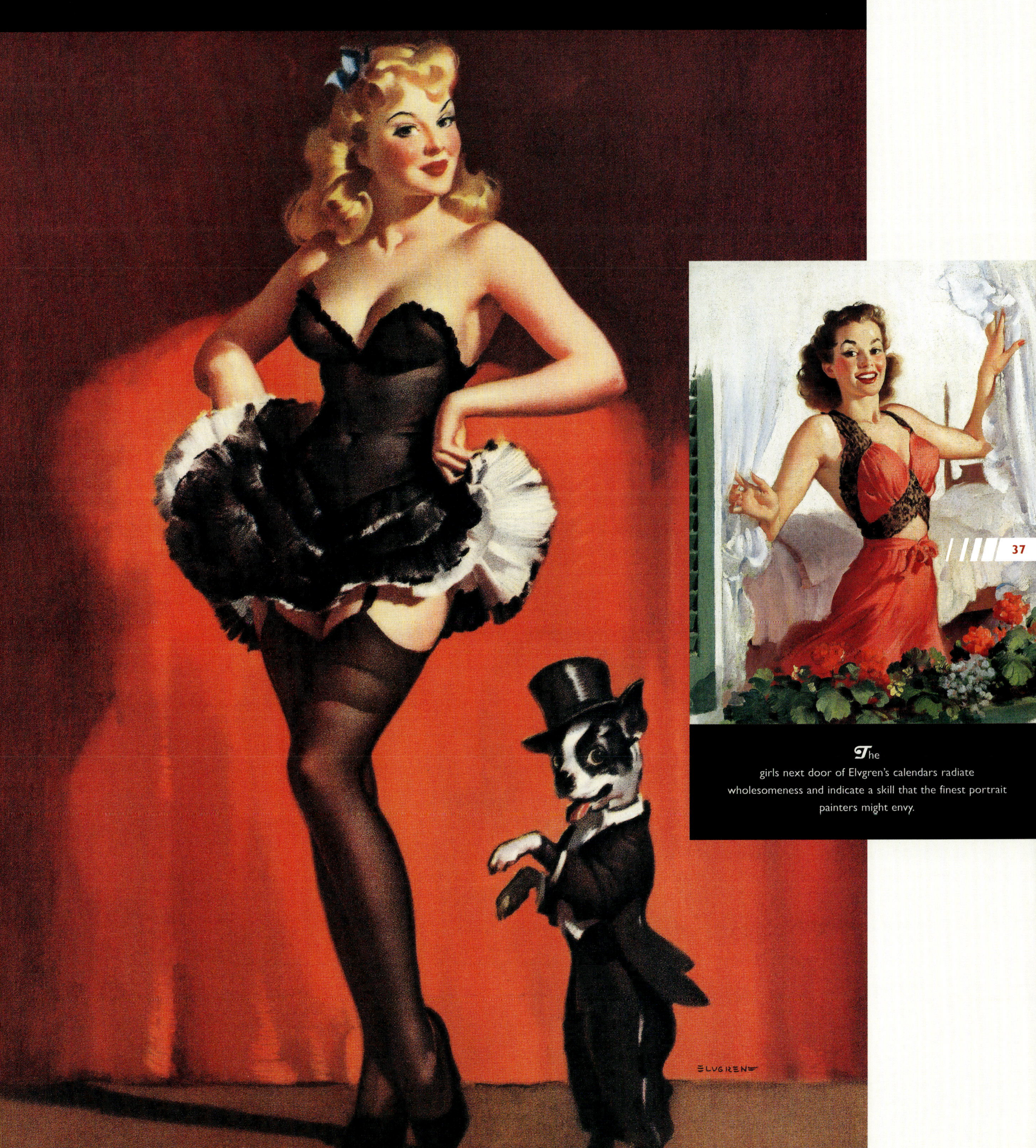

The girls next door of Elvgren's calendars radiate wholesomeness and indicate a skill that the finest portrait painters might envy.

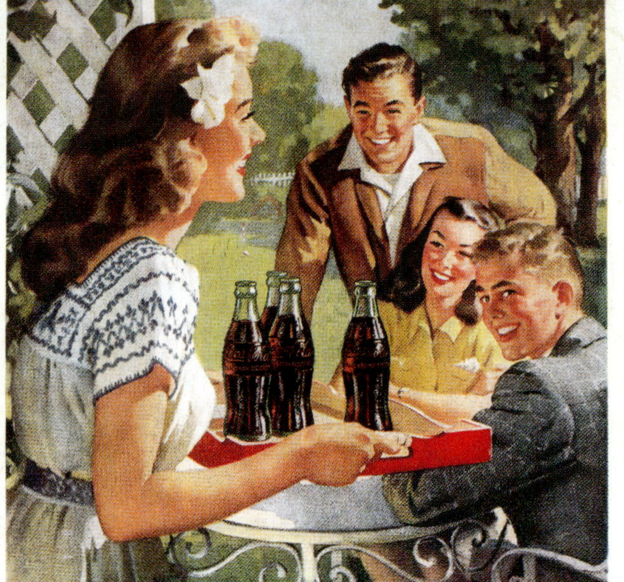

Hospitality... So Easy and Welcome

On warm summer days, guests like the terrace or the porch. Out of the family refrigerator comes ice-cold Coca-Cola. Hospitality has begun. *The pause that refreshes* with ice-cold Coke puts everyone at ease, makes people happy to be where they are. For refreshment at home, you can get Coca-Cola in the handy, easy-to-carry 6-bottle carton or in the 24-bottle case.

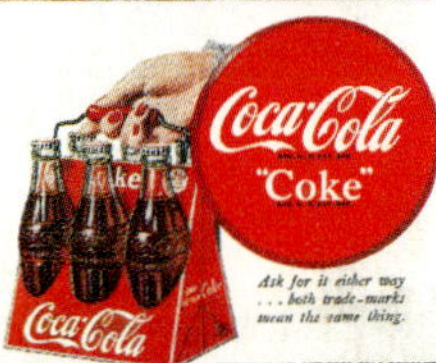

Ask for it either way ... both trade-marks mean the same thing.

Occasionally the guys get to be "on camera" in Elvgren's Coke ads, but these lovely girls in a Rockwell-esque Americana/romantic setting are pin-up worthy.

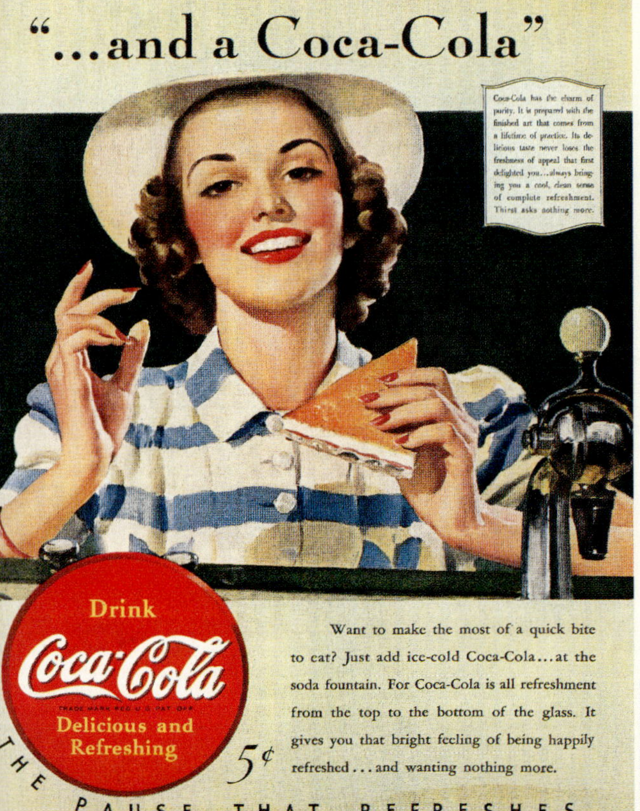

Elvgren's Coca-Cola girls — both before, during, and after the war — represented an idealized girl next door; the implied soda fountain was a symbol of both small-town and big-city America that resonated with servicemen.

Coca-Cola ads frequently feature an off-camera boyfriend handing a radiant Elvgren girl a Coke; the carousel pose is one Elvgren (and other pin-up artists) uses frequently, with its obvious but innocent phallic elements.

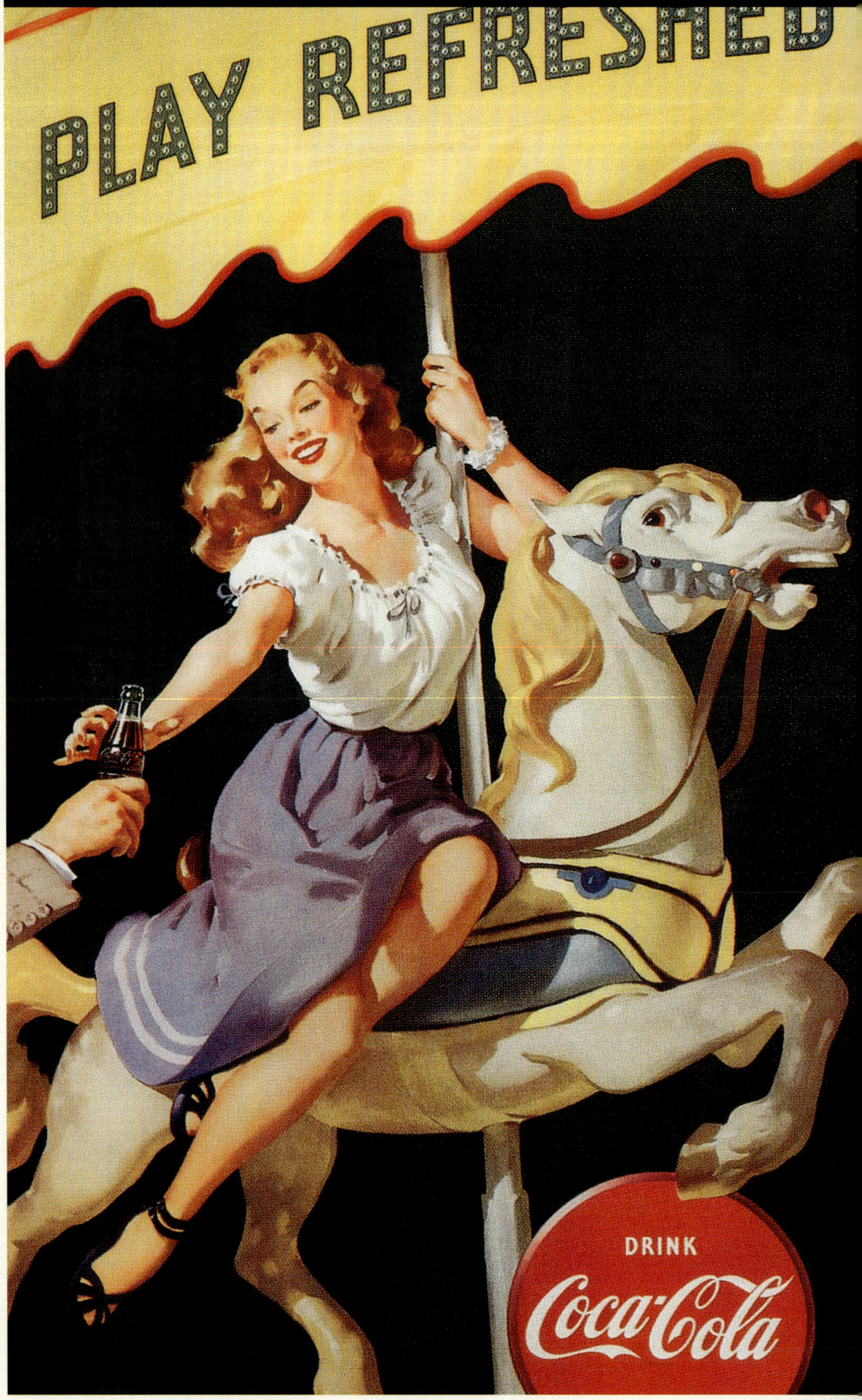

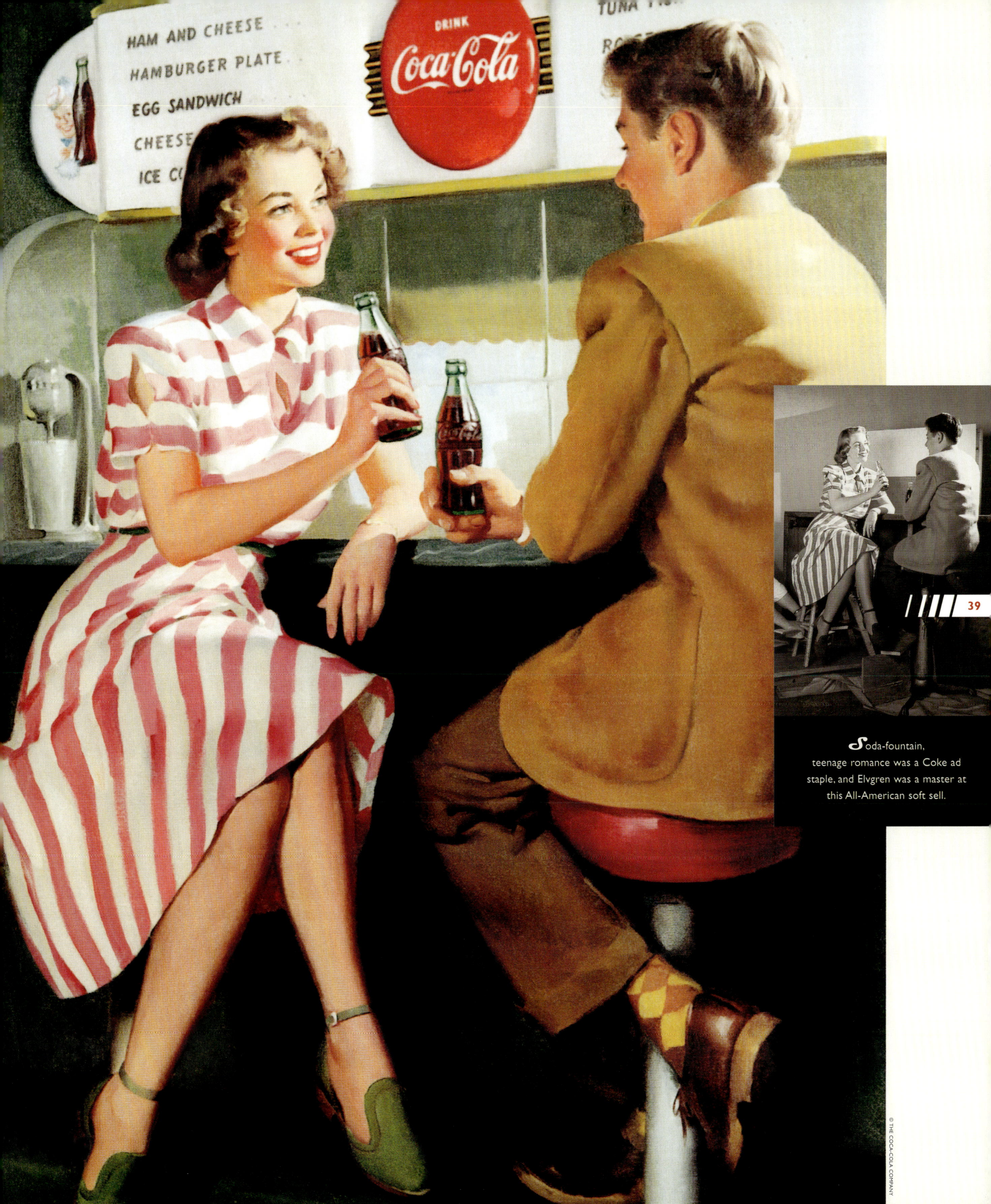

Soda-fountain, teenage romance was a Coke ad staple, and Elvgren was a master at this All-American soft sell.

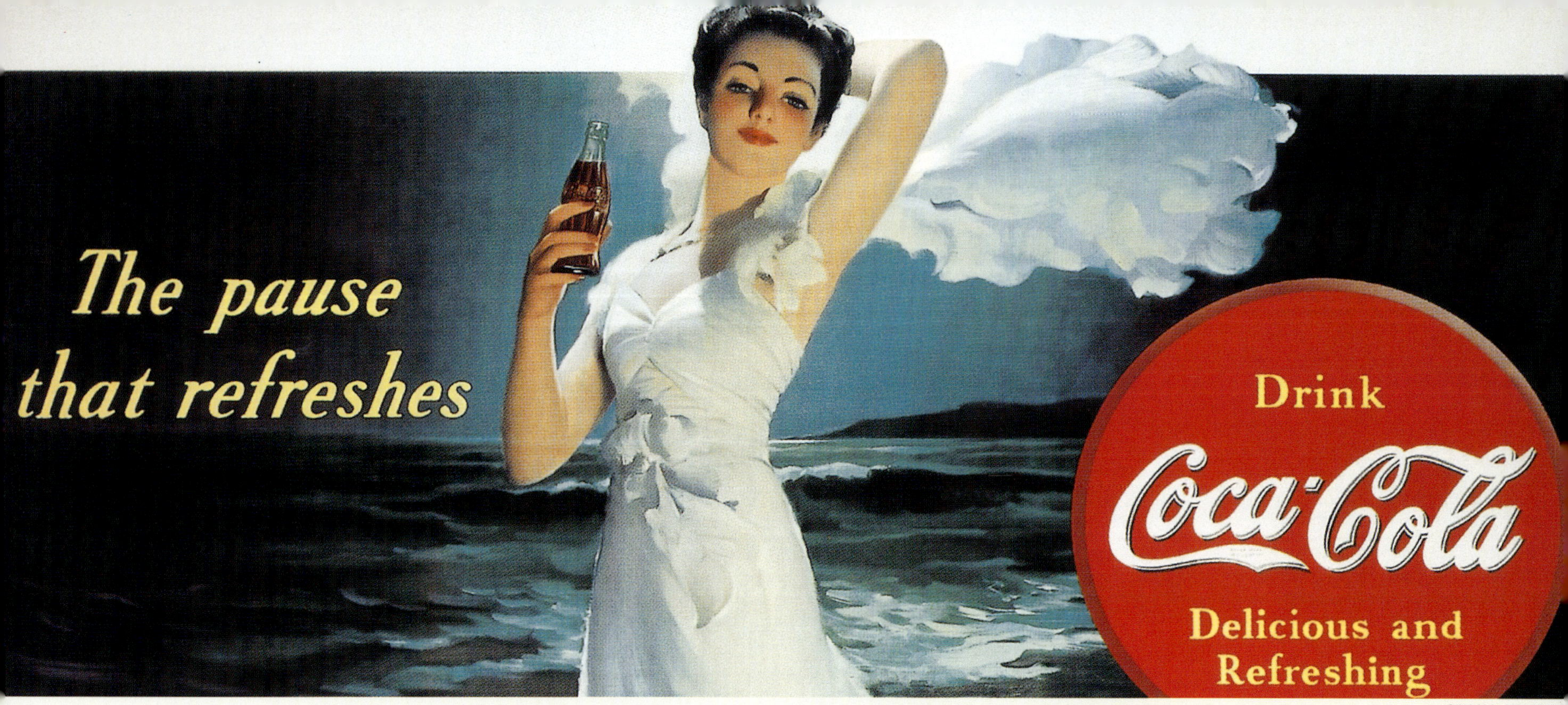

The pause
that refreshes

Drink
Coca-Cola
Delicious and
Refreshing

Probably
dating to the early 1940s, Elvgren is working in the gently sexy pin-up style perfected by his mentor, Haddon Sundblom.

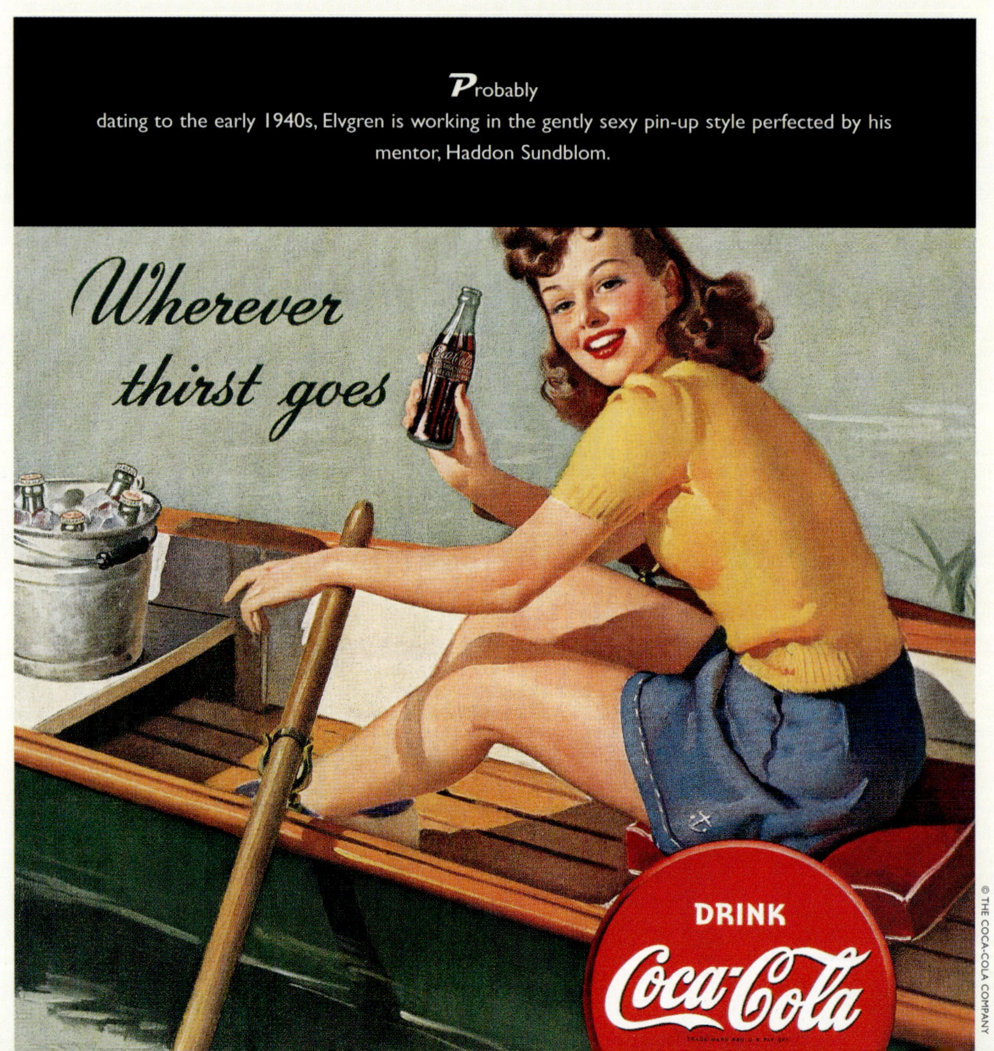

Women aren't always Elvgren's subjects; lovingly depicted by outdoorsman Gil, this working-class man — probably a farmer — loves his beer as much as the outdoors.

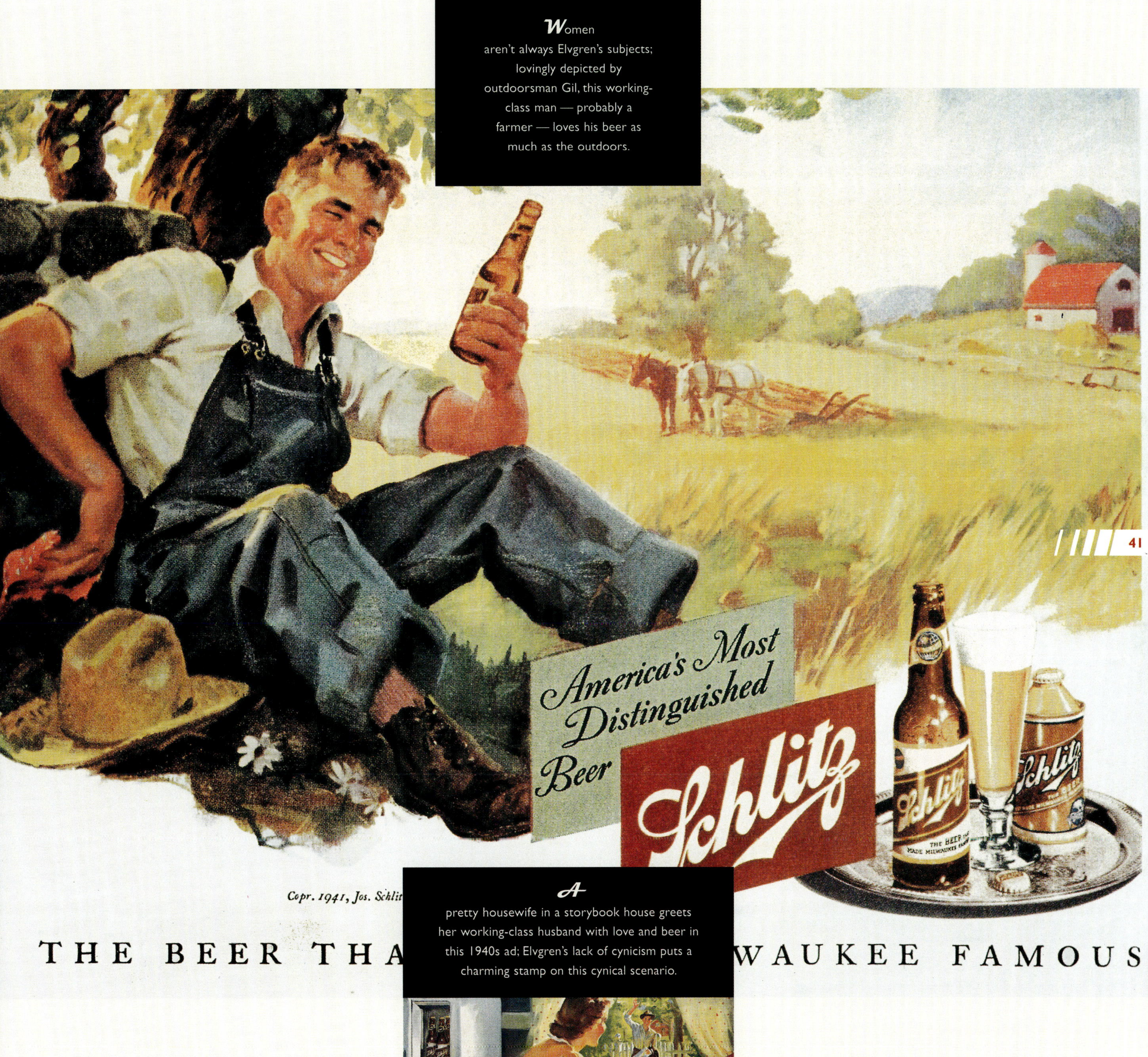

A pretty housewife in a storybook house greets her working-class husband with love and beer in this 1940s ad; Elvgren's lack of cynicism puts a charming stamp on this cynical scenario.

Beaming though she is, the Good Luck Dutch girl reveals Elvgren's lack of enthusiasm for child subjects.

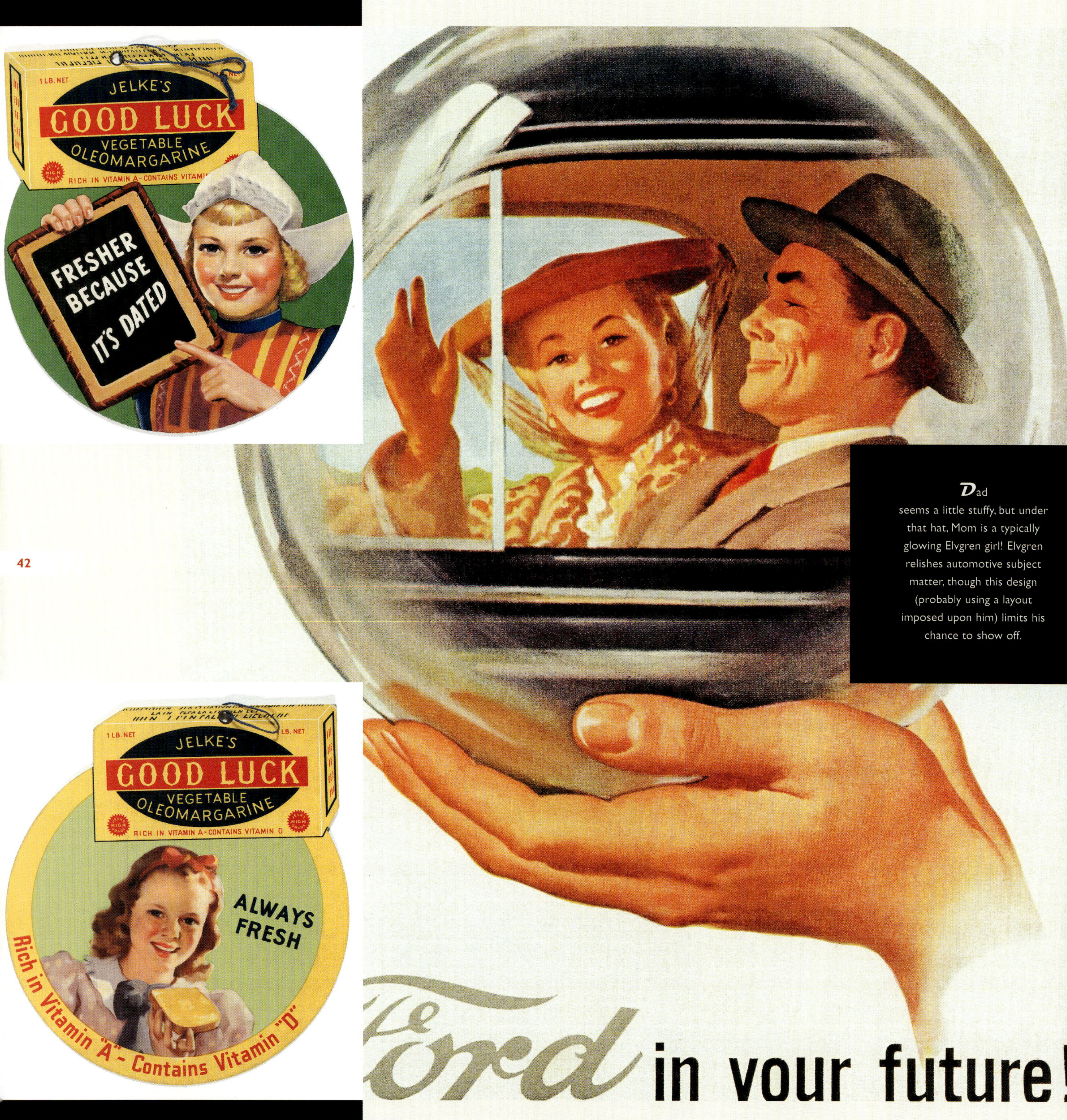

Dad seems a little stuffy, but under that hat, Mom is a typically glowing Elvgren girl! Elvgren relishes automotive subject matter, though this design (probably using a layout imposed upon him) limits his chance to show off.

Vaguely Shirley Temple-ish, this brunette is more realistic and winning than Elvgren's Dutch girl for the same product; but his lack of delight in drawing children is evident.

AREFREE TIRES are essential to carefree days. Many people, of
urse, buy Generals first of all for the economy of their famous long
leage. But, every user realizes that maximum blowout protection
uicker, straight stops – and freedom from trouble – are equally
portant features of General's Top-Quality. And they are worth so
ch more than the few cents difference per tire they cost to obtain.

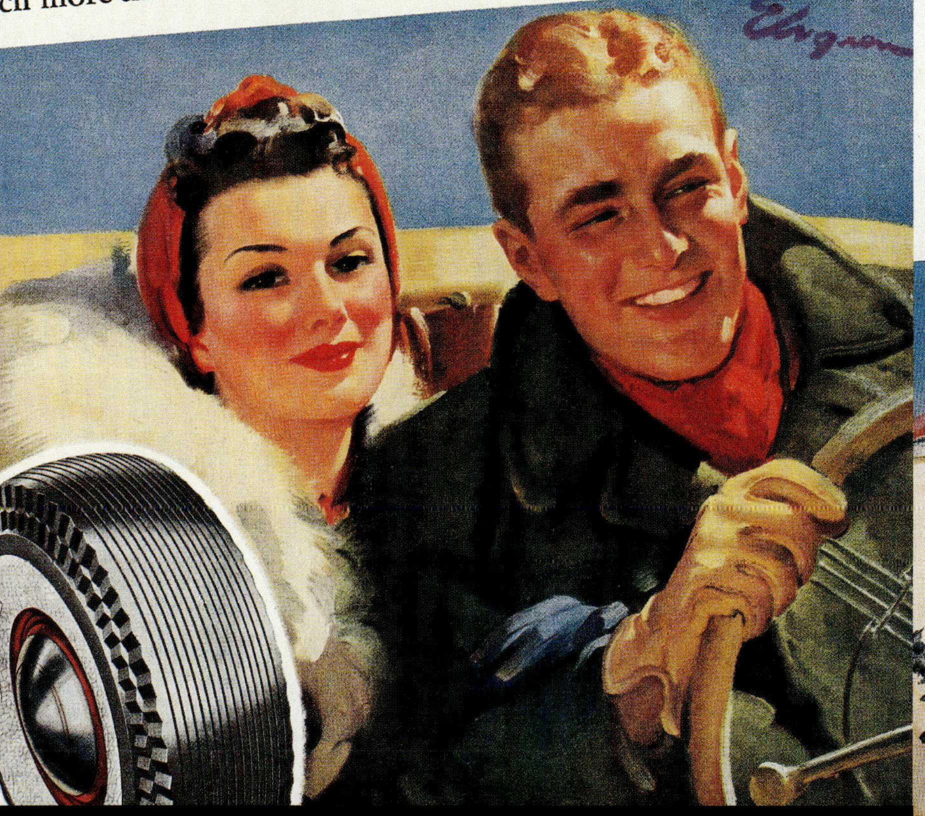

This General Tire advertisement features a sophisticated couple this time and shows Elvgren's Sundblom and Leyendecker influences merging pleasantly.

This tire ad — presumably appearing shortly before the start of World War II — is rather cluttered, but that's not Elvgren's fault: his central image is straightforward and naively romantic.

THERE IS A SENSE OF SECURITY when riding on Generals that you seem to experience with no other tire. For sheer peace of mind you need the quick-stopping safety, blowout protection and trouble-free travel that General's Top-Quality assures. On a dollar and "sense" basis, the famous long mileage of General Tires makes them by all odds your wisest investment.

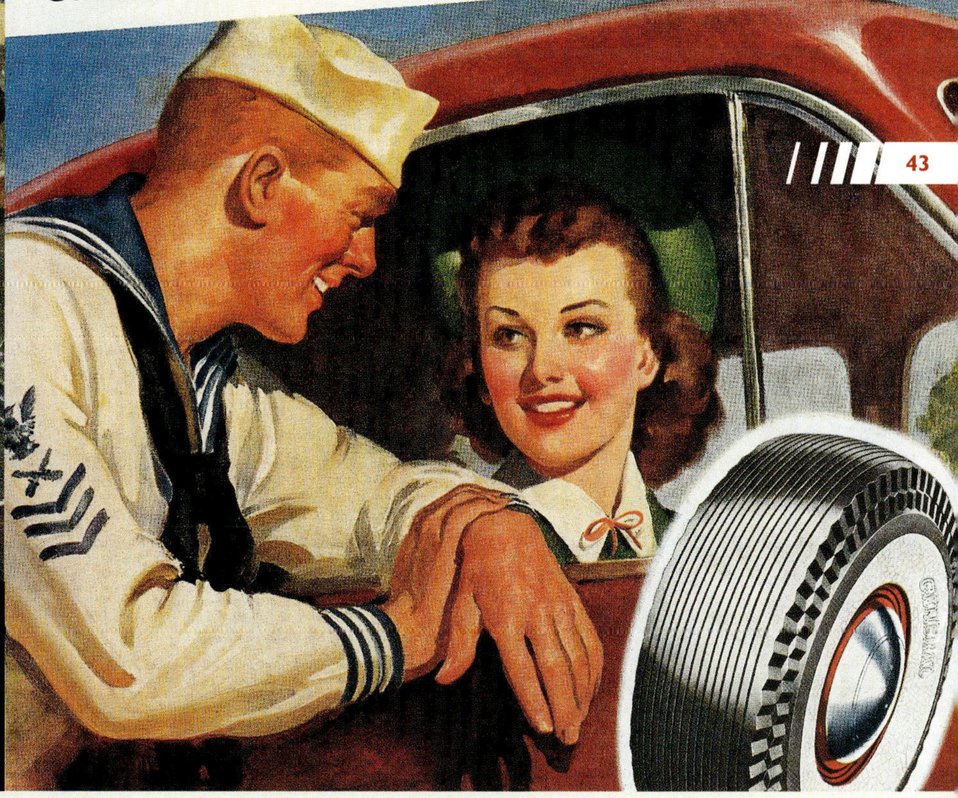

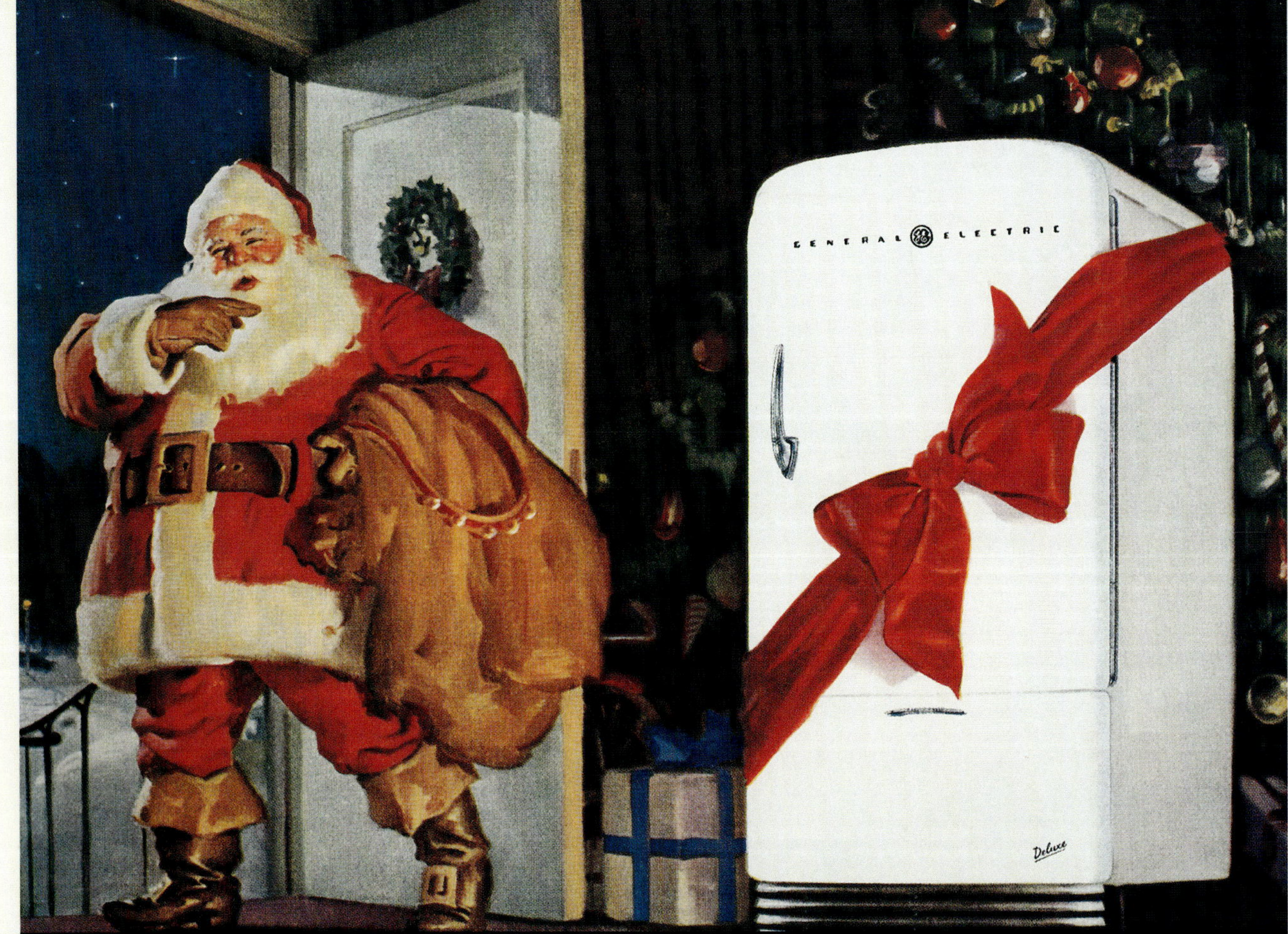

Seven-Up backed away from Elvgren's Santa Claus because it was too close to Coke's Haddon Sundblom version; but that didn't stop other clients — like General Electric — from taking advantage of the talents of Sundblom's protégé.

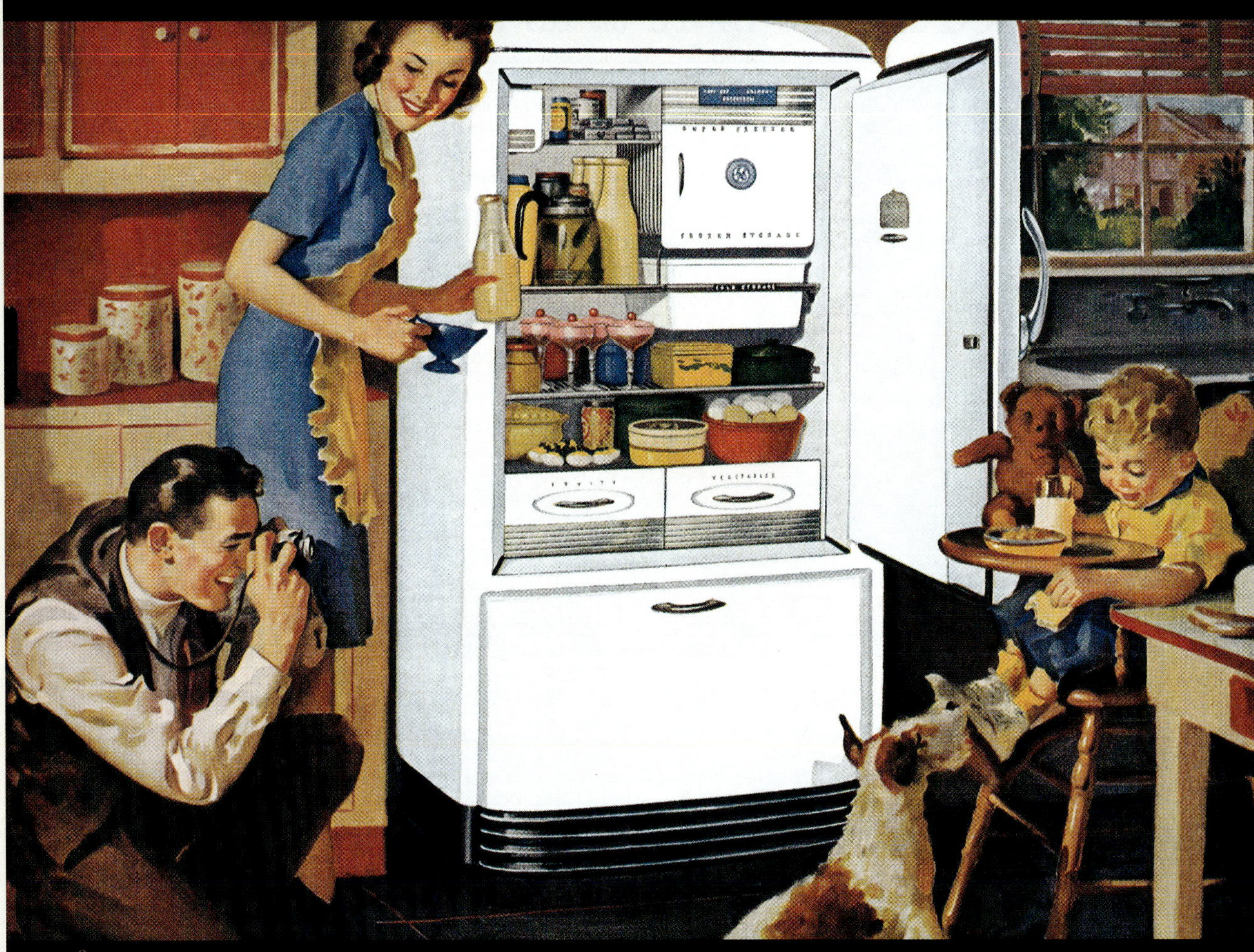

This 1940s refrigerator ad portrays an idyllic family life in the patented *Saturday Evening Post* manner.

Elvgren's Santa for G.E. tops his mentor Haddon Sundblom's Santa by adding a beautiful, page-boy-sporting secretary; no elves for Gil Elvgren!

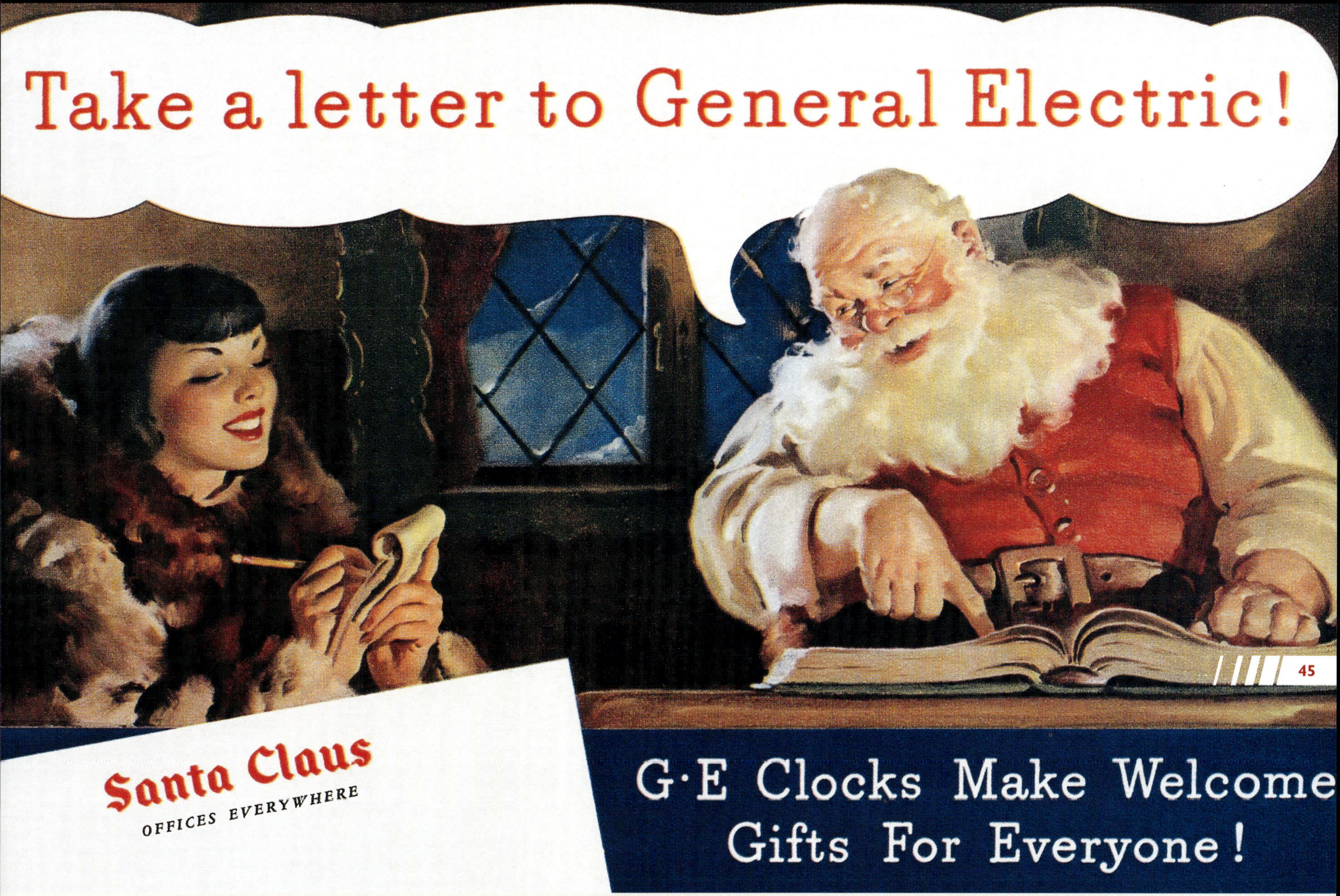

Take a letter to General Electric!

Santa Claus
OFFICES EVERYWHERE

G·E Clocks Make Welcome Gifts For Everyone!

The Rockwell of the pin-up depicts an idyllic family at Christmas; that's no Haddon Sundblom Santa but Dad in disguise.

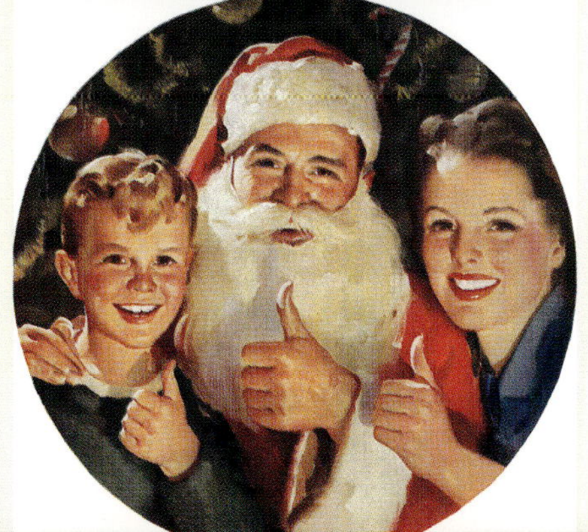

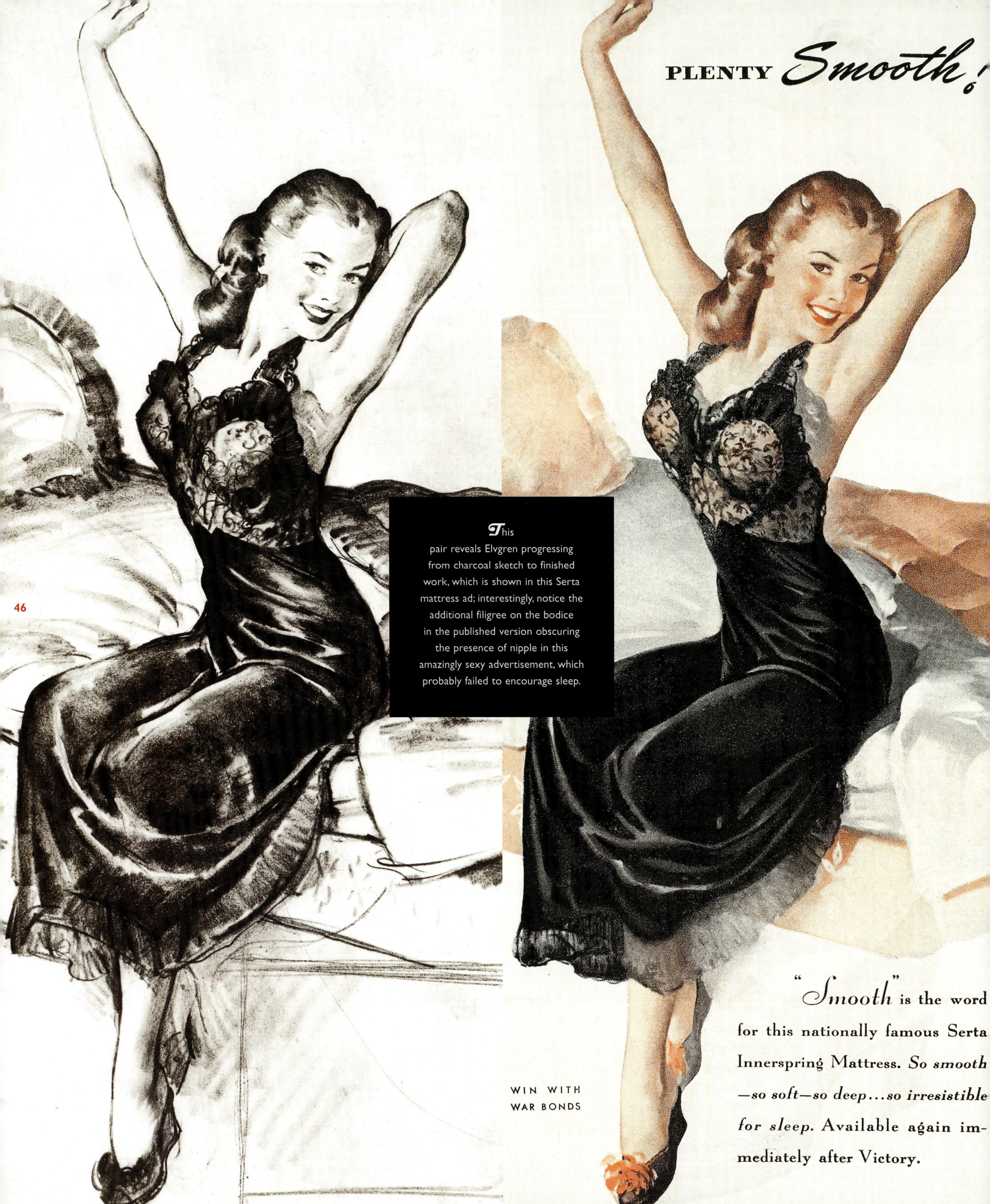

This pair reveals Elvgren progressing from charcoal sketch to finished work, which is shown in this Serta mattress ad; interestingly, notice the additional filigree on the bodice in the published version obscuring the presence of nipple in this amazingly sexy advertisement, which probably failed to encourage sleep.

Could actress Barbara Hale (Della Street herself) have posed for this Ovaltine ad? She was one of Elvgren's models in the early 1940s.

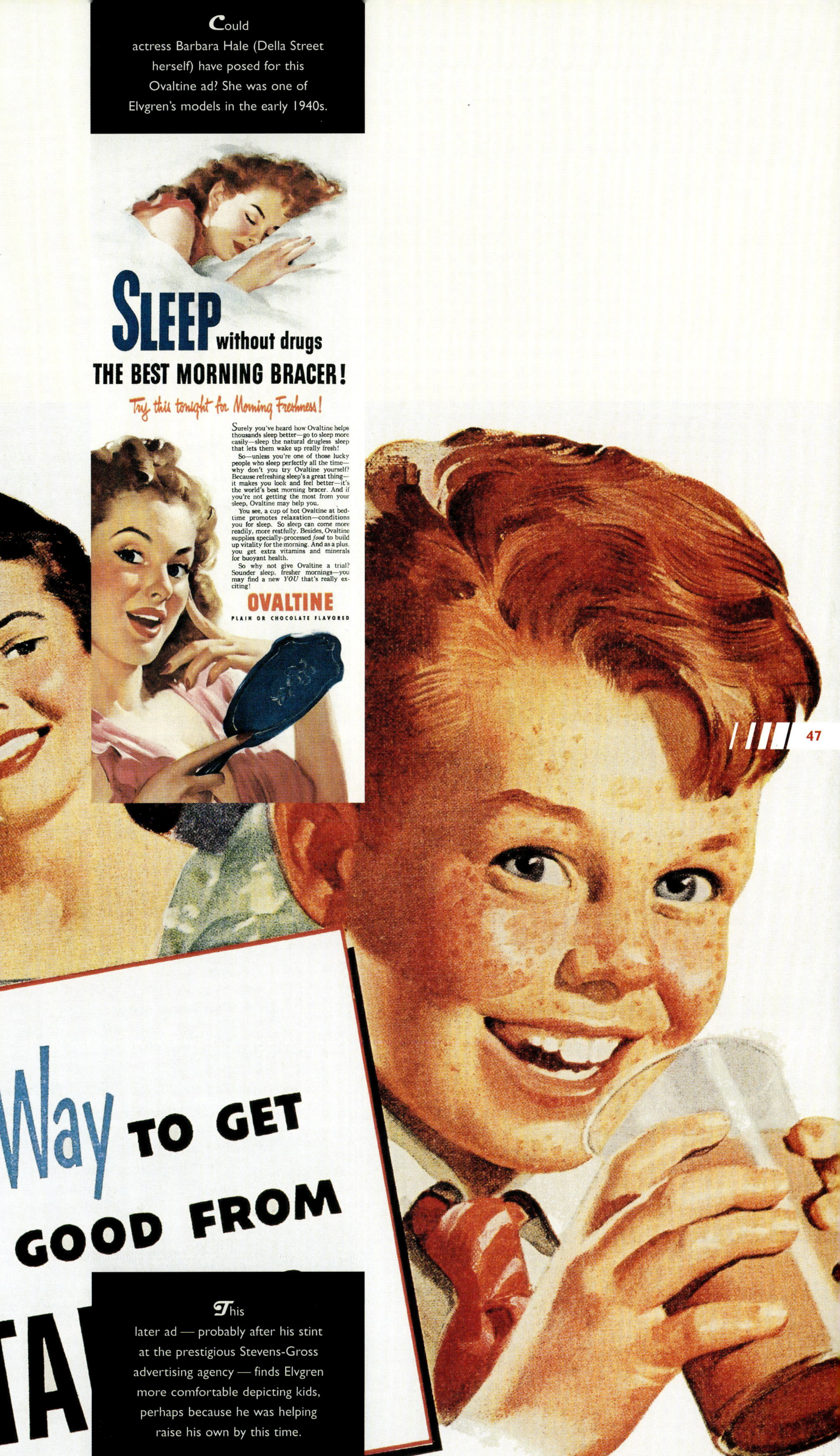

This later ad — probably after his stint at the prestigious Stevens-Gross advertising agency — finds Elvgren more comfortable depicting kids, perhaps because he was helping raise his own by this time.

What better way to sell toothbrushes than by showing a radiant blonde with perfect teeth?

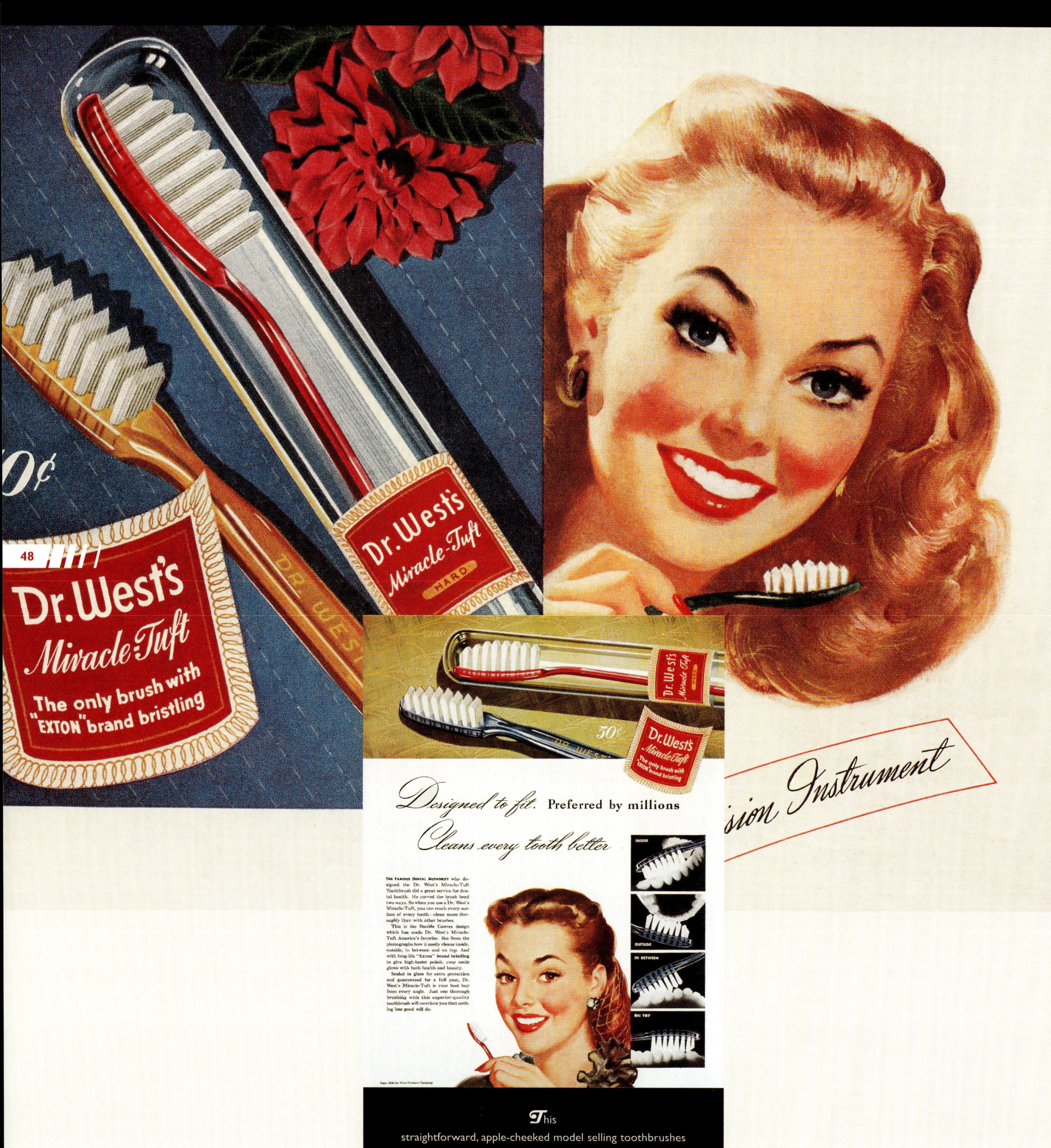

This straightforward, apple-cheeked model selling toothbrushes is a perfect example of Elvgren's wholesome, all-American girl next door.

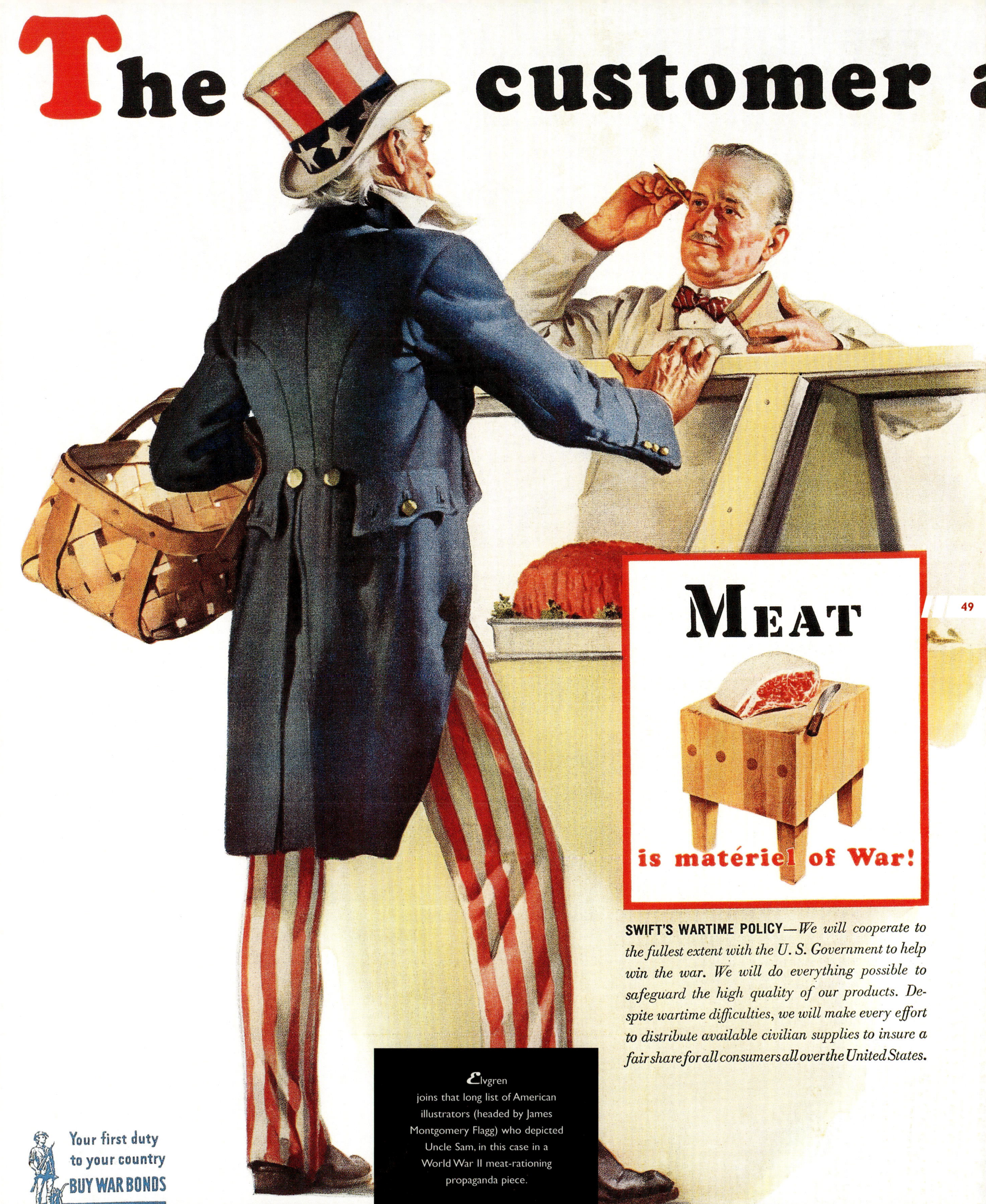

Elvgren joins that long list of American illustrators (headed by James Montgomery Flagg) who depicted Uncle Sam, in this case in a World War II meat-rationing propaganda piece.

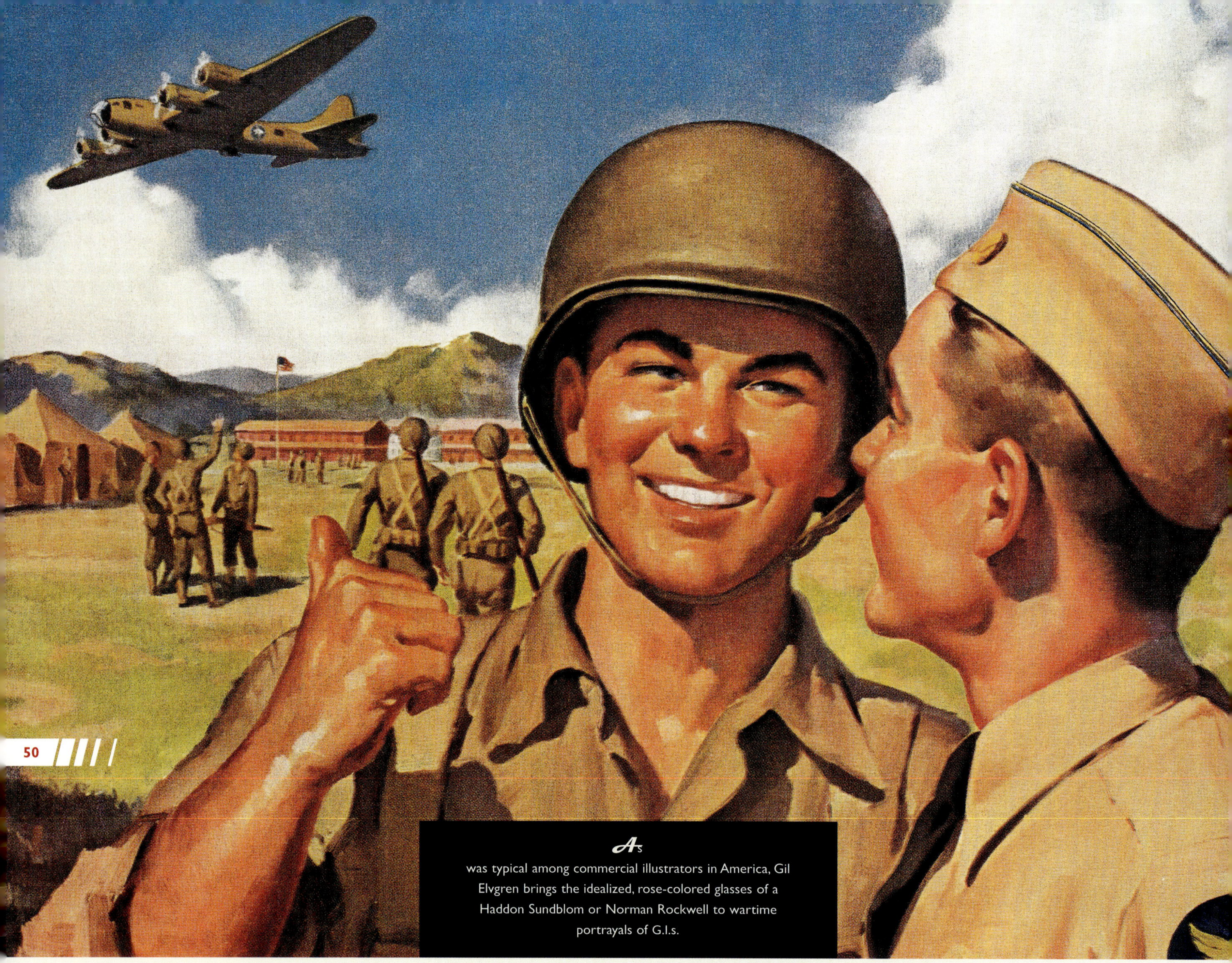

As was typical among commercial illustrators in America, Gil Elvgren brings the idealized, rose-colored glasses of a Haddon Sundblom or Norman Rockwell to wartime portrayals of G.I.s.

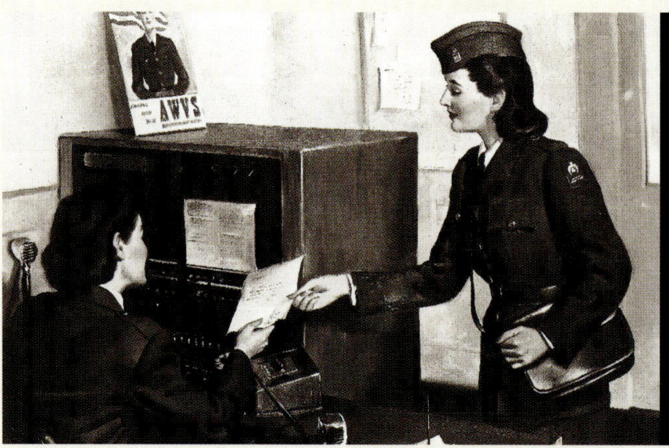

Like most American illustrators, Elvgren created many home-front propaganda pieces; though he did not serve in the armed services, Elvgren was public-spirited and shared his knowledge of firearms as a civilian instructor of military personnel.

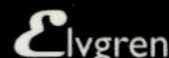

Elvgren was aware that the subject matter of this illustration — cheerful G.I.s behind the lines — was home-front propaganda; he must have been gratified to know his pin-ups brought pleasure to the American fighting man.

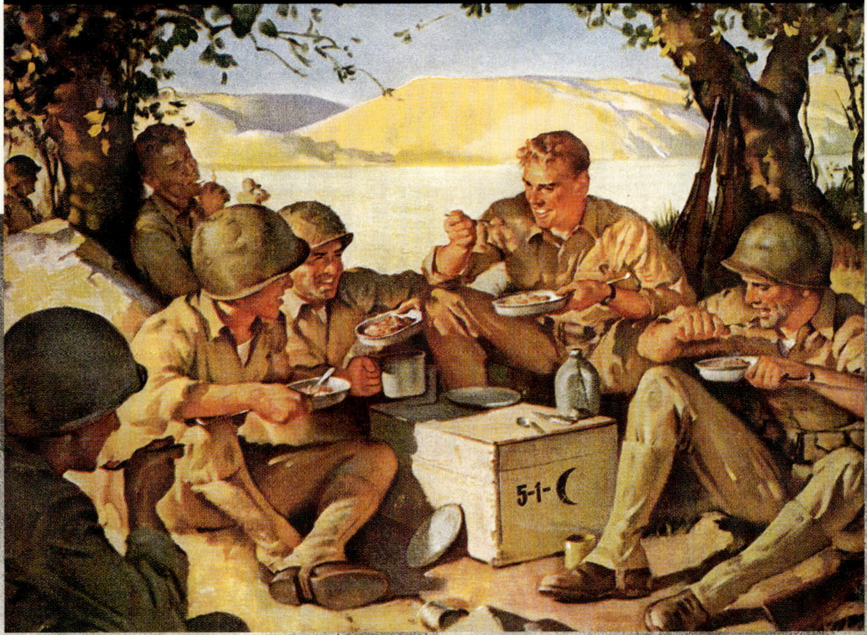

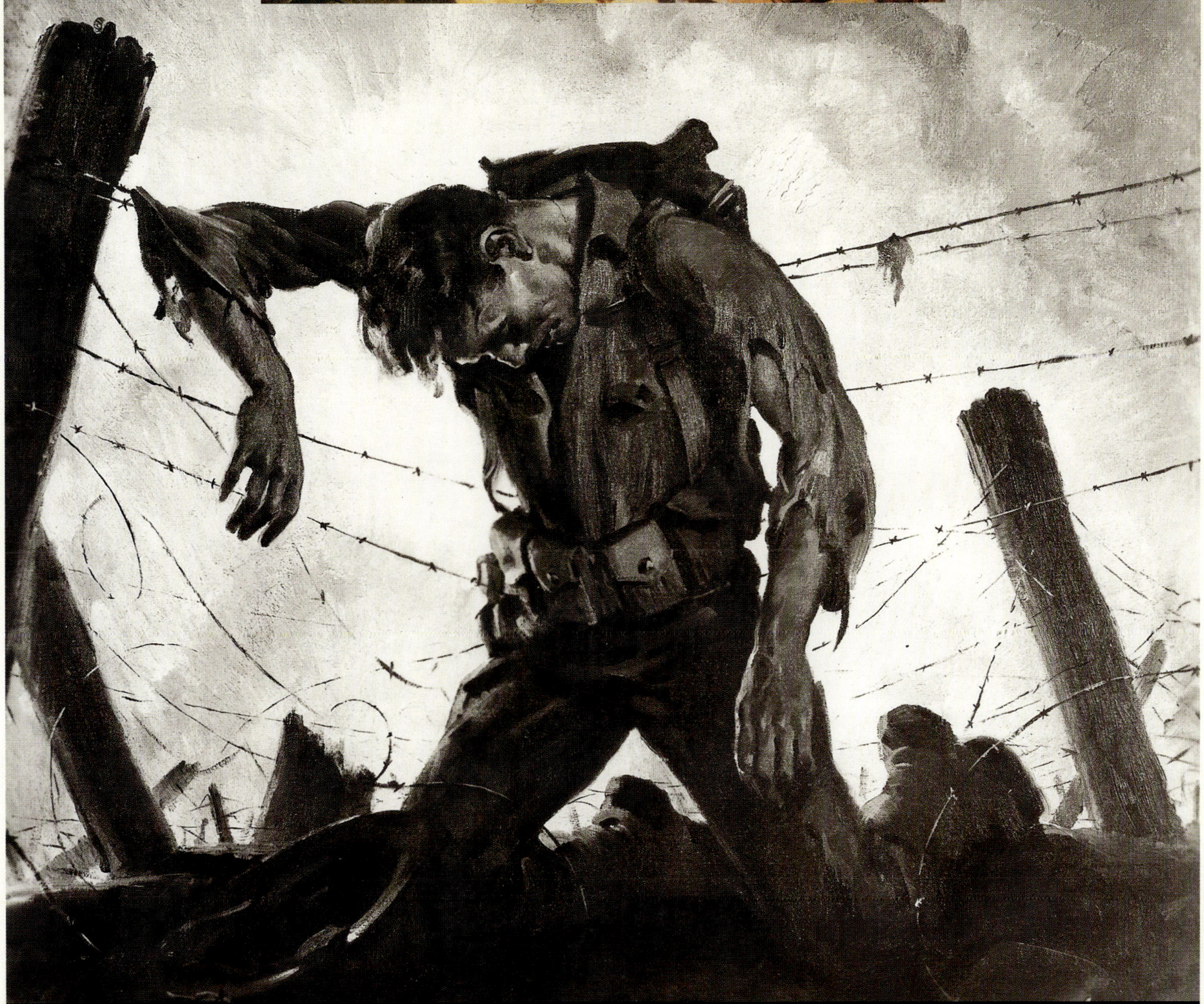

When the occasion called, Elvgren could abandon the light touch that so dominated his career; here he suggests the tragedy and even horror of war in this classically composed illustration with its Christ-like central figure.

This outstanding magazine illustration conveys tenderness and sorrow, heightened by superb design, again hinting at Gil Elvgren's warm family feelings.

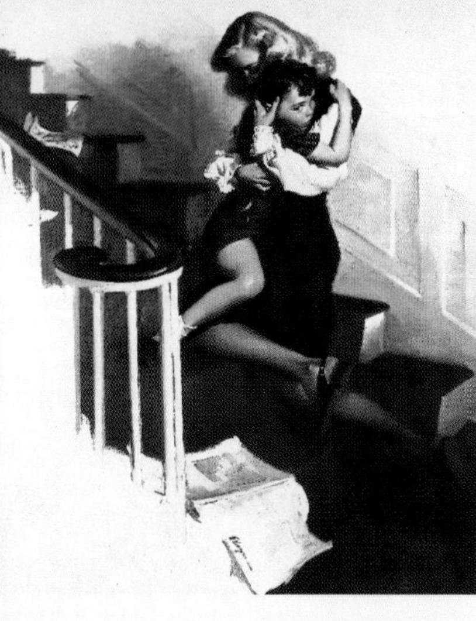

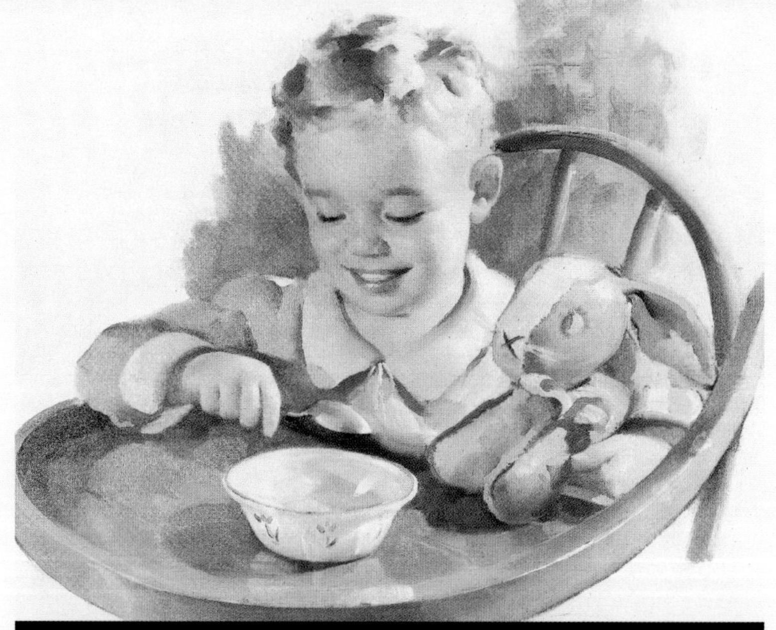

Elvgren professed to despise painting children, though this cute kid and his cuter toy bunny is an accomplished work, perhaps echoing his own happy childhood.

This moody illustration of a glowering male is worlds away from Elvgren's sunny world of pin-ups; but it is evocative evidence that his illustration skills are wide-ranging.

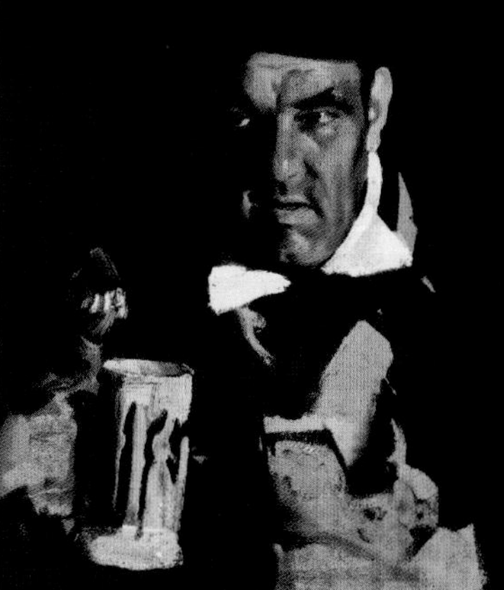

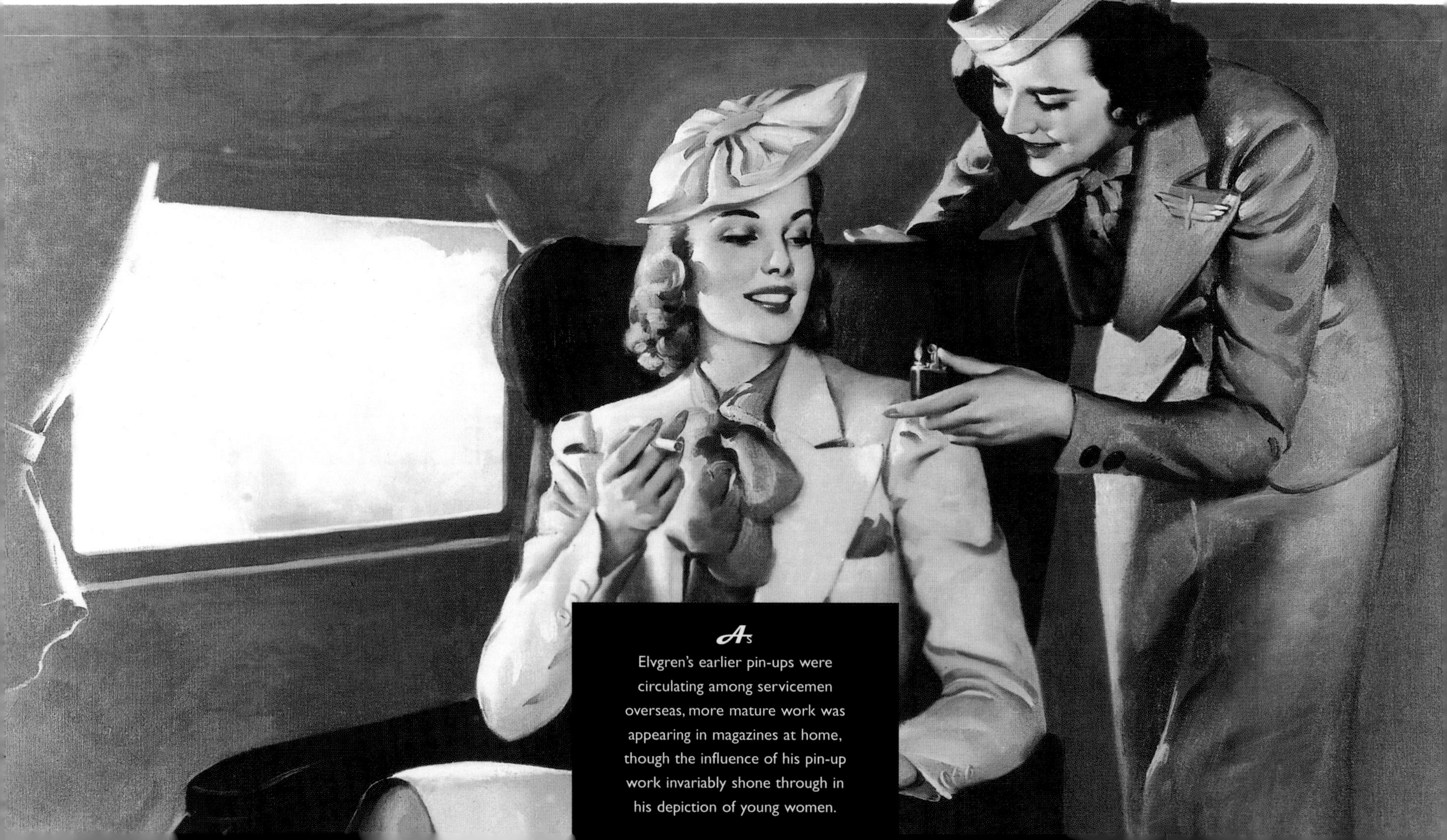

As Elvgren's earlier pin-ups were circulating among servicemen overseas, more mature work was appearing in magazines at home, though the influence of his pin-up work invariably shone through in his depiction of young women.

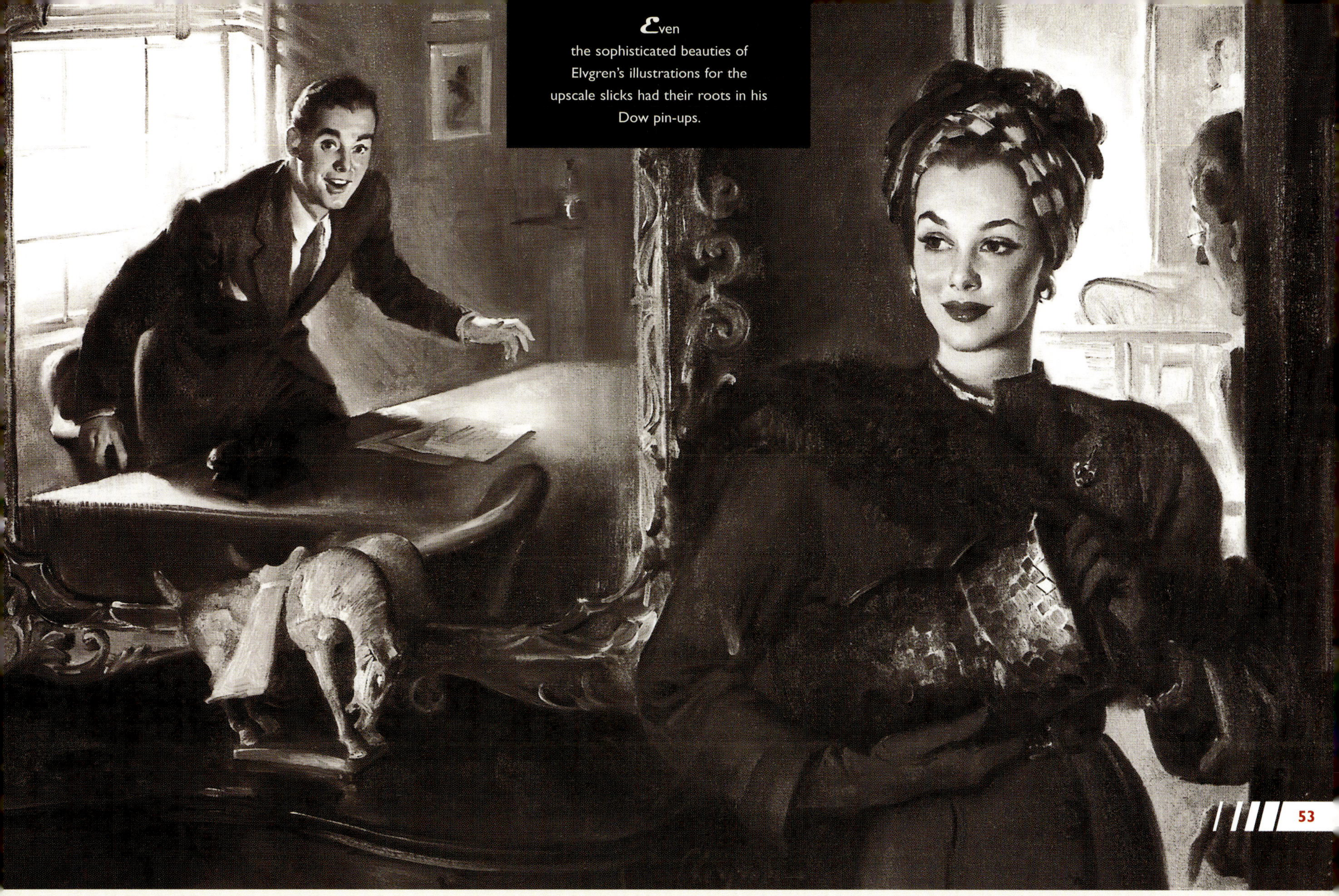

Even
the sophisticated beauties of Elvgren's illustrations for the upscale slicks had their roots in his Dow pin-ups.

Elvgren,
in another rare portrayal of a child (this time a father and son), perhaps draws upon his own warm feelings for his father, whom he much admired.

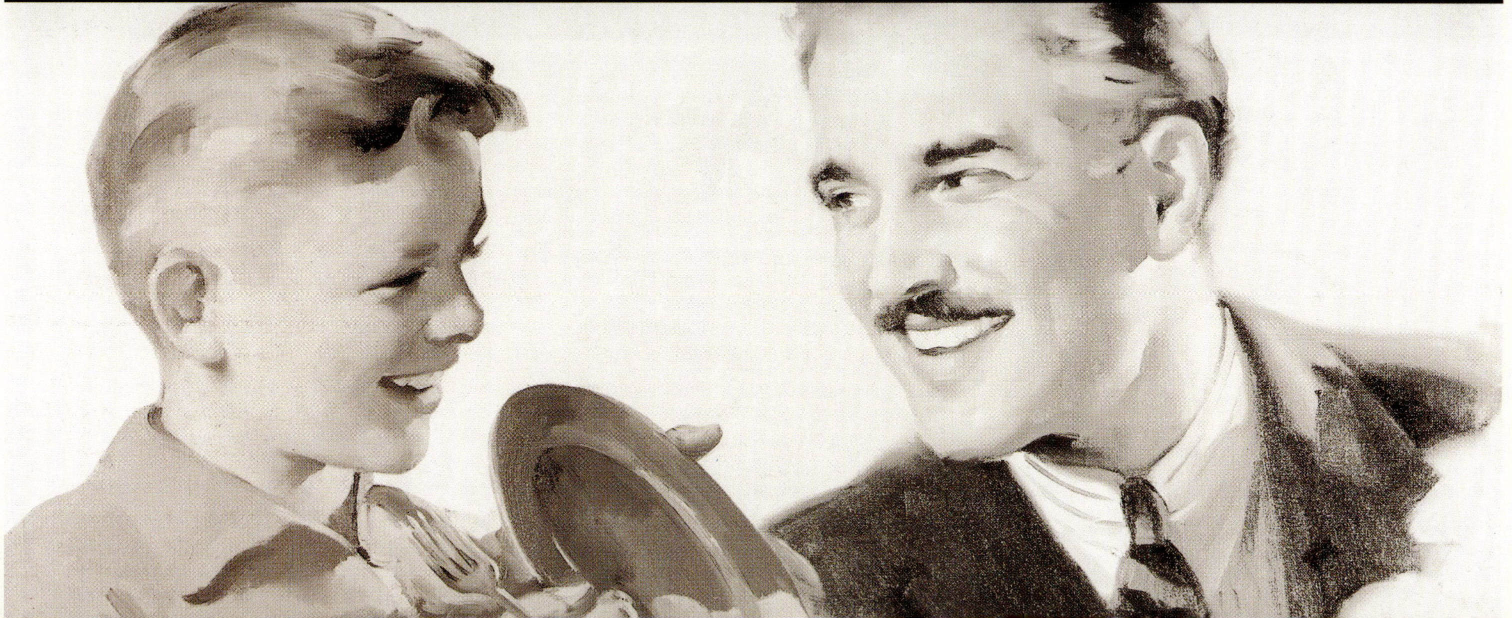

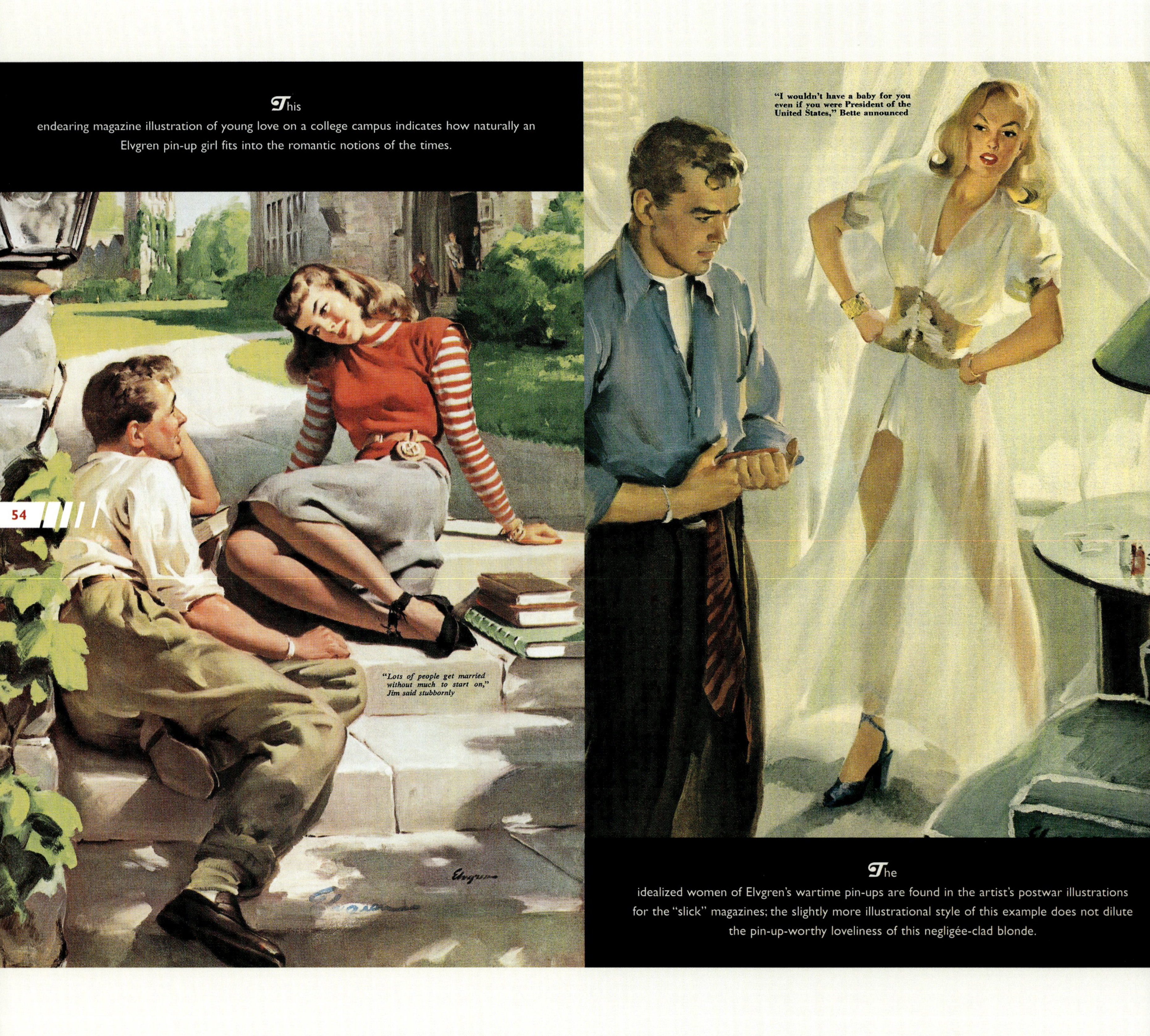

This endearing magazine illustration of young love on a college campus indicates how naturally an Elvgren pin-up girl fits into the romantic notions of the times.

The idealized women of Elvgren's wartime pin-ups are found in the artist's postwar illustrations for the "slick" magazines; the slightly more illustrational style of this example does not dilute the pin-up-worthy loveliness of this negligée-clad blonde.

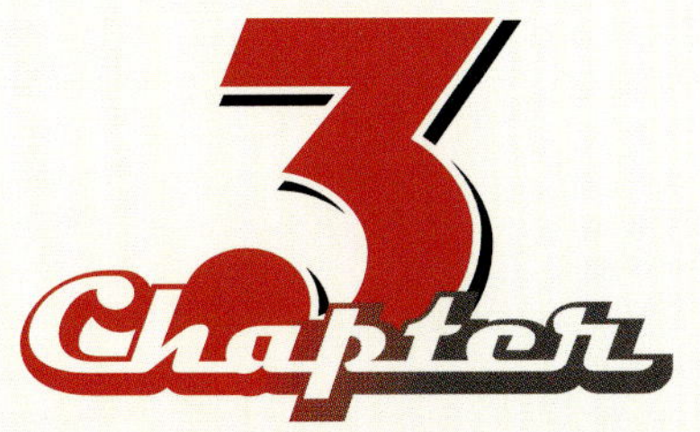

The Stevens-Gross Years

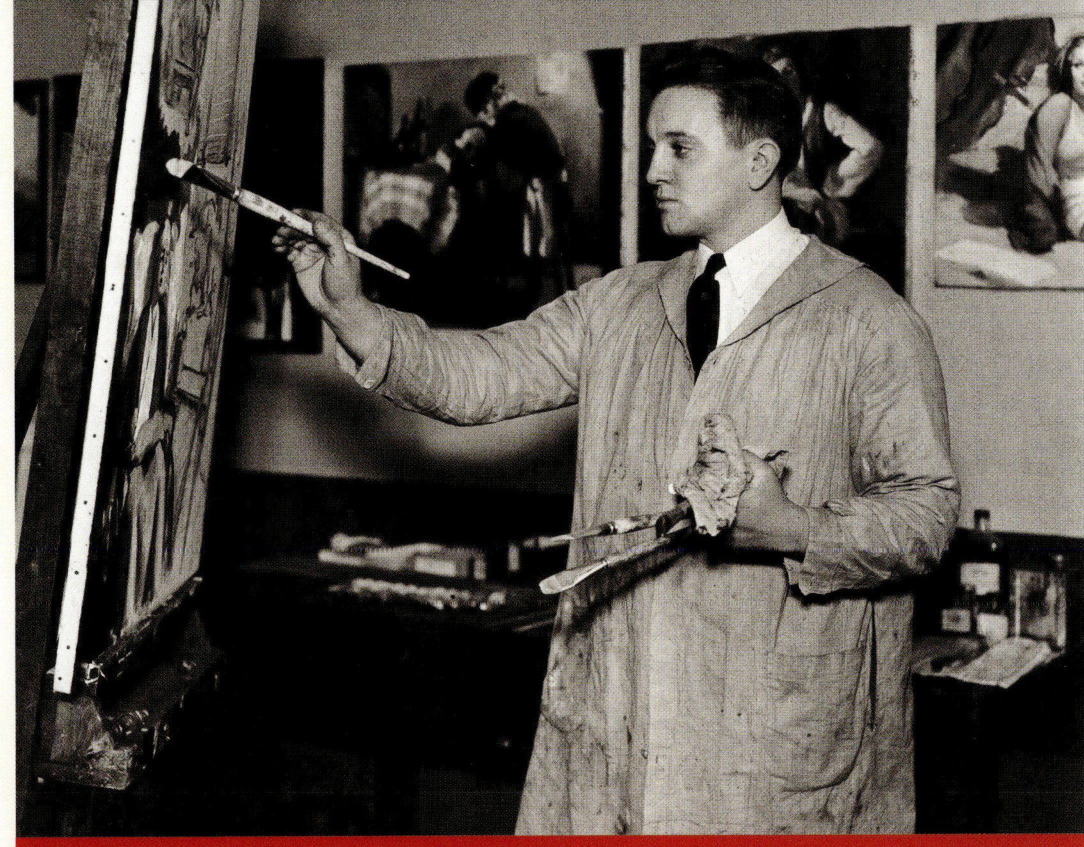

Early in his career, Gil strikes a painterly pose; later Elvgren photos inevitably portray an artist comfortable with himself and his studio.

At the academy, Elvgren's fellow students had included Al Buell, Coby Whitmore, and Andrew Loomis, among a number of other future luminaries of illustration; like Elvgren, some would go on to work for that top commercial client, Coca-Cola. A graduate at twenty-two, the confident Elvgren immediately became a full-time freelance artist, returning to St. Paul and briefly opening his own studio before returning to Chicago, where he began a lengthy stint working for the prestigious Stevens-Gross advertising agency. One of his first professional jobs was a high-profile one: he submitted a painting of a cute little brunette girl to be considered for Brown & Bigelow's Dionne Quintuplets calendars. The Quints, the object of public media interest rivaled in later years only by Jackie Kennedy and Princess Diana, were considered a national treasure (and resource) by their native Canada. Elvgren's audition got him the job, and the first two calendars appeared in 1937 and 1938. One of his Dionne portraits is said to hang in the Canadian House of Parliament, but Elvgren himself saw the Quints only once, when they were on tour and separated from the crowds by a wall of glass.

The Quints only technically began the artist's long association with top calendar producer, Brown & Bigelow; his famous series of pin-ups for them was several years away. Ironically, Elvgren disliked drawing or painting children and shied away from them, when possible, when doing portrait work or when on advertising assignments. At Stevens-Gross, Elvgren encountered the artist who most influenced his style: Haddon Sundblom, whose lush brushstrokes were responsible for the soft-focus romanticism of beautiful Coca-Cola girls sitting at idyllic small-town soda fountains, as well as those rosy-cheeked plump Santa Clauses who have defined the image of St. Nick for every subsequent generation. Like Art Frahm and the aforementioned Buell and Loomis, Elvgren fell under Sundblom's spell.

Haddon H. Sundblom was born June 22, 1899, in Muskegon, Michigan. Following the death of his mother when he was thirteen, the boy worked construction on the day shift while taking night-school classes, pursuing a dream of becoming an architect. In 1920 he became an office boy at one of Chicago's biggest art agencies, Charles Everett Johnson Studios, where his gift for illustration soon became known, and five years later joined two colleagues in starting his own firm. This was the heyday of advertising illustration, and Chicago's advertising industry was booming. Here, Sundblom flourished, painting ads for major firms such as Cream of Wheat, Nabisco, Aunt Jemima, Maxwell House, Palmolive, Cashmere Bouquet, Whitman Chocolates, Goodyear, Four Roses Whiskey, Budweiser, Schlitz, Pabst, Ford, Packard, Lincoln, Buick, Pierce-Arrow, and the United States Marines. His magazine assignments were just as prestigious: *The Saturday Evening Post*, *Ladies' Home Journal*, *Cosmopolitan*, and *Good*

Housekeeping. And of course, one of Sundblom's first and most prominent clients—and the one with which he'd be identified during and after his life—was Coca-Cola. His first ad campaign for Coke was in 1925, and by the 1940s, Sundblom was illustrating better than half of all billboard art for Coke. He created Santa Claus paintings for Coca-Cola as late as 1964 and enjoyed acclaim from the fans and media during his later years rarely enjoyed by an "advertising artist." He died in 1976, semi-retired. That one artist could so dominate a major company's image, in this illustration-dominated period of advertising, says volumes about Sundblom and his skills, particularly considering the list of *other* artists Coke employed during this same period: Frederic Mizen, Norman Rockwell, N.C. Wyeth, and Bradshaw Crandell, among other notables. Sundblom, the older, legendarily successful artist—a commanding figure standing six feet three with a booming voice and an ebullient personality—became a mentor to Elvgren, who mastered (and in the minds of some, improved upon) his teacher's technique. Son Drake admits that, in examining various Coca-Cola advertisements, he frequently cannot tell his father's work from Sundblom's. 7Up once commissioned a Santa Claus from Elvgren, but it was never published, when the soft drink company's lawyers advised the firm that Elvgren's Santa was virtually indistinguishable from Sundblom's, and lawsuits could result. It is the Sundblom technique, that glowing style so rightly associated with Coca-Cola ads, that characterizes not only Elvgren's technique but that of the vast majority of the pin-up artists who worked in oil, a group that far outnumbered the watercolor/airbrush followers of Petty and Vargas. The other major schools of pin-up art were the "sketchbook" style of Earl MacPherson and his imitators, which combined charcoal with pastels, and the descendants of pastel master Rolf Armstrong, notably Zoë Mozert, Earl Moran, and Billy DeVorss. But even these artists (Armstrong excepted) were influenced by the subject matter and approach of Elvgren's Sundblom-like pin-ups. Elvgren's long run of calendar girls for Brown & Bigelow, then and now the nation's leading calendar company, represents the artist at his peak (from 1944 until the early 1970s) and constitutes the major body of work for which he is remembered. But it was not at Brown & Bigelow that he developed his style and formulated the girl-next-door approach that would so influence his peers. Throughout his tenure at Stevens-Gross, Elvgren worked for many prestigious advertising accounts, most notably, Coca-Cola. "Sundblom probably had some influence getting Dad in at Coke," Drake recalls. And indeed Elvgren is probably second only to Sundblom himself in having his artistic images identified with Coca-Cola, his sunny, wholesomely sexy girls outshining those of his mentor. Coca-Cola was only one of the prominent accounts to receive the Elvgren touch. His artwork, usually featuring his trademark pretty girls, adorned the ads of Coca-Cola, Schlitz Beer, Ovaltine, Ford, General Electric, Sylvania (the "Miss Sylvania" calendar), Ditzler Paint, Serta mattresses, Orange Crush, Pangburn Chocolates, General Tire, among others; and his magazine illustrations appeared in the high-profile likes of *Saturday Evening Post* and *McCall's*. But it was the first major, post-Dionne Quints assignment at Stevens-Gross that set the tone of, and created the pattern for, Gil Elvgren's career. In 1937 one of Brown & Bigelow's chief rivals, the Louis F. Dow Company, hired Elvgren to paint a series of pin-ups. In these pin-ups Elvgren first transferred the apple-cheeked Sundblom-style sweetheart of advertising to straight calendar-girl pin-up. Equally important was Elvgren's exploration of what he called the "compromising" situation. Most Elvgren girls expose their graceful nyloned limbs inadvertently, often to their embarrassment, though they are never humiliated, and in fact one suspects these girls don't mind showing off their charms a little, if there's a dog on a leash or a windy day to blame it on. In what is regarded as perhaps Elvgren's finest early pin-up, "Thar She Blows," a breathtakingly lovely blonde is surprised but takes in stride the inevitable funhouse gust of air that lifts her pretty green skirt above perfect shapely legs and reveals even a hint of lacy pink step-in. Elvgren's secondary theme has a beautiful girl looking directly, unabashedly at the viewer, smiling, as if caught in the act of undressing (or exercising scantily, or slipping on nylons) by her lover—and not minding. Yet there is never anything vaguely salacious about even these more frankly sexual situations. The Coca-Cola sweetness of their smiles tells us these are "nice girls" (as Elvgren insisted they all were). The Dow pin-ups are undoubtedly uneven. A few—"A Live Wire" and "Short on Sails" come to mind—pleasant, pretty girls whose features have a baby-like softness, as if they (and Elvgren's art) aren't yet fully formed. Still others—"Weight Control" and "A Knockout," for instance—rival his best Brown & Bigelow work. Perhaps most fascinatingly, the late thirties period of their birth lend many of these pin-ups an art-moderne feel, both in props and design, that the later, more polished pin-ups lack—notably, "Station WOW" and "Out on a Limb." Still others are such full-blown examples of the Elvgren art that they could have been published a decade or more later, amid the Brown & Bigelow masterworks, and fit right in—the definitive "Sport Model" and "Tail Wind," for instance. Elvgren left Stevens-Gross around 1952, taking his Brown & Bigelow account with him, his most glorious pin-ups yet to come. But those years, under the influence and guiding eye of Haddon Sundblom, were crucial and formative, and had his career ended when he left the prestigious agency, his position in the history of American advertising and calendar art still would be secure.

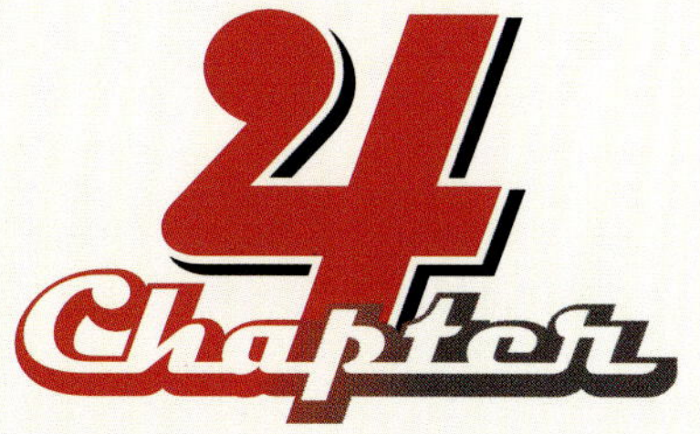

Chapter 4

Wartime Pin-ups

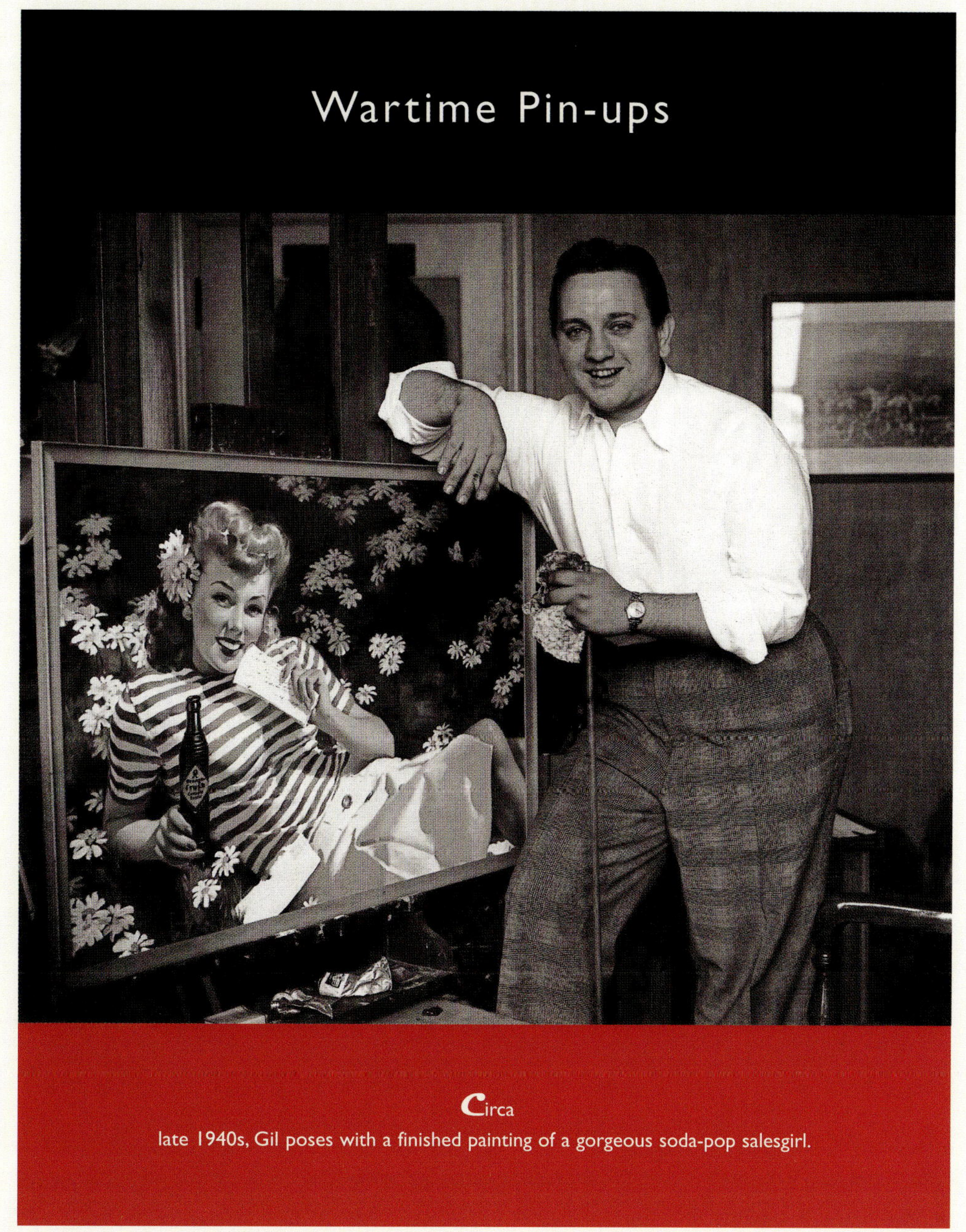

Circa late 1940s, Gil poses with a finished painting of a gorgeous soda-pop salesgirl.

The Louis F. Dow Company certainly got its money's worth from Elvgren's batch of pin-ups. Long after Elvgren left for the greener pastures of Brown & Bigelow, Dow recycled the Elvgren pin-ups, having other staff artists (notably Vaughn Bass, a second-tier pin-up artist) rework the paintings, varying apparel and subject matter, turning a roadside hitchhiker pouring dirt from her shoe ("The High Sign") into a woman in a shoe store about to try on a high heel. "Dow would pay Dad around $350 a painting," Drake recalls, "and then later on they would get some other artist to paint another background over it for about a tenth of that amount, getting two paintings for a lot less." Bass, an accomplished artist himself, knew enough not to fool with Elvgren's girls, and skin texture, nyloned legs, and to some extent the clothing itself tended to be left alone. (Hats were often added or embellished.) The unfortunate aftermath of Dow's recycling was the reworked paintings themselves: most of the surviving originals of the Dow pin-ups are the so-called "over-painted" mutations. Calendar girls have been around forever (or at least since about the turn of the century); but *pin-up* girls constitute one of the happiest by-products of World War II. Wherever G.I.s went, pinned-up reminders of the pretty girls back home accompanied them, as *Terry and the Pirates* cartoonist Milton Caniff chronicled in his classic wartime strip *Male Call* (which appeared exclusively in army camp newspapers), itself starring one of the era's most popular pin-up girls—Miss Lace, who posed and preened for the delight of various hapless soldiers in the strip (and out). Certainly a share of real-life beauties could be found on the walls of barracks and bulkheads—girls from back home, whether in a prom dress or maybe a sunsuit, providing fetching snapshot reminders of what awaited their gallant soldier and sailor boys in the glorious postwar world. And when it wasn't a real hometown sweetheart, it was the Hollywood variety: Betty Grable in a swimsuit or Rita Hayworth in her famous negligée or maybe Dorothy Lamour in a sarong. But the tradition of the calendar girl—the idealized vision of female pulchritude as imagined by illustrators, primarily for advertising purposes, flowing directly from the Gibson Girl and *Police Gazette* to Rolf Armstrong and *Esquire*—played into the yearning of the G.I.s for a glorified girl next door. And no artist before or since has done for the girl next door what Gil Elvgren did.

While Alberto Vargas has, justifiably, become famous for his superb Esquire girls, the Vargas reputation as the key pin-up artist of World War II is, as noted earlier, at least partly revisionist history. By war's end, Vargas (and a series of *Esquire* calendars created especially for servicemen) had made an indelible mark; but at the time of Pearl Harbor, George Petty was the superstar among pin-up artists, and Elvgren's images were probably the most widely circulated of any pin-up artist's. From the earliest days of the war, Elvgren's girls found themselves constantly reworked by the aviator amateur artists decorating aircraft nose art and flight jackets. While the single most imitated pin-up image seen on U.S. military aircraft during World War II was probably Vargas' "Sleepy Time Gal," which depicted a yawning blonde apparently ready for bed, the next most frequently seen recycled image may well have been Elvgren's "Double Exposure," in which a lovely blonde covers herself with a towel. Two versions of this classic pin-up exist, one of them censored with a "reflection" (both included in this volume). The nose cone versions omit the "gag," i.e., that as the blonde covers herself up in front, we are seeing the reflection of her lovely back (and backside) in the mirror behind her. In Gary M. Valant's *Vintage Aircraft Nose Art* (1987, Motorbooks International), amateur reworkings can be seen of Elvgren paintings (included in this volume) such as "Is My Face Red," "Out on a Limb," and "Kneeding a Lift," among others from the artist's relatively brief stint with the Dow company. These and other images inspired by Elvgren can be found in virtually all the numerous books chronicling the practice of adding pin-up "mascots" to the nose cones of planes. All this adds to the significance of the Louis Dow pin-ups, giving them a permanent pop-culture position that threatens to overshadow the artist's later work, and it's perhaps ironic that a number of Elvgren's most famous images are clearly not his best work. It is, of course, Elvgren's long association with Brown & Bigelow that produced the lush, mature work that has made him the latter-day favorite of pin-up aficionados, paintings whose brush strokes are every bit as sensuous as the supple curves of the painter's subjects. This is not to say the Dow paintings are lackluster; in fact, had Elvgren stopped painting pretty girls after the Dow series, he would still inhabit a position of prominence in the history of pin-up art. If these paintings did not have charm and freshness and a wholesome sex appeal, they would not have become such wartime favorites. Elvgren created most of these wartime pin-ups before the war, beginning in 1937; originally published as calendar images and "mutoscope" cards (vending-machine pin-ups about the size of a postcard), the images were recycled (a common Dow practice), published in eight-by-ten-inch format and gathered in loose-leaf packets for shipment to military personnel stationed overseas. The eight-by-ten-inch format was ideal for pinning up by soldiers and sailors, and Elvgren's Dow images were among the first widely distributed pin-ups of World War II, easily predating the "Varga" *Esquire* calendars that dominated the later years of the war. The same was true of Earl MacPherson's work (his images turn up on numerous nose cones, as well), whose first two Brown & Bigelow calendars were recycled in a manner that would have made Dow proud. Even in these early, sometimes formative works, Elvgren reveals himself as the quintessential American pin-up artist. His subject matter is far more appealing to the mom-flag-and-apple-pie instincts of World War II-era American males than the B-17-sleek Petty girls or Vargas' perhaps too idealized Greek Goddess-style beauties. The pin-ups of both these legendary artists usually floated in a nonspecific background, often with a single prop (usually a phone, with Petty; often a hat, with Vargas). A number of the Dow images show Elvgren following this pattern (imitating Petty, not Vargas, the latter not being a formidable presence in the field, as yet) and isolating his images, girls floating in a sea of solid color—often yellow or blue, occasionally a mauve-ish pink. Now and then, the telephone—Petty's favorite prop, a virtual pin-up cliché—turns up, as in "A Live Wire." Still, the winsome wench on the phone exists in at least a hint of a realistic setting, with other props present, including colorful pillows she rests upon, and an art deco table for the base of the phone. There are even hints of the cartoony line drawings that Petty (and, in imitation, Vargas) frequently intermingled with their girls, the real world around the pin-up girls being reduced to squiggles and quick strokes ("Double Exposure," "Going Up"). The conceit of phones and stools and other props in a Petty pin-up being a simple line drawing (usually red) was the artist's crafty way of sending the message that the girl is the only important "object" in this stripped-down world. This technique evolved from Petty, at *Esquire*, initially being a glorified panel cartoonist. And, like Petty and (albeit to a lesser extent) Vargas, Elvgren *was* in the cartoon tradition—his pin-ups (and this remained true throughout his career) were designed to accompany clever captions that turned his lush paintings into overblown panel cartoons. These captions are part of the nostalgic charm of Elvgren's work and ultimately take nothing away from his standing as the Rockwell of pin-up artists. Yet Elvgren—while understandably paying lip service to various conventions and clichés of a genre that even then was viewed by its most avid proponents as a low-brow one—rejected much of what the most popular pin-up artists of the day were doing. Petty was a watercolor and airbrush master; Rolf Armstrong, a virtuoso of pastels, as was Earl Moran. These were the examples a young artist in 1937 might be expected to follow. Instead Elvgren brought to the (female) form his painterly style, his full palette of oils on canvas, clearly caring more about Haddon Sundblom and John Singer Sargent than George Petty and Rolf Armstrong. In doing so, he created a new style of pin-up and soon headed a sub-genre that included such talents as Joyce Ballantyne, Edward Runci, Bill Medcalf, Al Buell, Edward D'Ancona, and Harry Ekman. Perhaps it was this painterly approach that made the simplistic, pin-up image on a field of solid (or no) color seem, somehow, lacking; but even in these Dow paintings, we find Elvgren presenting (or at least suggesting) a real, complete world for his fantasy females to inhabit.

Even in many of the more simplistic images — which seem at first glance to contain nothing but the girl — objects and background items make themselves known. In "What Hoe," a bed of flowers centers and balances the composition; and in "Out on a Limb," the beautiful blonde is perched on a delightful deco foot stool whose roundness (like the blonde's) is echoed by an equally round, equally deco window. Other Dow images suggest the more complete backgrounds more common in later Elvgren works: "On De-Fence" (an unusual painting in that the subject's face is never shown) finds a girl in a red dress caught on a very real barbed-wire fence as a bull peeks from behind bushes; the lyrical untitled study of a nude on the beach, her hair flowing in the wind, is a full seascape: sky, sand, rolling waves. Like Rockwell, Elvgren is at heart an illustrator, and an illustrator needs a premise, a situation, to depict. The Dow images, for all their unevenness (and a few are downright amateur-ish — "Just the Type" and "Doctor's Orders" come to mind), tell little stories, stories frequently tied to everyday American life. Whether whimsical ("Tree for Two") or outright sensual ("Out on a Limb"), these paintings depict all-American girls who, in the musings of G.I.s dreaming of the postwar world, might well live next door. It was a fantasy that Hugh Hefner would build an empire upon, and though Hef hired Vargas to work for *Playboy*, it is still Elvgren who defined and refined that fantasy. A story common to many of the Dow paintings (and later Elvgren pin-ups, as well) is the embarrassed young woman whose dress is caught by, say, an elevator door ("Going Up") or, frequently, an awkward positioning of the leash of a dog or dogs she happens to be out walking ("Tree for Two," "Help Wanted"). The charm of these subjects relates to the girl gazing directly at the viewer with such coy chagrin that the suspicion arises that the girl has somehow orchestrated this "embarrassment" to occur, to entice and attract. Now and then a voyeuristic situation is depicted by Elvgren — both "Skirtin' Trouble" and "A Hitch in Time" have us viewing, without their knowledge, lovely dog-walkers hiking up nylons. One of the best of the Dow paintings — "A Peek-A'-Knees" — has a lovely girl sitting with her Pekingese held up for her to get a better look, unwittingly giving the viewer an even better look. Slightly less voyeuristic are the images that depict a hitchhiking cutie hiking her skirt in the time-honored Claudette Colbert *It Happened One Night* manner ("Kneeding a Lift," "Foot-Loose"). But more often, the caught-in-the-act cutie knows of our presence, and this is somehow more wholesome; after all, we didn't *mean* to peek. . . . Elvgren's favorite subject matter was the exposed nyloned graceful "gam" — and his favored female expression was the kiss of surprised embarrassment — but some of his strongest (if most uncharacteristic) paintings, among the Dow wartime images, feature more unabashed, uninhibited subjects. The women in paintings such as "French Dressing" (in which a topless damsel beams at us as she steps into her dress) and "Foil Proof" (in which a redhead in her underthings and nylons thrusts a sword our way) are brazenly, boldly showing off their beauty. A blonde housewife wearing only an apron and nylons kneads at a kitchen counter in "In the Dough," giving us a smile only a husband deserves; and a nurse in a miniskirt beamingly brings us some medicine, in the somewhat crudely painted "Doctor's Orders." The best of these paintings suggests the mature Elvgren of the Brown & Bigelow period — in "Miss-Placed Confidence" a puppy has watered a coat tree to the displeasure of a nyloned and sheerly undied mistress; "A Hitch in Time" shows a sunny, embarrassed blonde who could hold her own next to most any Brown & Bigelow gal. At the end of the war, when American G.I.s returned to family and friends, one of the friends waiting for them was Gil Elvgren. The artist painted a number of memorable images of soldiers romancing their Coke-swilling sweeties, as the Coca-Cola Company celebrated "the joyous homecoming of American soldiers" under such designations as "Just Like Old Times" and "Home-Refreshment." The girls these returning soldiers courted were sunny, Sundblom-cheeked girls next door who, despite their more modest garments, were clearly the same subjects as the racier Brown & Bigelow calendar images that also awaited G.I.s, sweetly sexy images of nylons, swimming suits, and lingerie, which no doubt more closely mirrored the returning warriors' fantasies than that of sharing a Coke with a cutie in saddle shoes. Whether soft-drink ad or calendar pin-up, it is fitting that Elvgren planted the image of the perfect girl next door in the minds and hearts (among other places) of sailors and soldiers and flyboys. After Elvgren helped create the idealized woman every man was fighting for, that perfect sensual, romantic dream of the postwar wife, he chronicled that same idealized woman in illustrations for the magazines that shaped and recorded postwar attitudes — *The Saturday Evening Post*, *Cosmopolitan*, *McCall's*, *Redbook*, *The Women's Home Companion* — and, of course, in his classic series of Brown & Bigelow calendars, beginning in 1944. It's further fitting that Elvgren helped define, chart, and record the postwar era in all its commercial glory, with advertising accounts from Coca-Cola, General Electric, various beer companies, NAPA auto parts, and even Ovaltine for the kids those beautiful wives produced.

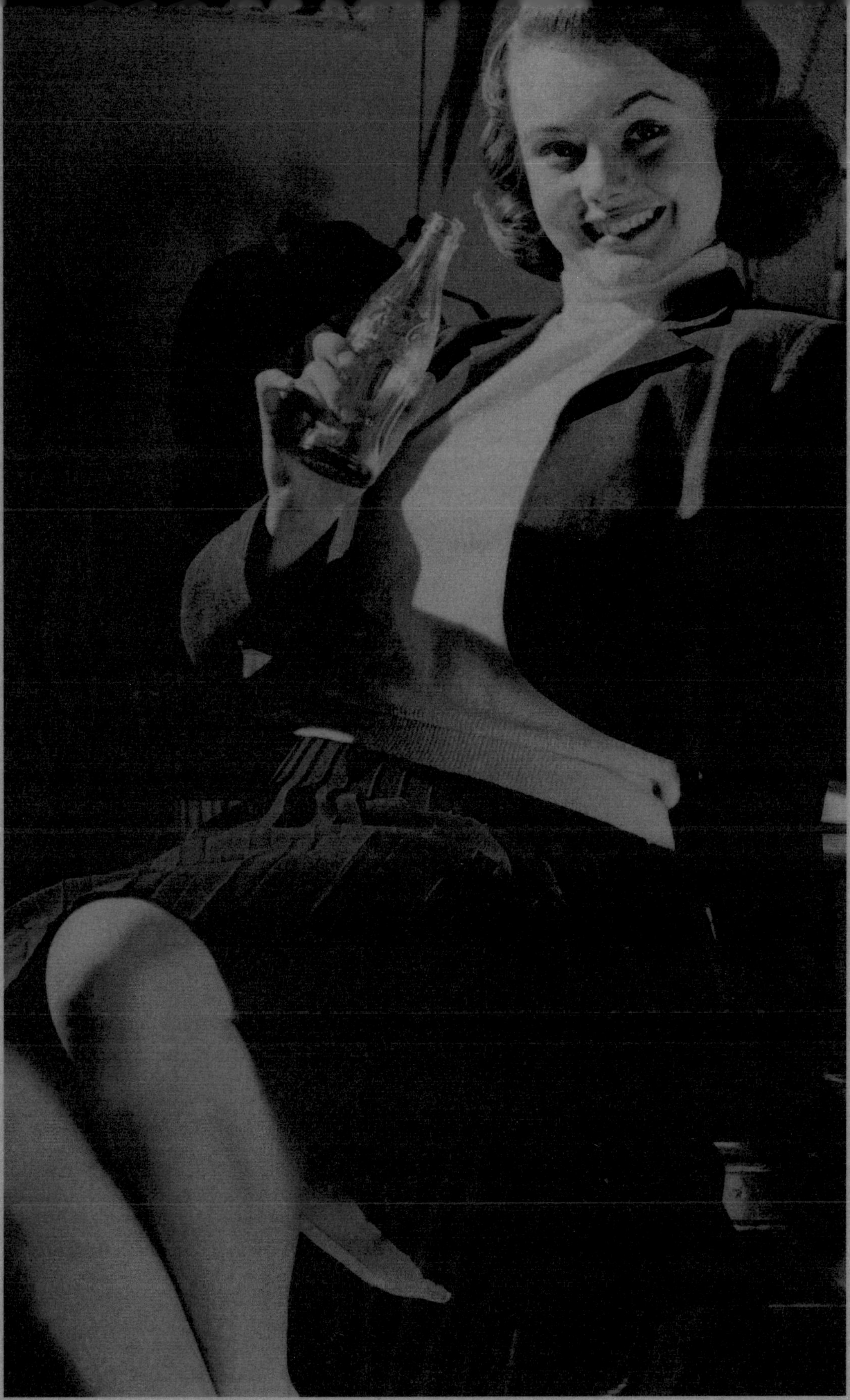

1950s Portfolio

65

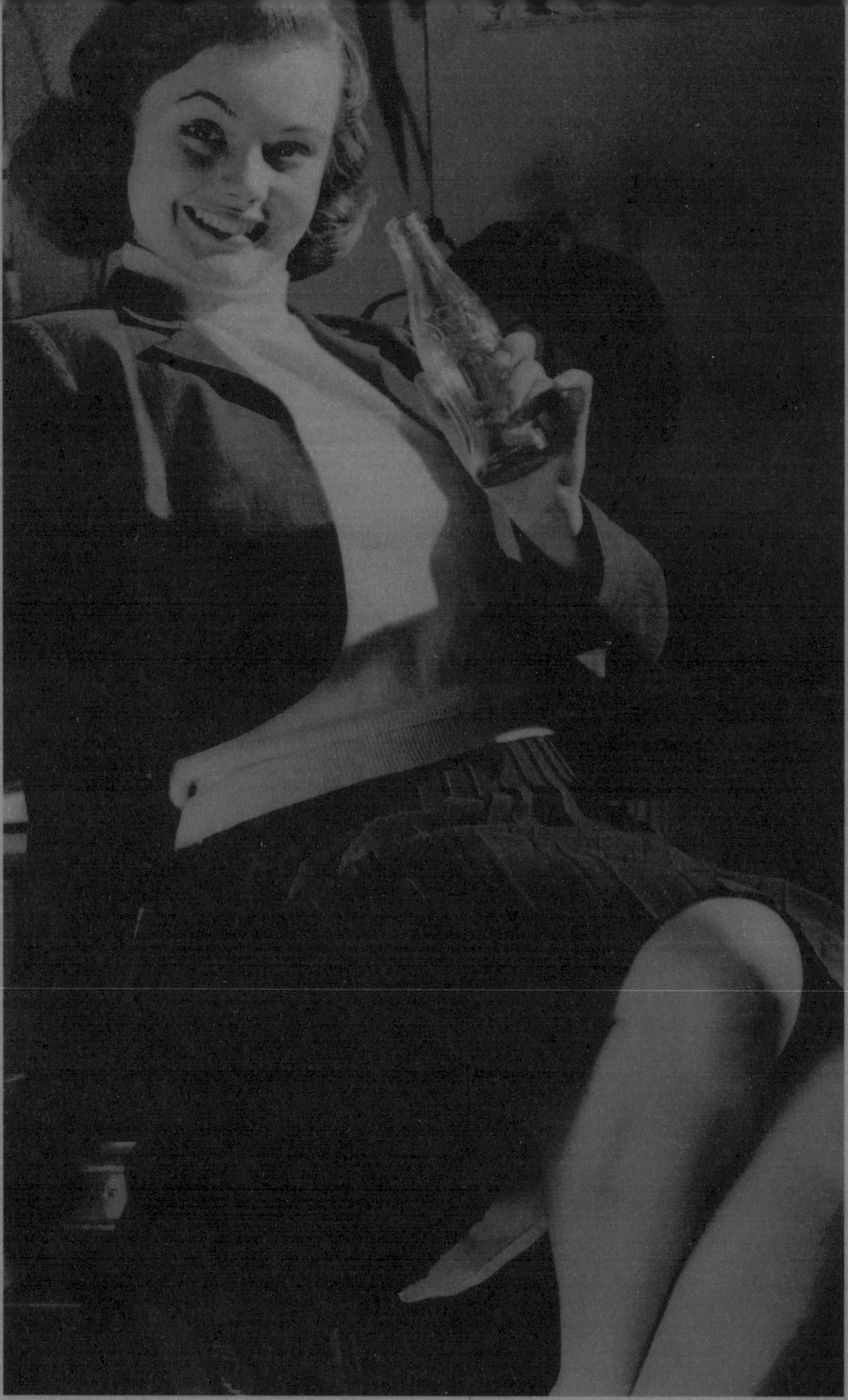

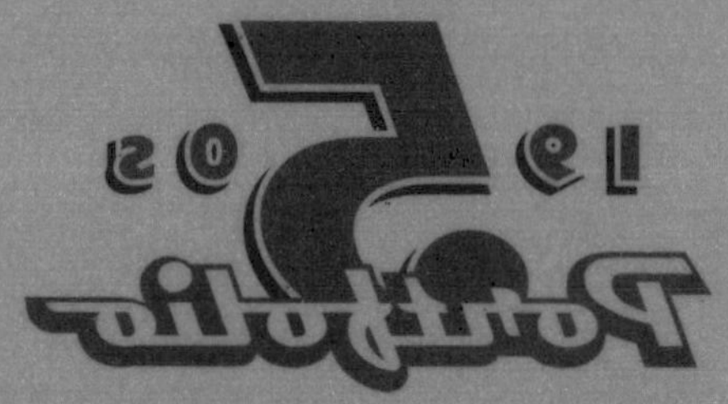
1950s
Portfolio

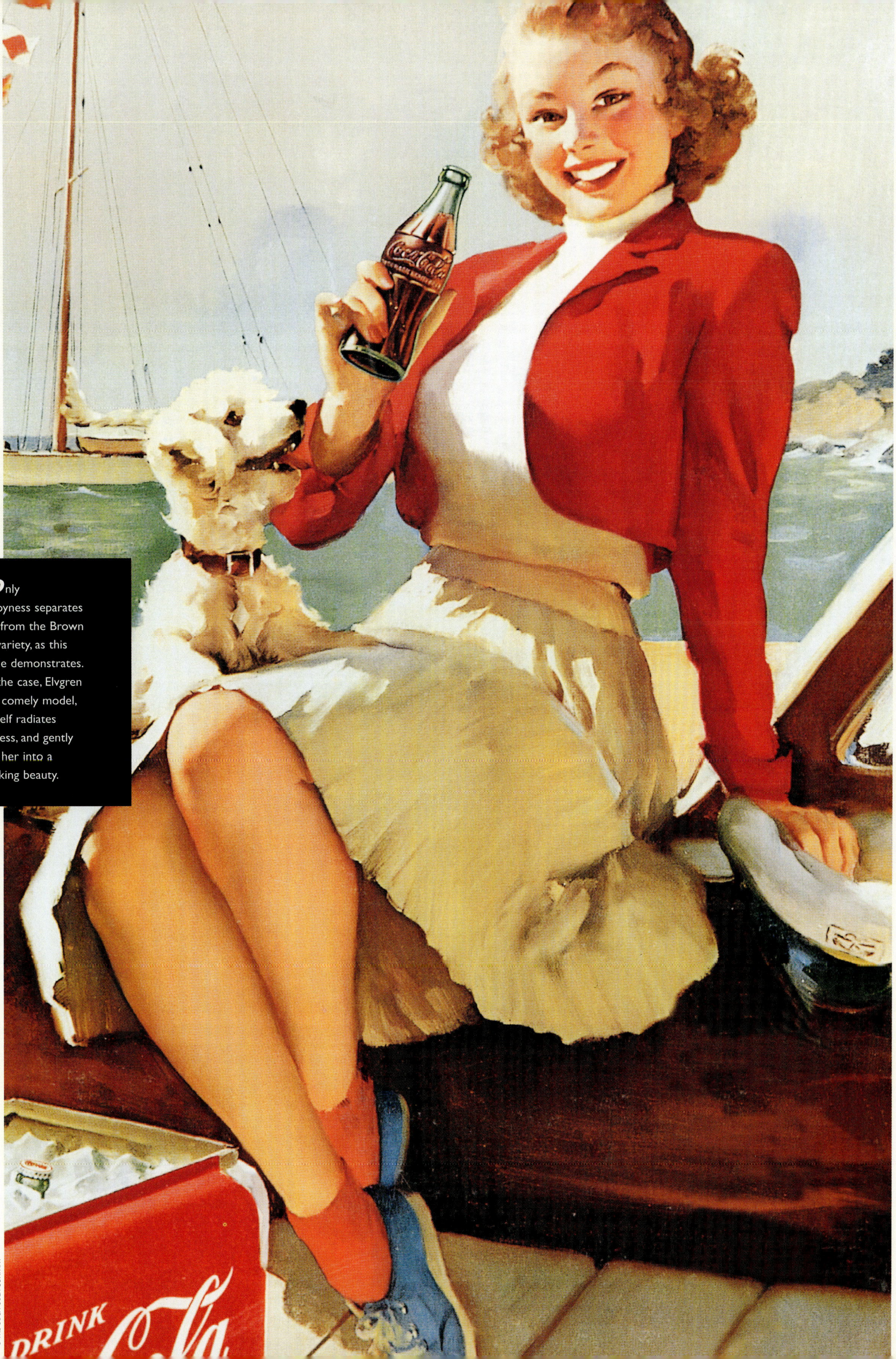

Only their lack of coyness separates the Coke girls from the Brown & Bigelow variety, as this mature example demonstrates. As was often the case, Elvgren begins with a comely model, who herself radiates wholesomeness, and gently idealizes her into a heartbreaking beauty.

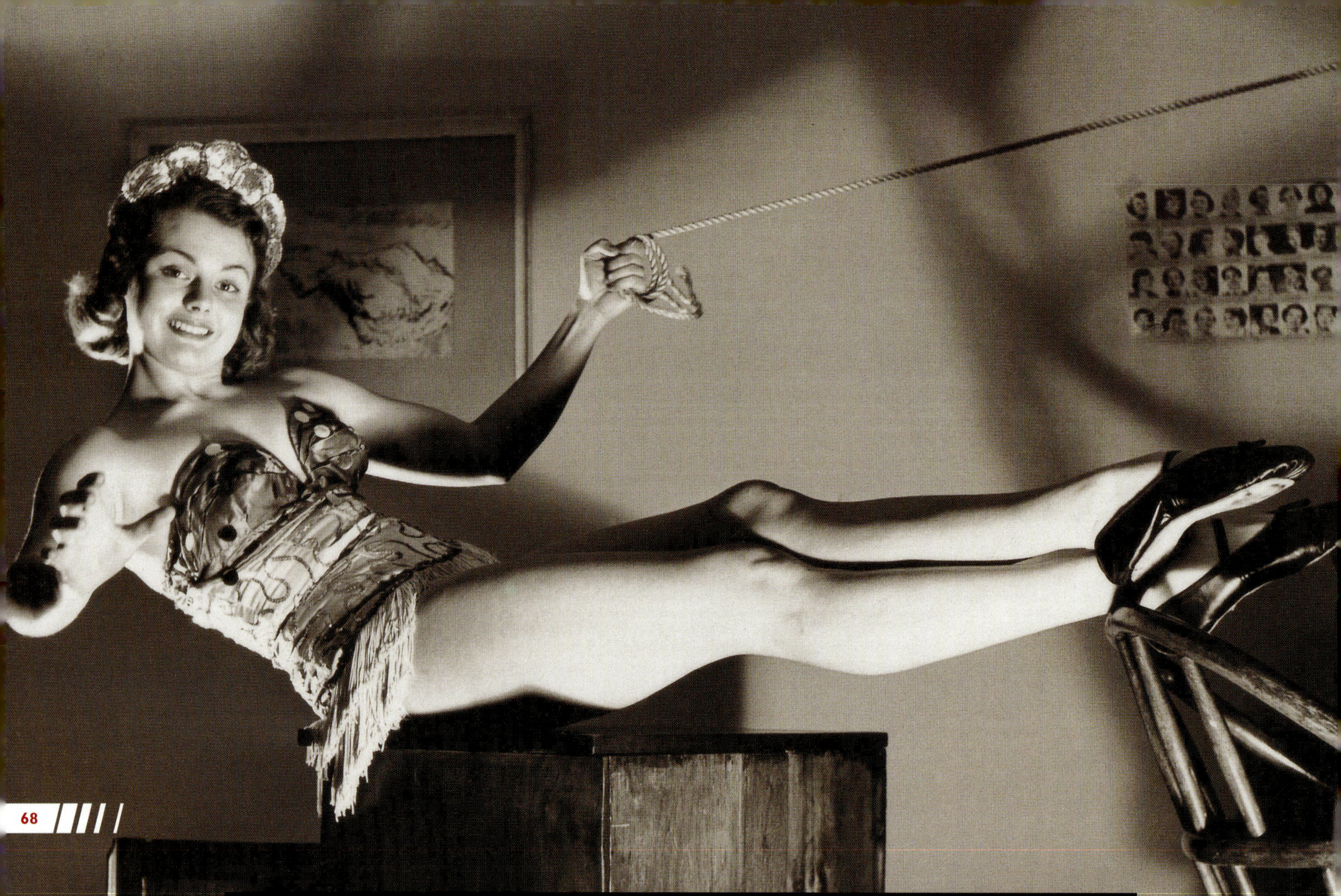

In one of Elvgren's cleverest Coca-Cola ads, this circus girl ready to accept a Coke — poised large in the frame, midair, for our perusal — is a dazzling example of 1950s illustrational advertising at its best. Note the skillful and elaborate studio staging of the reference photo.

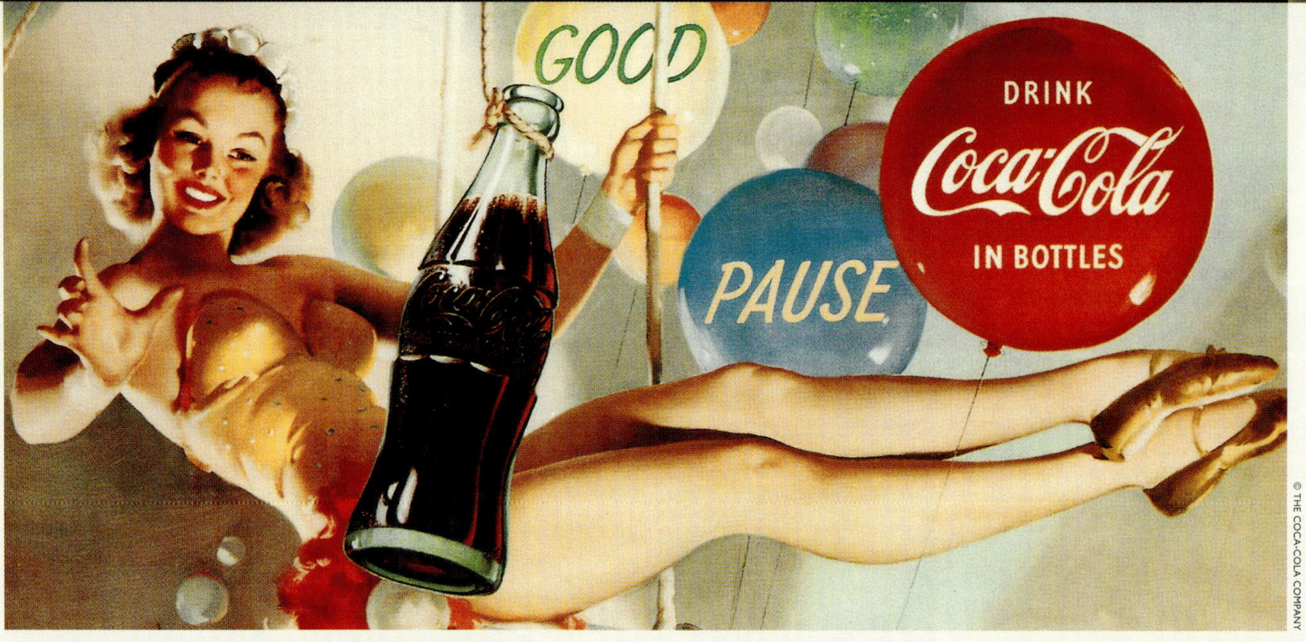

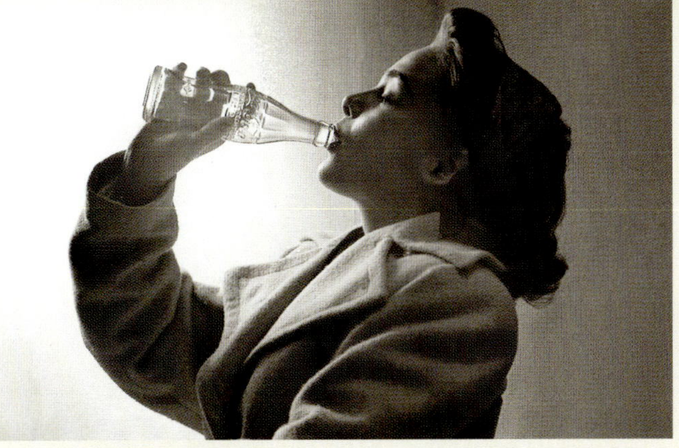

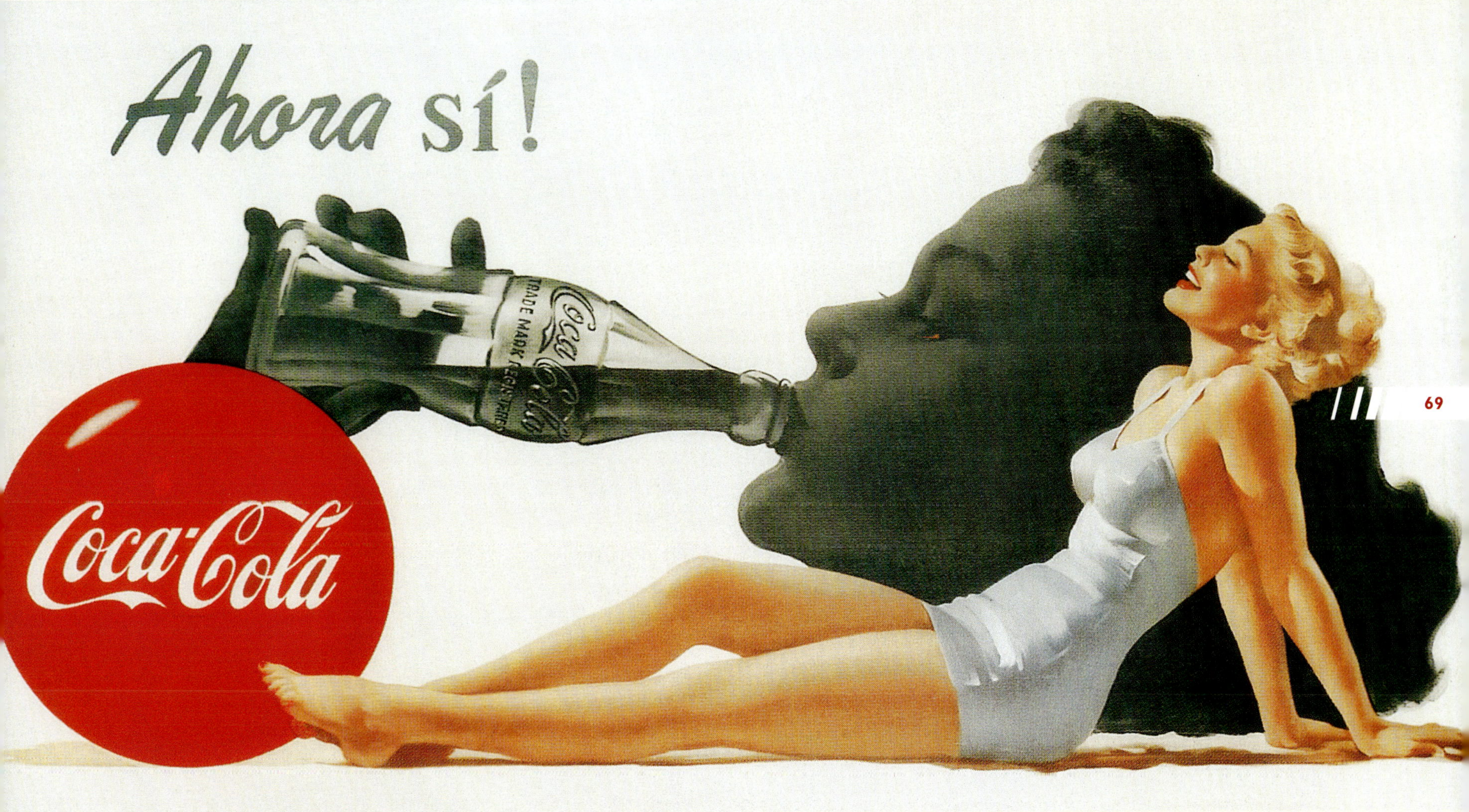

Ahora sí!

Coca-Cola

THE COCA-COLA COMPANY

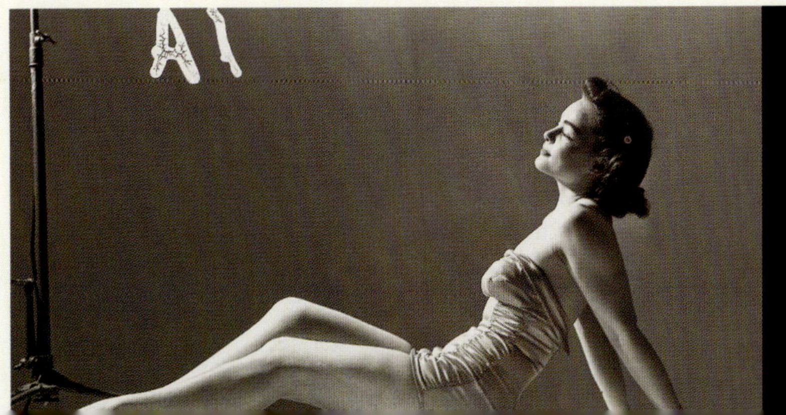

Photos for both elements of this strikingly well-designed Coca-Cola billboard reveal Elvgren's attitude to his self-created reference: unerringly faithful to his under-lighted, near-silhouette of the Coke-drinking girl, he plays fast and loose with his swimsuit model, subtly repositioning her legs, lifting her breasts, and trading the pretty brunette's face for that of a beautiful blonde, glorying in the wonders of the outdoors and Coca-Cola.

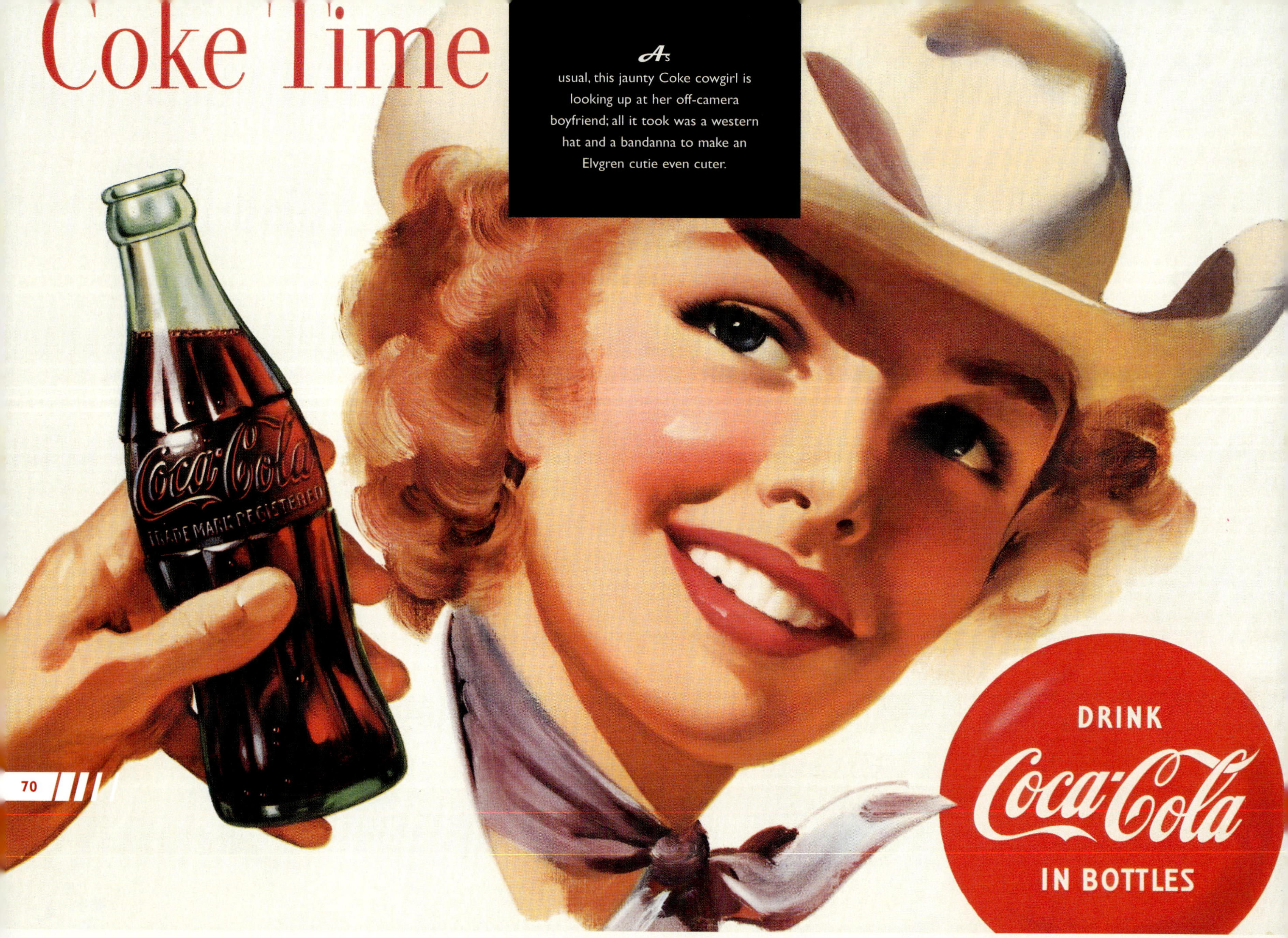

Coke Time

As usual, this jaunty Coke cowgirl is looking up at her off-camera boyfriend; all it took was a western hat and a bandanna to make an Elvgren cutie even cuter.

DRINK
Coca-Cola
IN BOTTLES

This Coca-Cola gal is looking at us, for a change, and she's about to swig that Coke clutched in her mitten; part of the secret of an Elvgren girl's beauty is the happiness he conveys in their luminous faces.

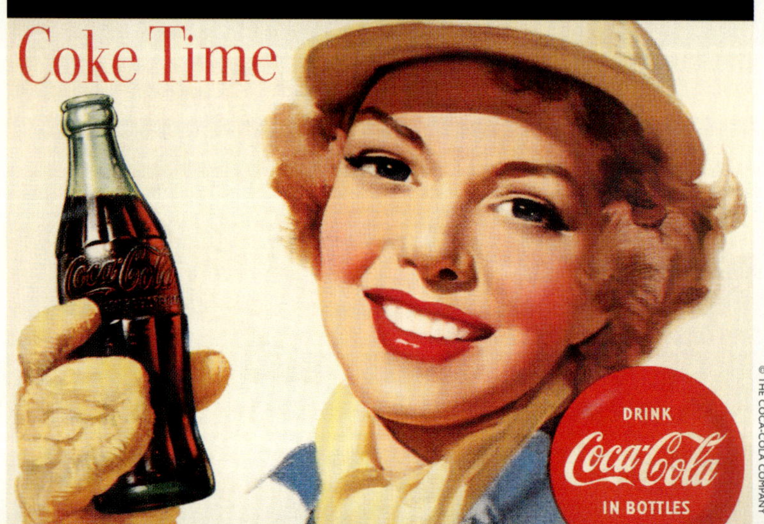

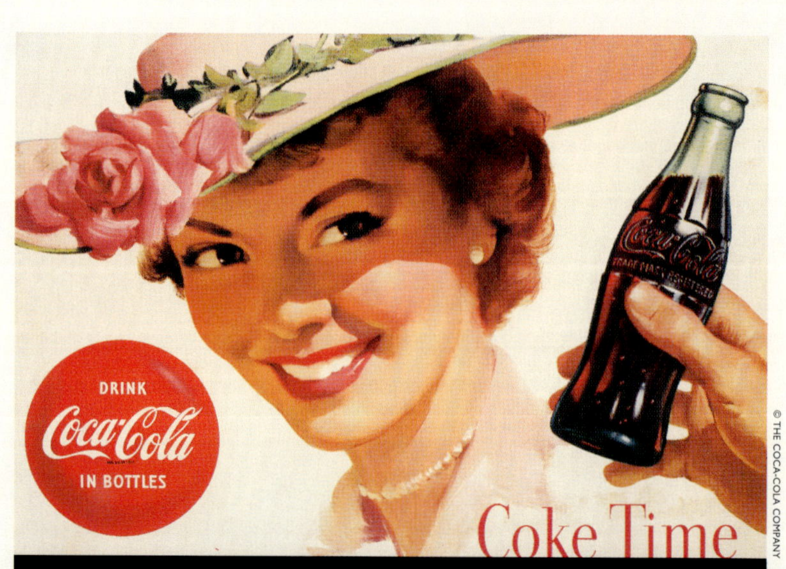

This beauty in a spiffy bonnet is looking up at her off-camera, Coke-offering beau, the standard pose in this Elvgren series.

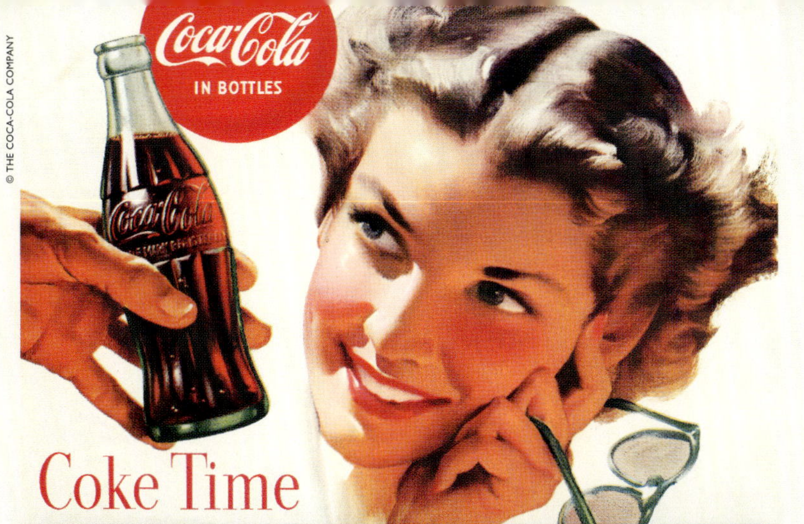

*T*his sophisticated Coke girl (those sunglasses are probably prescription!) typically looks up at her Cola-proffering fella; whether she loves him or the soft drink more is open to speculation.

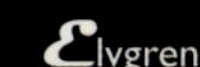

*E*lvgren's Coca-Cola calendar girls are frequently head shots, not full pin-up poses, as this beaming winter beauty demonstrates.

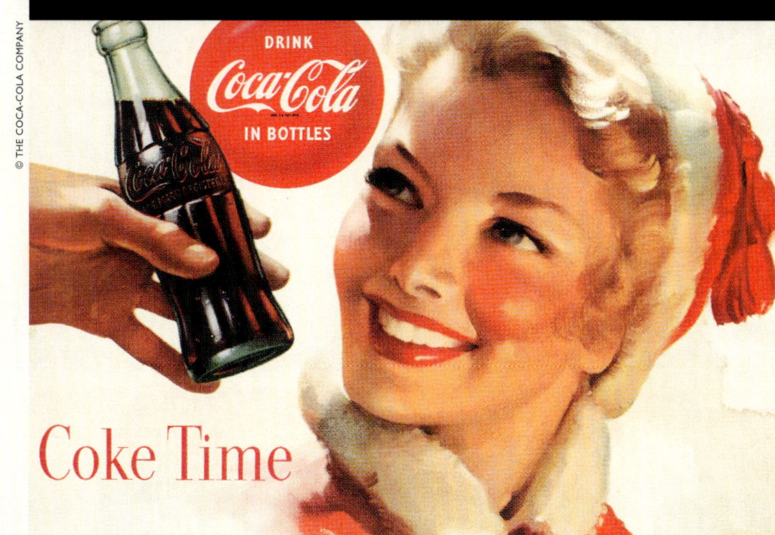

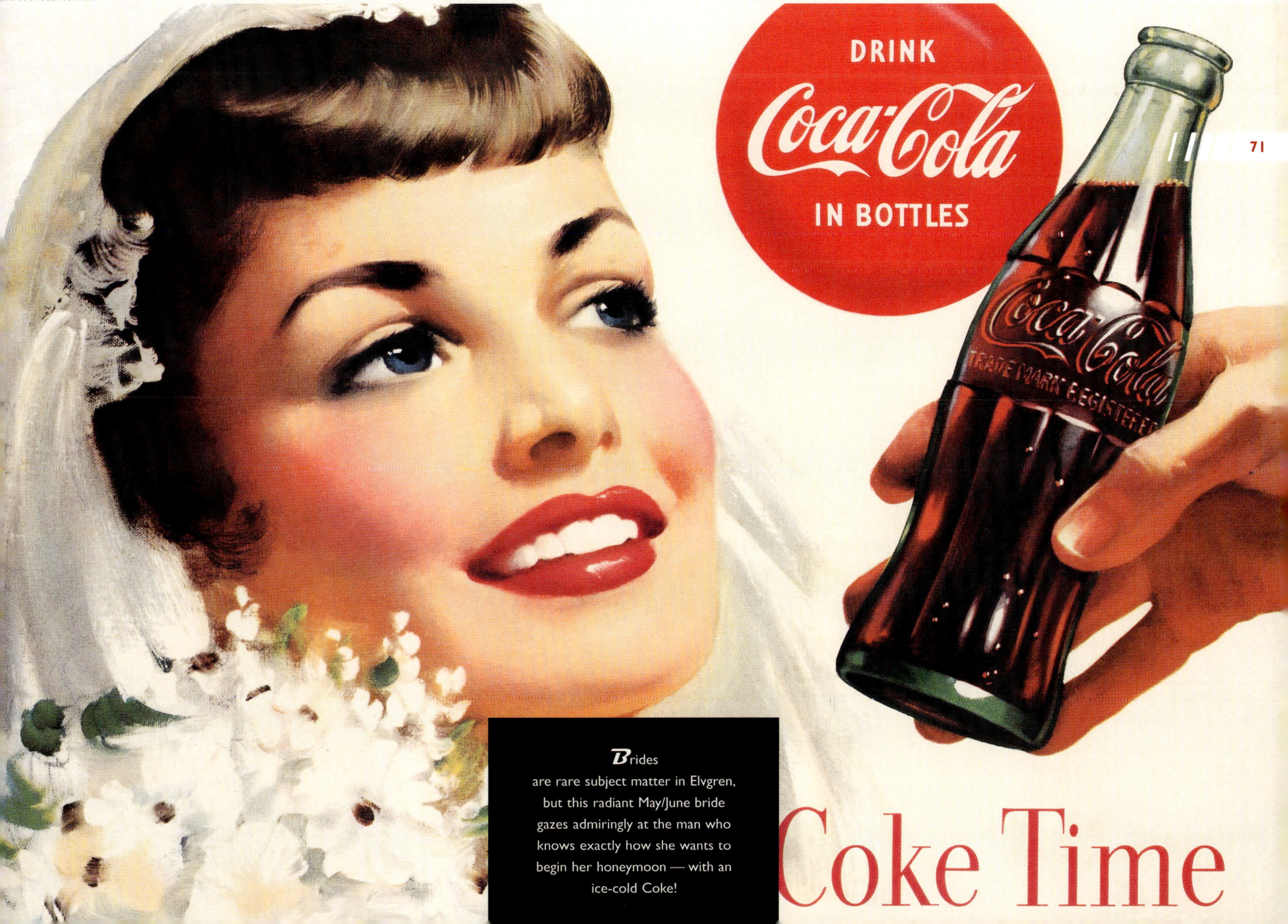

*B*rides are rare subject matter in Elvgren, but this radiant May/June bride gazes admiringly at the man who knows exactly how she wants to begin her honeymoon — with an ice-cold Coke!

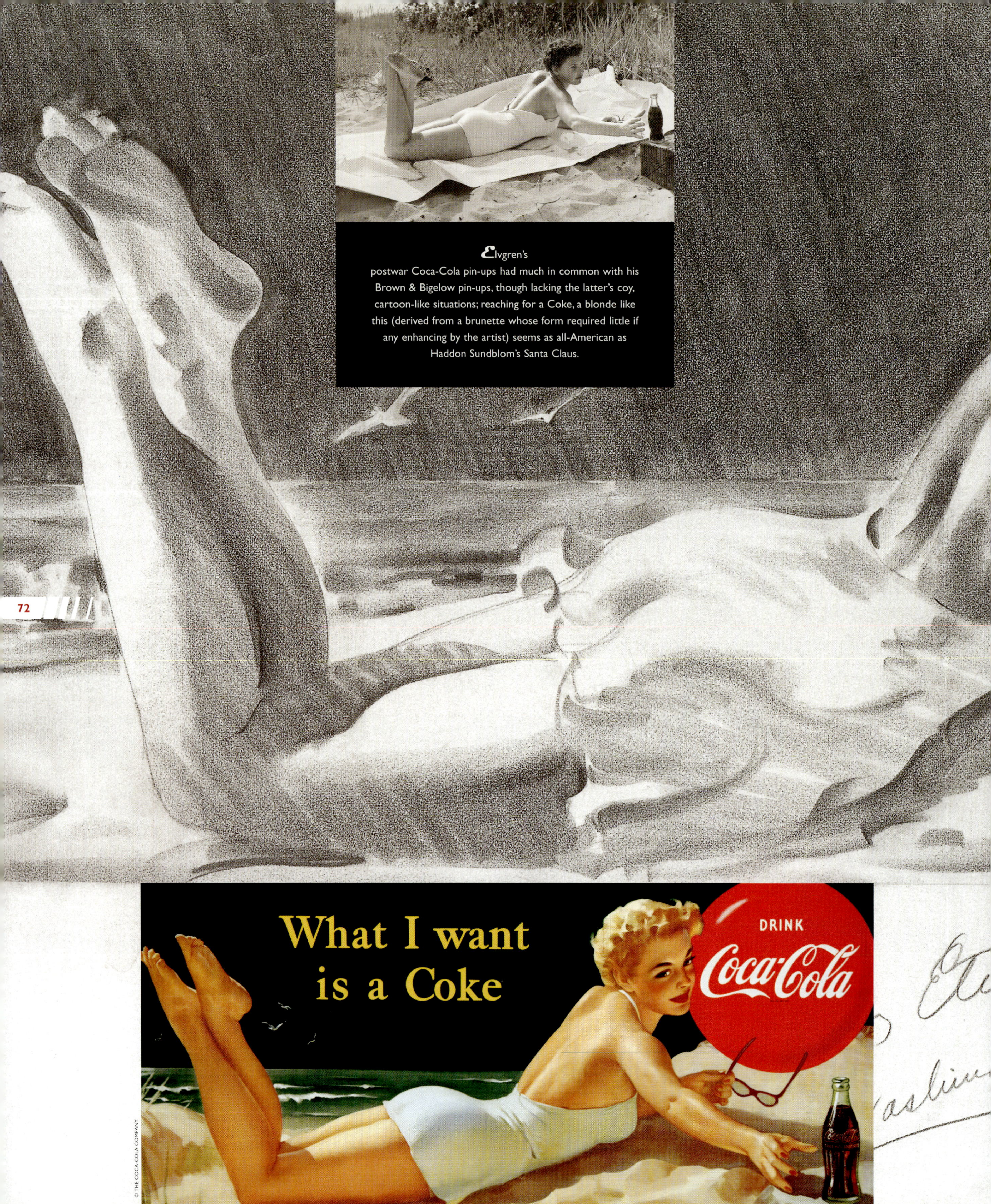

Elvgren's postwar Coca-Cola pin-ups had much in common with his Brown & Bigelow pin-ups, though lacking the latter's coy, cartoon-like situations; reaching for a Coke, a blonde like this (derived from a brunette whose form required little if any enhancing by the artist) seems as all-American as Haddon Sundblom's Santa Claus.

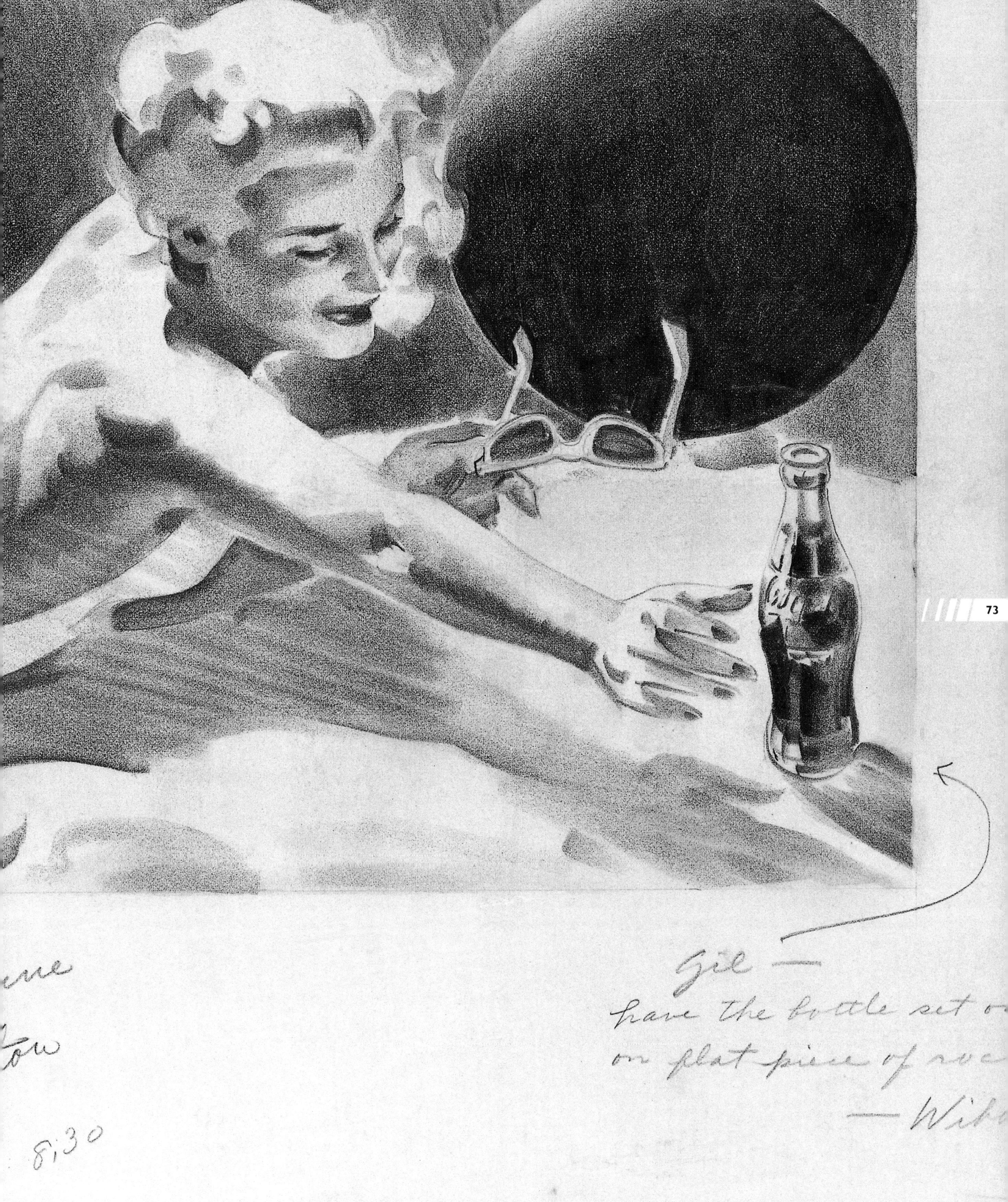
Gil —
have the bottle set
on flat piece of
8:30

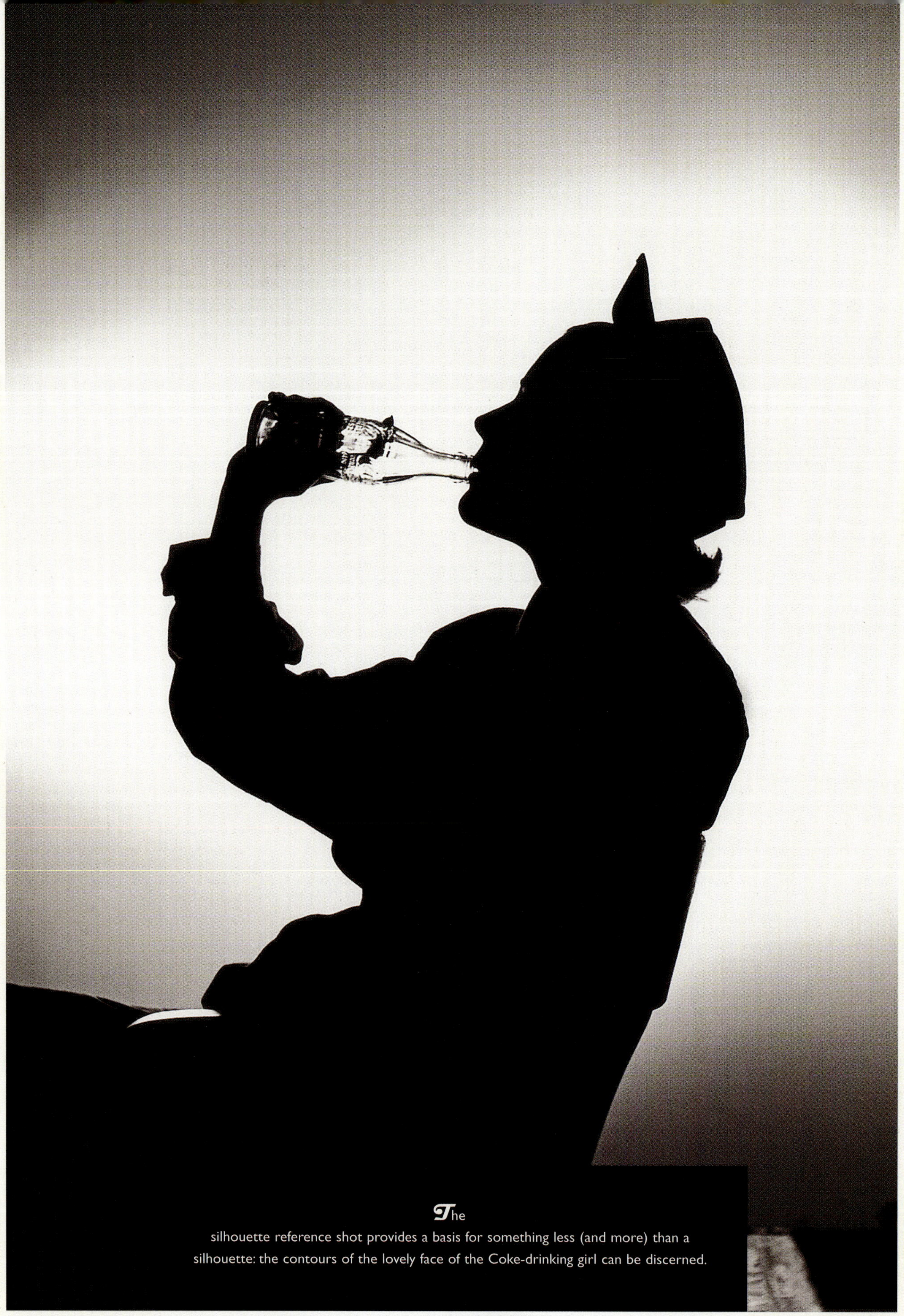

The silhouette reference shot provides a basis for something less (and more) than a silhouette: the contours of the lovely face of the Coke-drinking girl can be discerned.

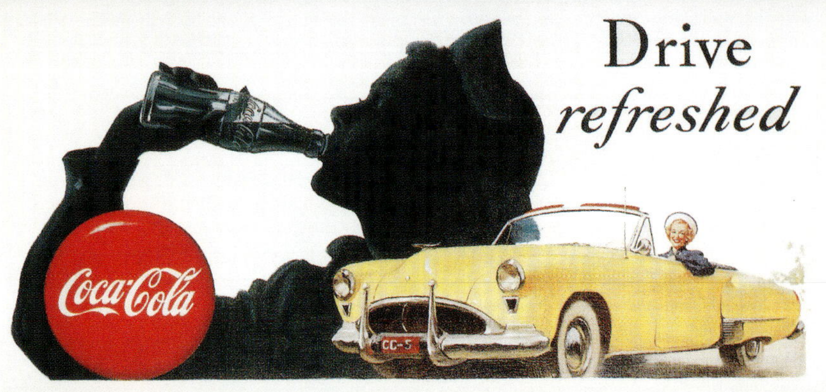

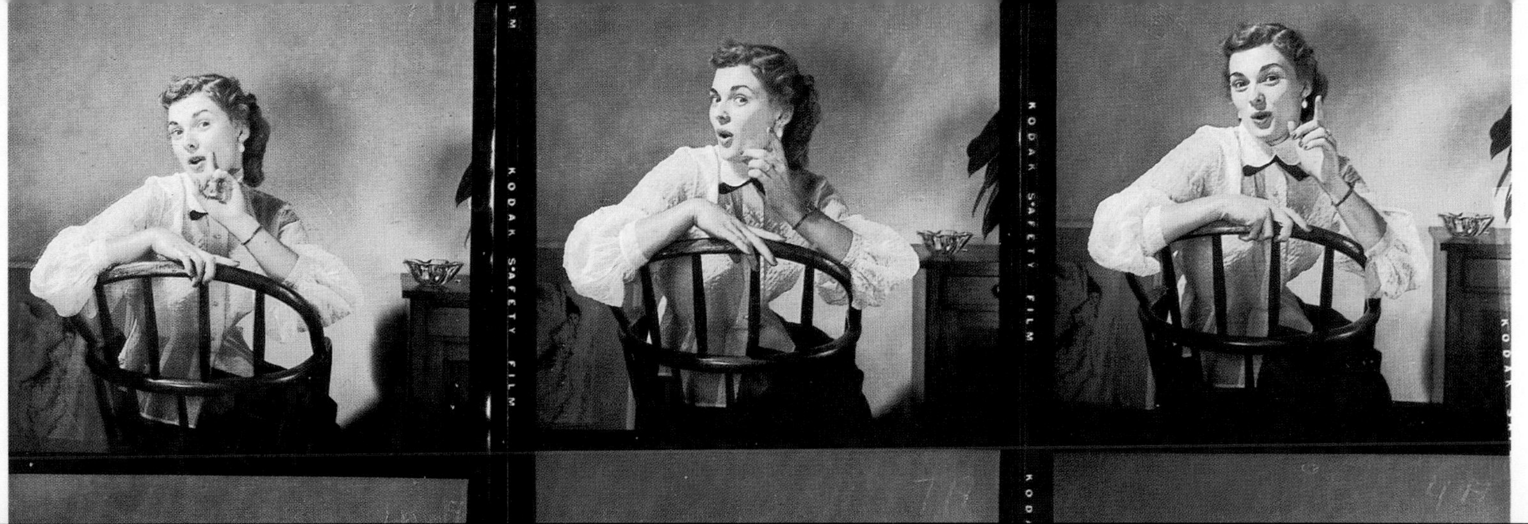

Rather
more elaborately posed than most of Elvgren's beer advertisements, this one presents an improbably elegant saleswoman for so blue-collar a product.

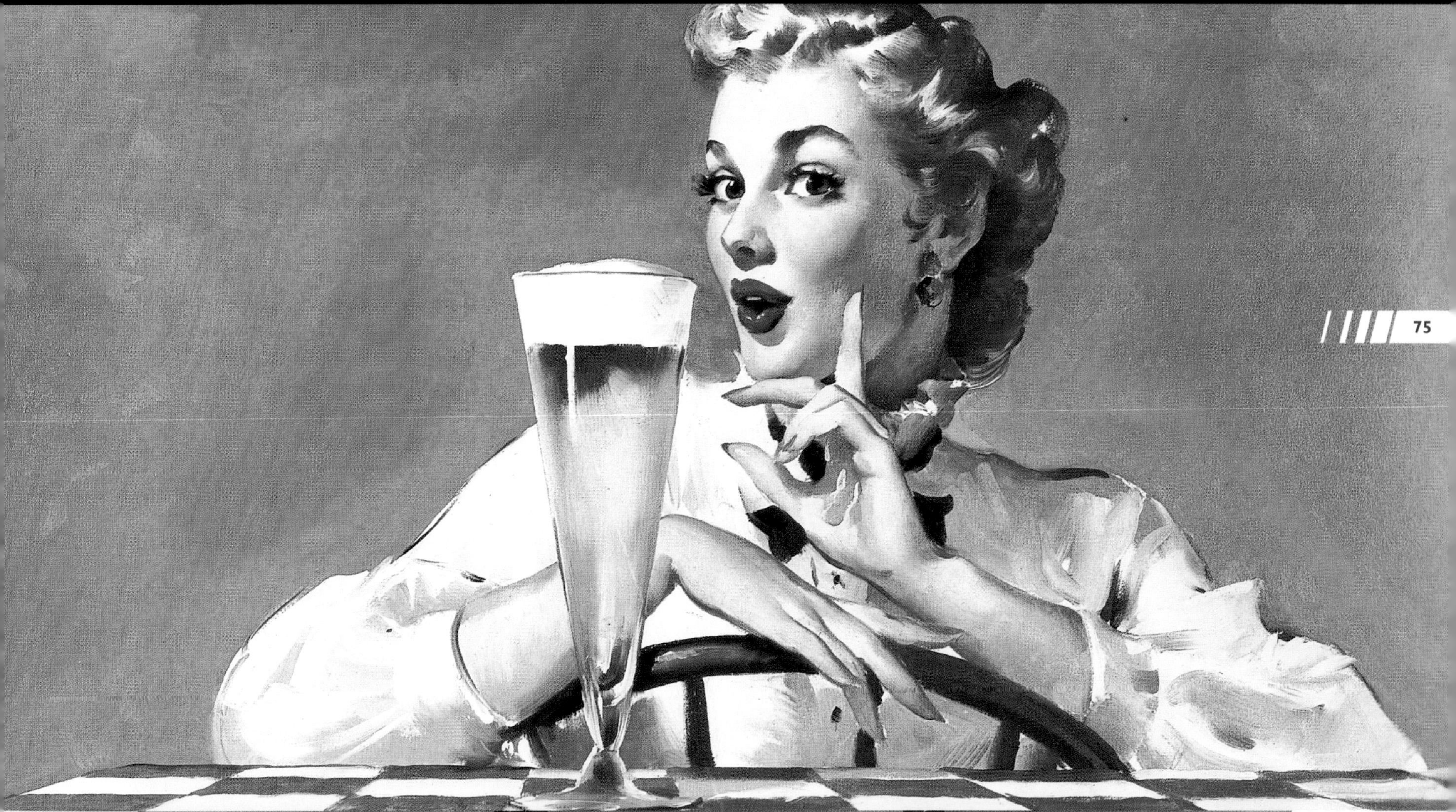

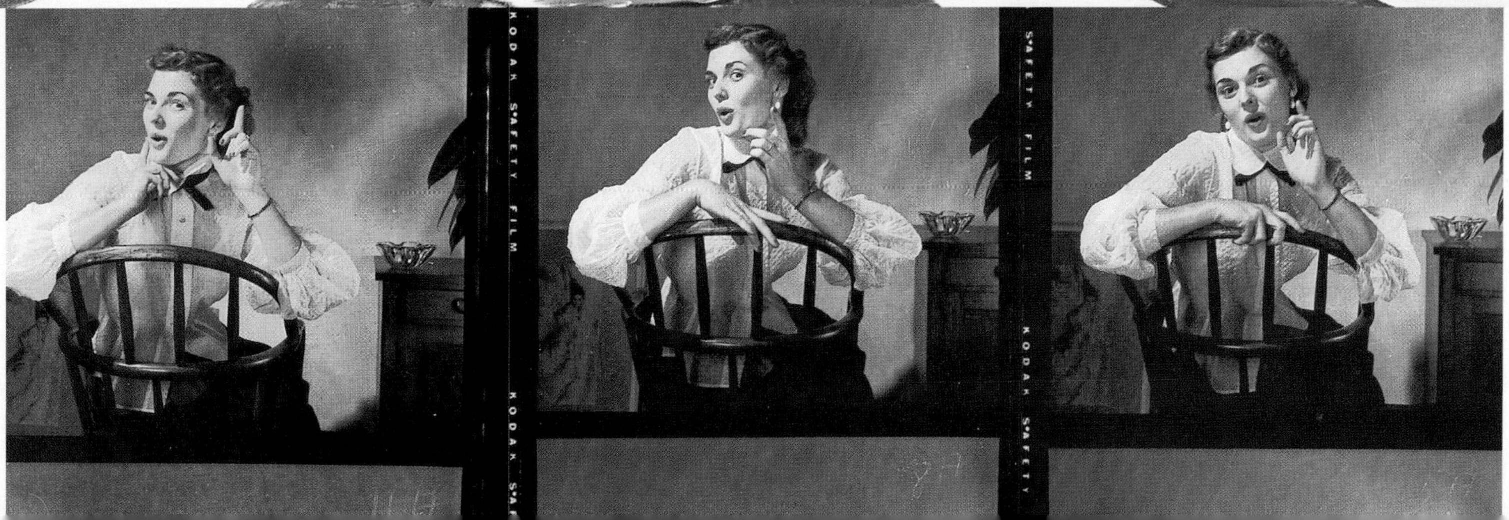

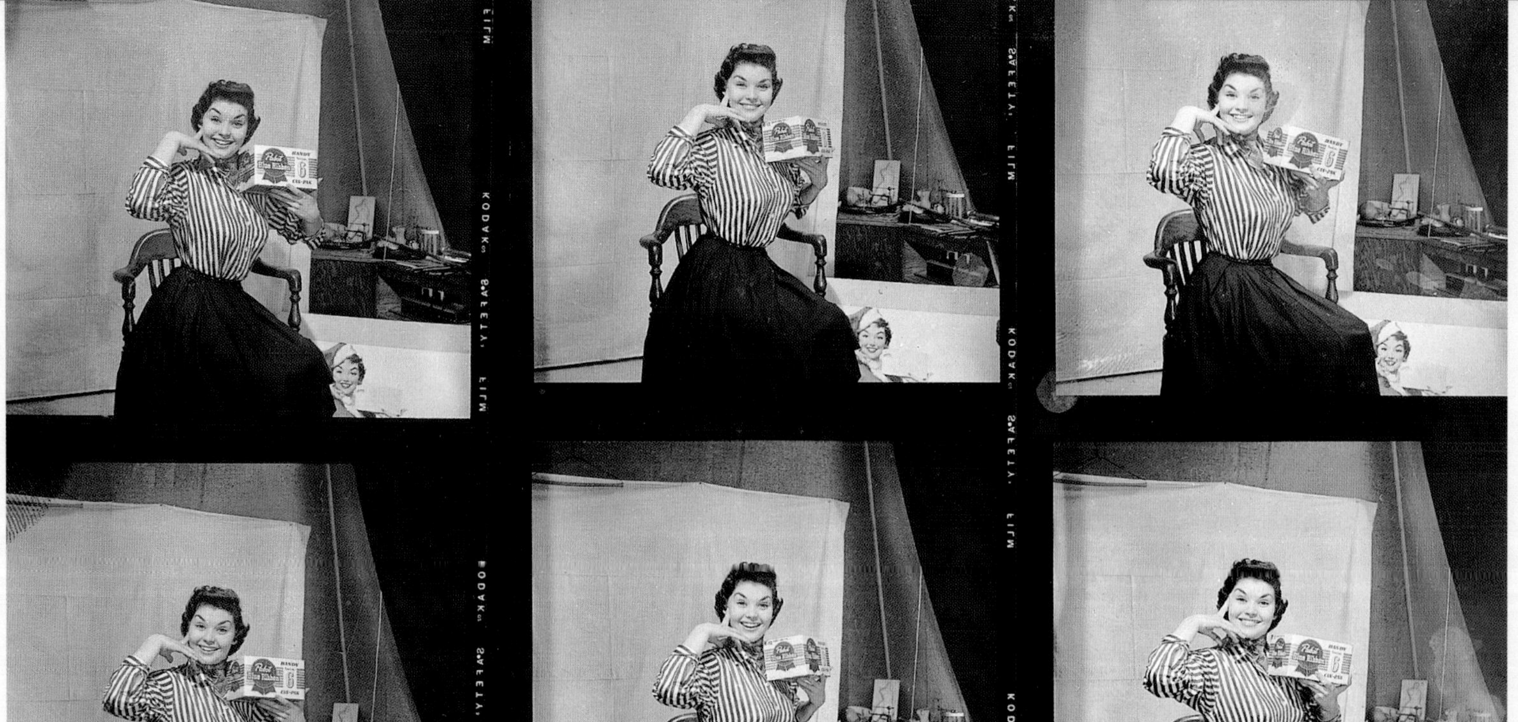

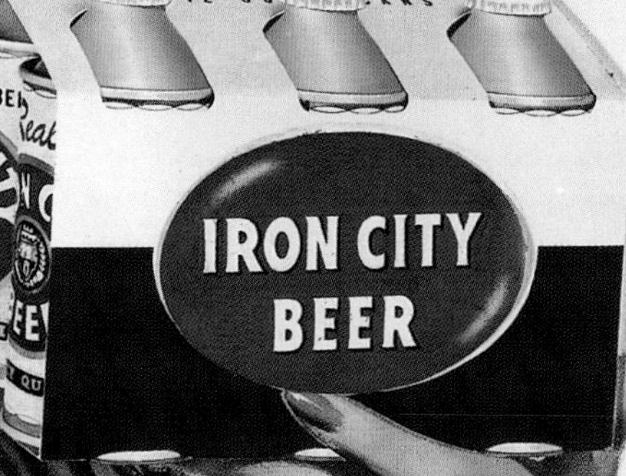

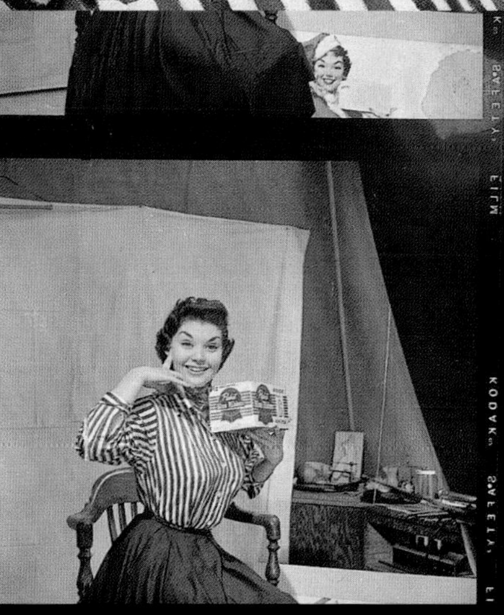

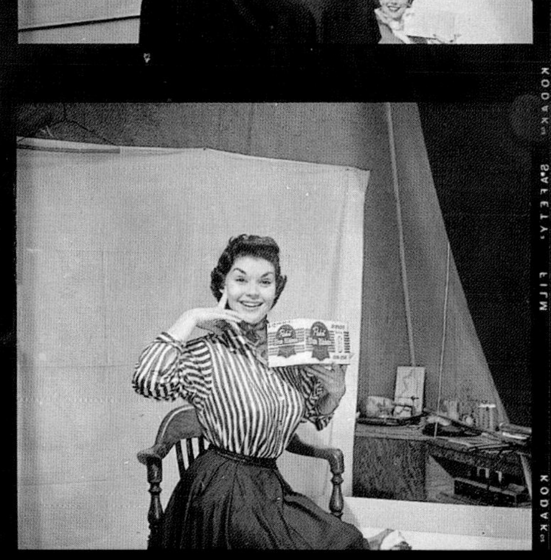

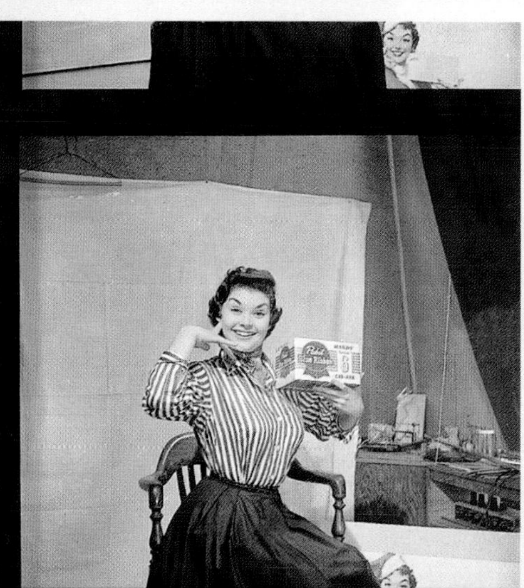

Jaunty

1950s fashions with their horizontal and vertical stripes and bold colors are perfect fodder for Elvgren; a wholesomely sexy woman gives her seal of approval to Iron City Beer. The proof sheet shows the lengths artist and model go to capture that casual, graceful pose.

Elvgren puts his glowing, robust touch on a model, already cheery and healthy-looking; the sporty casualness of the pixie-haired, probable housewife on the phone imparts wholesomeness to the product she and Elvgren are selling: beer.

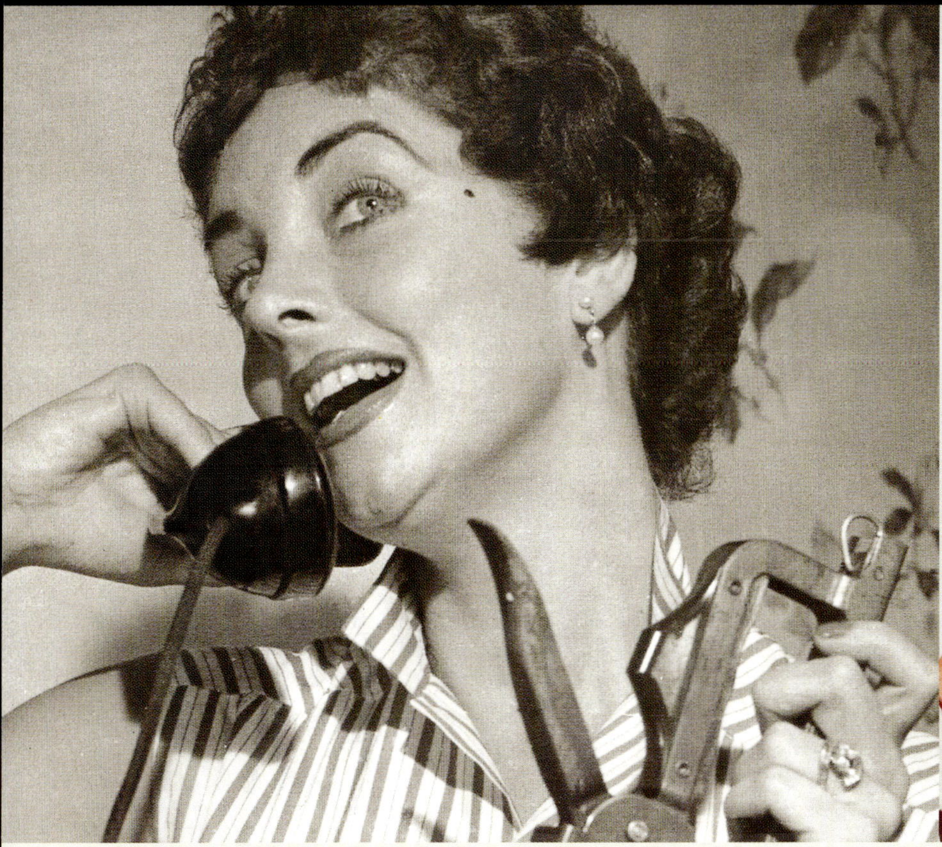

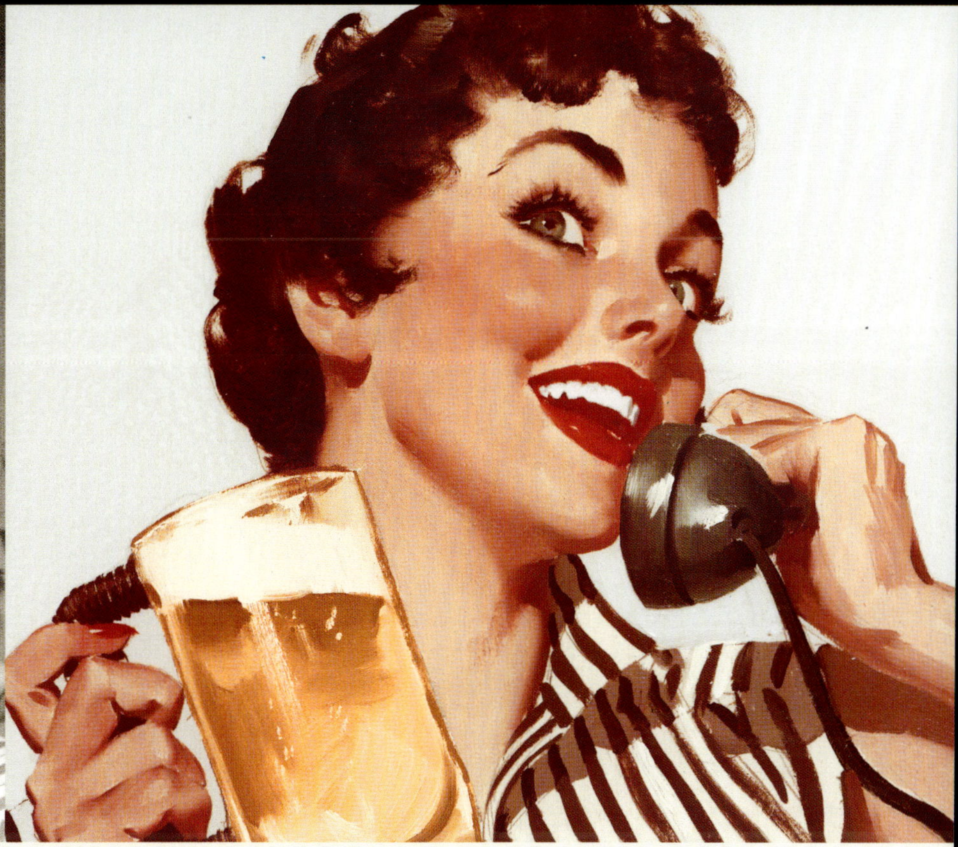

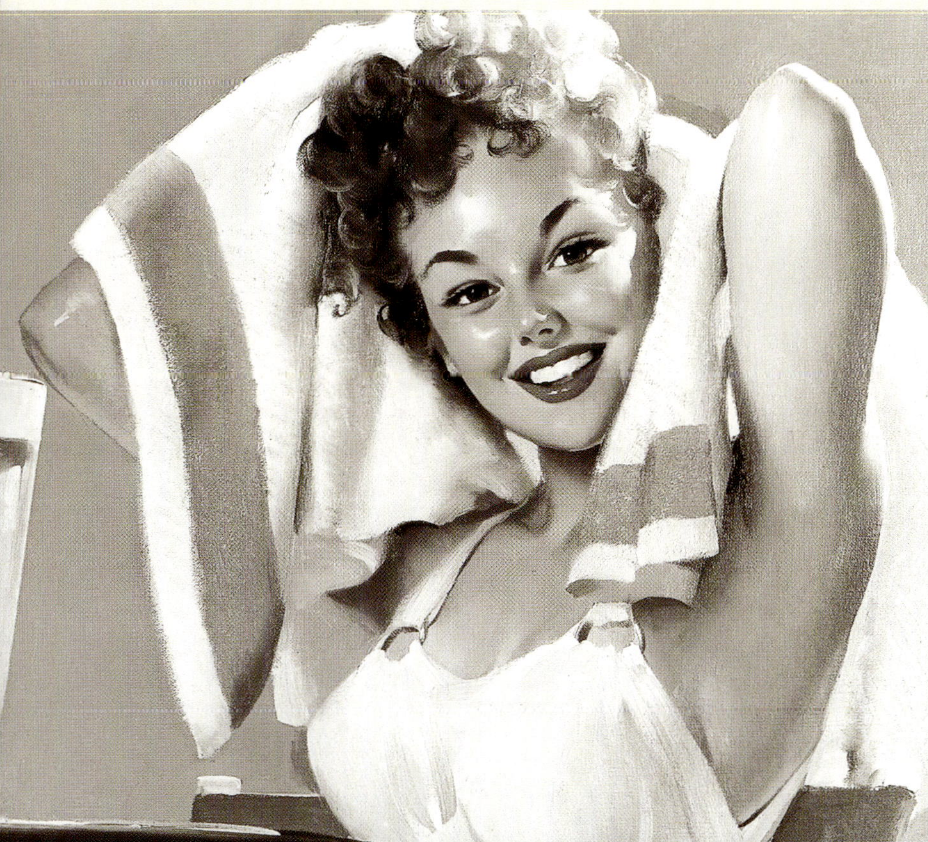

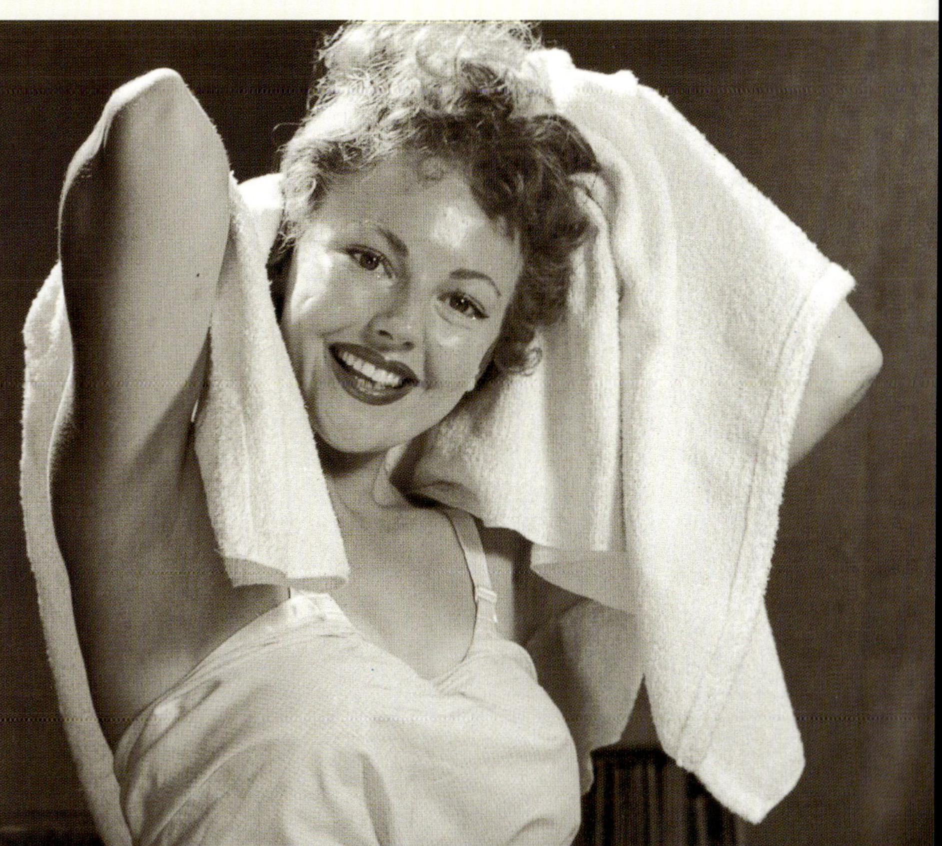

The astonishingly sexy photograph of this model is a rare instance when the Elvgren combination of sex appeal and wholesomeness exists in the flesh; the beer in the ad seems a mere afterthought in this outstanding painting.

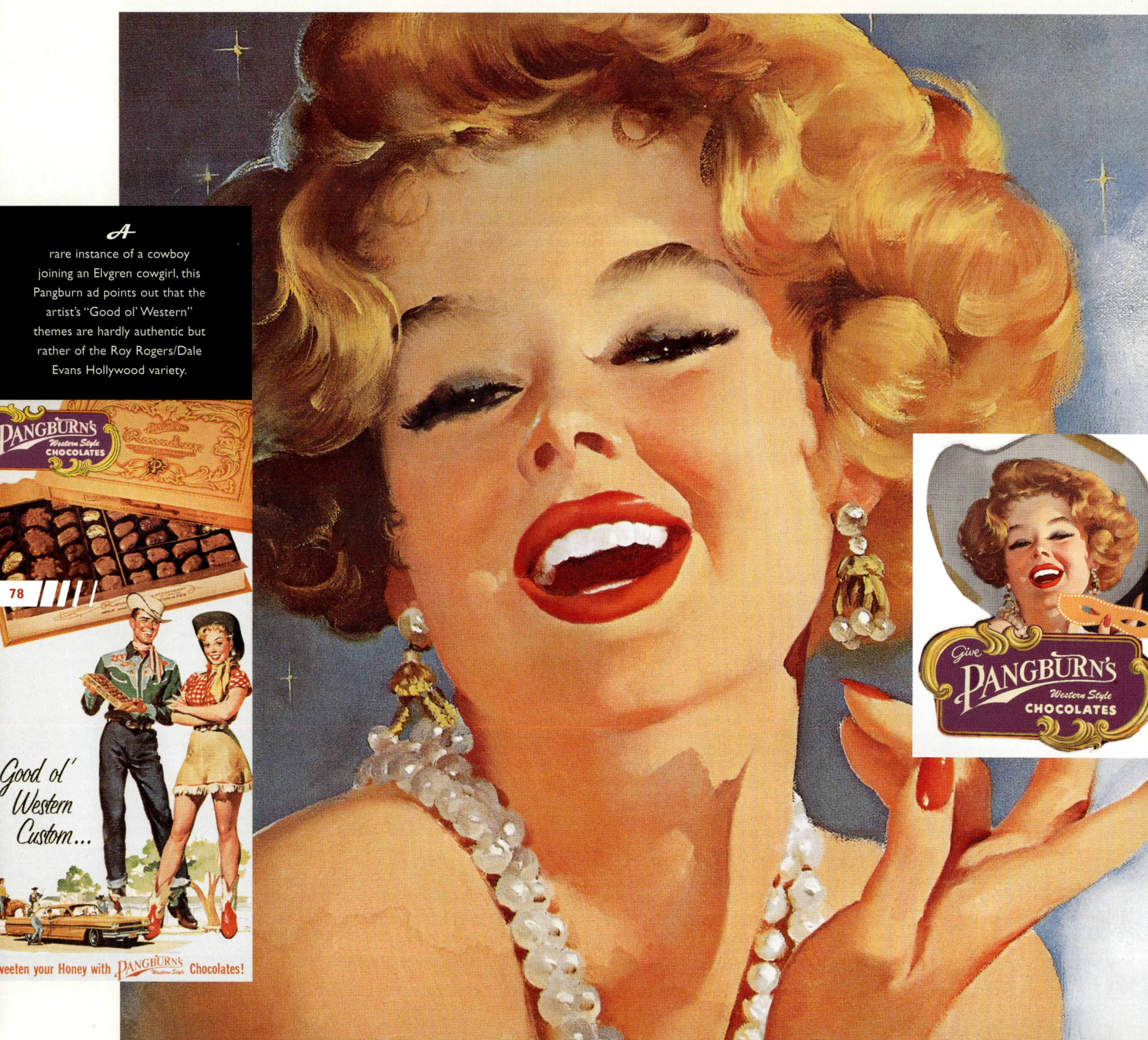

A rare instance of a cowboy joining an Elvgren cowgirl, this Pangburn ad points out that the artist's "Good ol' Western" themes are hardly authentic but rather of the Roy Rogers/Dale Evans Hollywood variety.

A generic, bubbly, sophisticated showgirl is somewhat clumsily reworked (probably not by Elvgren himself) into a cowboy-hat-wearing, masquerade-mask-bearing salesgirl for "Western-Style" chocolate.

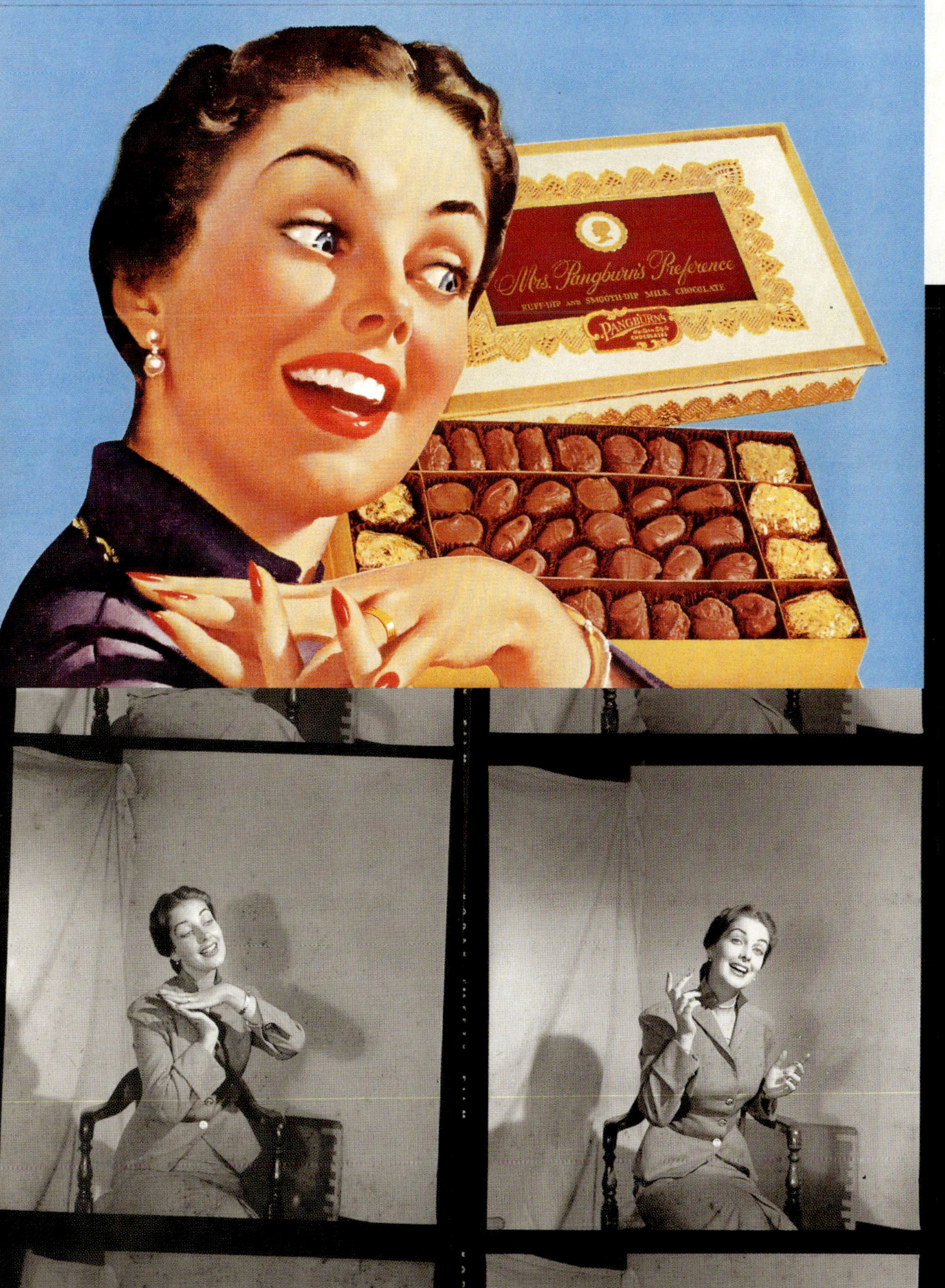

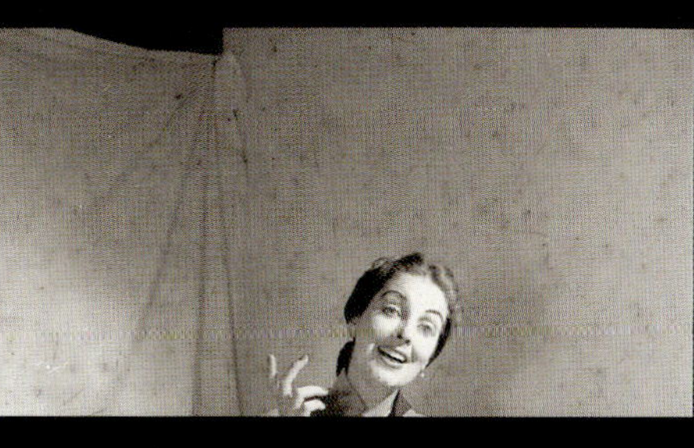

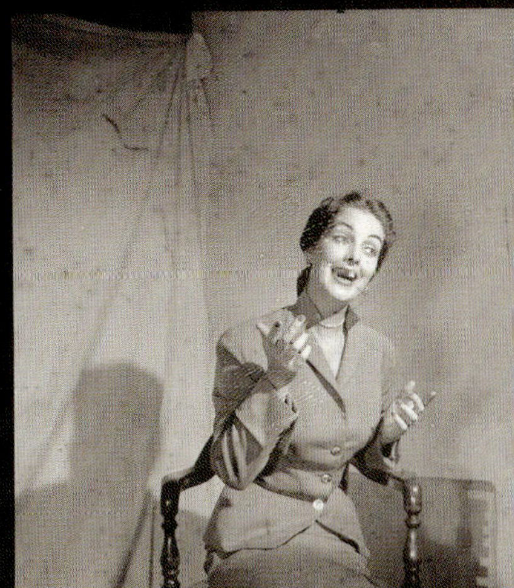

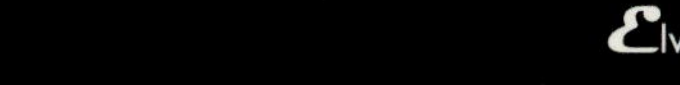

*E*lvgren
often creates generic images that could be adapted to sell any number of products — this rather upscale housewife is equally excited about chocolates and cottage cheese!

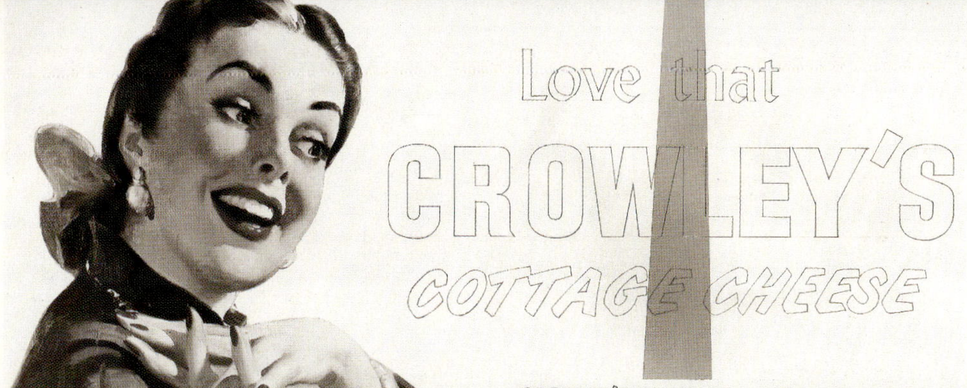

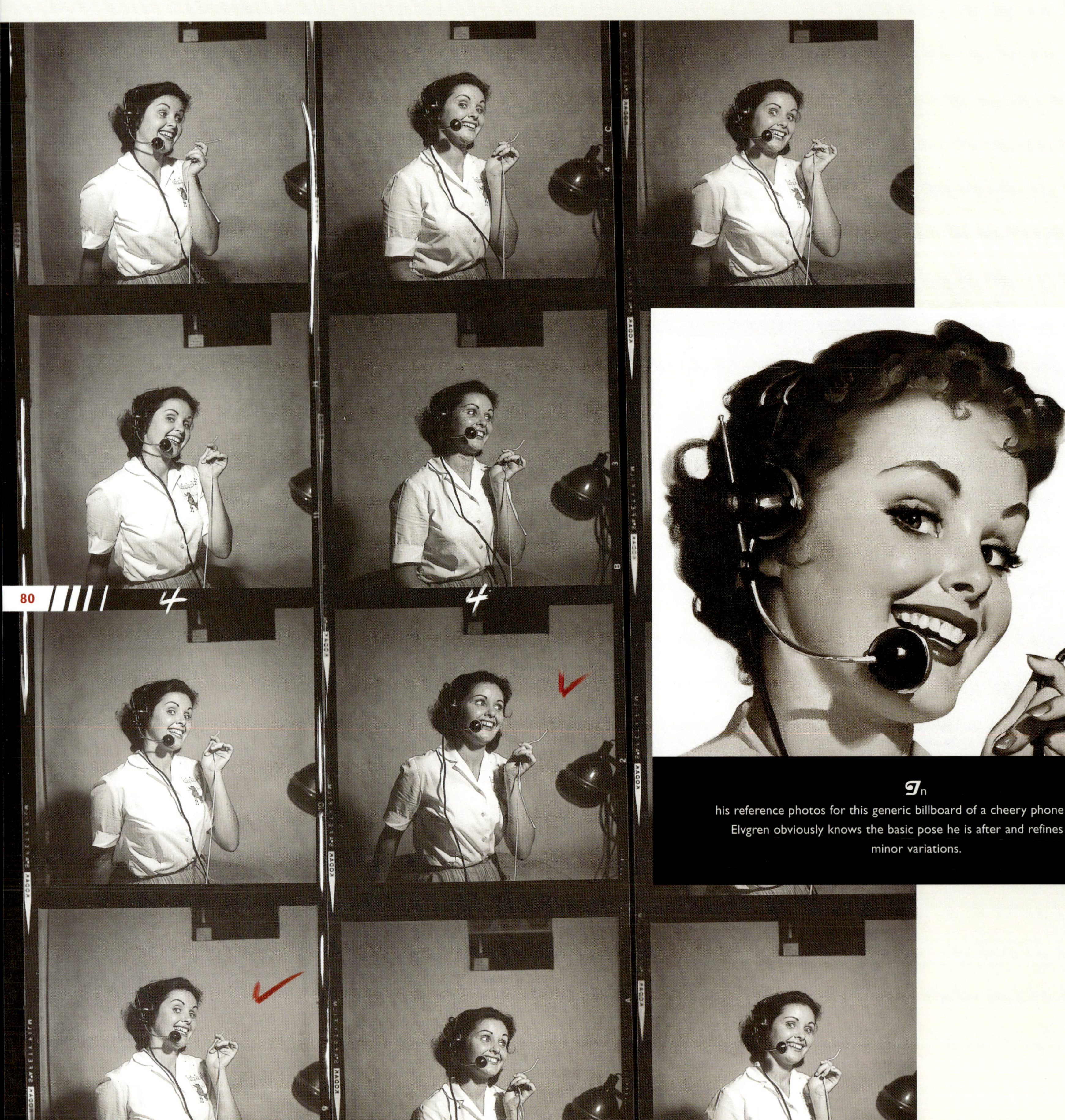

In his reference photos for this generic billboard of a cheery phone operator, Elvgren obviously knows the basic pose he is after and refines it with minor variations.

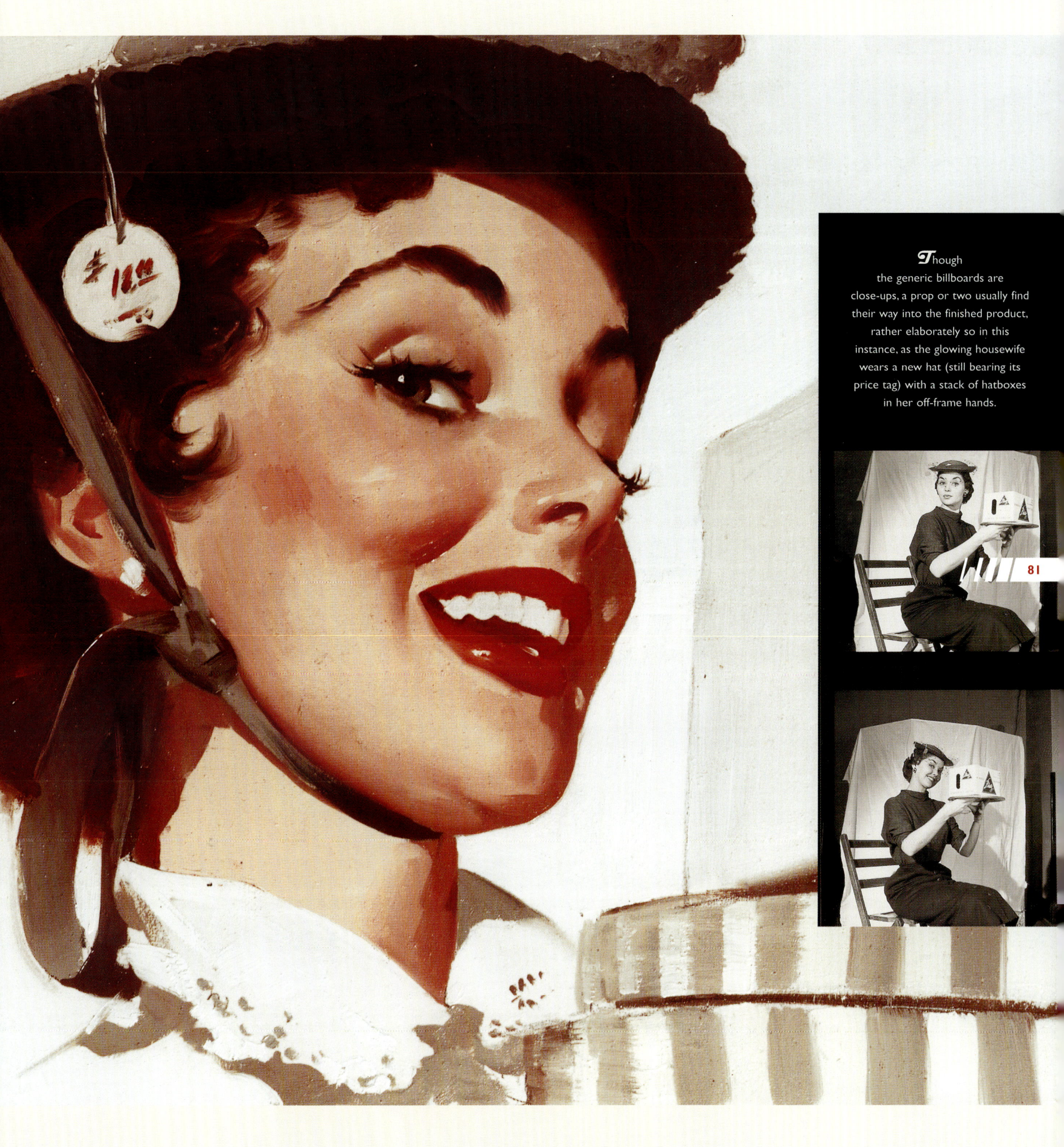

Though the generic billboards are close-ups, a prop or two usually find their way into the finished product, rather elaborately so in this instance, as the glowing housewife wears a new hat (still bearing its price tag) with a stack of hatboxes in her off-frame hands.

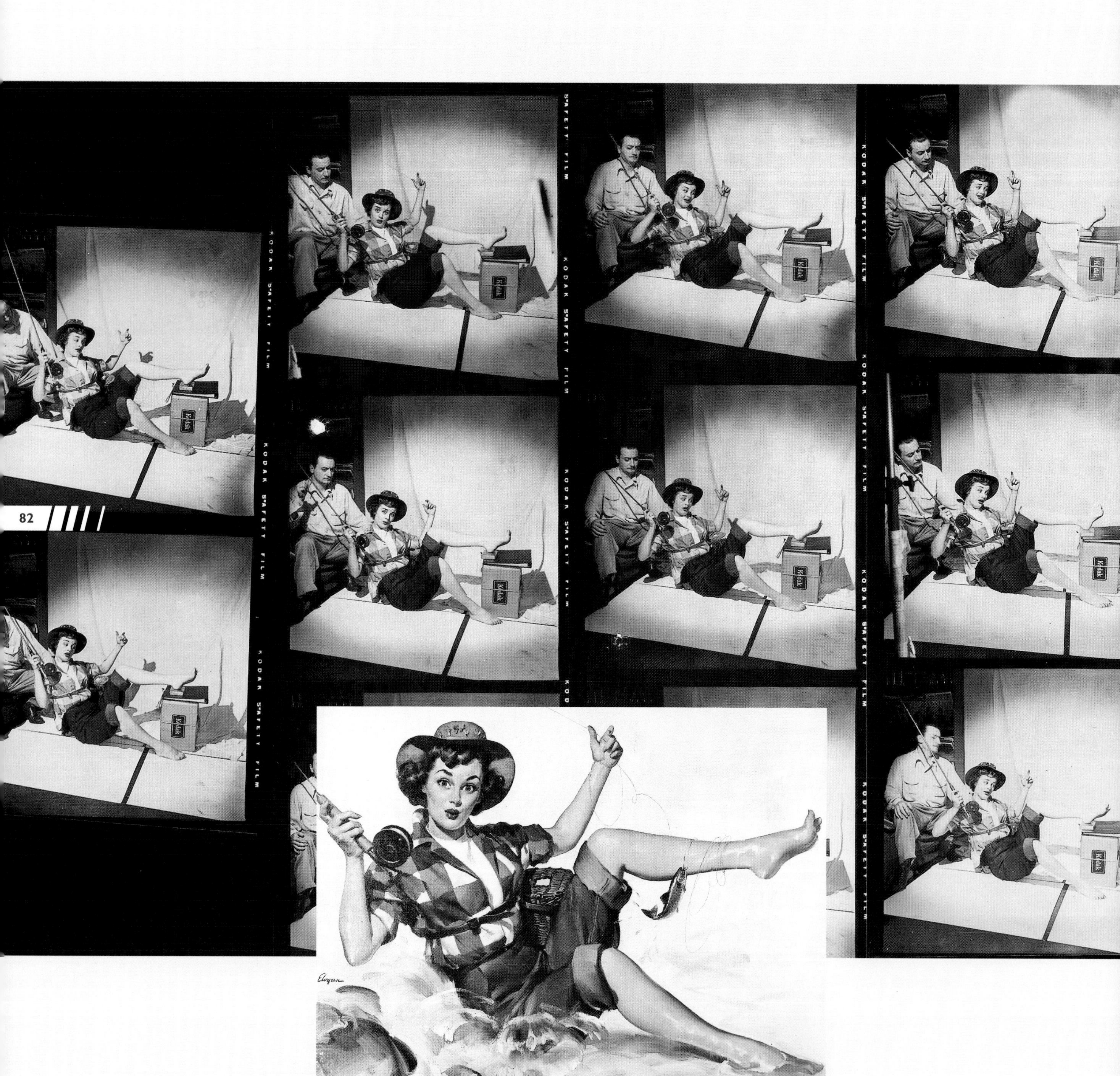

Inveterate
outdoor sportsman Elvgren uses fishing as a theme in this advertising piece (product unknown). Note the elaborate and varied staging of this situation in proof-sheet photos.

Elvgren's
advertising and magazine pieces frequently featured girls lovely enough to appear in one of his pin-ups, as this bathing-beauty blonde attests.

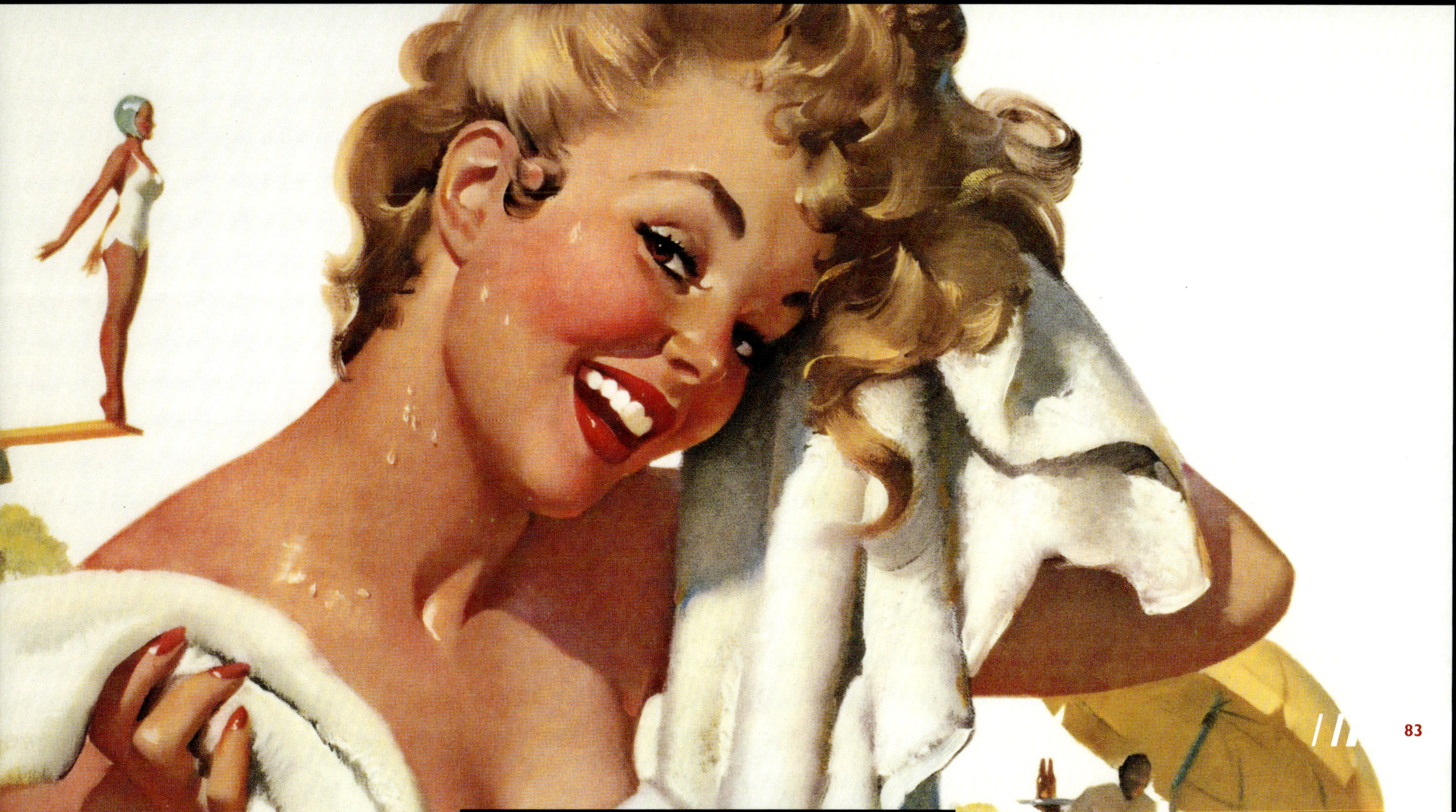

This
illustration reveals the full romantic equation: not just the pretty girl but her hunky boyfriend, as well, in a romanticized outdoors — the sexual symbolism of the lifesaver straddling the bench is surely no accident.

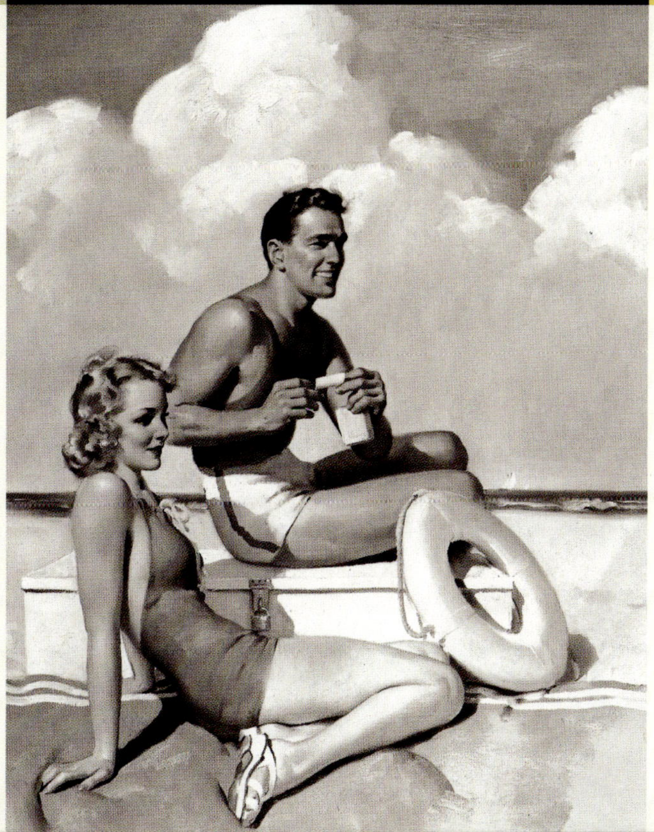

His
fondness for outdoors sports themes dates to even this early Elvgren mirror-image bathing beauty.

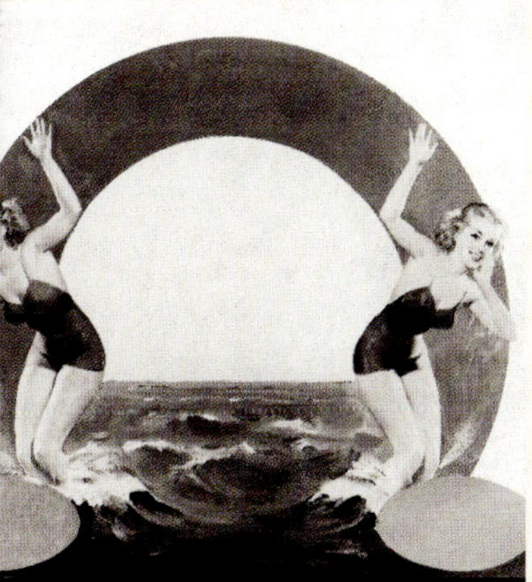

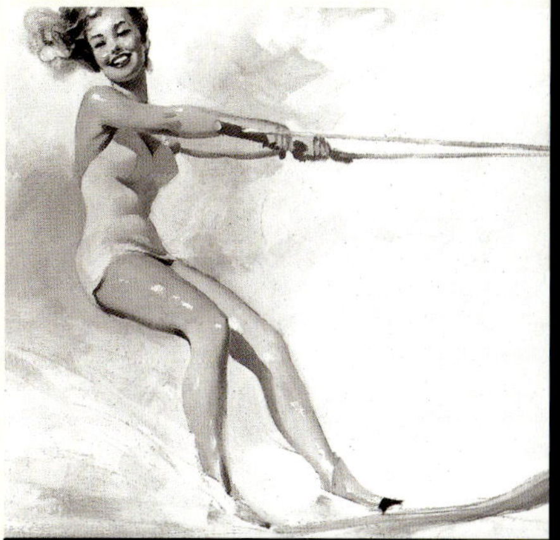

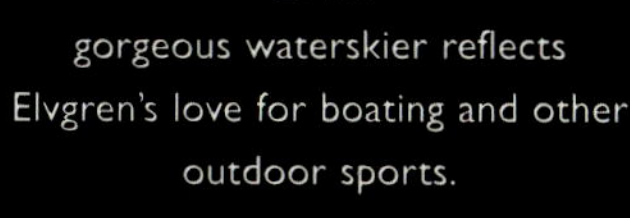
This
gorgeous waterskier reflects Elvgren's love for boating and other outdoor sports.

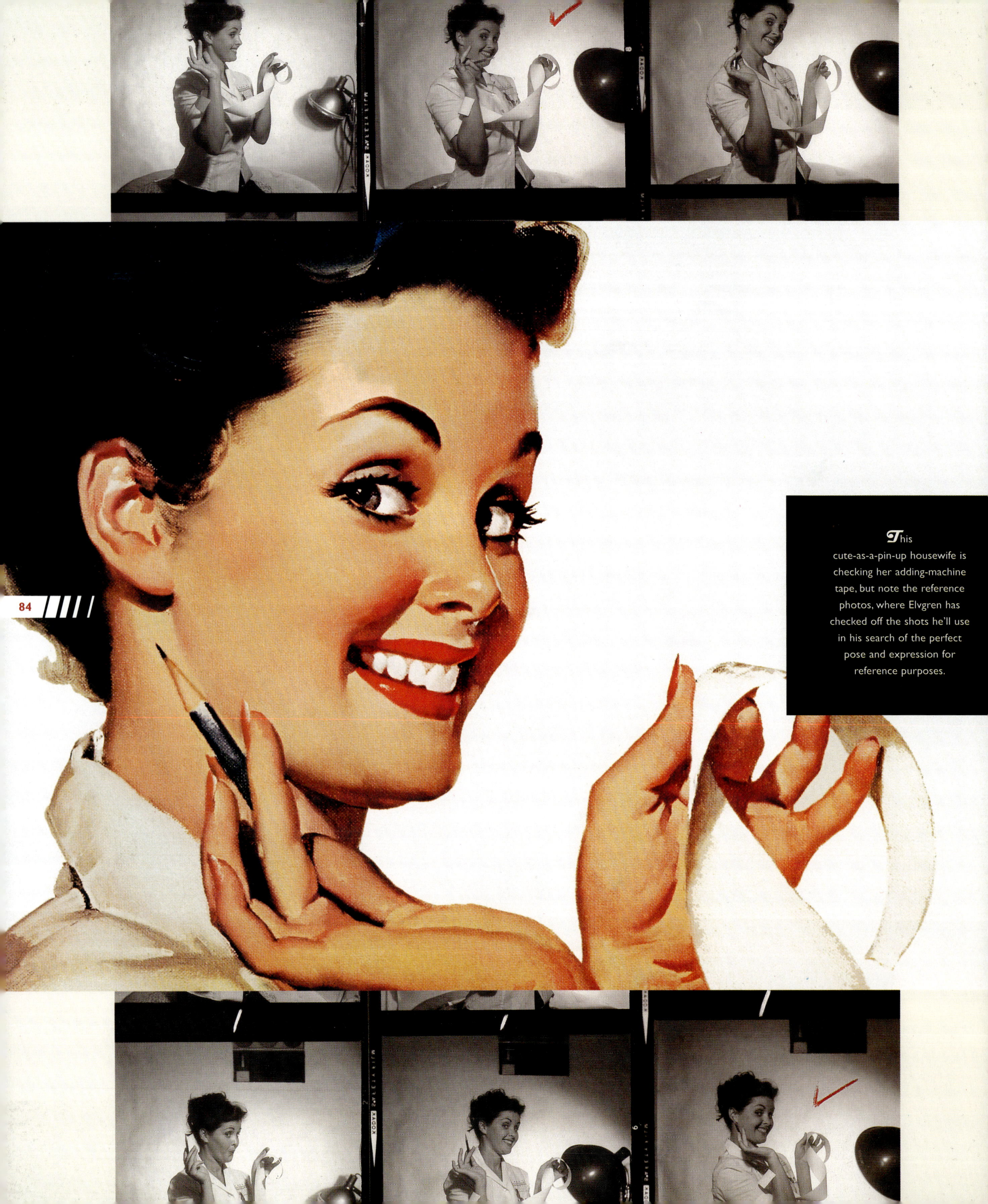

This cute-as-a-pin-up housewife is checking her adding-machine tape, but note the reference photos, where Elvgren has checked off the shots he'll use in his search of the perfect pose and expression for reference purposes.

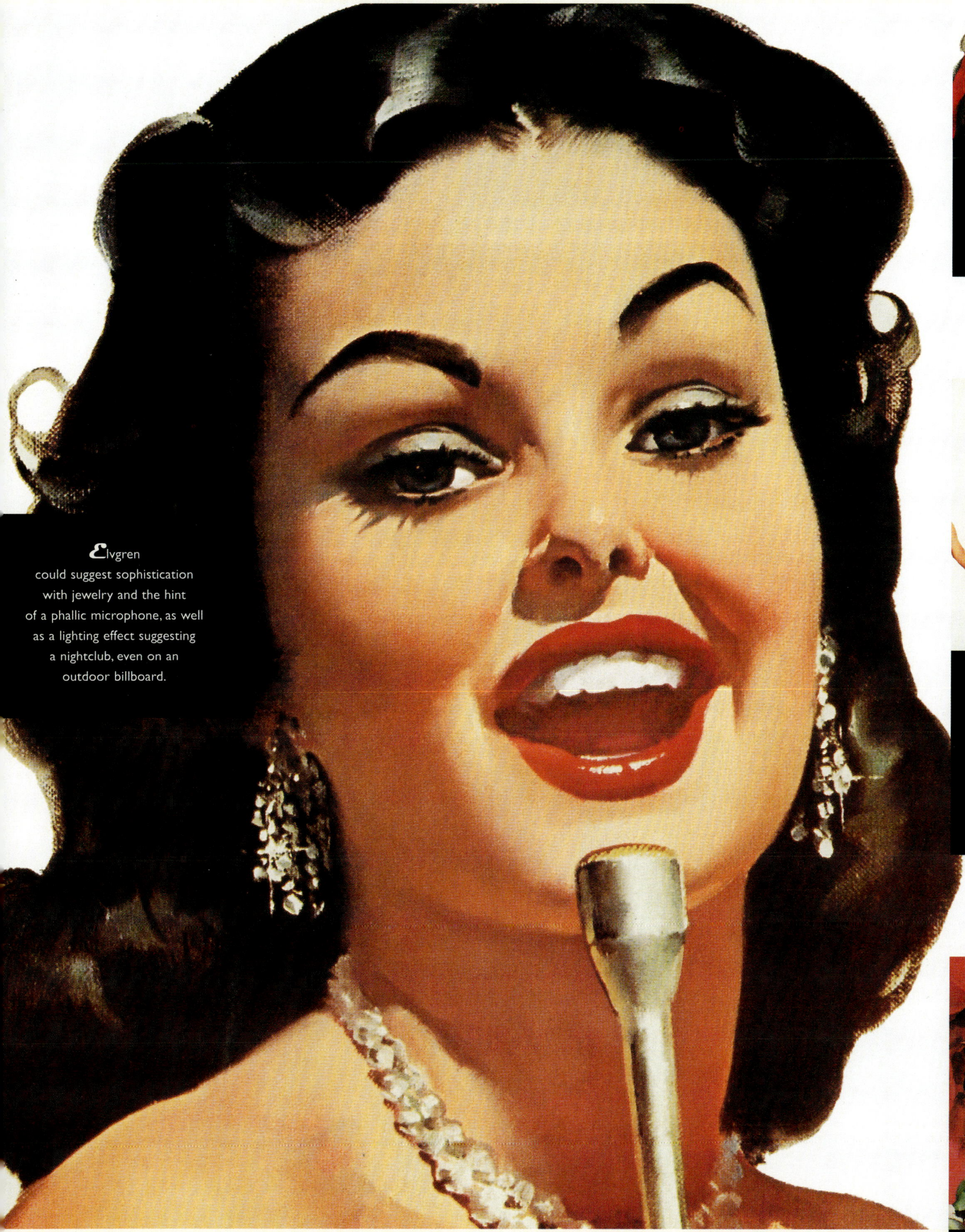

Elvgren could suggest sophistication with jewelry and the hint of a phallic microphone, as well as a lighting effect suggesting a nightclub, even on an outdoor billboard.

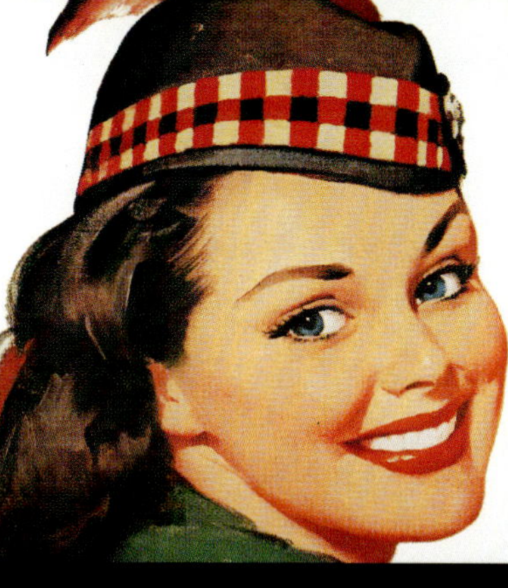

Elvgren was capable of muting his sexy girls into more wholesome images, as in this generic billboard painting, though they retained a sparkle.

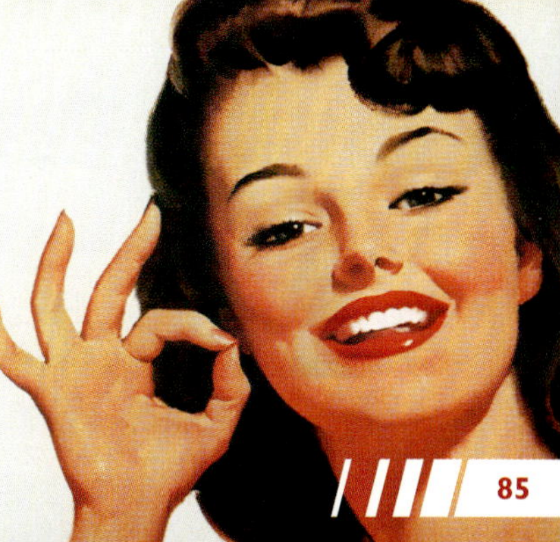

With their big eyes, pert noses, apple cheeks, and lush, lipsticked lips — not to mention perfect, usually cute coifs — an Elvgren "housewife" (as on this generic billboard) is only the slightly older sister of his Brown & Bigelow pin-up girls.

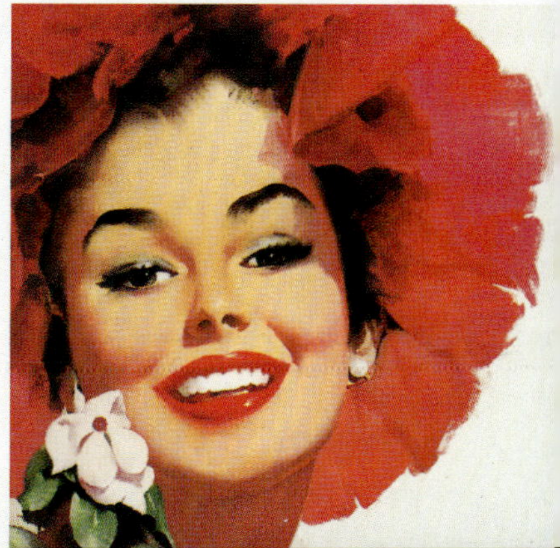

Elvgren's use of beautiful girls — like this sophisticate — on his "Universal billboards" could sell almost any product.

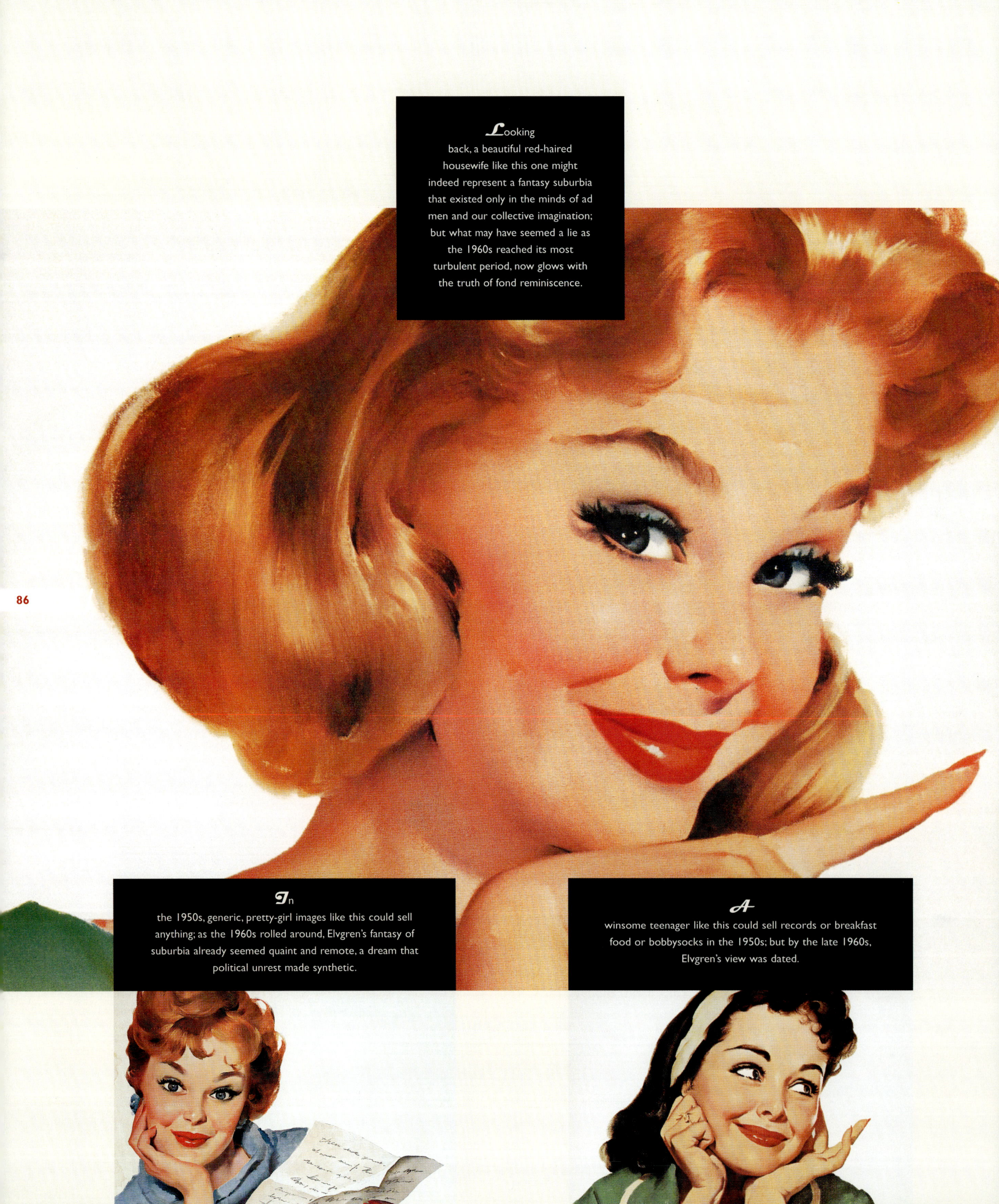

Looking back, a beautiful red-haired housewife like this one might indeed represent a fantasy suburbia that existed only in the minds of ad men and our collective imagination; but what may have seemed a lie as the 1960s reached its most turbulent period, now glows with the truth of fond reminiscence.

In the 1950s, generic, pretty-girl images like this could sell anything; as the 1960s rolled around, Elvgren's fantasy of suburbia already seemed quaint and remote, a dream that political unrest made synthetic.

A winsome teenager like this could sell records or breakfast food or bobbysocks in the 1950s; but by the late 1960s, Elvgren's view was dated.

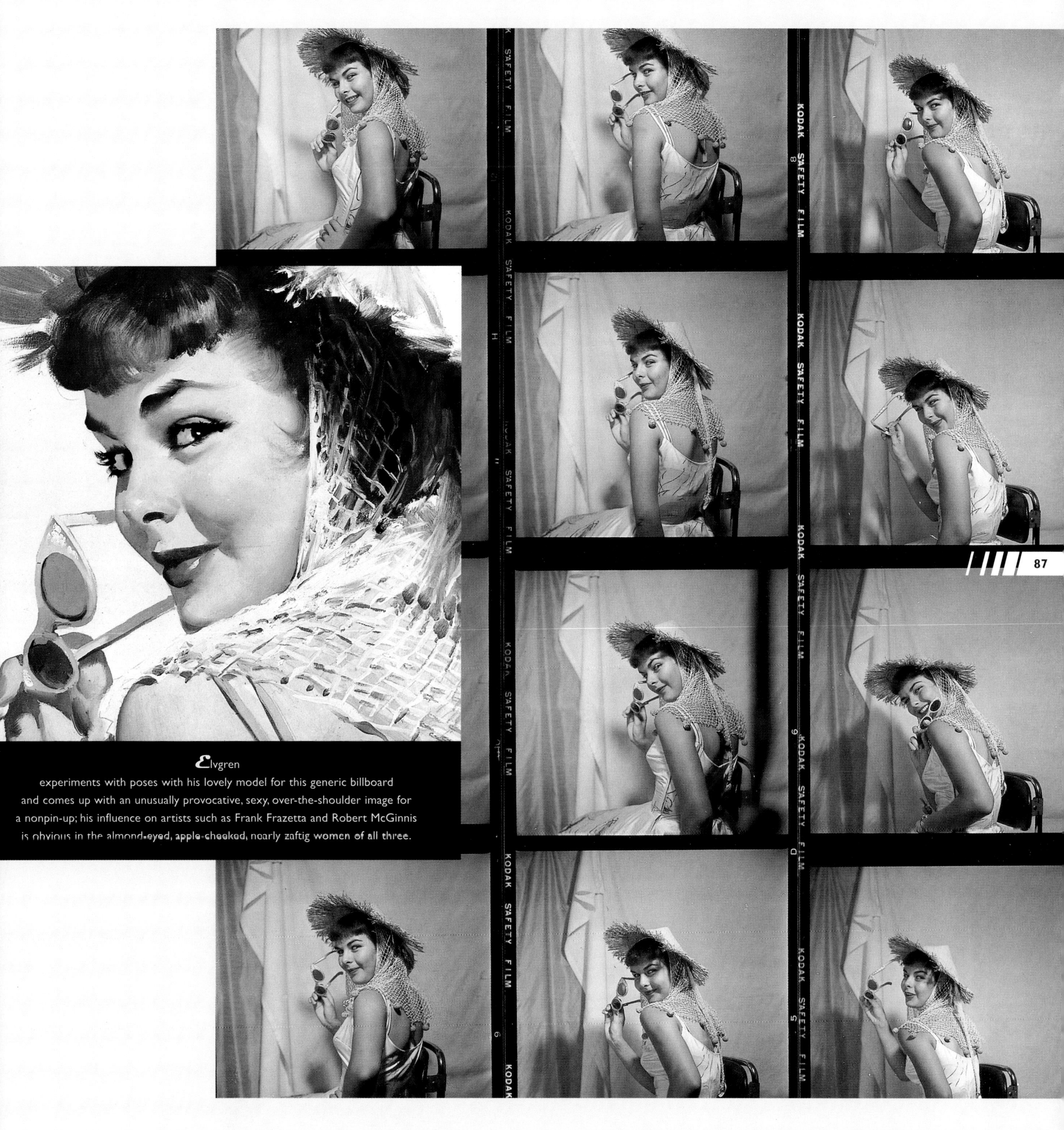

*E*lvgren
experiments with poses with his lovely model for this generic billboard and comes up with an unusually provocative, sexy, over-the-shoulder image for a nonpin-up; his influence on artists such as Frank Frazetta and Robert McGinnis is obvious in the almond-eyed, apple-cheeked, nearly zaftig women of all three.

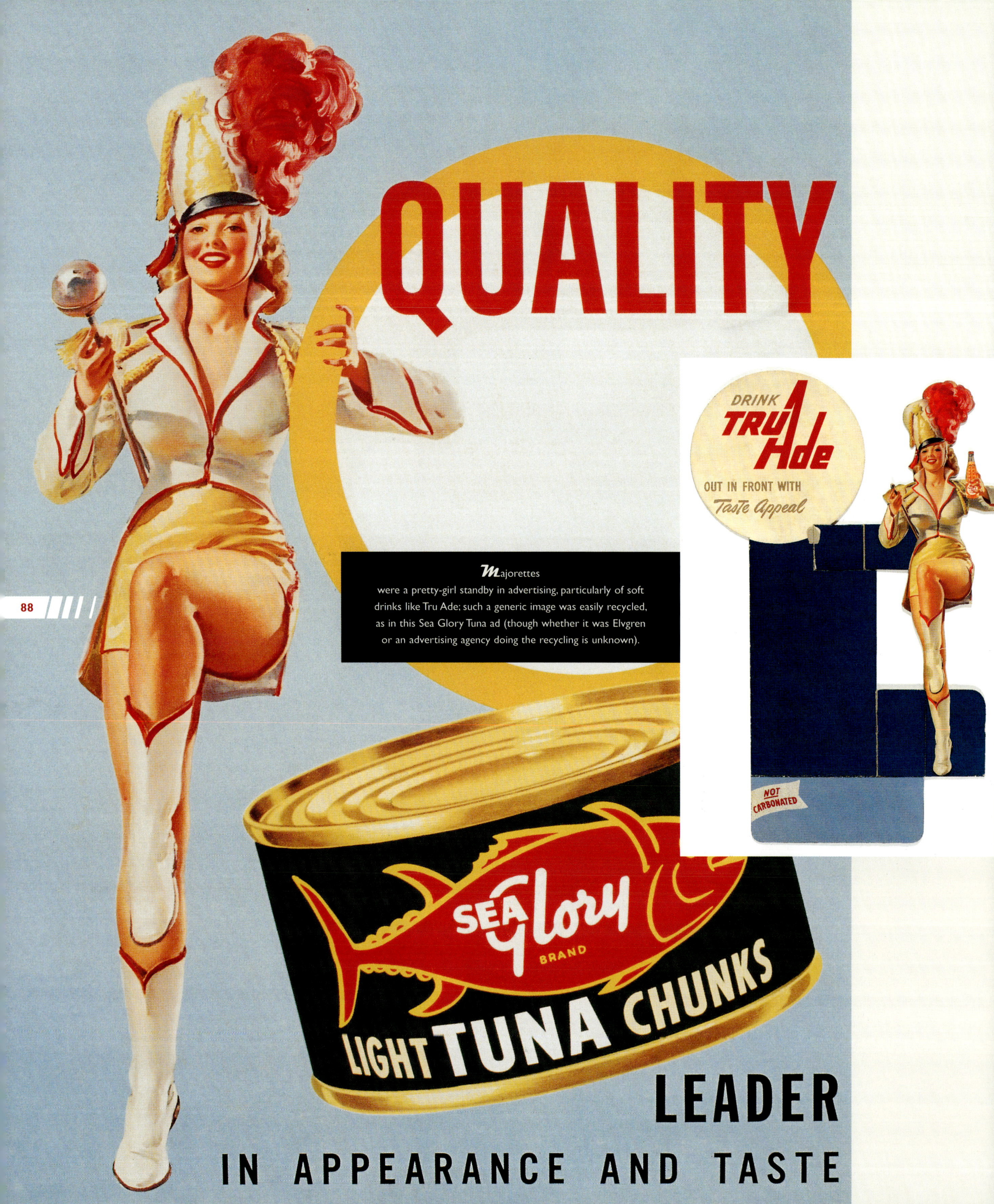

Majorettes were a pretty-girl standby in advertising, particularly of soft drinks like Tru Ade; such a generic image was easily recycled, as in this Sea Glory Tuna ad (though whether it was Elvgren or an advertising agency doing the recycling is unknown).

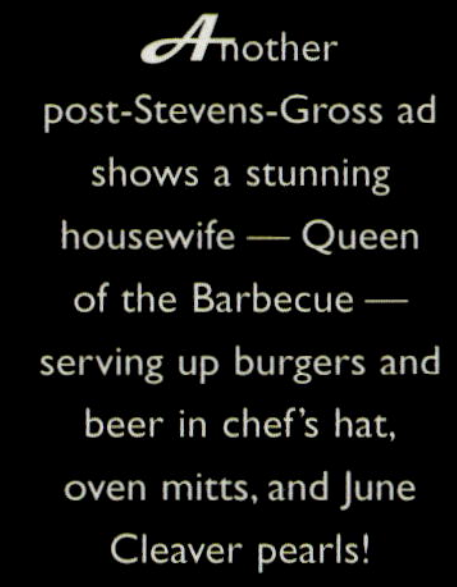

Another post-Stevens-Gross ad shows a stunning housewife — Queen of the Barbecue — serving up burgers and beer in chef's hat, oven mitts, and June Cleaver pearls!

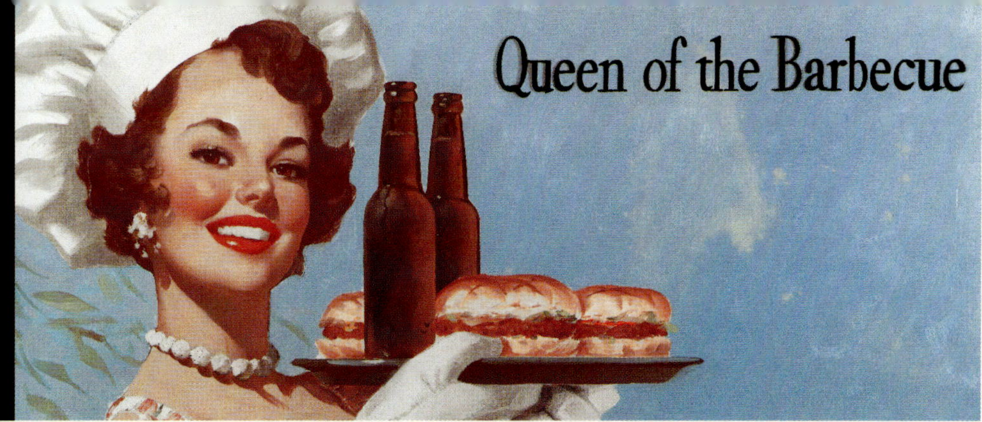

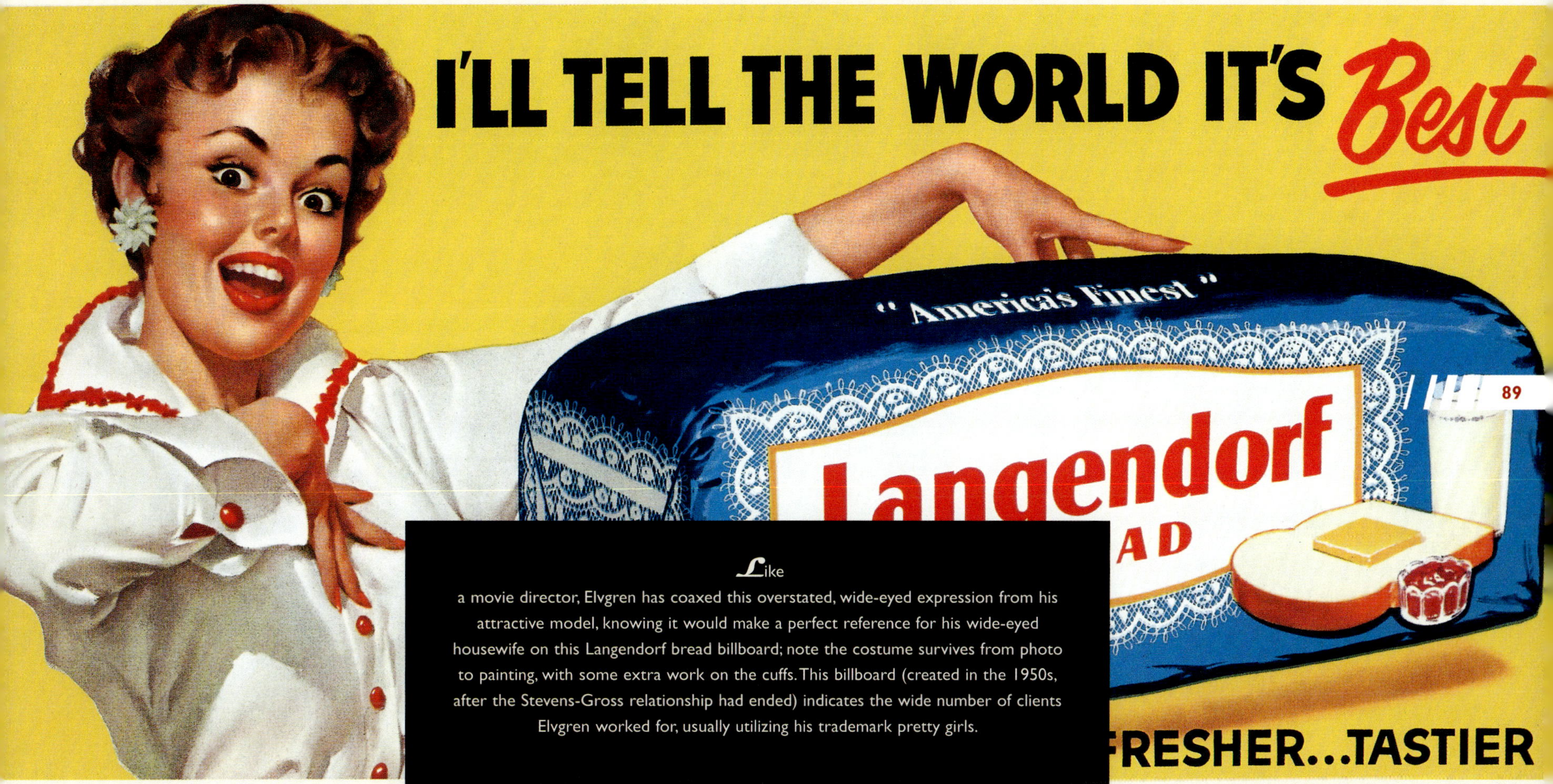

Like a movie director, Elvgren has coaxed this overstated, wide-eyed expression from his attractive model, knowing it would make a perfect reference for his wide-eyed housewife on this Langendorf bread billboard; note the costume survives from photo to painting, with some extra work on the cuffs. This billboard (created in the 1950s, after the Stevens-Gross relationship had ended) indicates the wide number of clients Elvgren worked for, usually utilizing his trademark pretty girls.

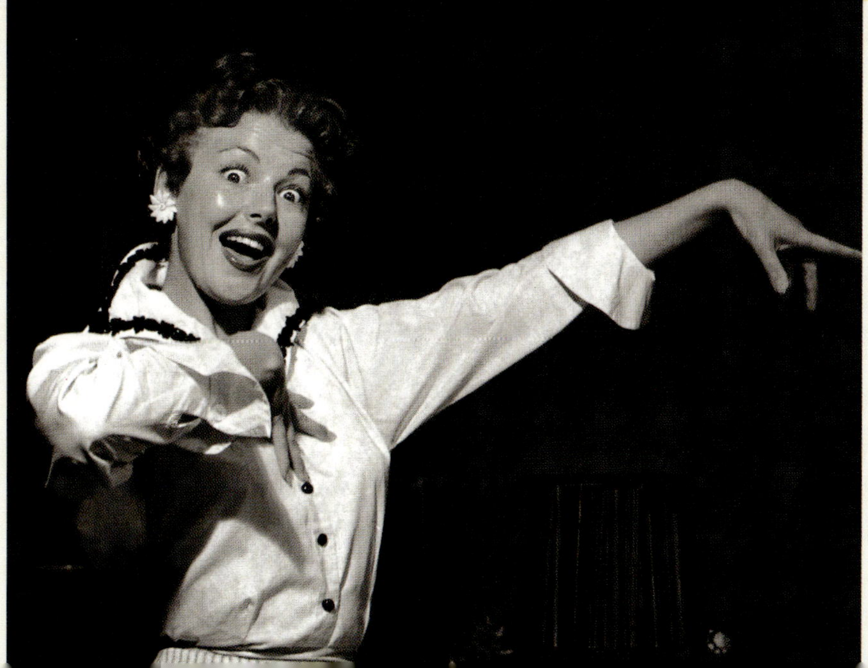

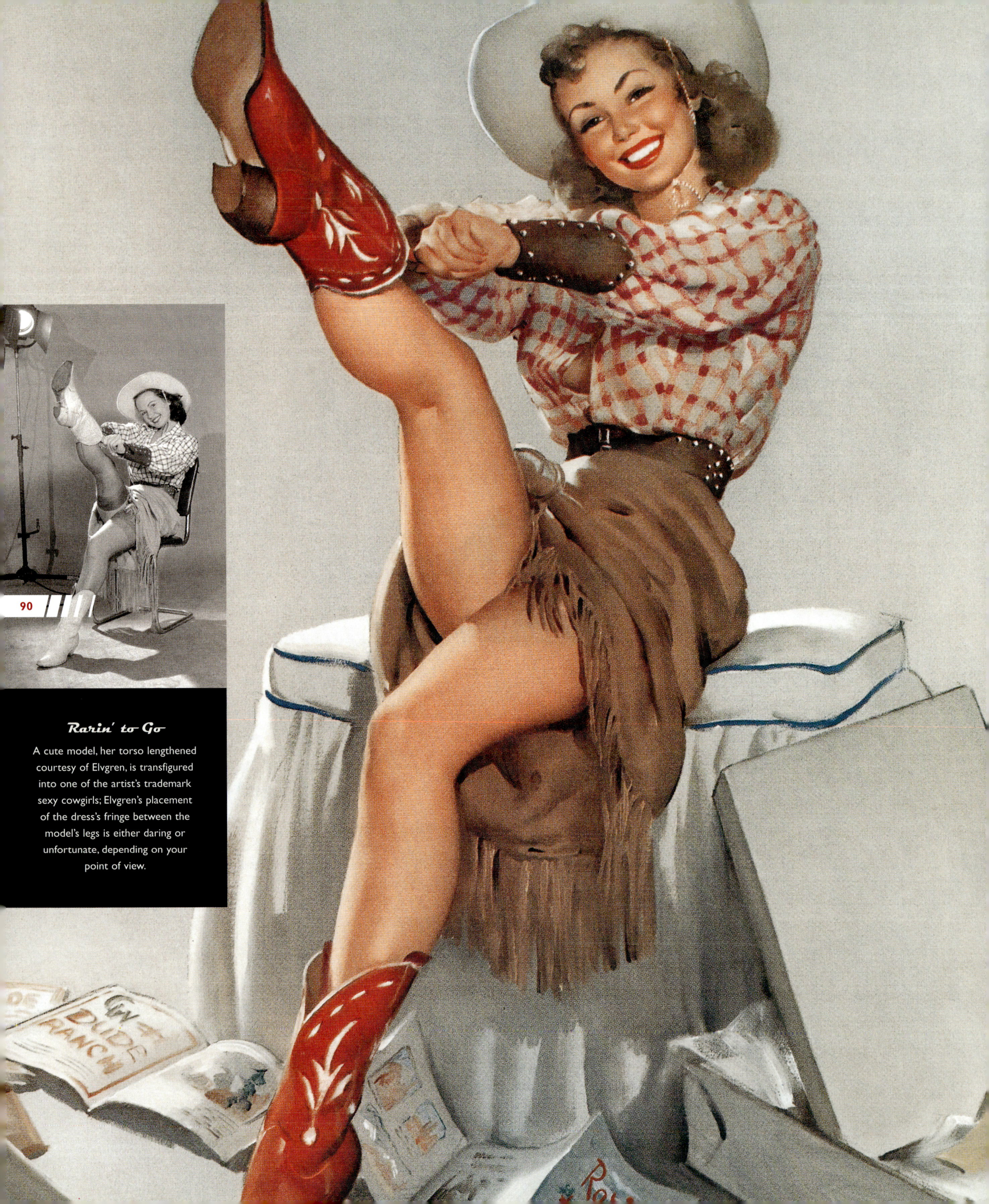

Rarin' to Go

A cute model, her torso lengthened courtesy of Elvgren, is transfigured into one of the artist's trademark sexy cowgirls; Elvgren's placement of the dress's fringe between the model's legs is either daring or unfortunate, depending on your point of view.

Worth Crowing About

It is comical and fascinating to note how precisely this pretty model is posed as compared to the makeshift or nonexistent props in the reference photos, elements Elvgren transmutes into eye-popping pin-ups like this one. Paint and hardware stores, in particular, would find this all-American subject matter appealing.

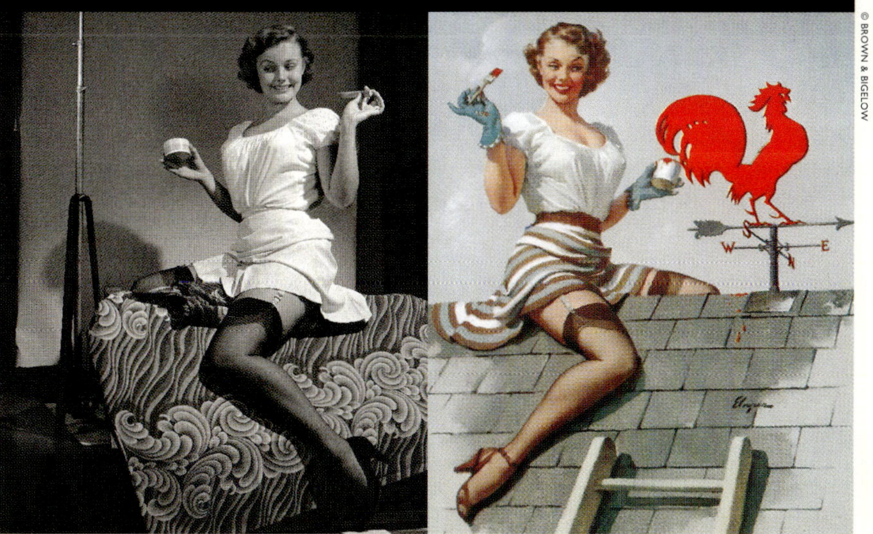

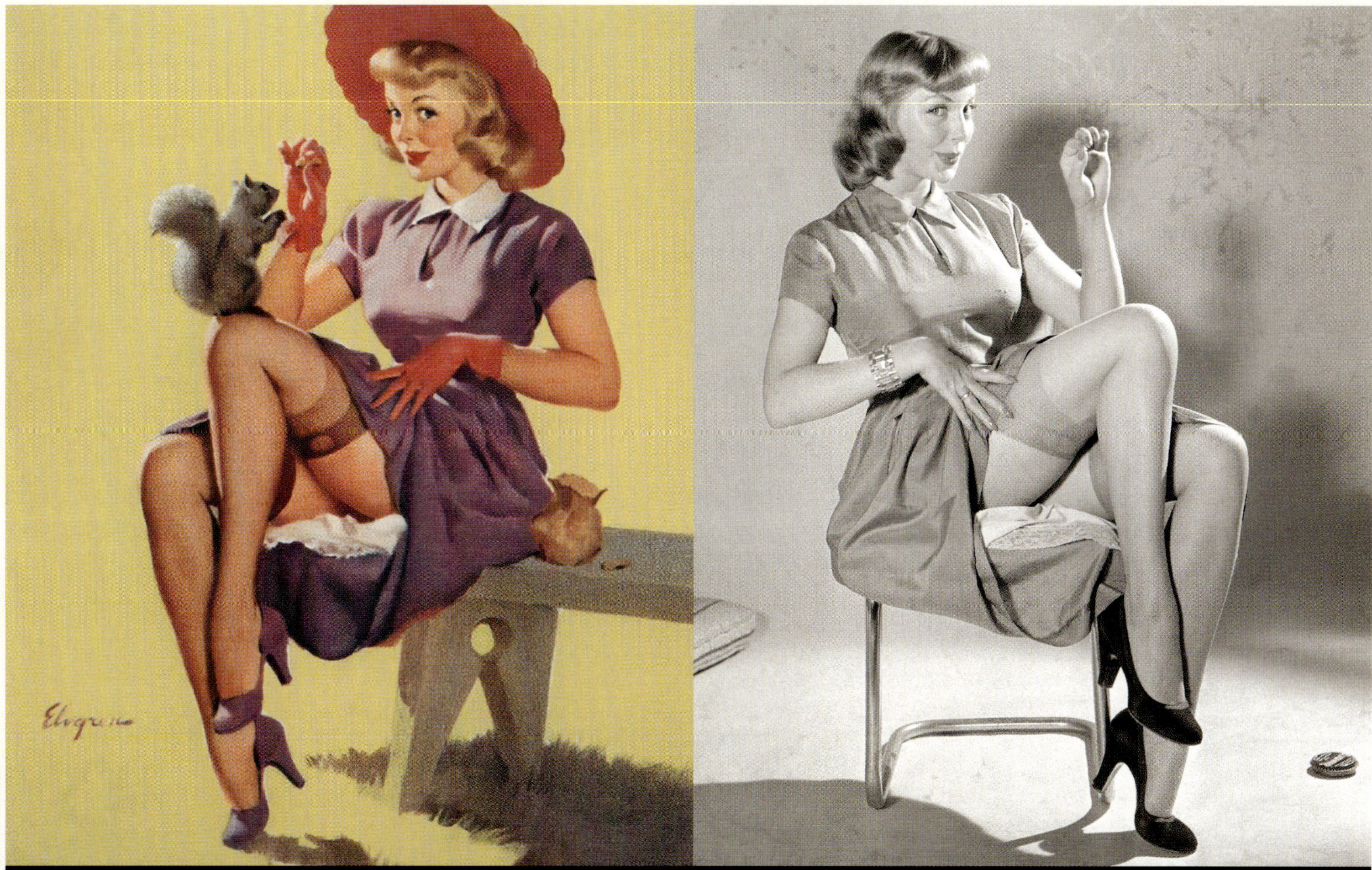

Making Friends

One of Elvgren's most charming models lends her grace to one of his most charming pin-ups; again, props and even costumes (not to mention the squirrel!) are nowhere to be seen in the reference photo of this alluring, page-boy blonde.

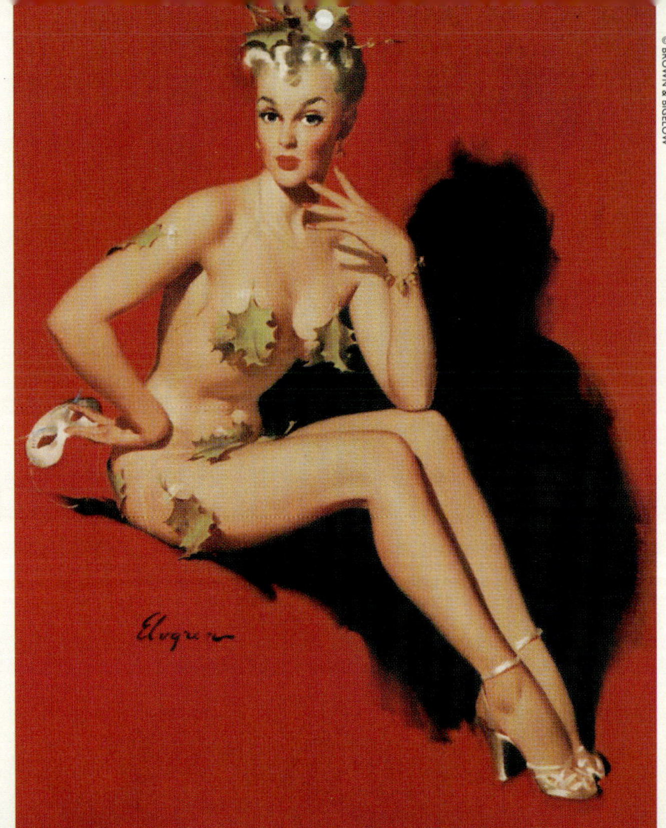

© BROWN & BIGELOW

Fall Change-over

A well-posed but prosaic shot of an attractive, if not stunning, model could be transformed by Elvgren into a magical pin-up like this.

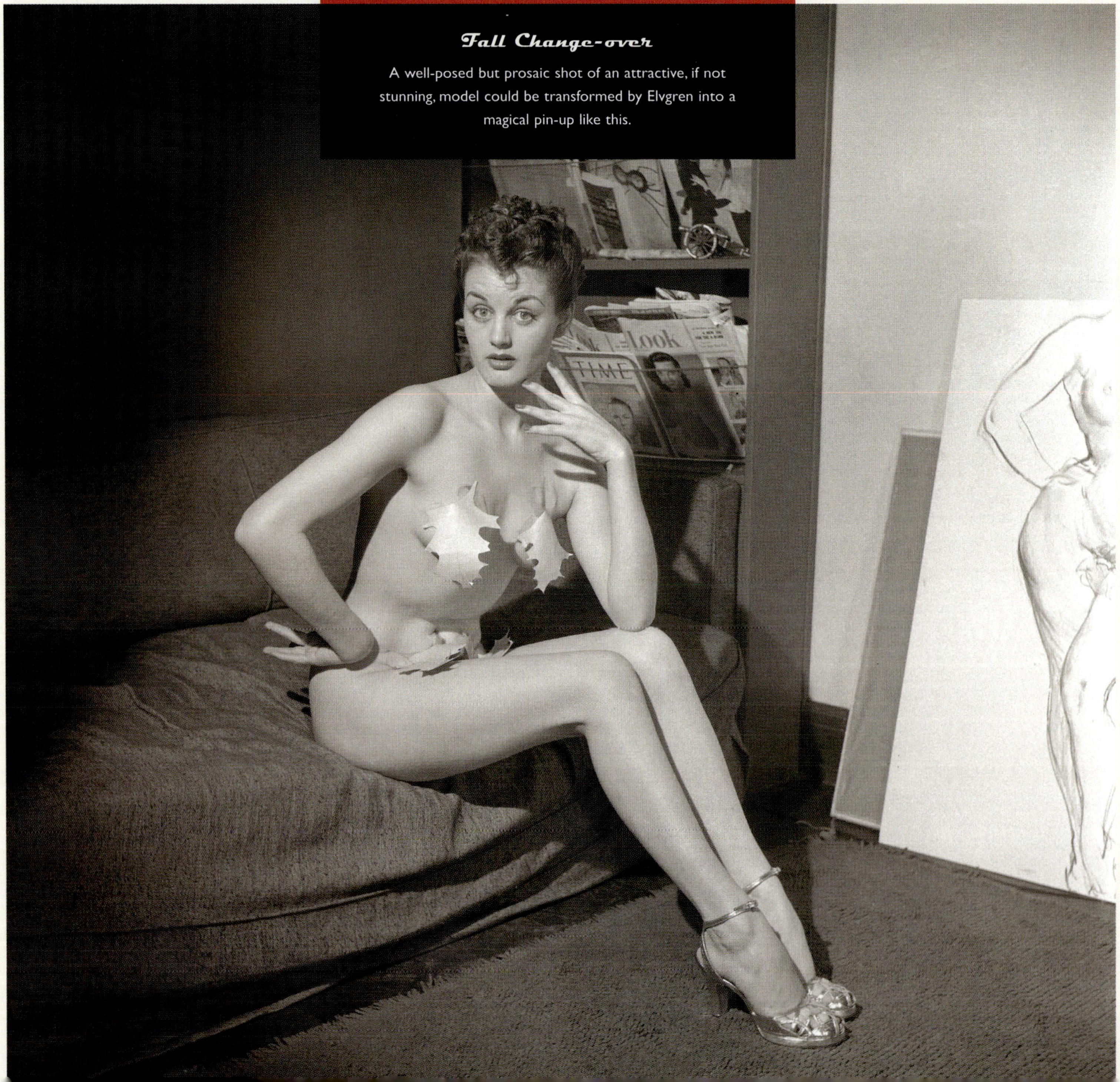

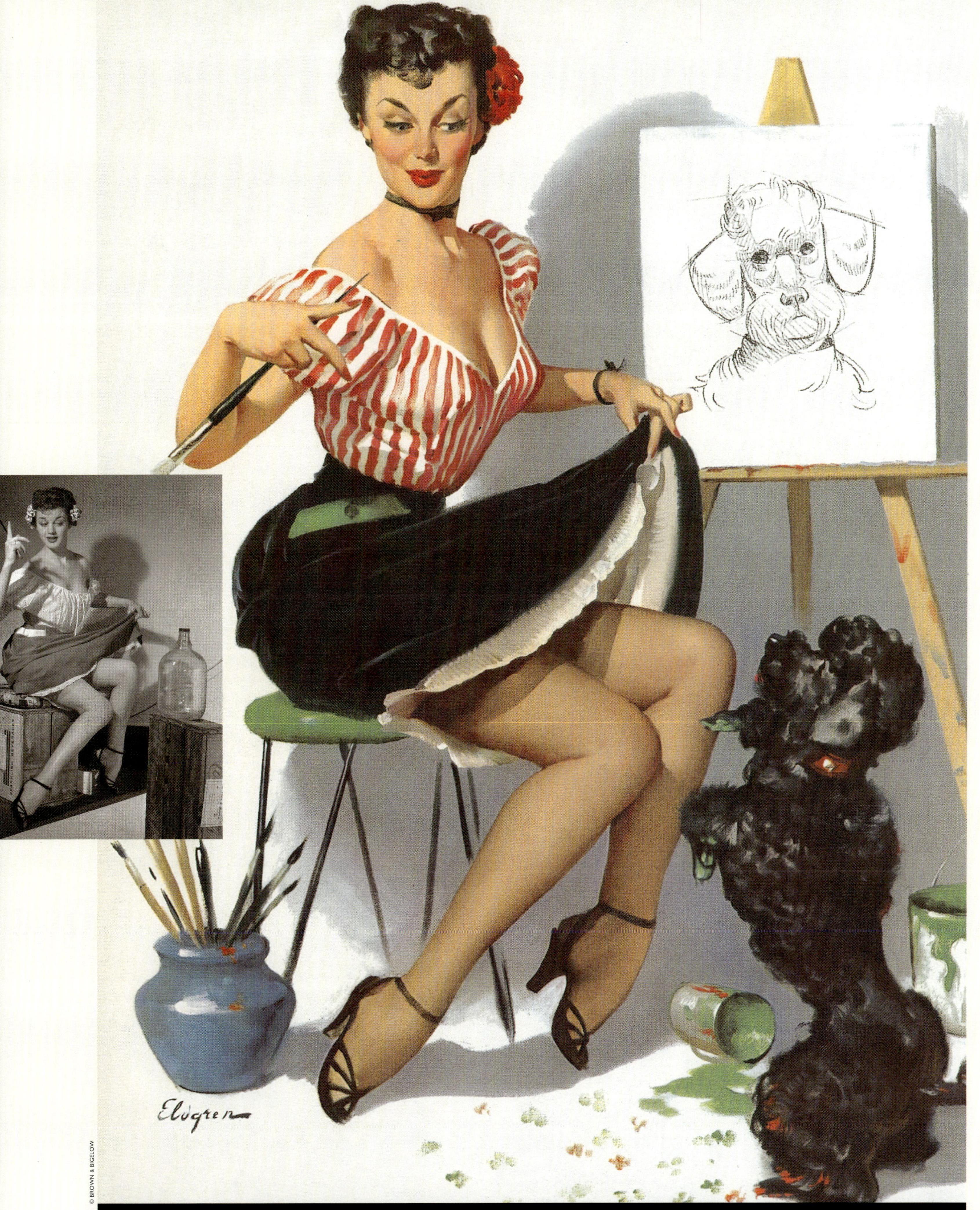

Down Boy!

Elvgren's propensity for selecting subject matter that would attract specific clients — a paint store like his father's might have chosen this calendar, for example — is well served here. Note the absence of props — a water jug on a crate standing in for the poodle — and Elvgren's subtle shifting of the model's pose.

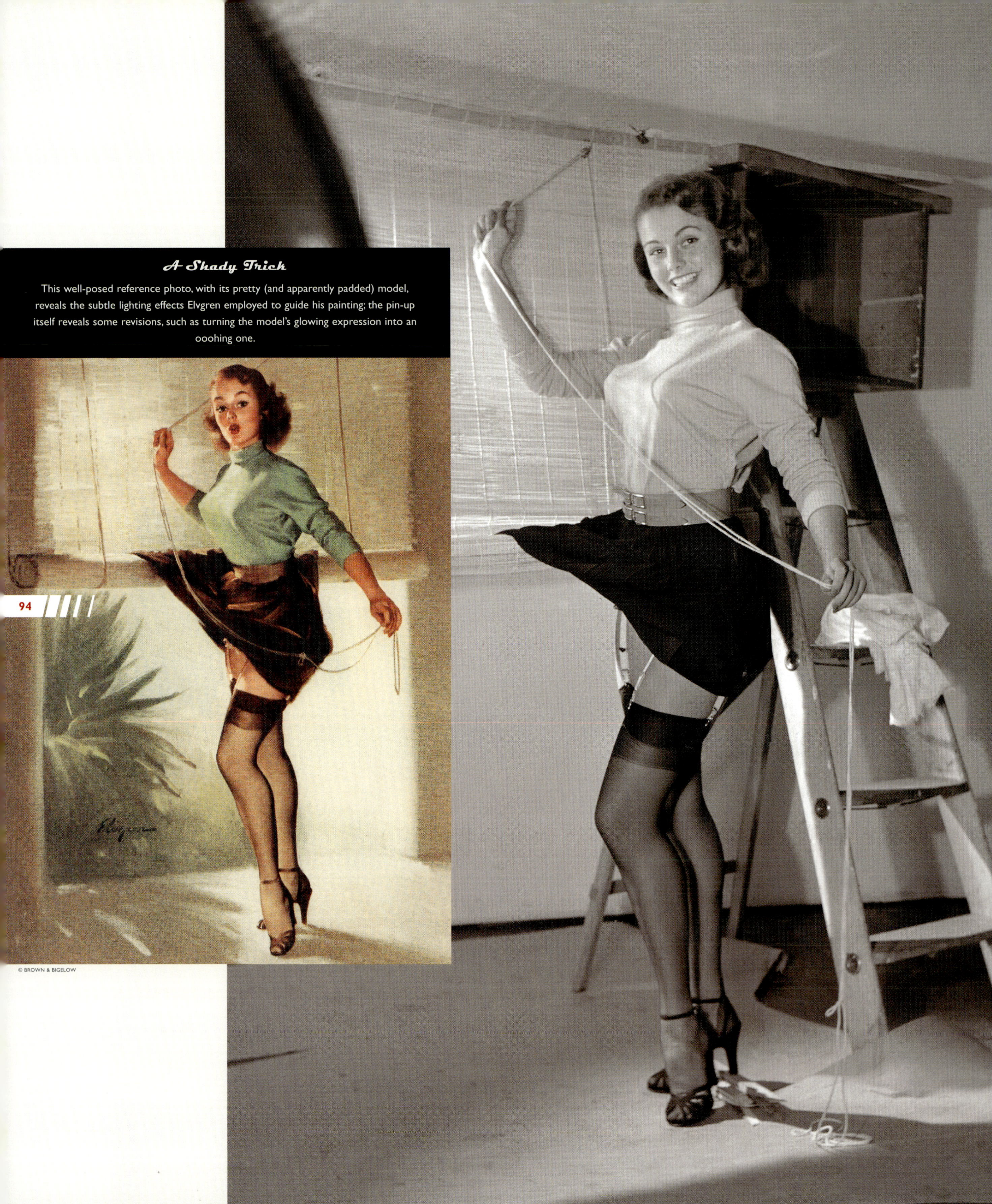

A Shady Trick

This well-posed reference photo, with its pretty (and apparently padded) model, reveals the subtle lighting effects Elvgren employed to guide his painting; the pin-up itself reveals some revisions, such as turning the model's glowing expression into an ooohing one.

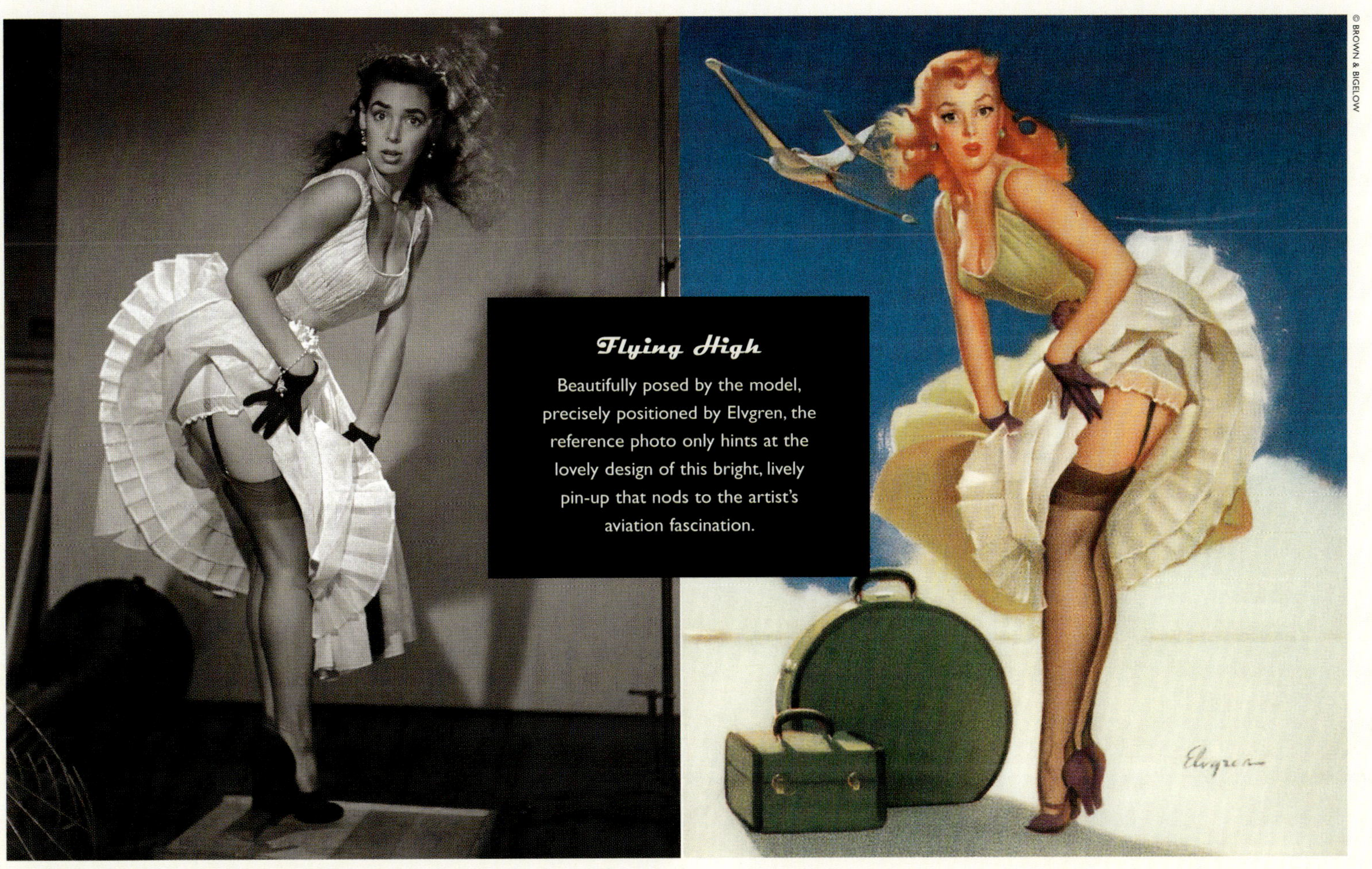

Flying High

Beautifully posed by the model, precisely positioned by Elvgren, the reference photo only hints at the lovely design of this bright, lively pin-up that nods to the artist's aviation fascination.

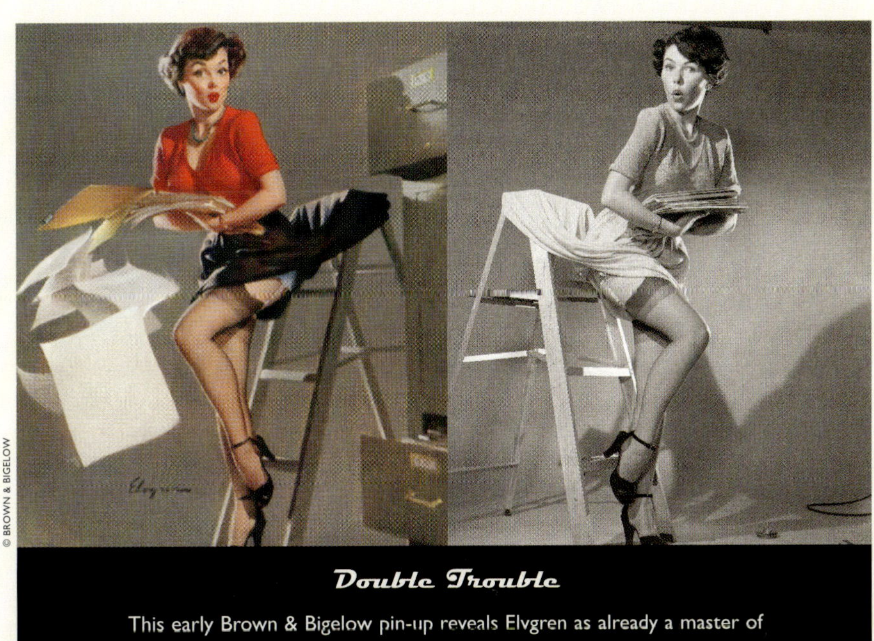

Double Trouble

This early Brown & Bigelow pin-up reveals Elvgren as already a master of staging reference photos, with a model whose expression and nyloned legs are the artist's fantasy in flesh and blood; note the subtle side-lighting reproduced in the painting itself.

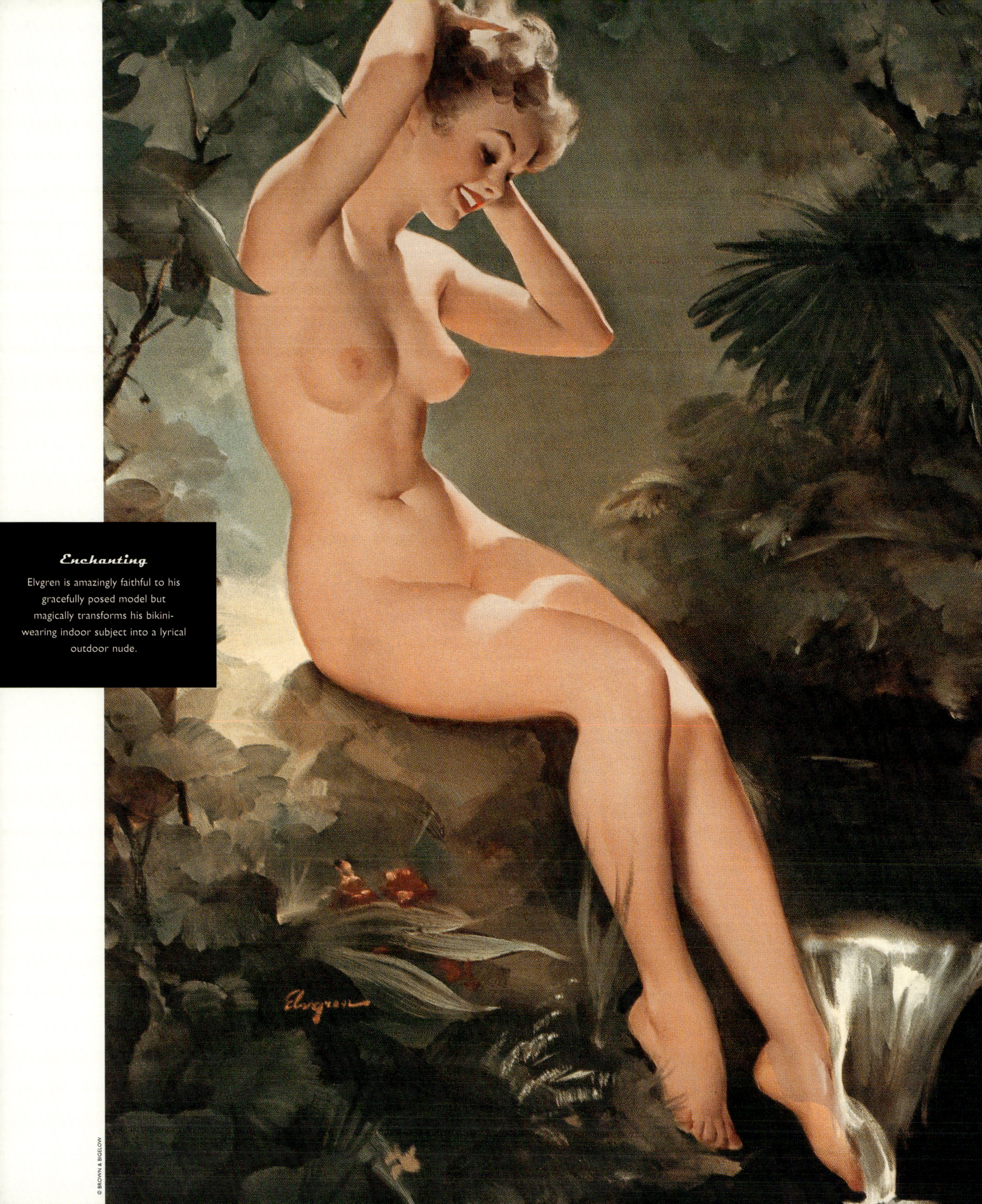

Enchanting

Elvgren is amazingly faithful to his gracefully posed model but magically transforms his bikini-wearing indoor subject into a lyrical outdoor nude.

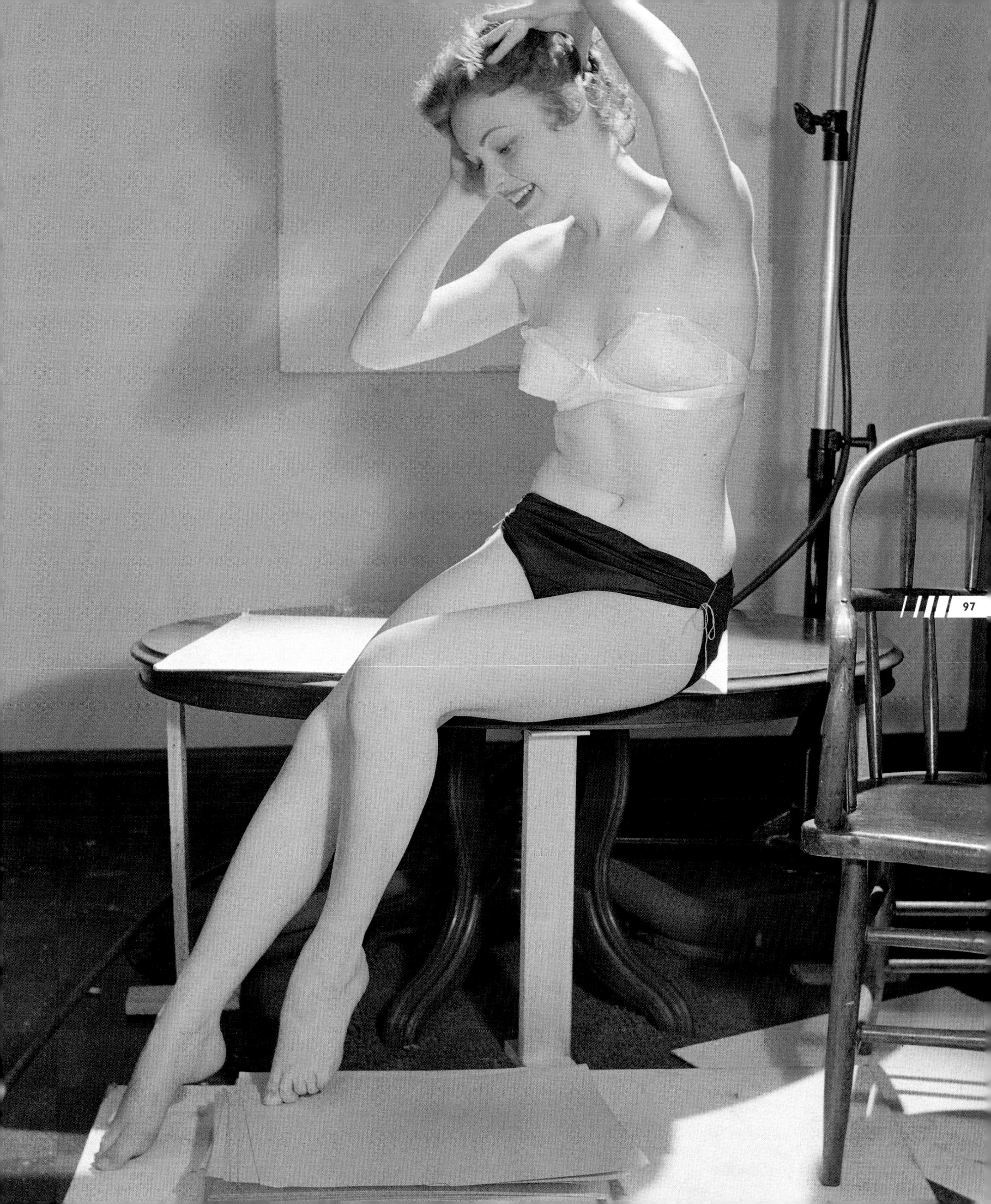

A-Cute Injury

The wholesome Coca-Cola girl image is underscored by the sports setting and the skater's legitimate reason for hiking her skirt; Elvgren's model is certainly shapely and attractive, but his change of hair color and decision to have her looking at her bruise, rather than showing it off to us, transform this into one of his most appealing pin-ups.

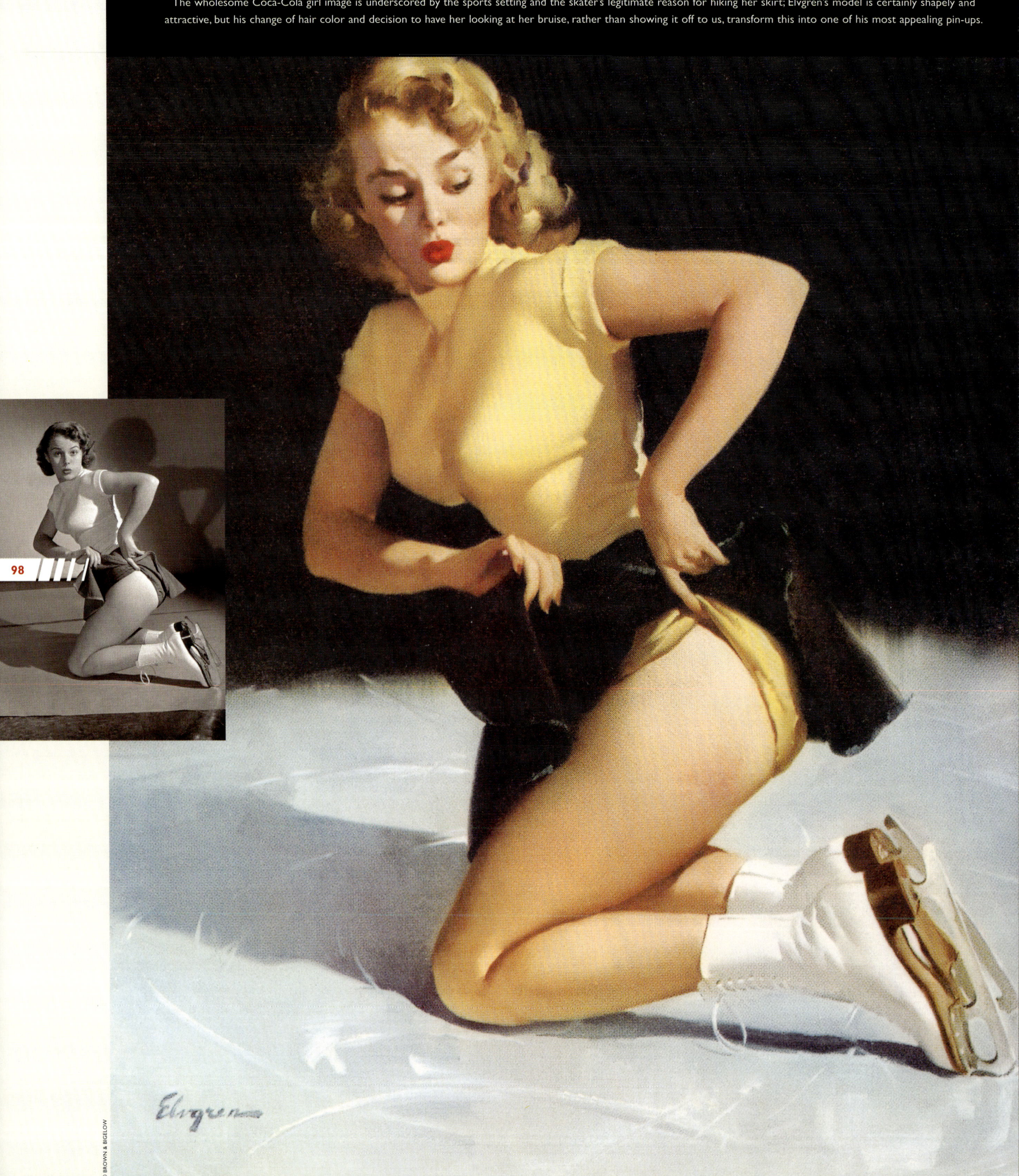

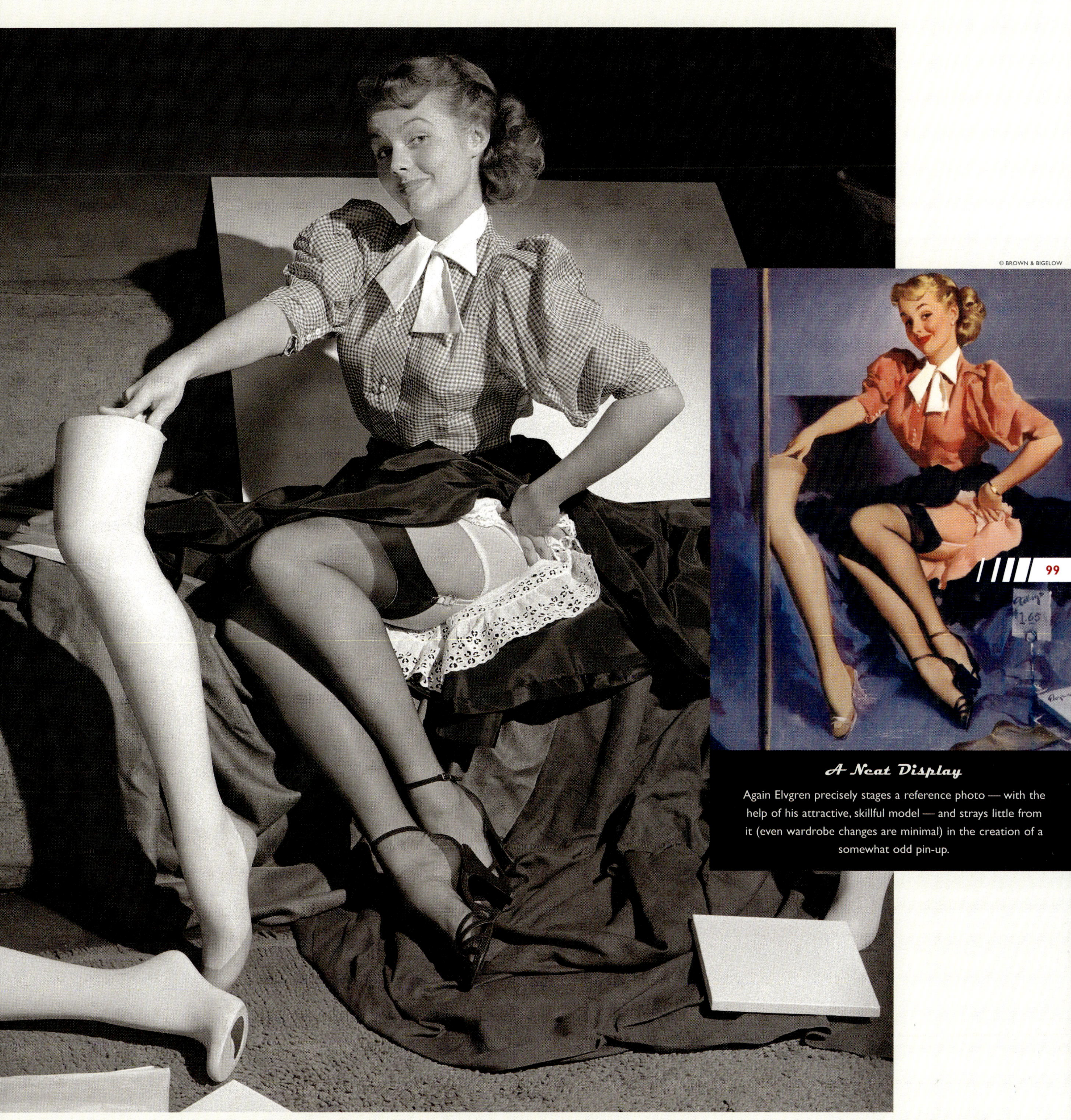

A Neat Display

Again Elvgren precisely stages a reference photo — with the help of his attractive, skillful model — and strays little from it (even wardrobe changes are minimal) in the creation of a somewhat odd pin-up.

One for the Money

Precise posing by a model is key to Elvgren's approach; note the lack of props — the "Kisses" sign, the heart archway, the drapery on the box, and the box itself are all inventions of the artist.

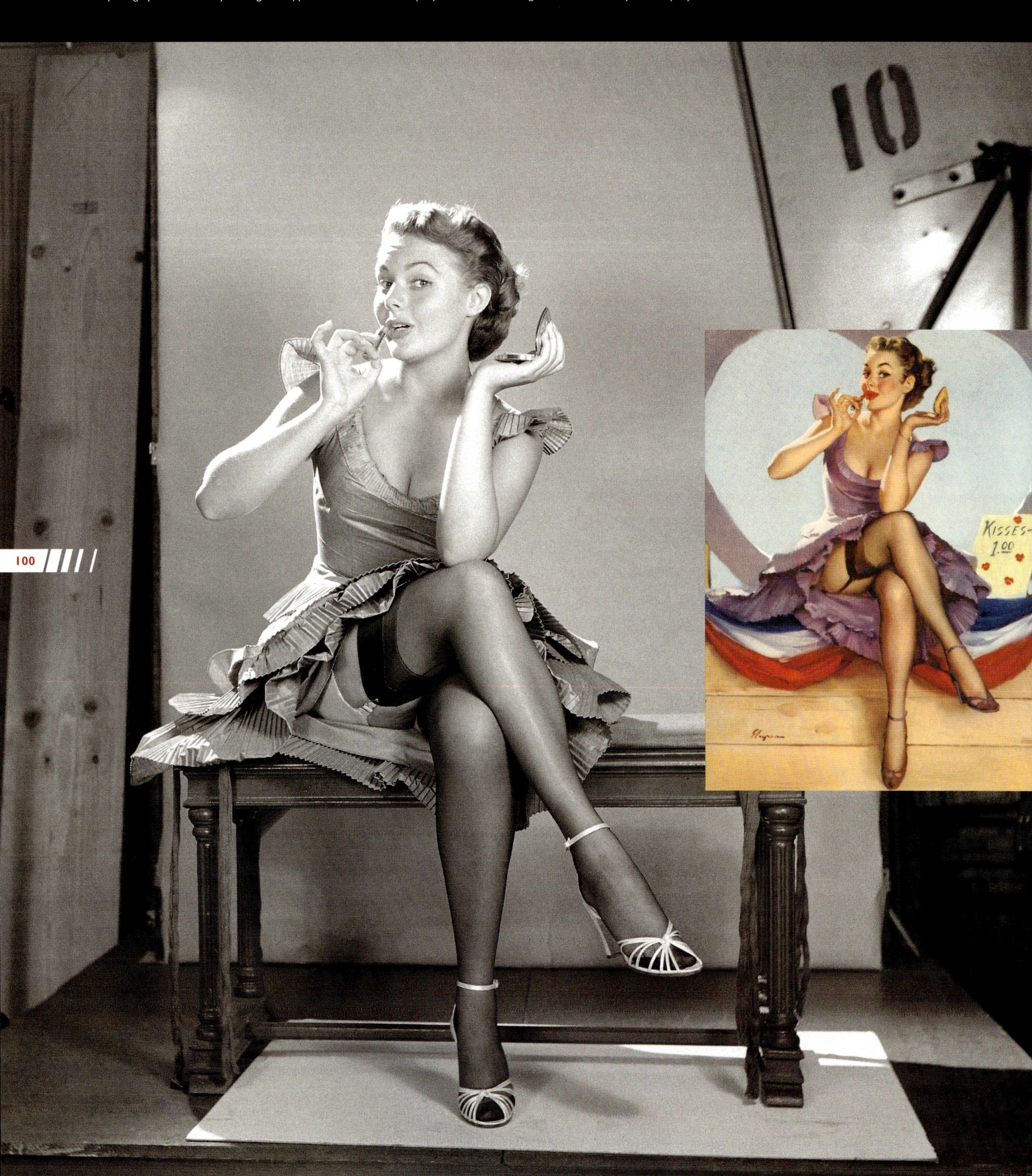

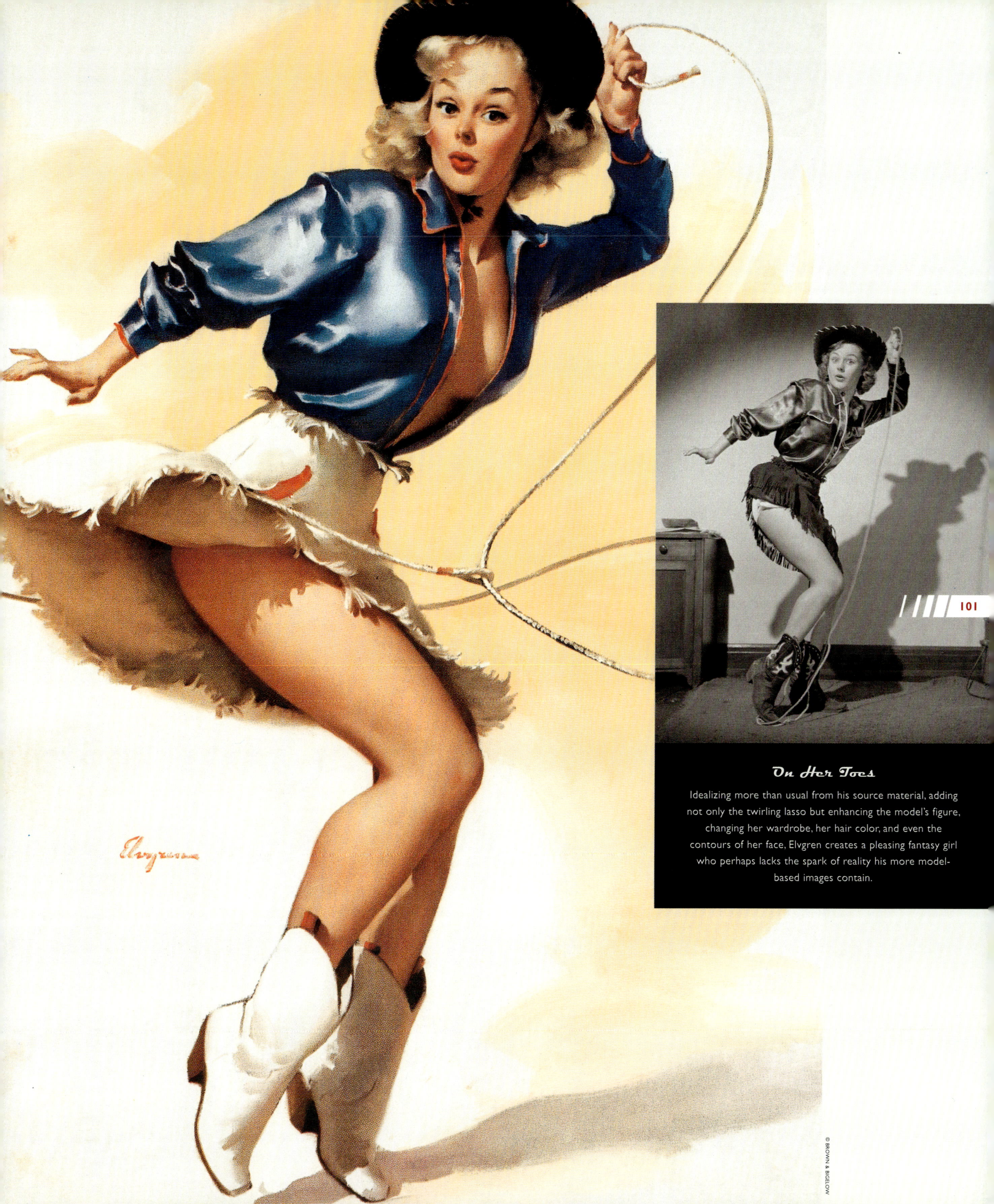

On Her Toes

Idealizing more than usual from his source material, adding not only the twirling lasso but enhancing the model's figure, changing her wardrobe, her hair color, and even the contours of her face, Elvgren creates a pleasing fantasy girl who perhaps lacks the spark of reality his more model-based images contain.

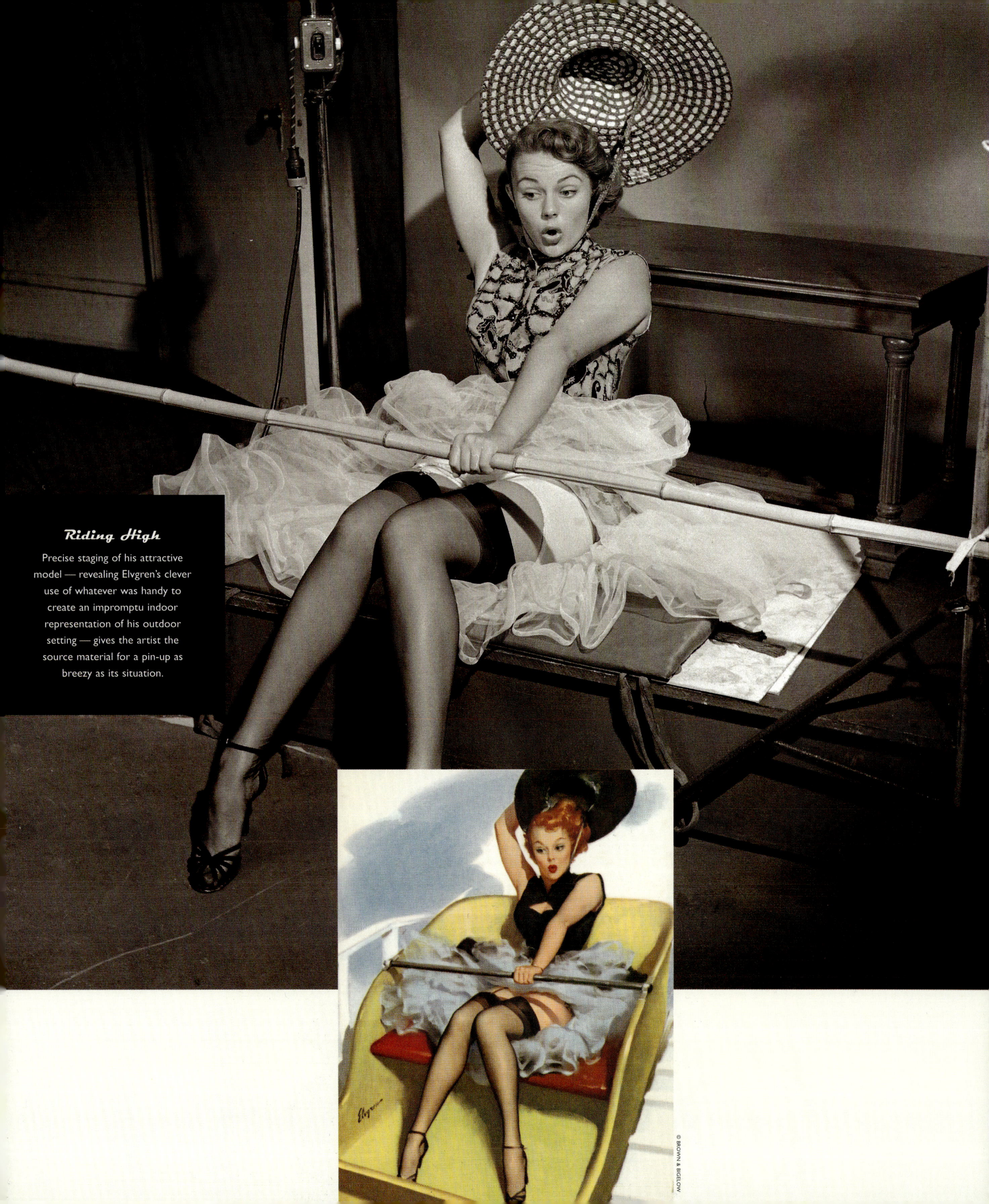

Riding High

Precise staging of his attractive model — revealing Elvgren's clever use of whatever was handy to create an impromptu indoor representation of his outdoor setting — gives the artist the source material for a pin-up as breezy as its situation.

Caught Napping

This graceful model's perfect form and pose make for one of Elvgren's most faithful-to-his-source pin-ups, with the romanticism of the setting (and the pussy cat) tastefully added.

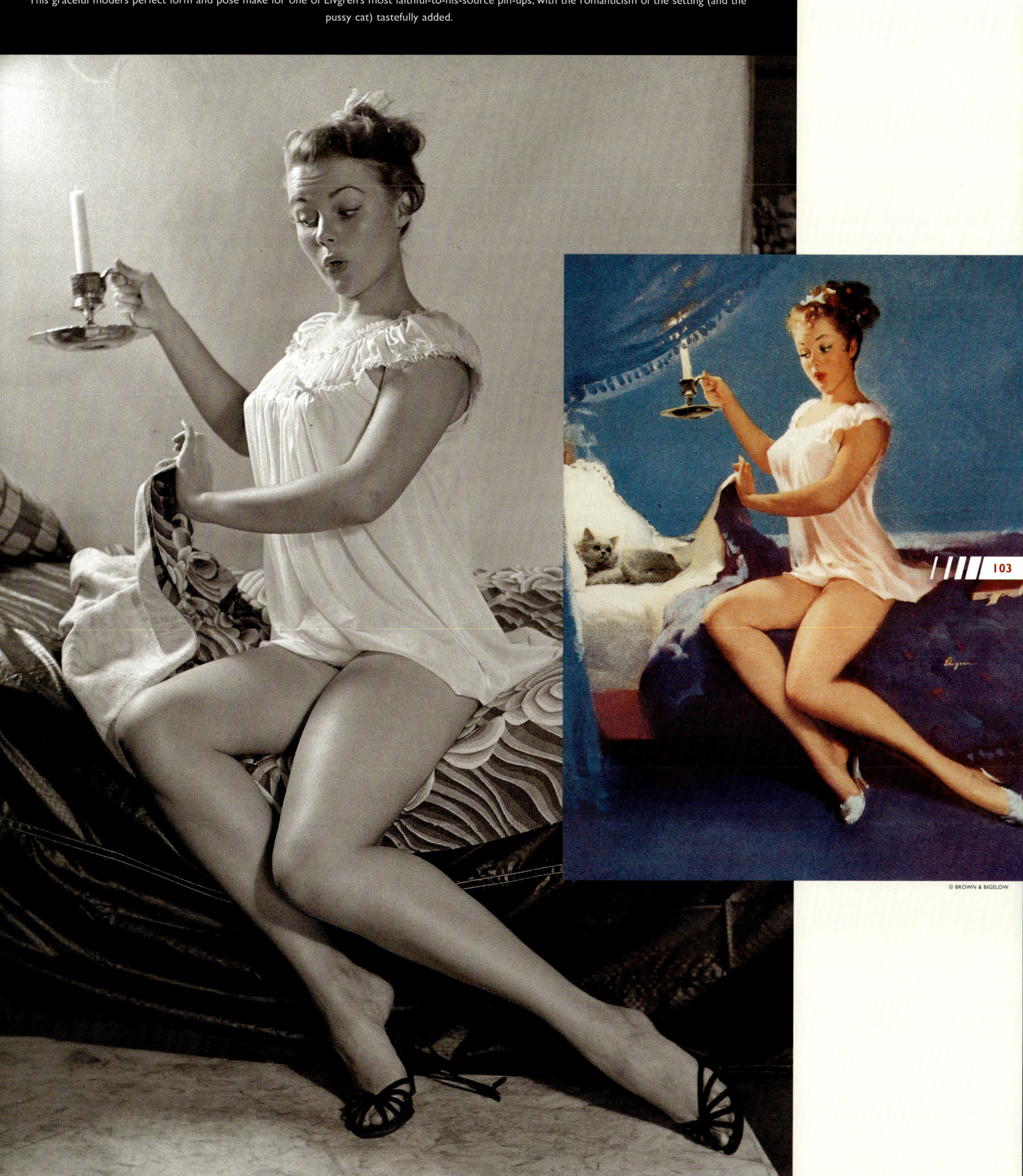

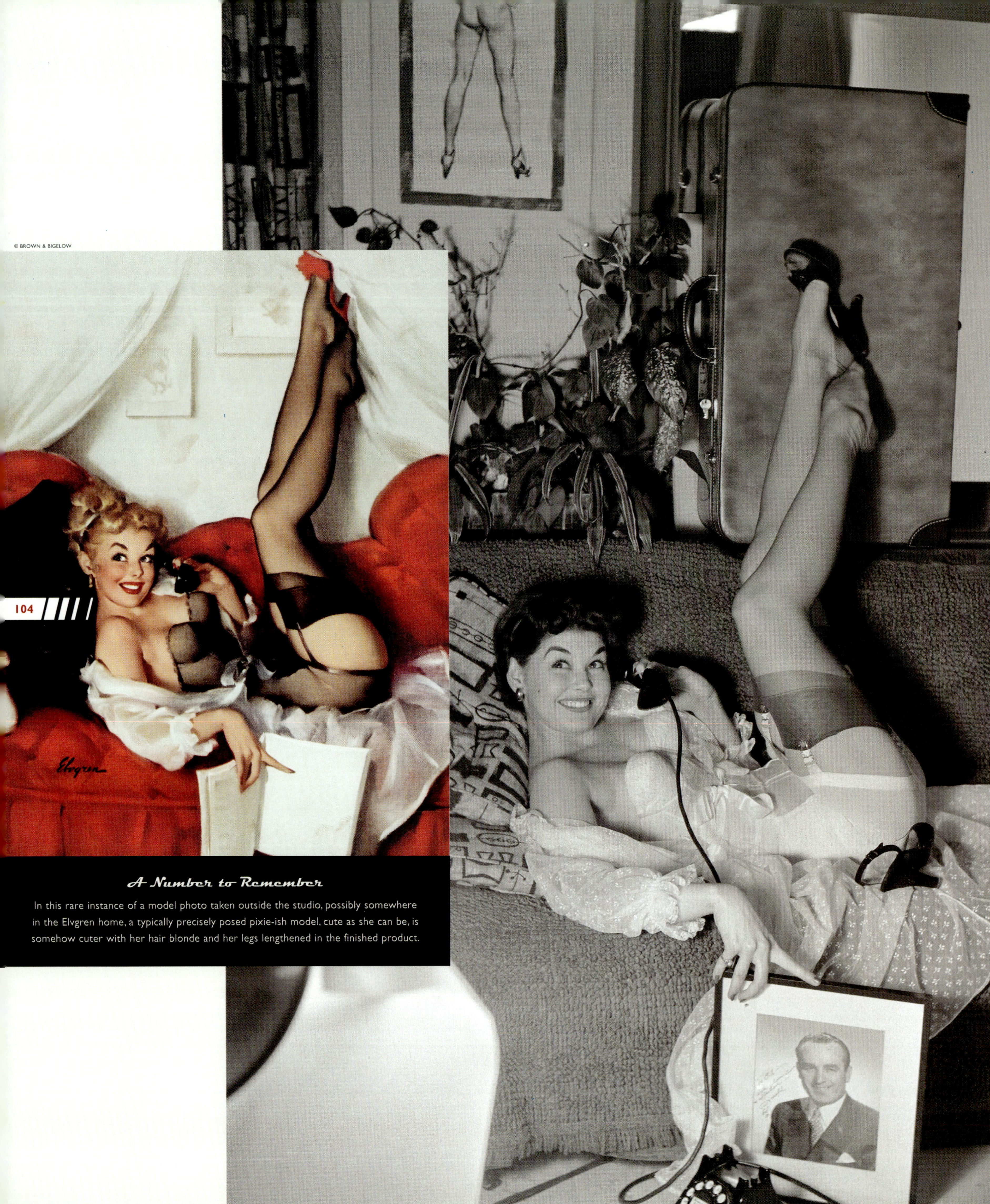

A Number to Remember

In this rare instance of a model photo taken outside the studio, possibly somewhere in the Elvgren home, a typically precisely posed pixie-ish model, cute as she can be, is somehow cuter with her hair blonde and her legs lengthened in the finished product.

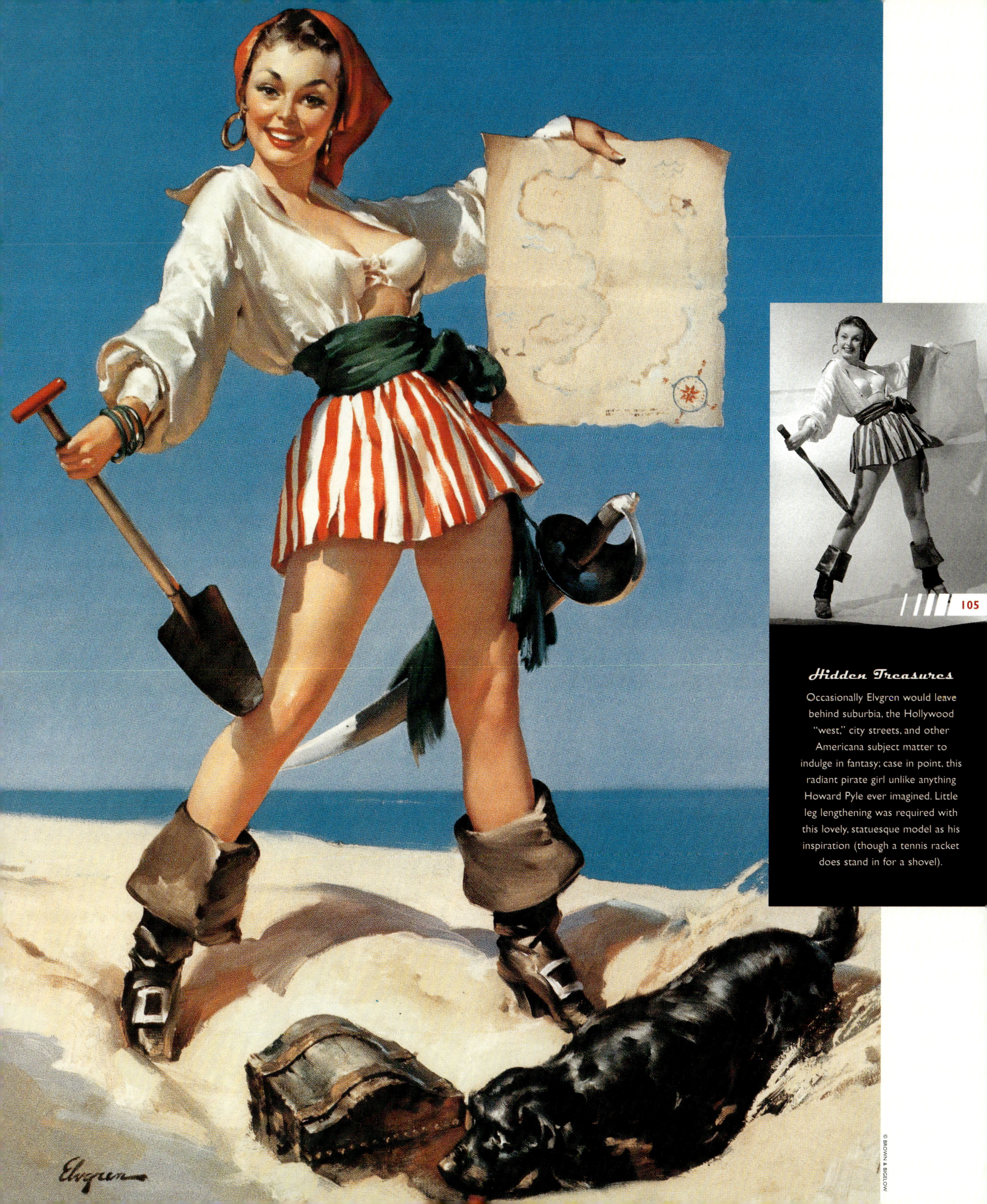

Hidden Treasures

Occasionally Elvgren would leave behind suburbia, the Hollywood "west," city streets, and other Americana subject matter to indulge in fantasy; case in point, this radiant pirate girl unlike anything Howard Pyle ever imagined. Little leg lengthening was required with this lovely, statuesque model as his inspiration (though a tennis racket does stand in for a shovel).

Cornered

The housewife of Elvgren's generic billboards finds herself painted into a corner; here, the reference photo seems to have been abandoned with the exception of the basic pose.

Time for Decision

This alluring, voluptuous model has been meticulously posed; but that doesn't stop Elvgren from changing the position of props, lengthening her torso, and changing her hair color.

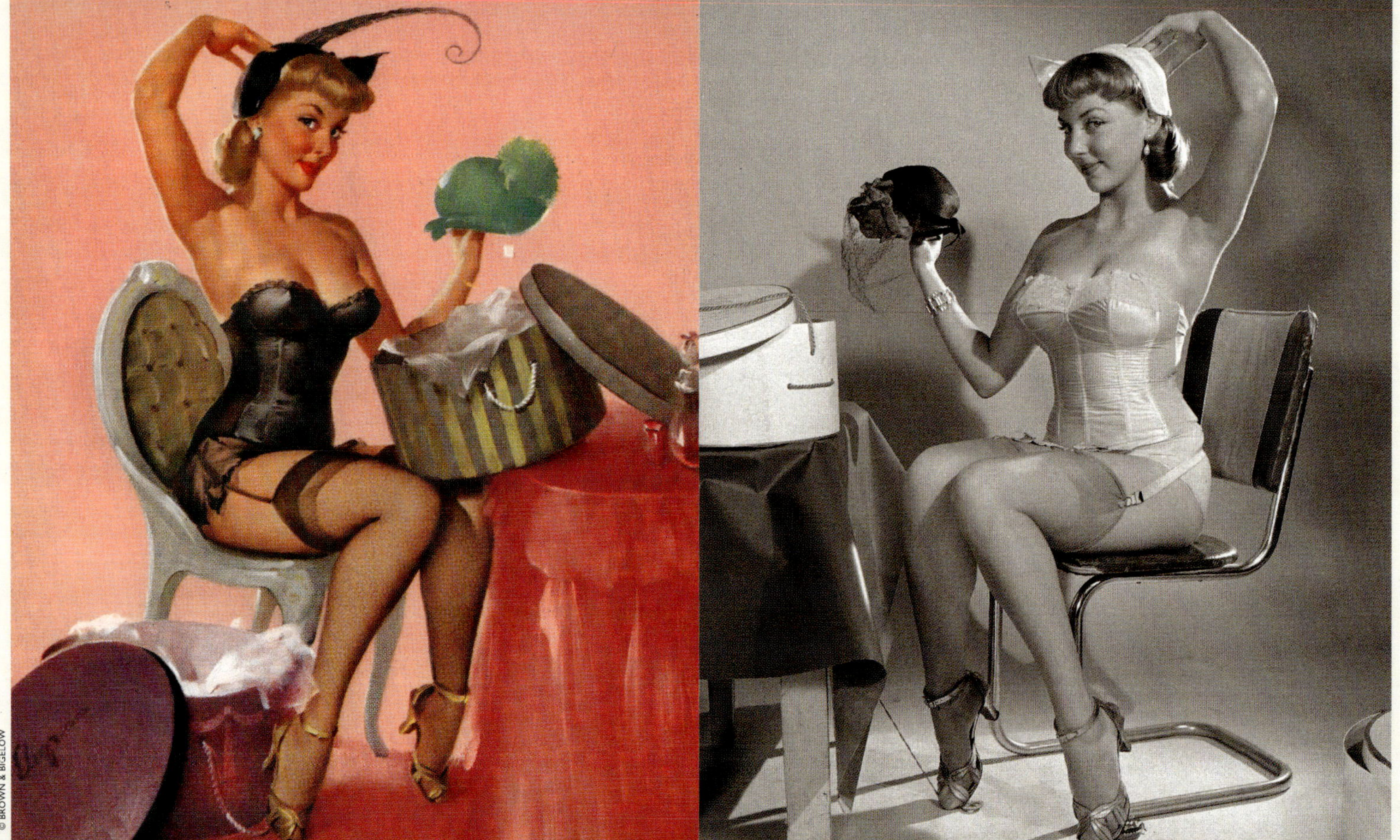

It's Easy

Elvgren is the true magician here, turning an attractive but not stunning model into a breathtaking beauty, not with a wand but a brush; how so faithful a rendering can so transform its source is pin-up wizardry.

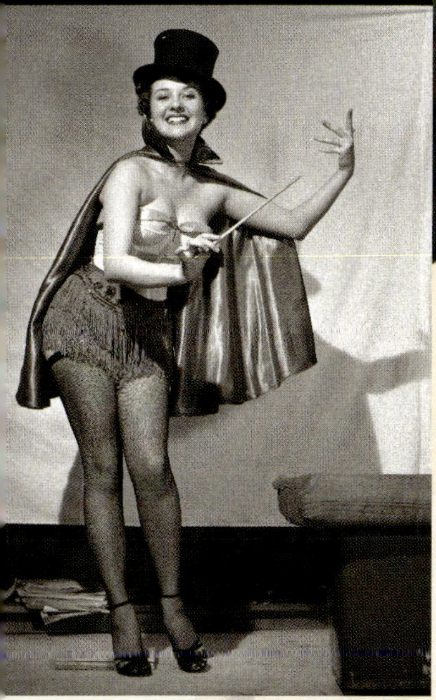

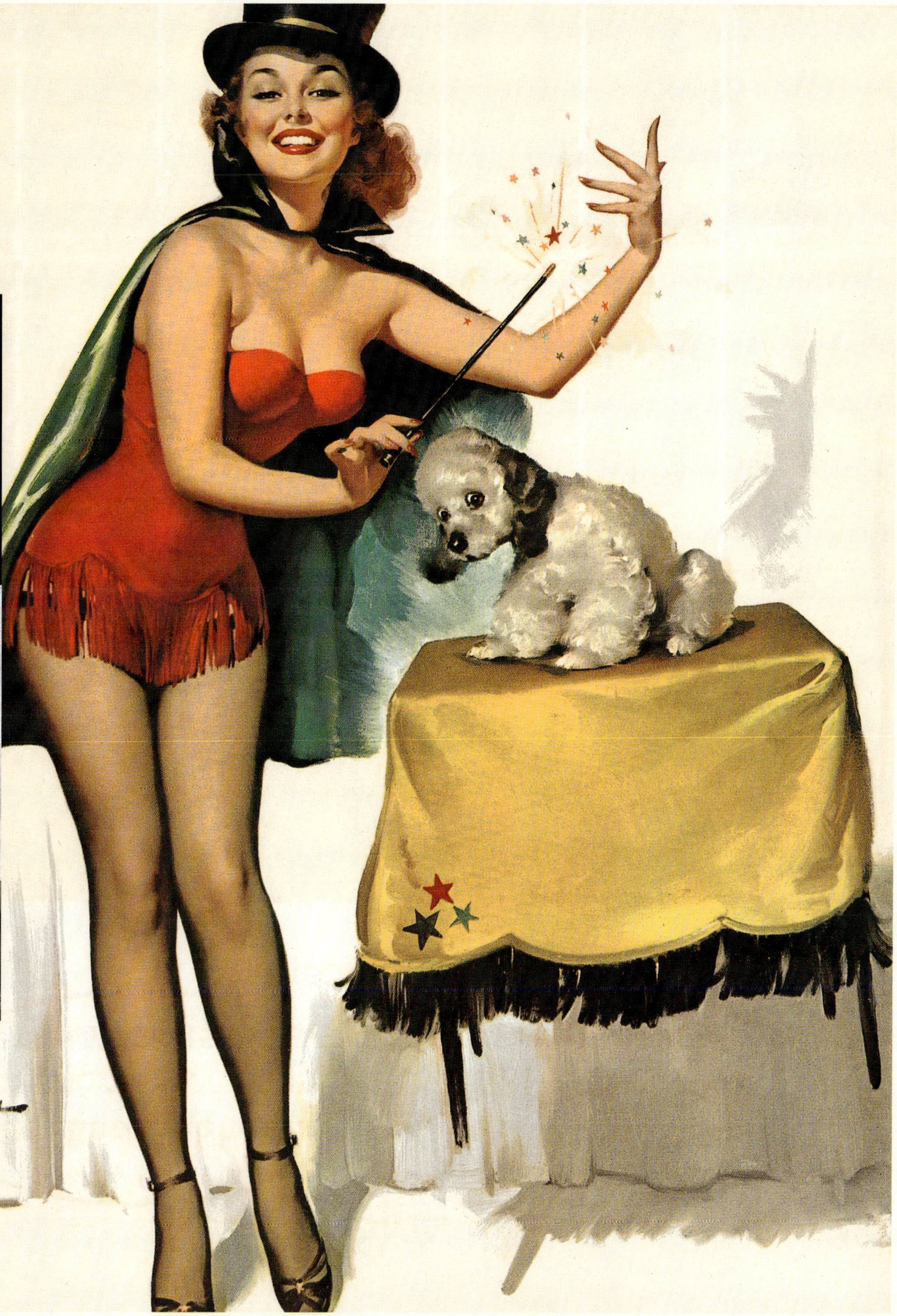

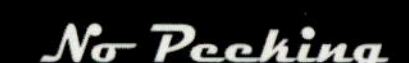

Again, a painfully pretty model strikes the exact pose Elvgren requests and duplicates, although he turns her head, substitutes an expression, and, as was often the case, a cute dog shows up for the gag.

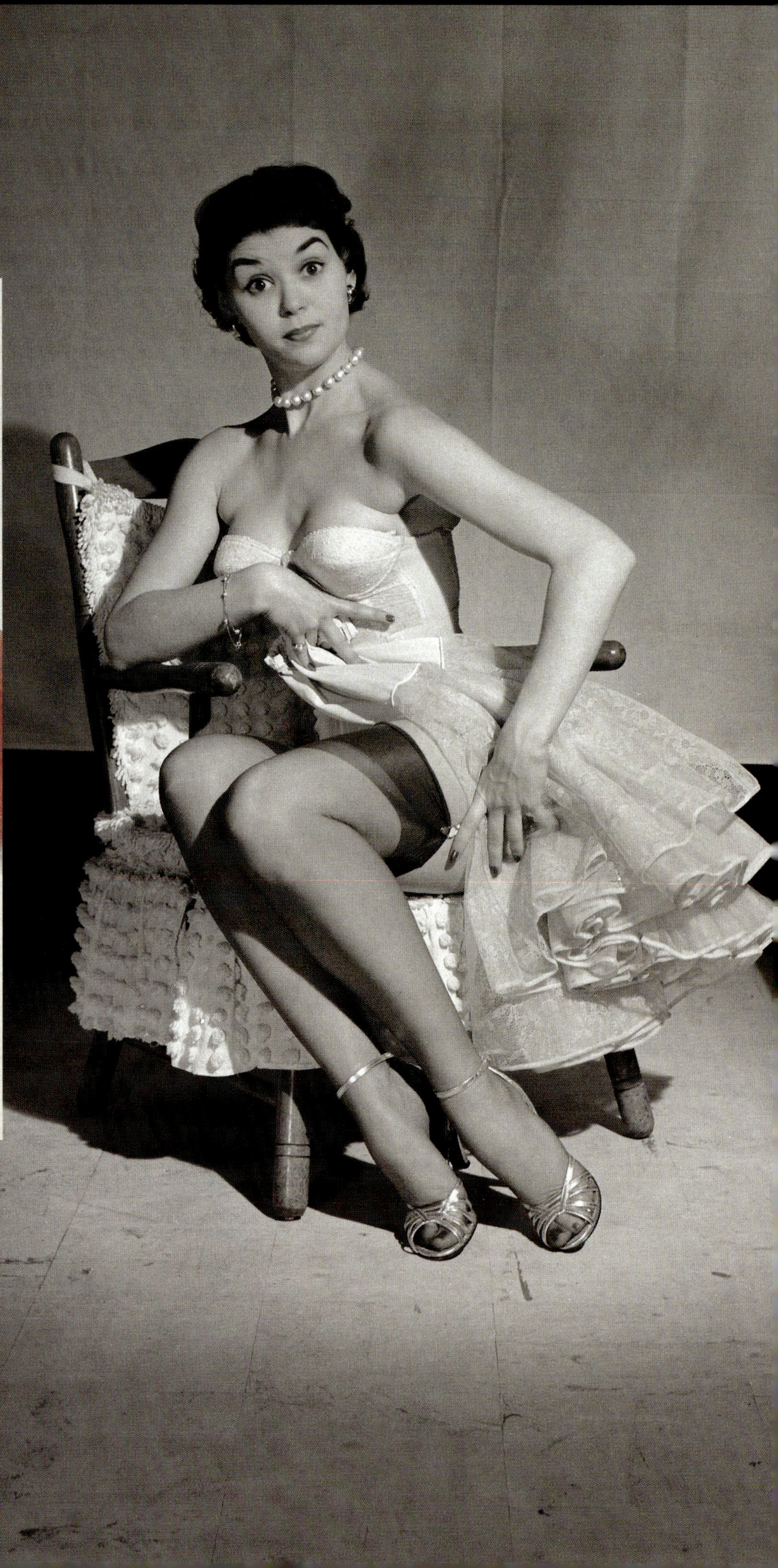

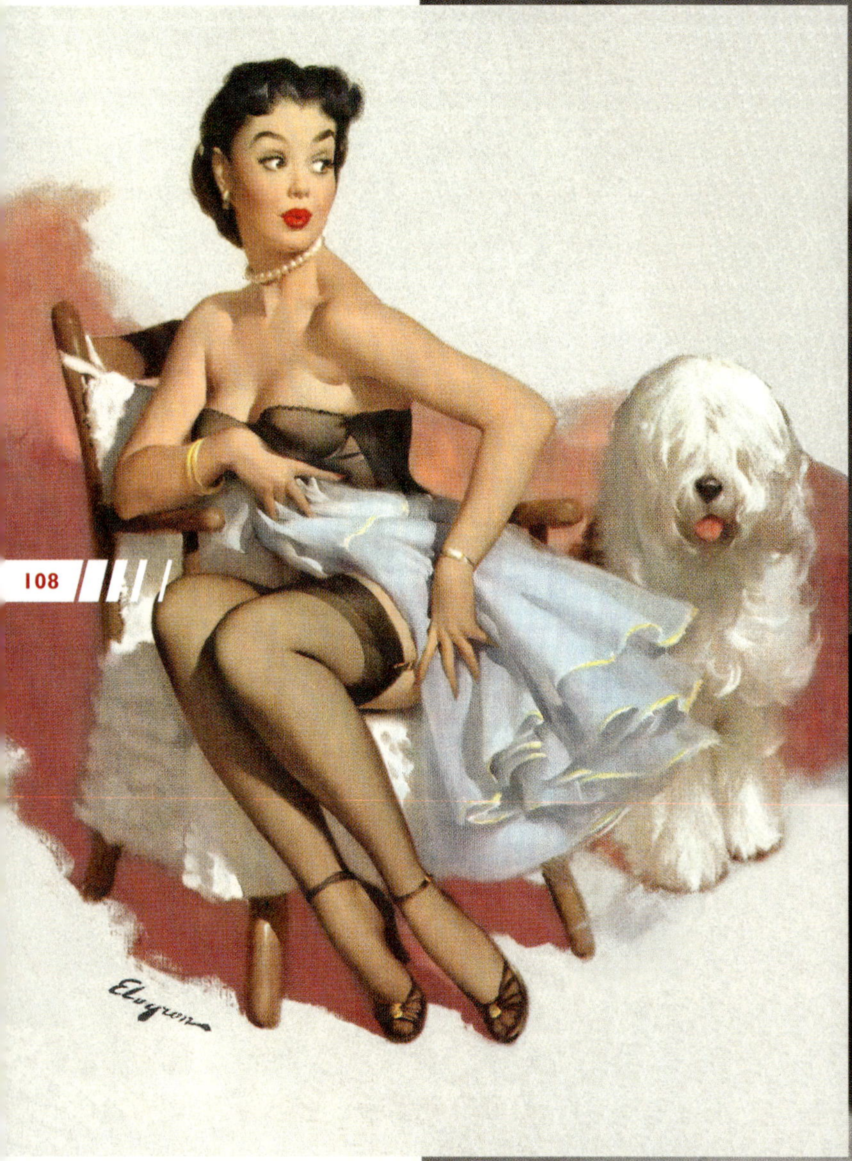

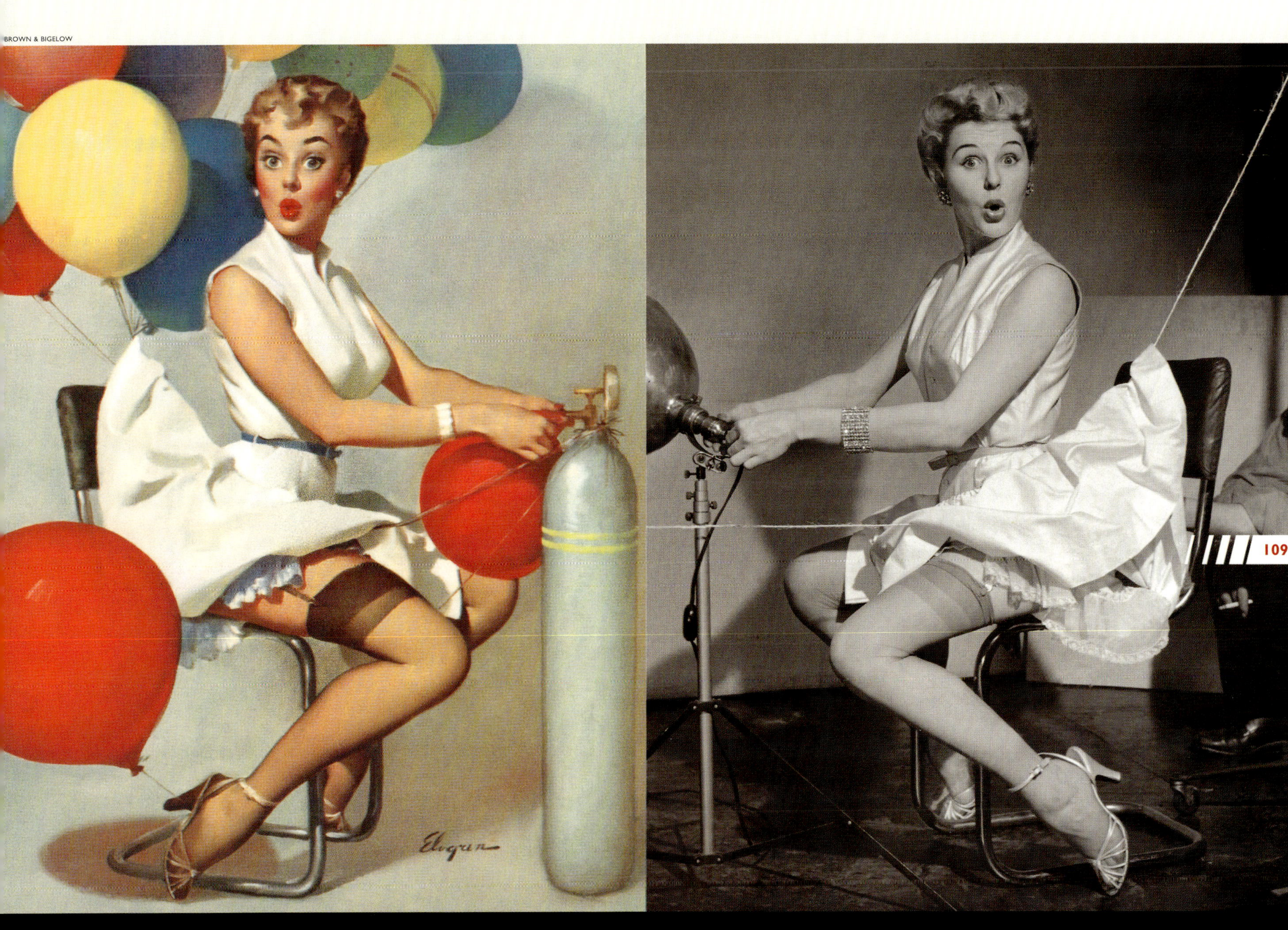

Taking Off

Elaborate staging and a perfectly posed model (assisted by Elvgren apprentice Peter Darson) are just a starting point for a colorful, outrageously well-designed pin-up, whose central phallic prop comes either from Elvgren's imagination or his clip file.

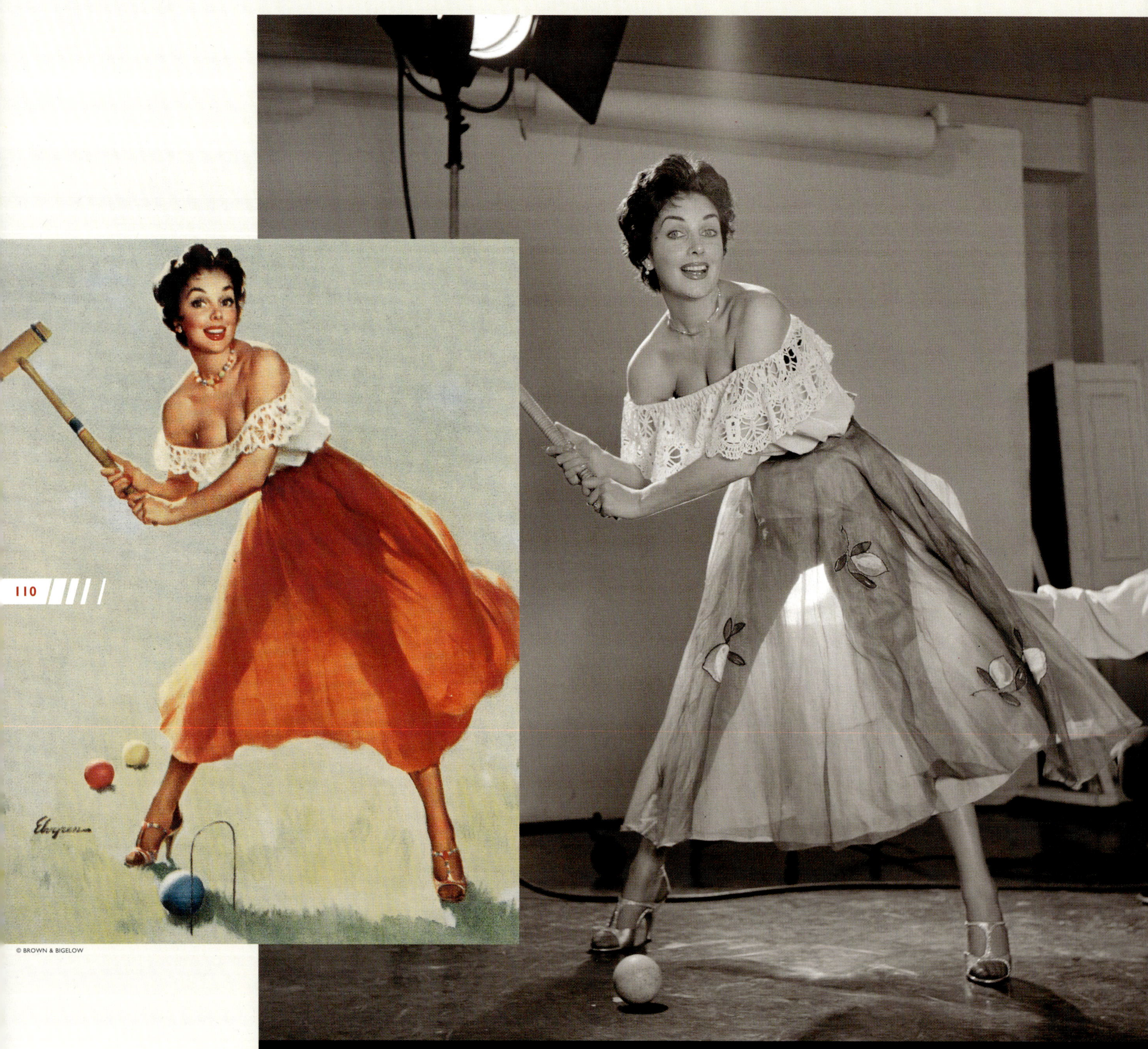

© BROWN & BIGELOW

Keep Your Eye on the Ball

Another cute, compliant, back-lighted model provides apt reference for Elvgren, faithful to his source but for a lowered neckline.

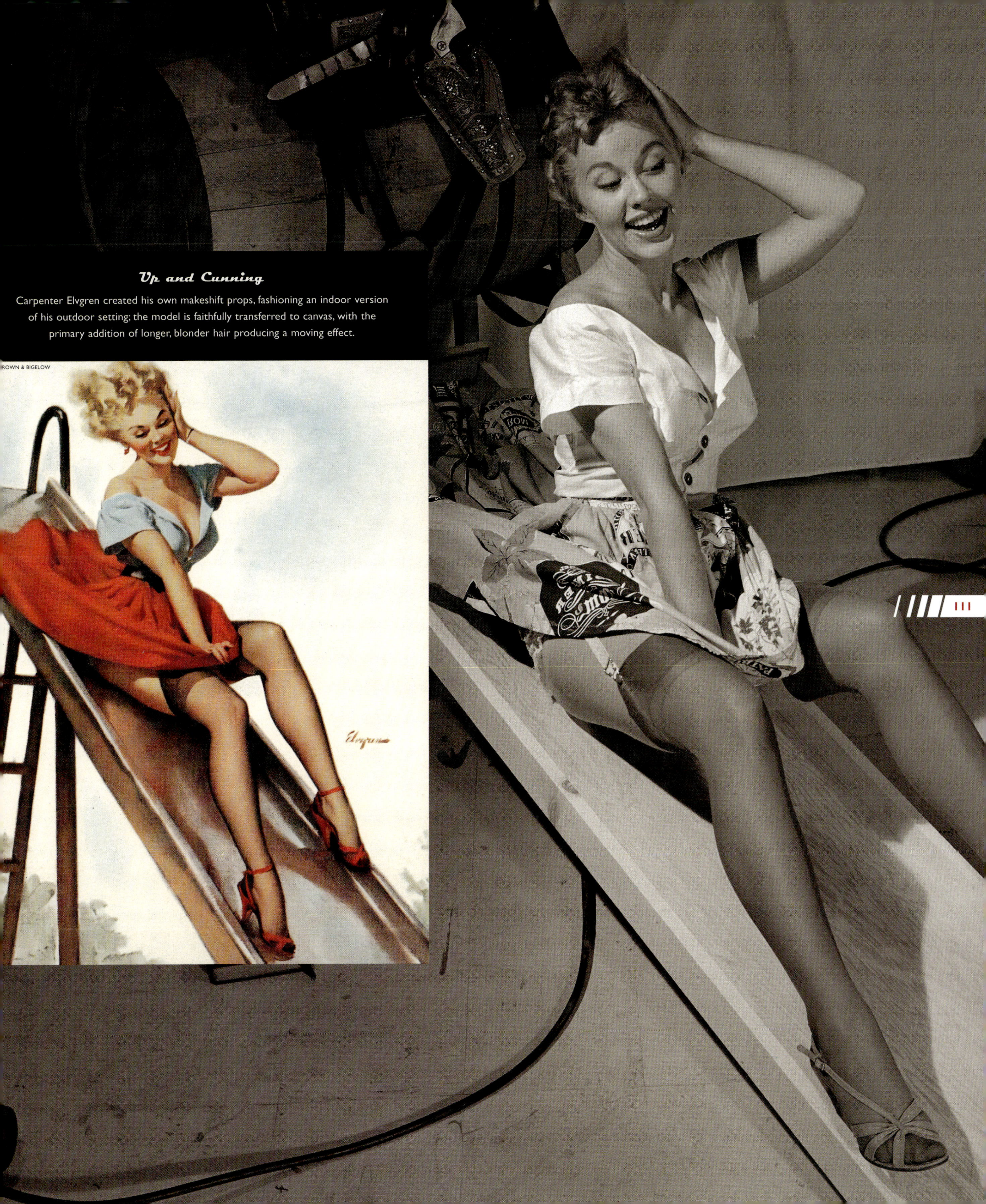

Up and Cunning

Carpenter Elvgren created his own makeshift props, fashioning an indoor version of his outdoor setting; the model is faithfully transferred to canvas, with the primary addition of longer, blonder hair producing a moving effect.

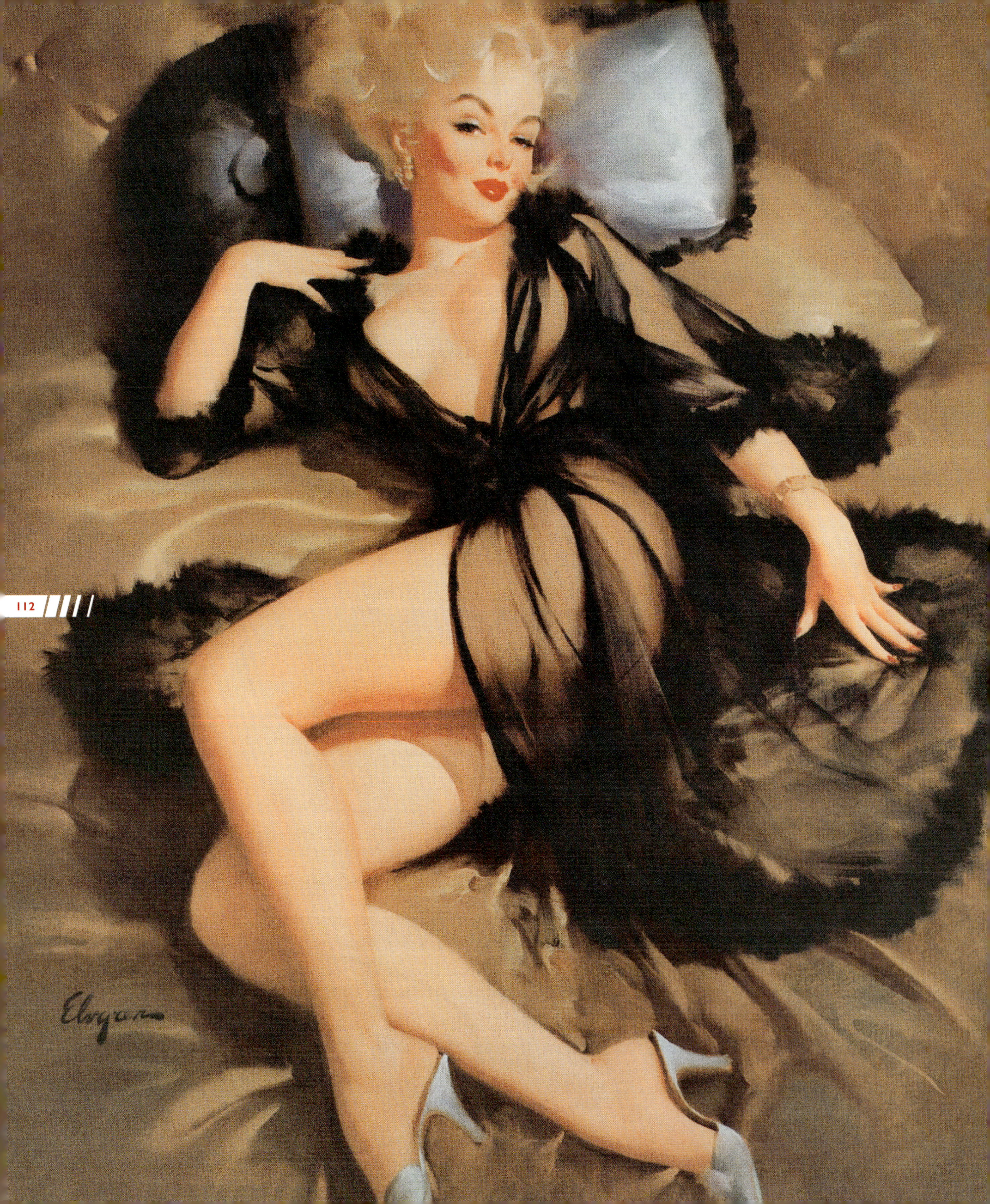
Elvgren

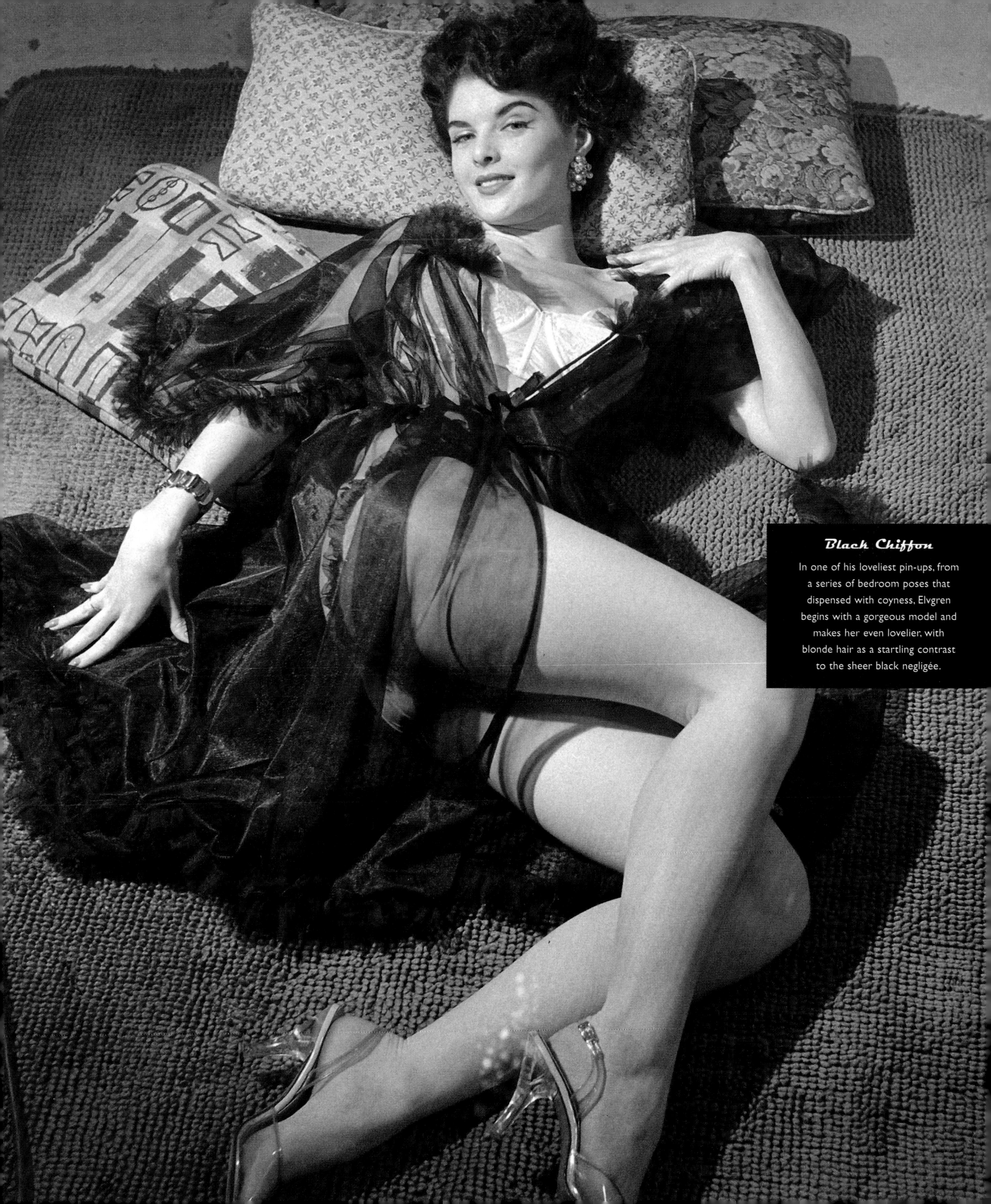

Black Chiffon

In one of his loveliest pin-ups, from a series of bedroom poses that dispensed with coyness, Elvgren begins with a gorgeous model and makes her even lovelier, with blonde hair as a startling contrast to the sheer black negligée.

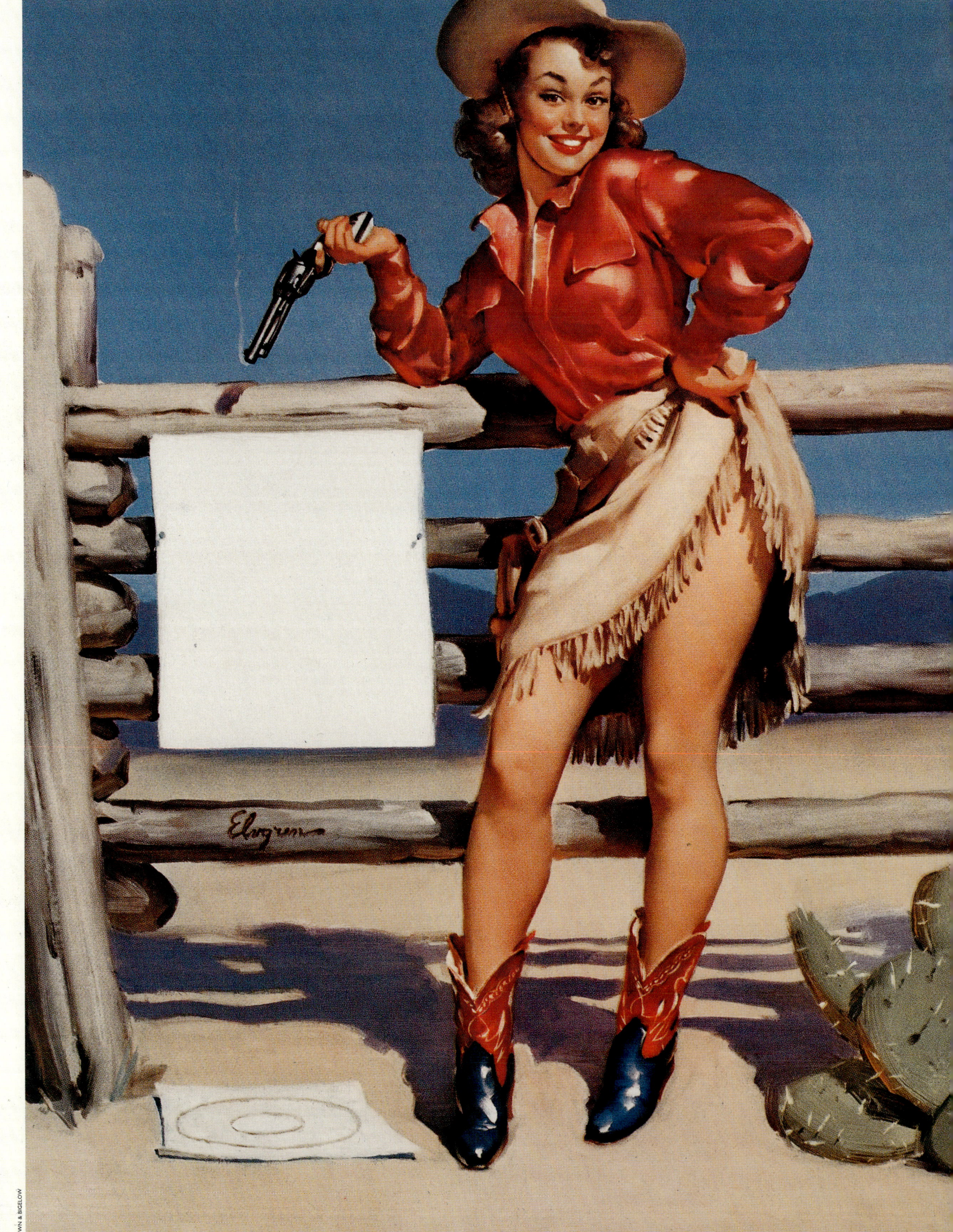
Elvgren

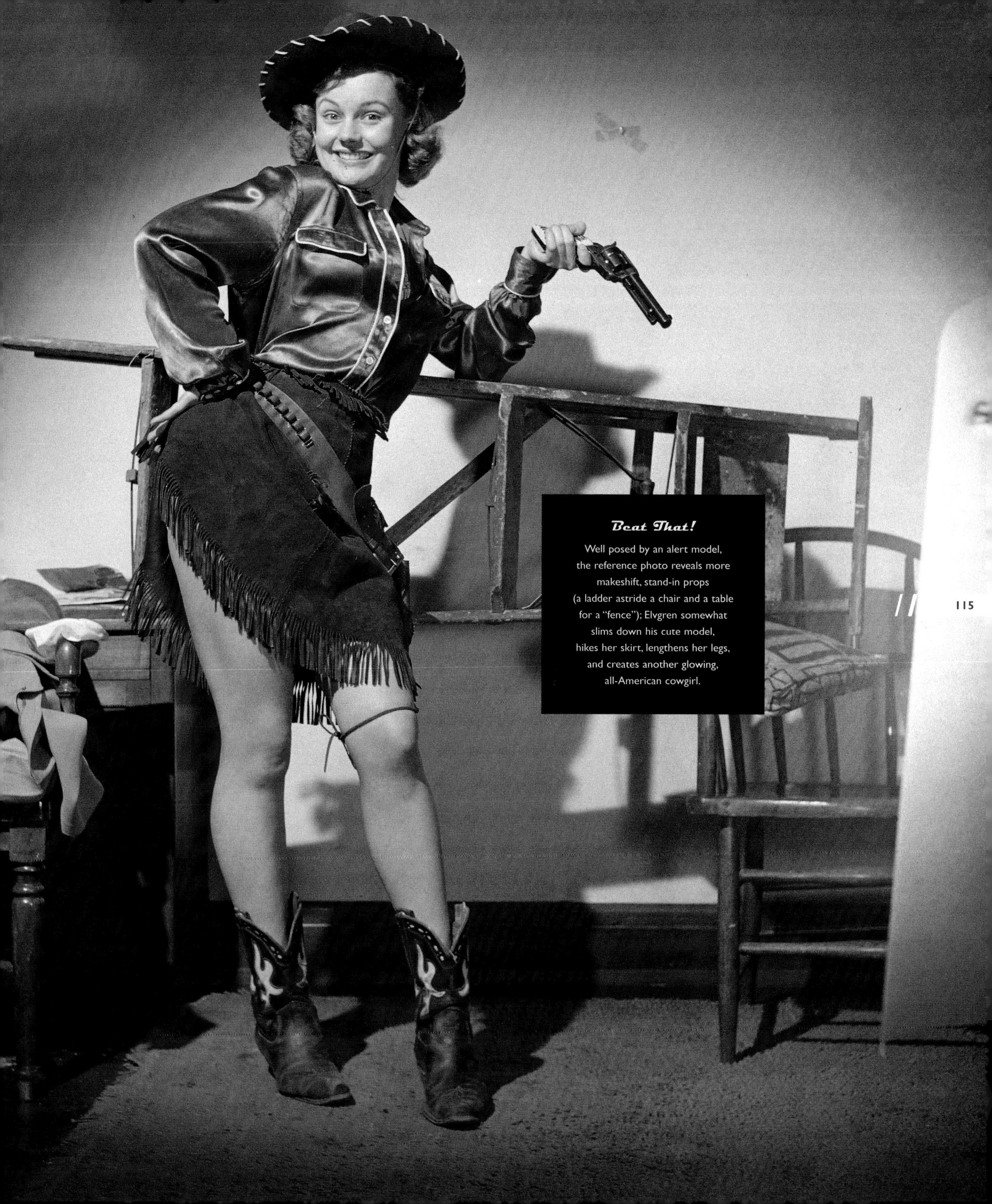

Beat That!

Well posed by an alert model, the reference photo reveals more makeshift, stand-in props (a ladder astride a chair and a table for a "fence"); Elvgren somewhat slims down his cute model, hikes her skirt, lengthens her legs, and creates another glowing, all-American cowgirl.

Hoops, My Dear!

Again, a lovely model is gently idealized, Coke-girl style, with emphasis provided by a full bustline, colorful skirt, and the trademark nylons.

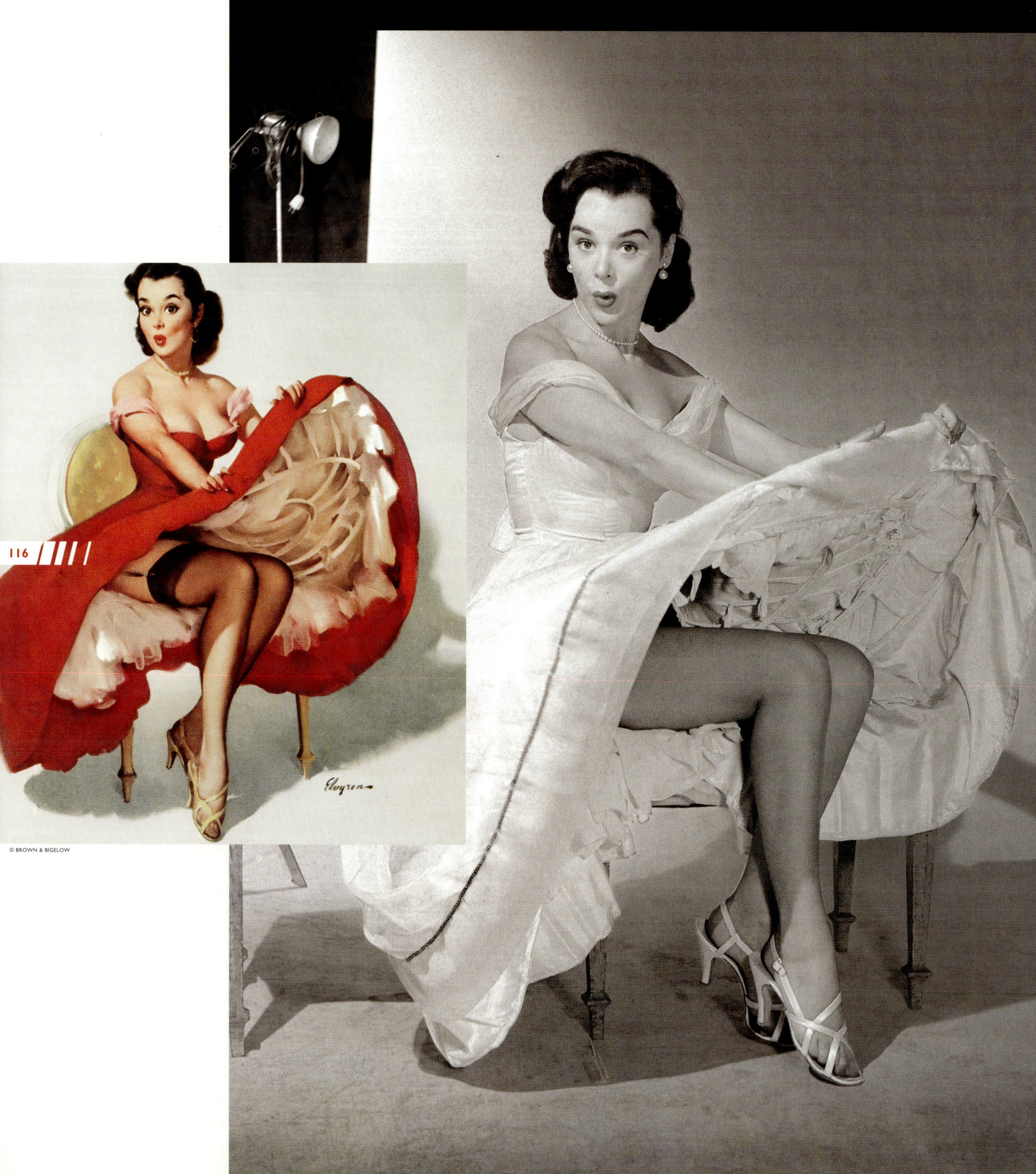

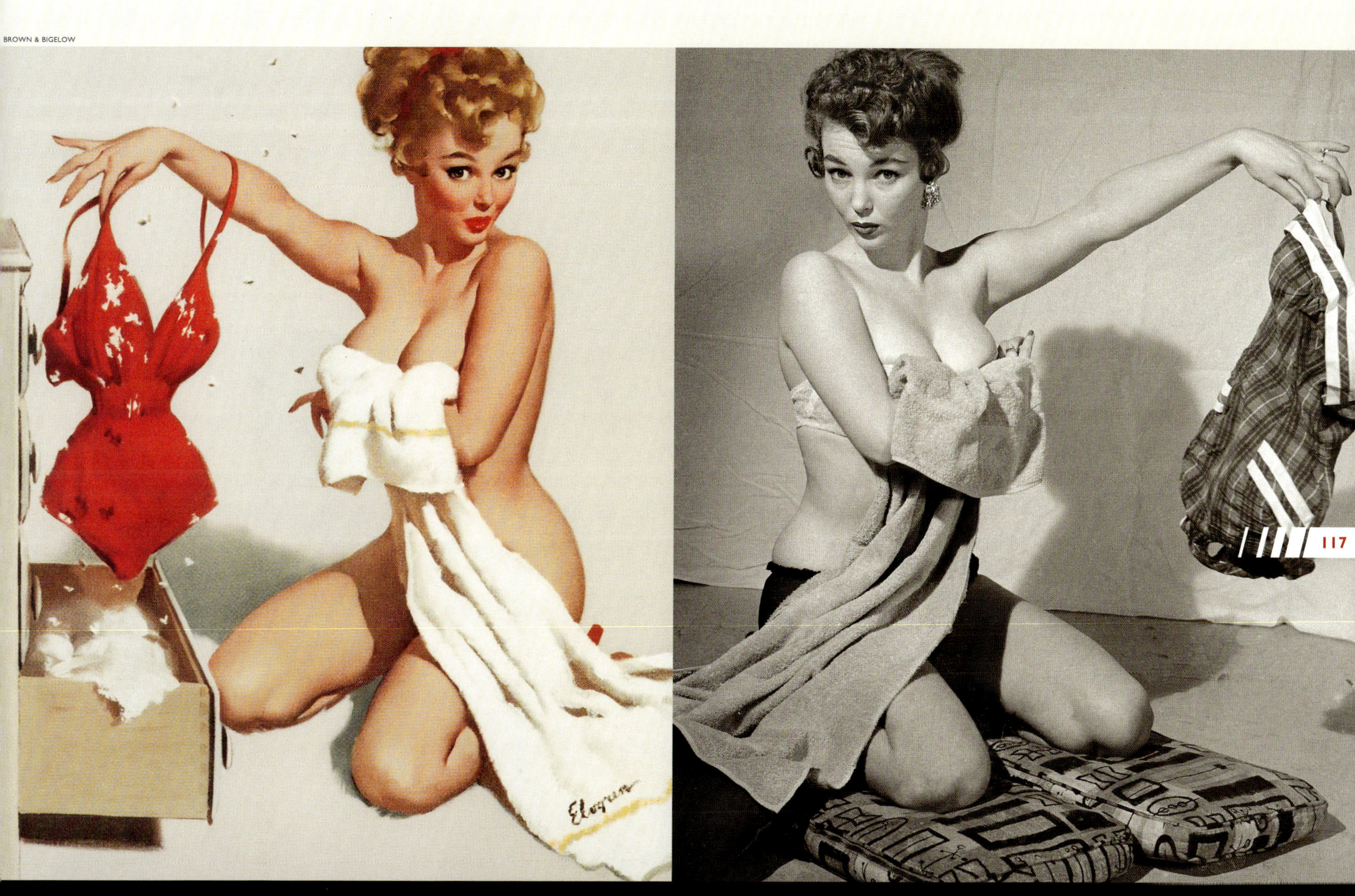

Partial Coverage

This later pin-up is racier than most, with a subject — somewhat hidden behind her towel — obviously acknowledging our presence; Elvgren is faithful to his reference photo of his voluptuous model but adds a touch of coquettish humor to her expression.

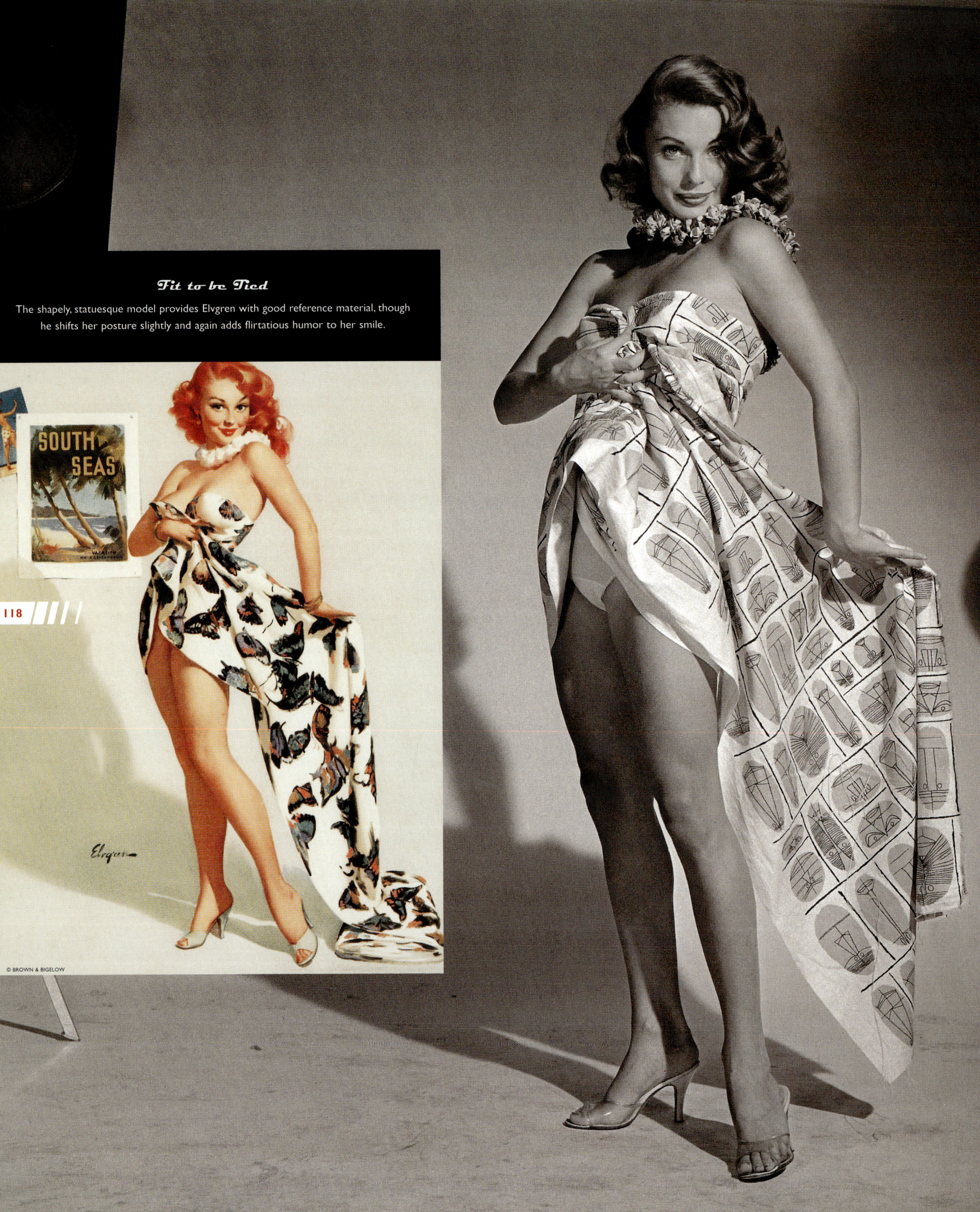

Fit to be Tied

The shapely, statuesque model provides Elvgren with good reference material, though he shifts her posture slightly and again adds flirtatious humor to her smile.

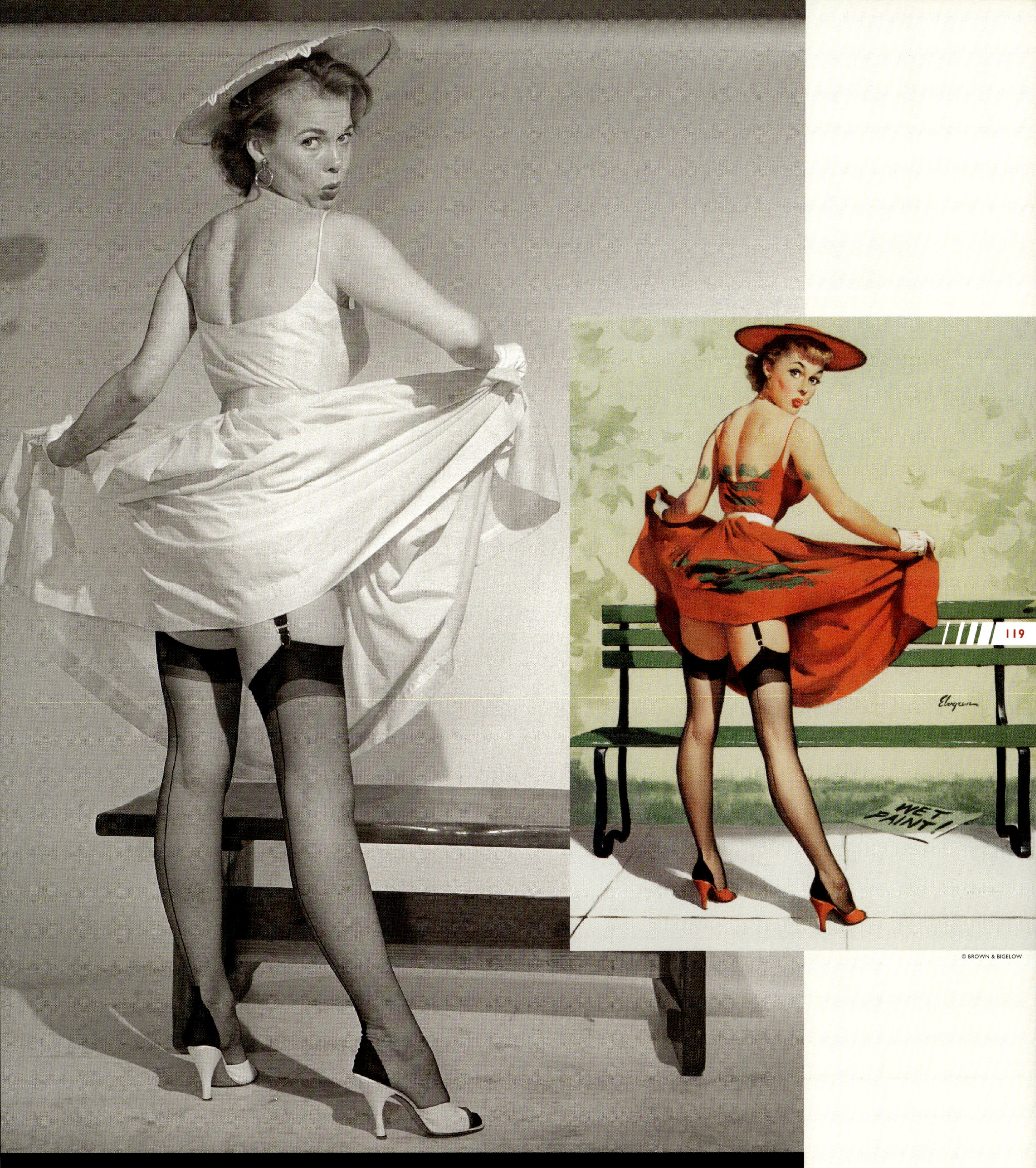

I've Been Spotted

Elvgren's models were, not surprisingly, pin-ups come to life; but even with a subject as appealing as this one, he lengthens her legs and adjusts her posture for his purposes.

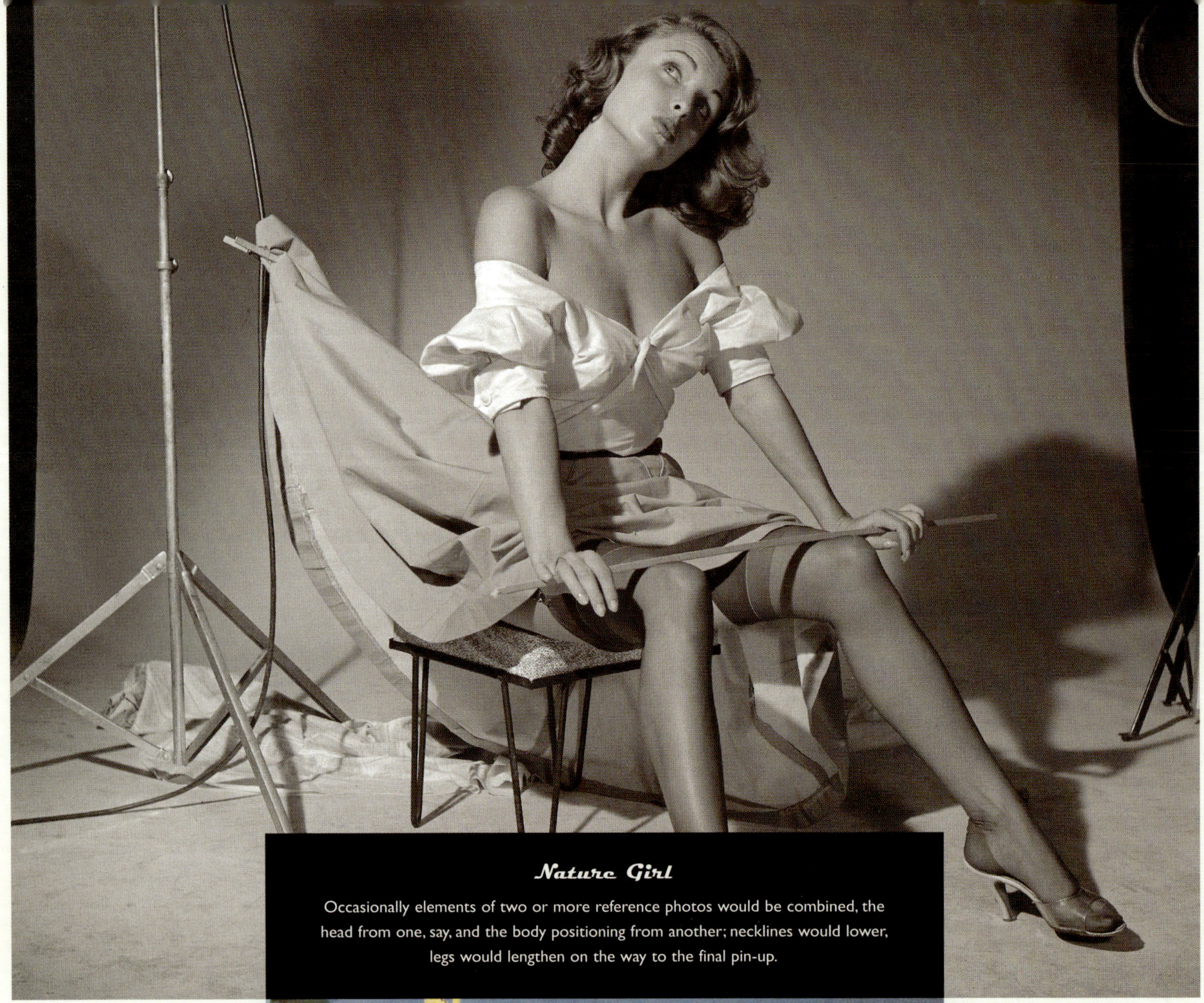

Nature Girl

Occasionally elements of two or more reference photos would be combined, the head from one, say, and the body positioning from another; necklines would lower, legs would lengthen on the way to the final pin-up.

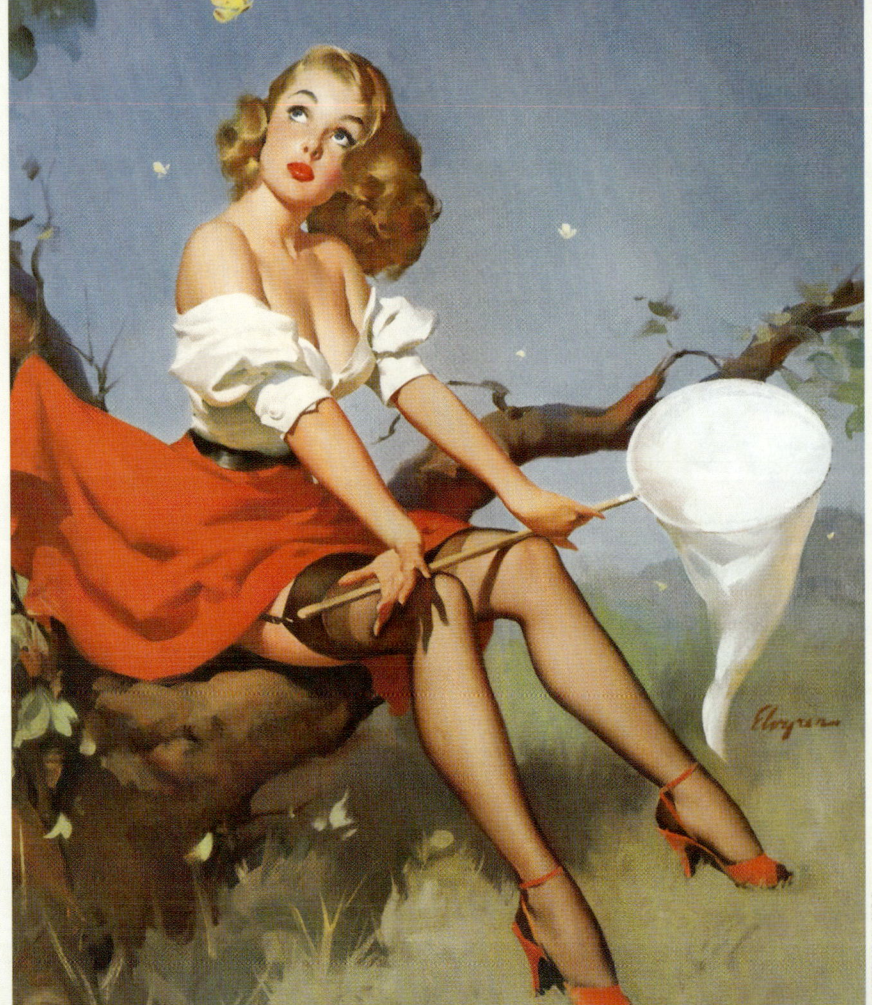

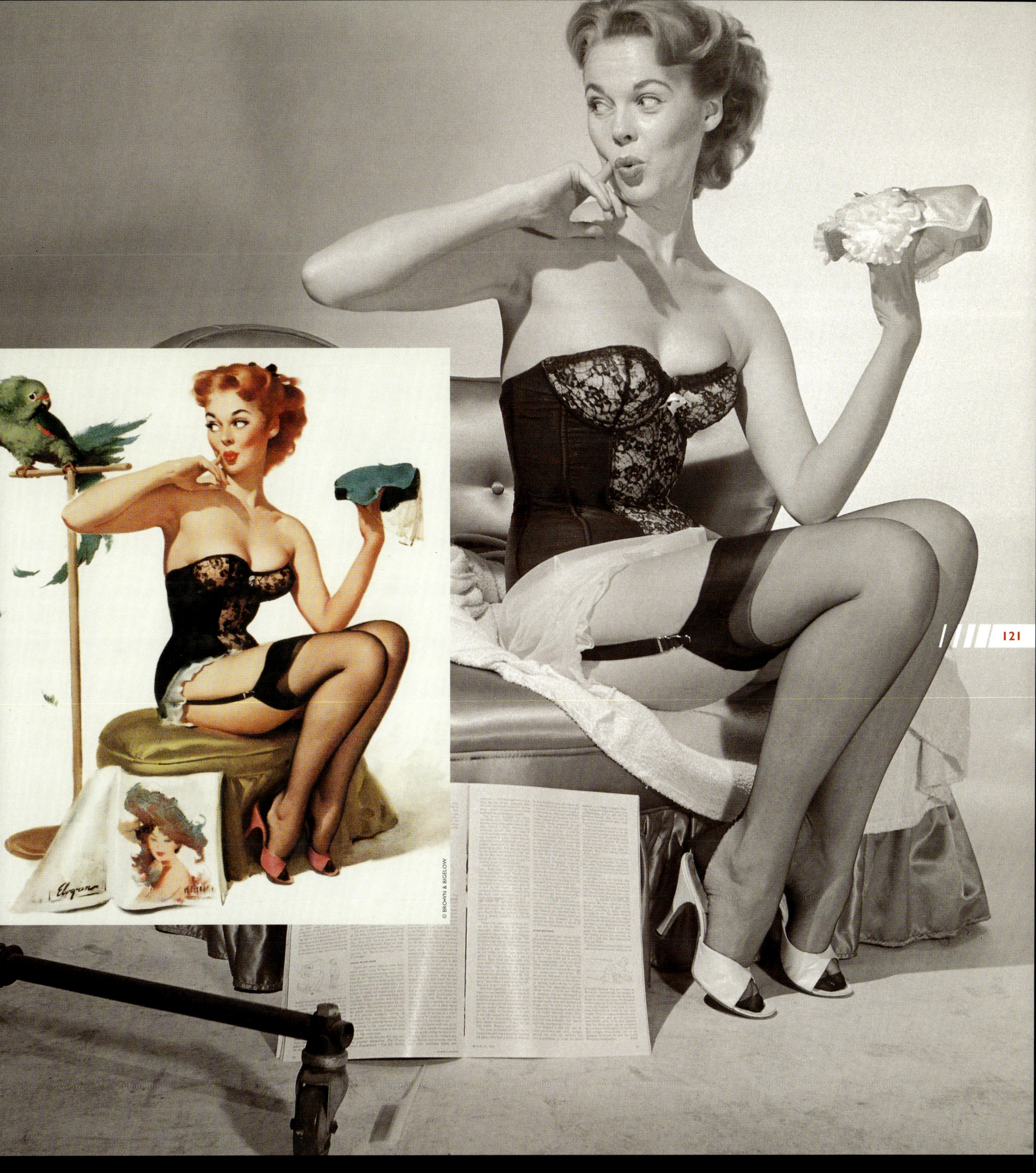

No You Don't

Birds, particularly parrots, are a typical prop in 1950s pin-ups; here Elvgren's lovely model is fairly accurately transferred to the painting, though her torso is lengthened.

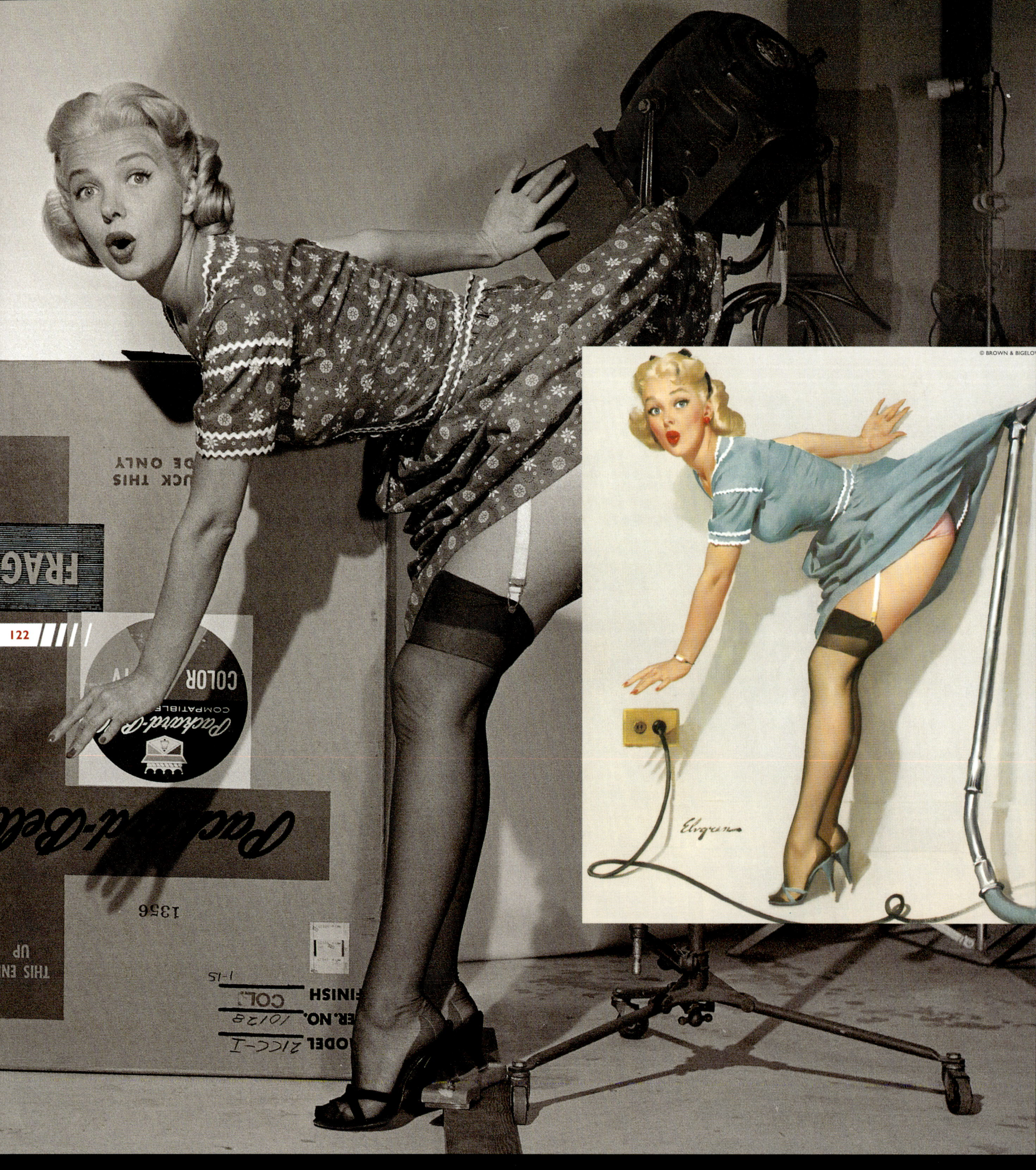

What's Up?

A well-posed, exquisite model provides the basis for this fun pin-up (a natural for vacuum-cleaner shops) and again suggests that housewives can be glamour girls, at least in Elvgren's fantasy suburbia.

Well Heeled

The subtle transformation of a good-looking model into a stunning pin-up is particularly impressive in instances, such as this one, where the artist does not vary much from his reference photo, keeping it faithful even as to wardrobe.

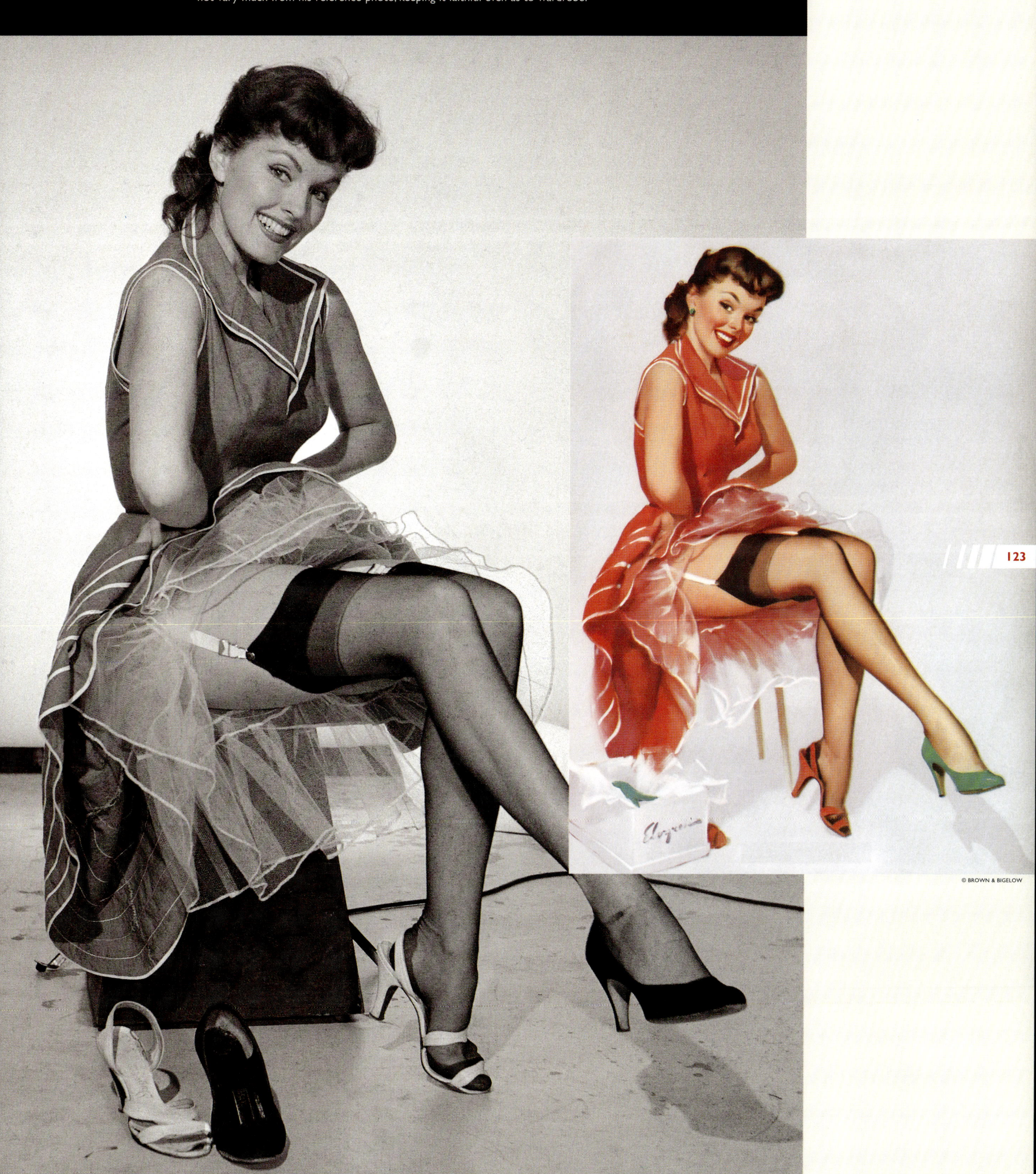

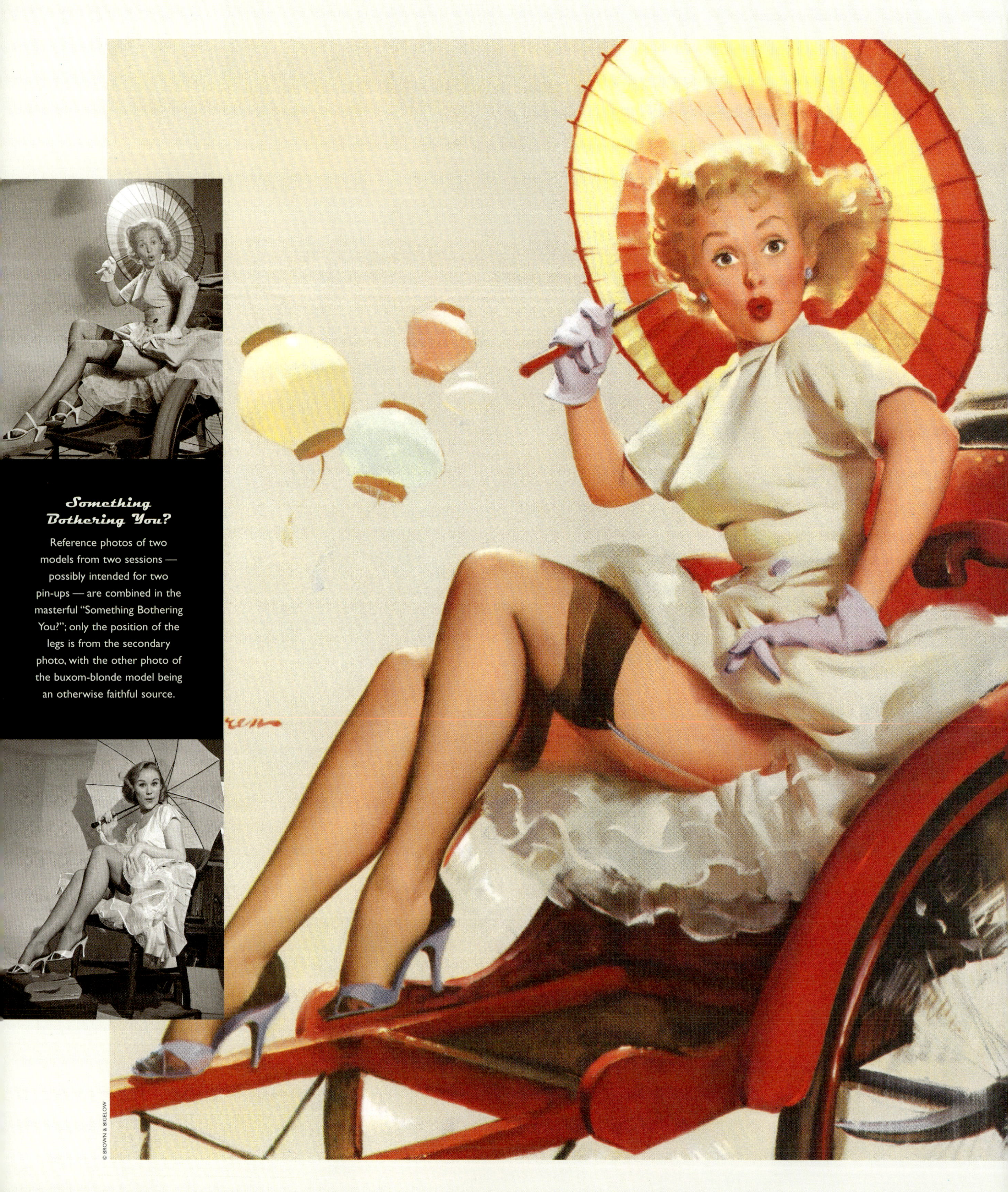

Something Bothering You?

Reference photos of two models from two sessions — possibly intended for two pin-ups — are combined in the masterful "Something Bothering You?"; only the position of the legs is from the secondary photo, with the other photo of the buxom-blonde model being an otherwise faithful source.

The Winner!

The model, already voluptuous, is pleasantly plumped into one of Elvgren's rare but always appealing, earthy, pseudo-Latin cuties; the brazen, if motivated, manner in which this temptress shows off and the bold, if odd, oral symbolism mark this as an unusual and unusually erotic Elvgren pin-up.

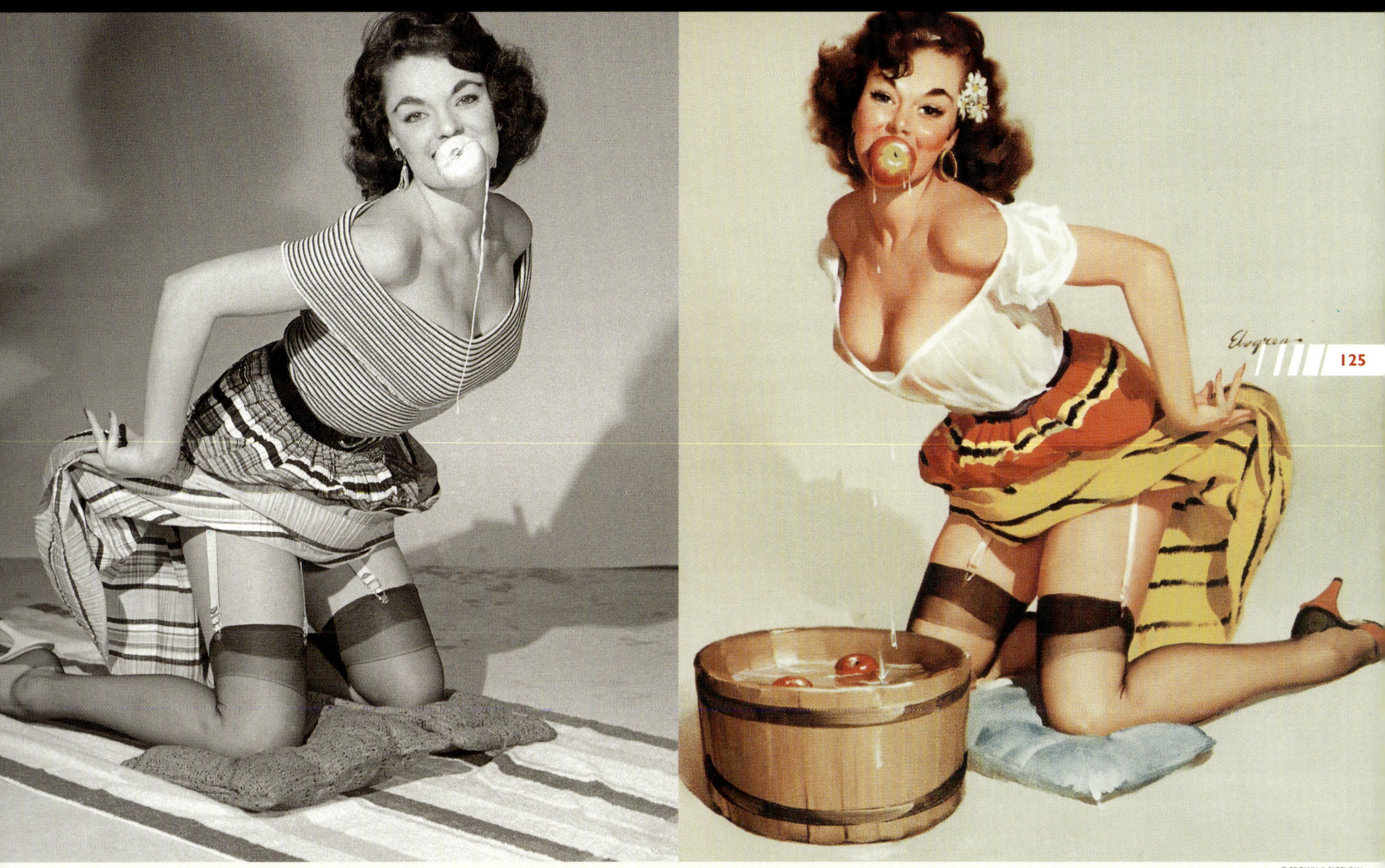

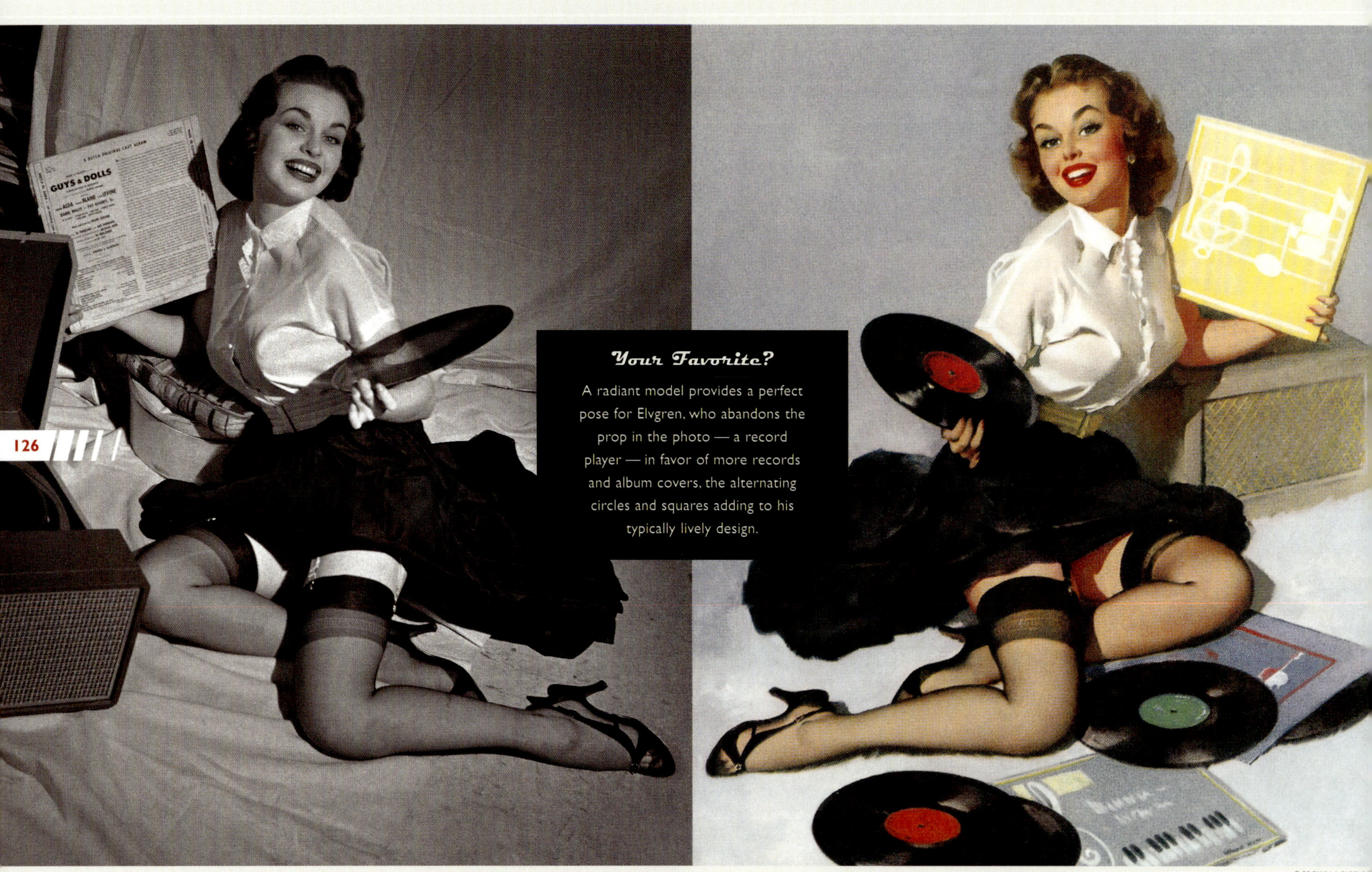

Your Favorite?

A radiant model provides a perfect pose for Elvgren, who abandons the prop in the photo — a record player — in favor of more records and album covers, the alternating circles and squares adding to his typically lively design.

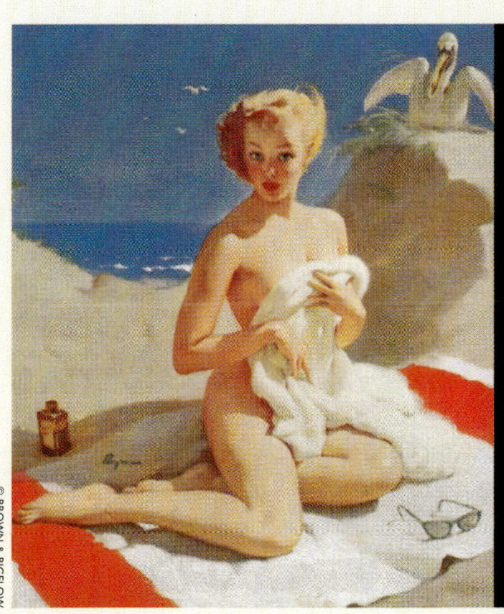

© BROWN & BIGELOW

A Peach on the Beach

For a 1950s image, this is a rare (if only suggested) instance of nudity in a pin-up (calendar nudes tended to be presented in a more artistic "study" manner); the reference photo also marks a rarity: an outdoors modeling session.

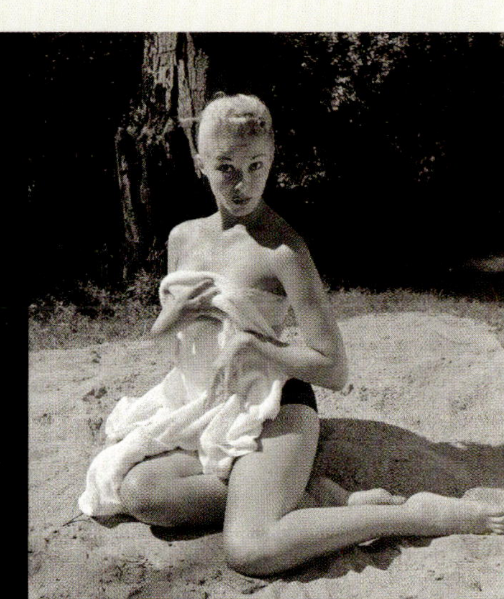

© BROWN & BIGELOW

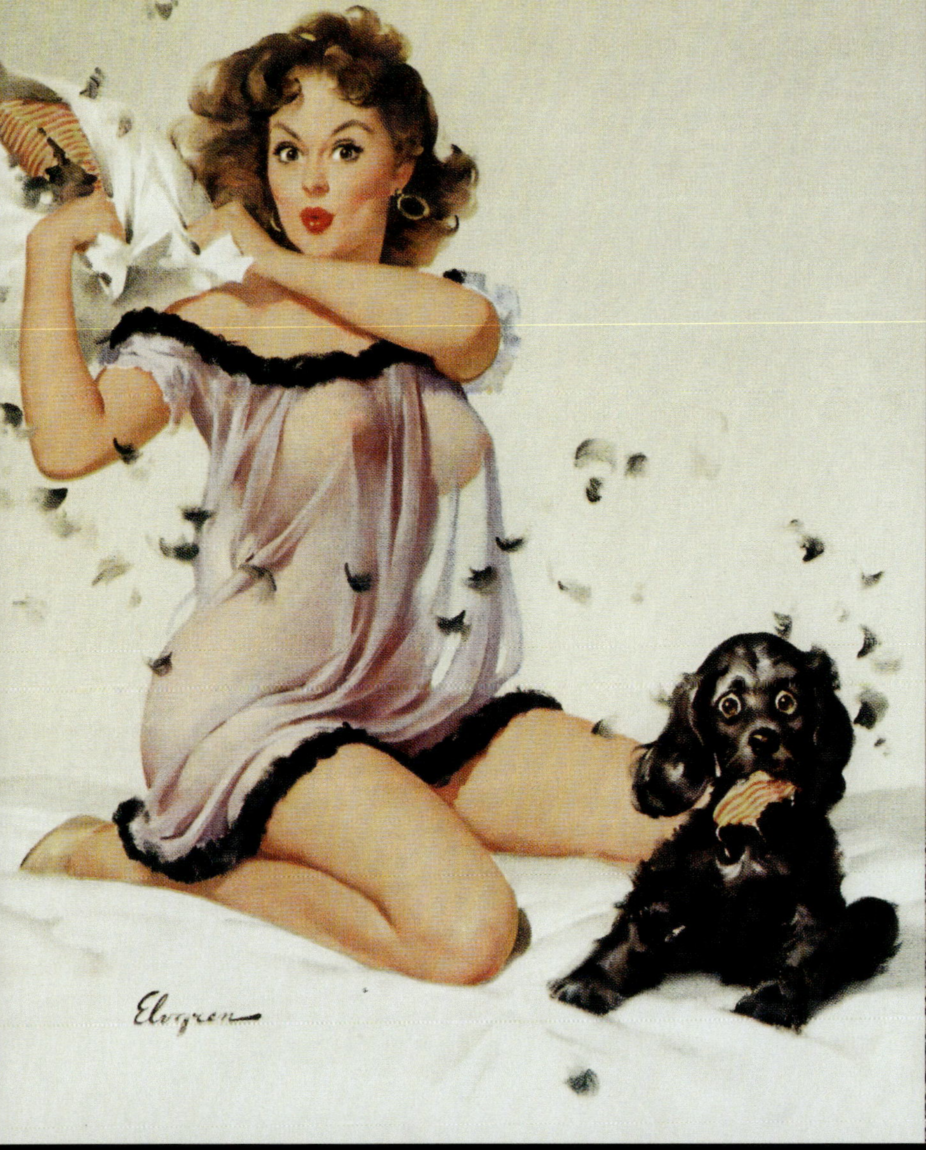

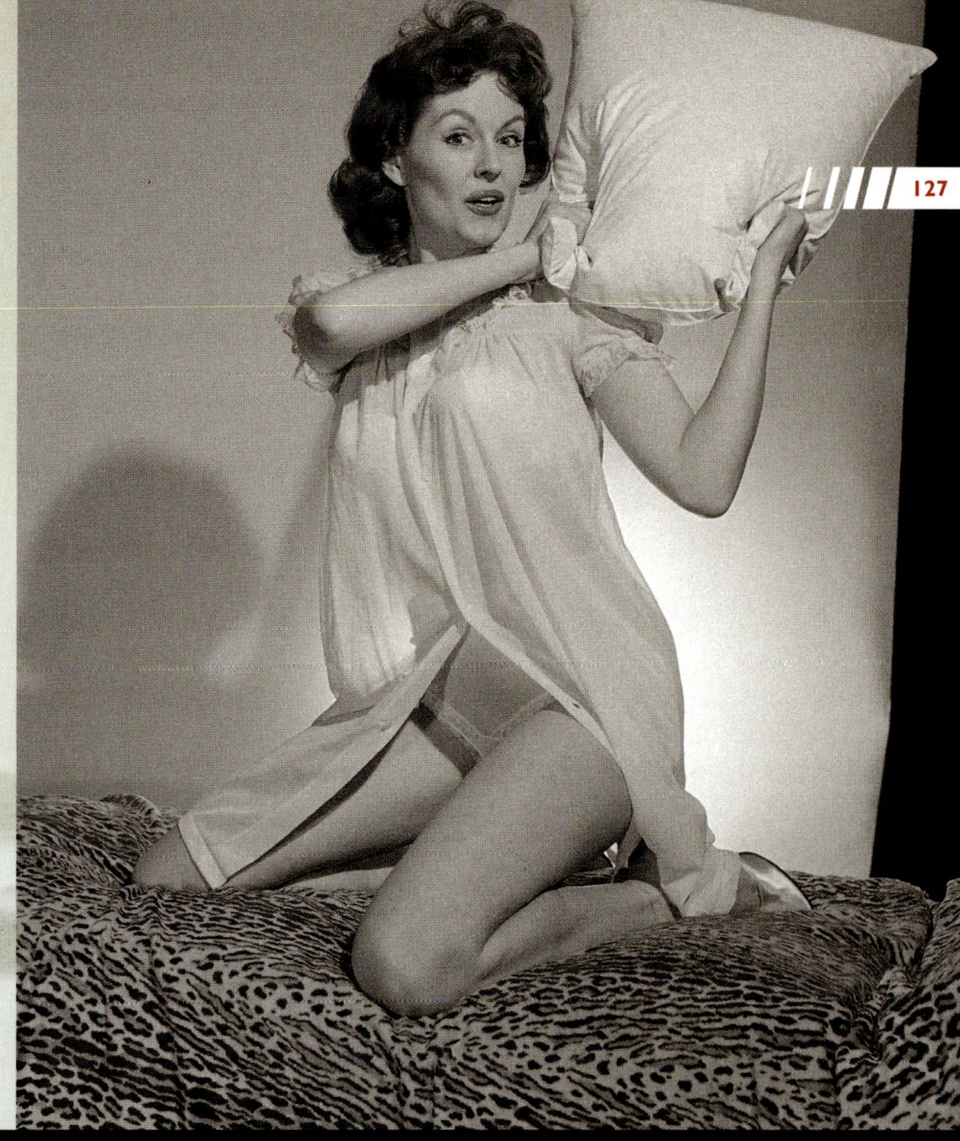

Ticklish Situation

Despite its attractive model, this reference photo is surprisingly pedestrian, considering the magical result. Elvgren emphasizes her curves, makes her nightie diaphanous, changes her hair style, and even adds an irresistible puppy.

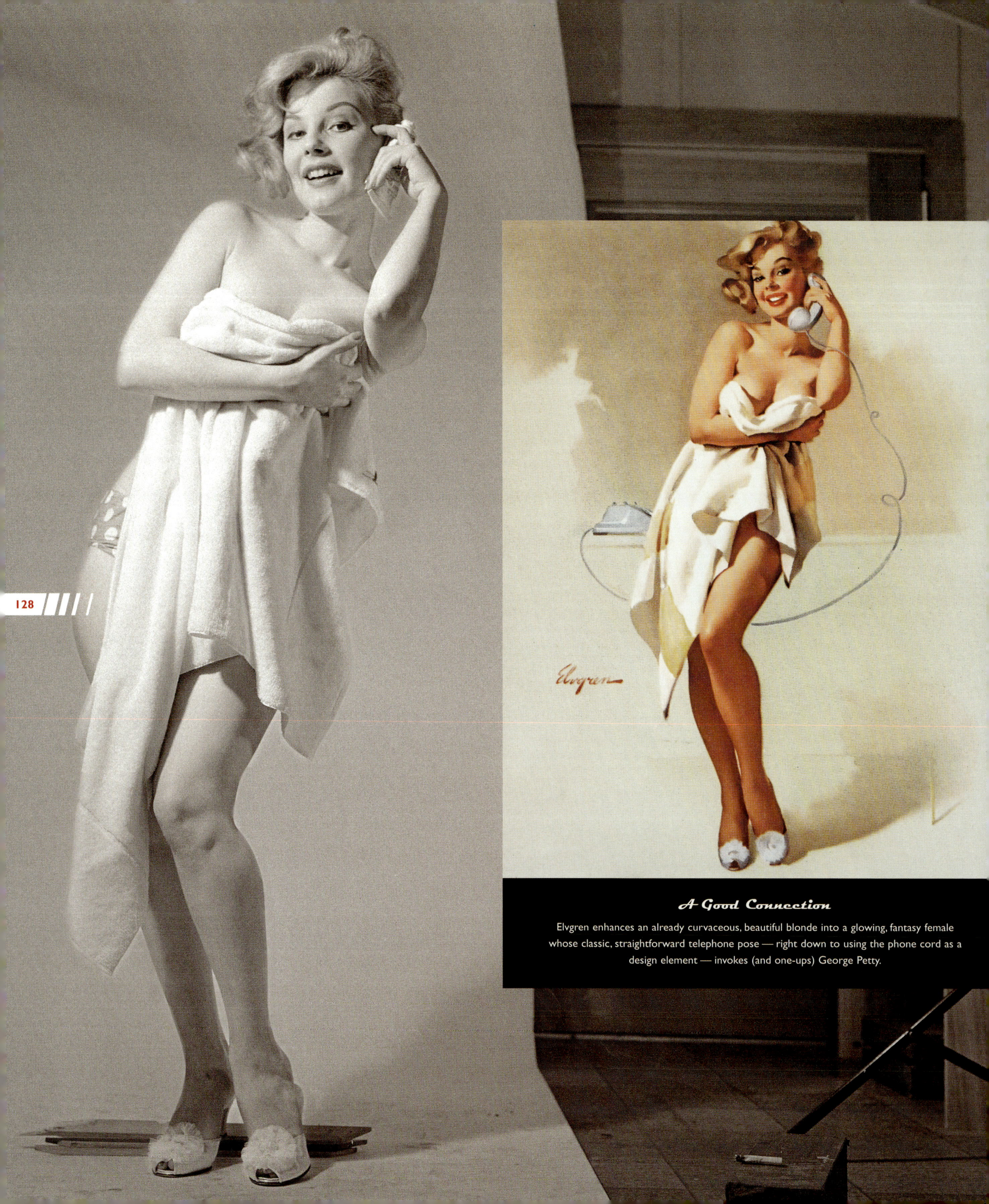

A Good Connection

Elvgren enhances an already curvaceous, beautiful blonde into a glowing, fantasy female whose classic, straightforward telephone pose — right down to using the phone cord as a design element — invokes (and one-ups) George Petty.

All Set

Operating with more props than usual, Elvgren's staging of his buxom, beautiful model provides a basis for a glowing pin-up; the addition of a sound-stage light in the background — and a Monroe-ish lightening of the hair and substitution of a closed-mouthed expression — are subtle, transforming touches.

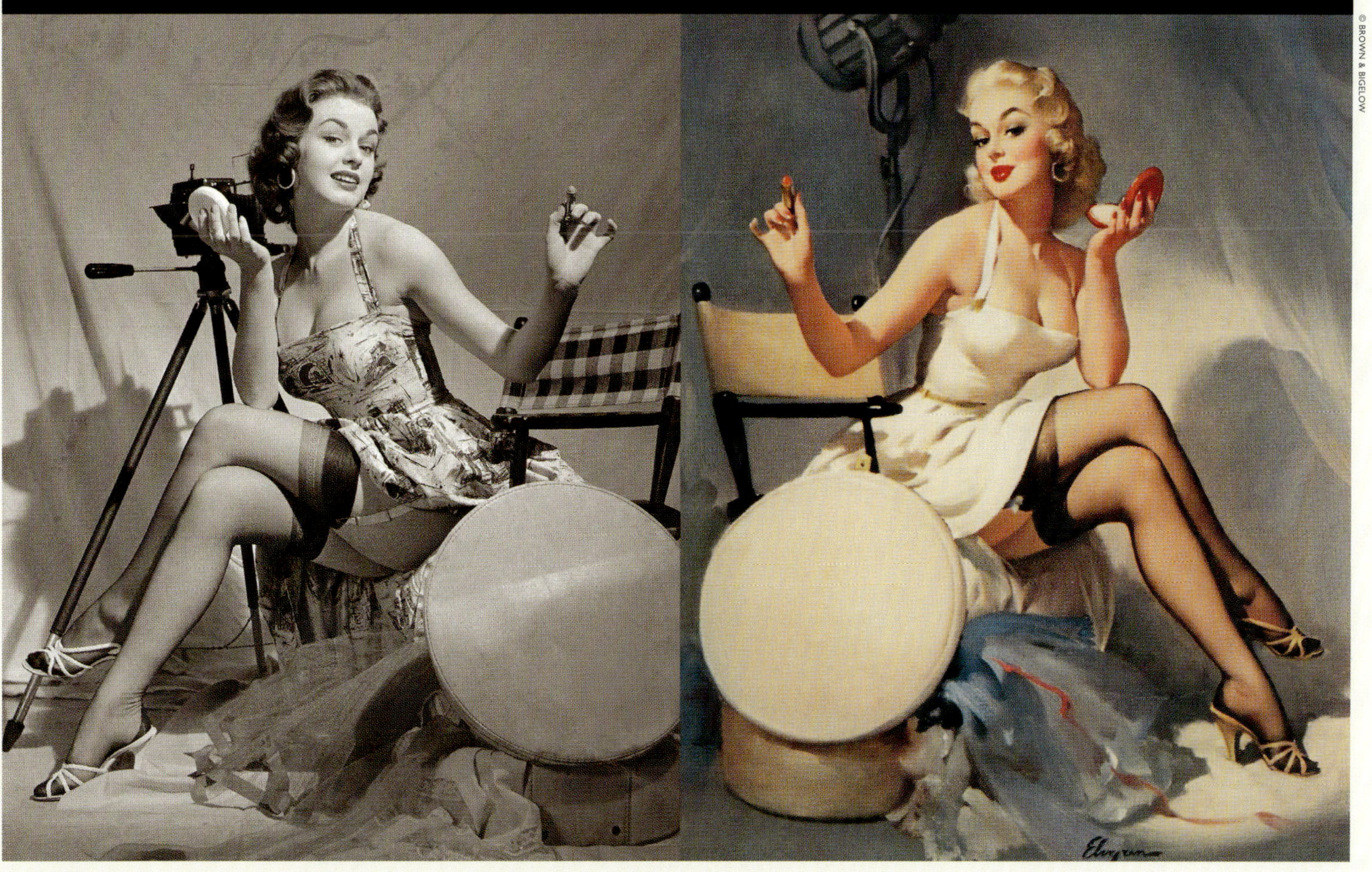

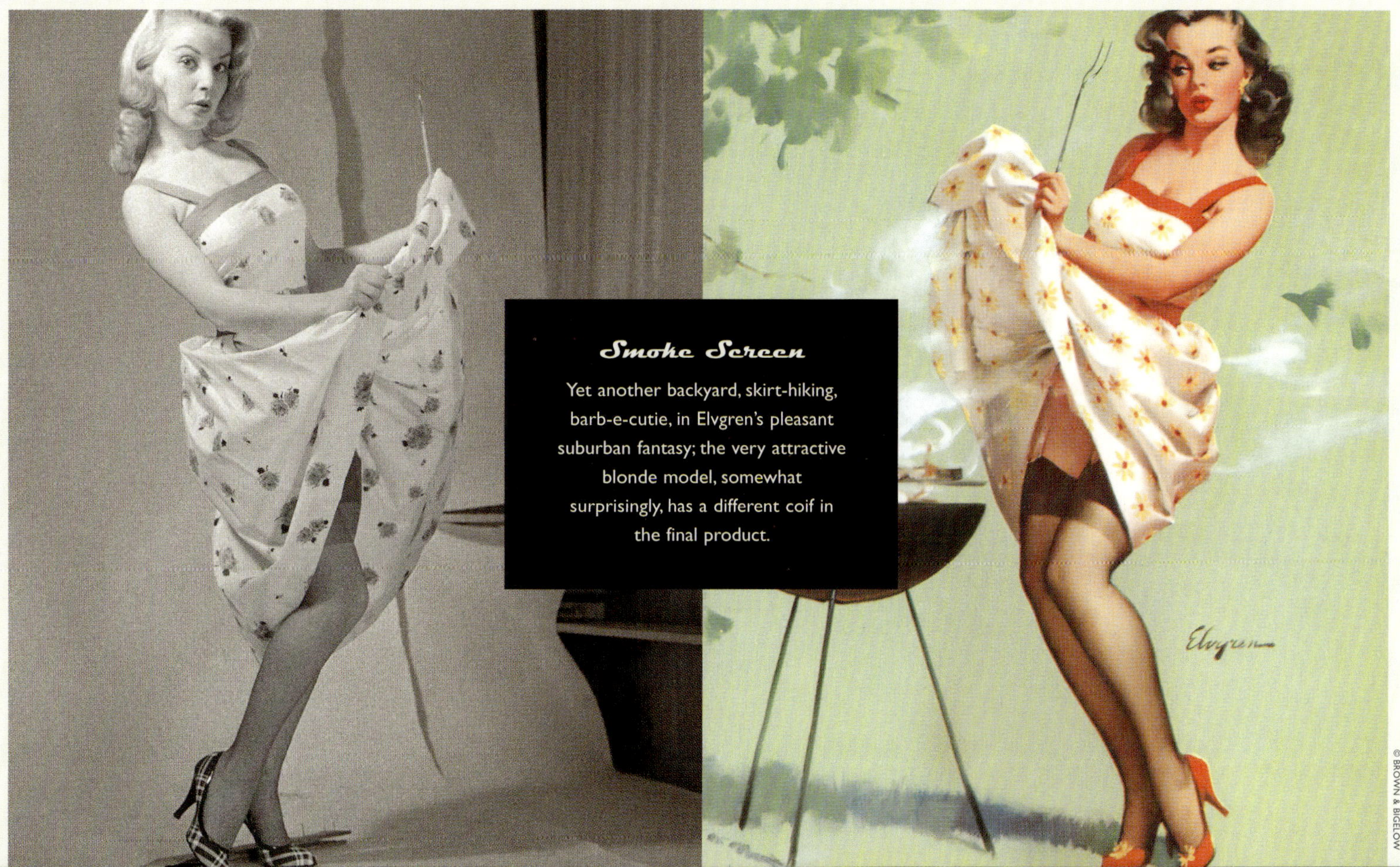

Smoke Screen

Yet another backyard, skirt-hiking, barb-e-cutie, in Elvgren's pleasant suburban fantasy; the very attractive blonde model, somewhat surprisingly, has a different coif in the final product.

Rude Awakening

A gorgeous, shapely model is somehow made even more gorgeous and shapely in this outrageous late Brown & Bigelow pin-up; the lightened hair color adds to the reworking of the model's face, suggesting actress Sherri North.

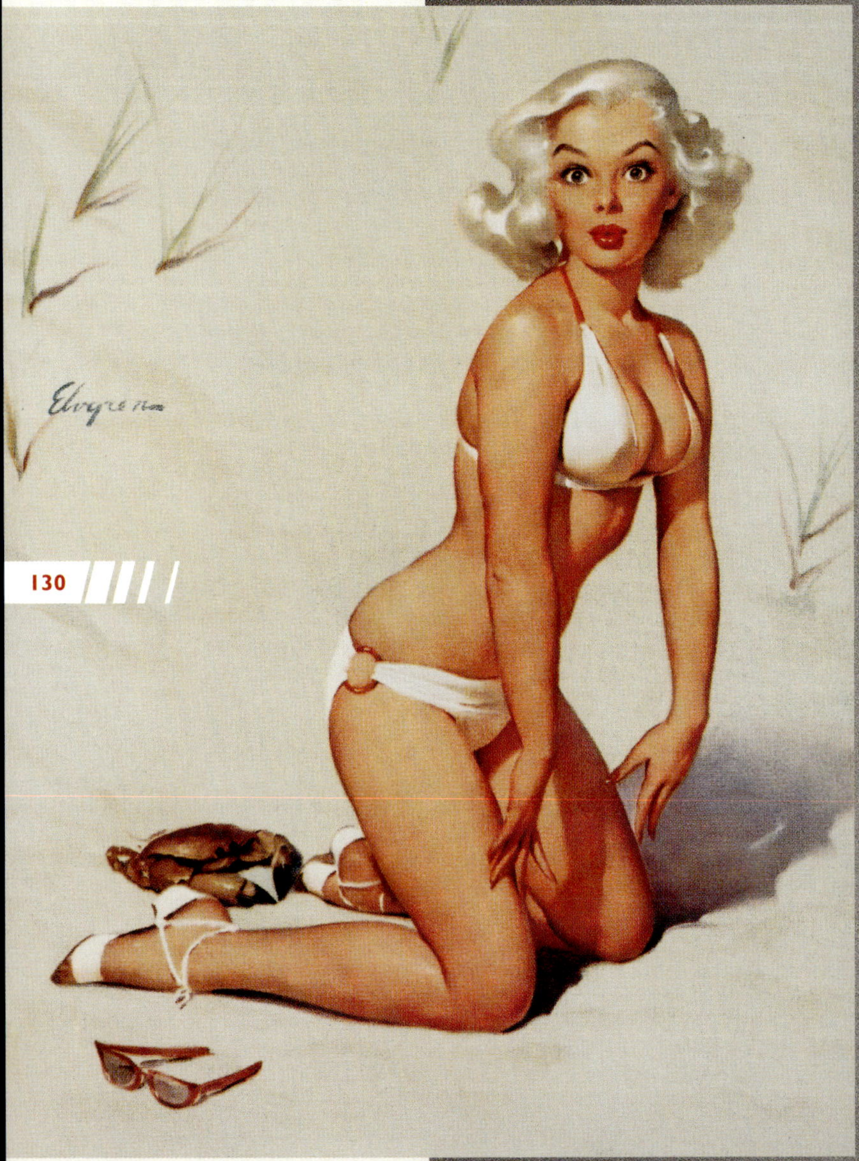

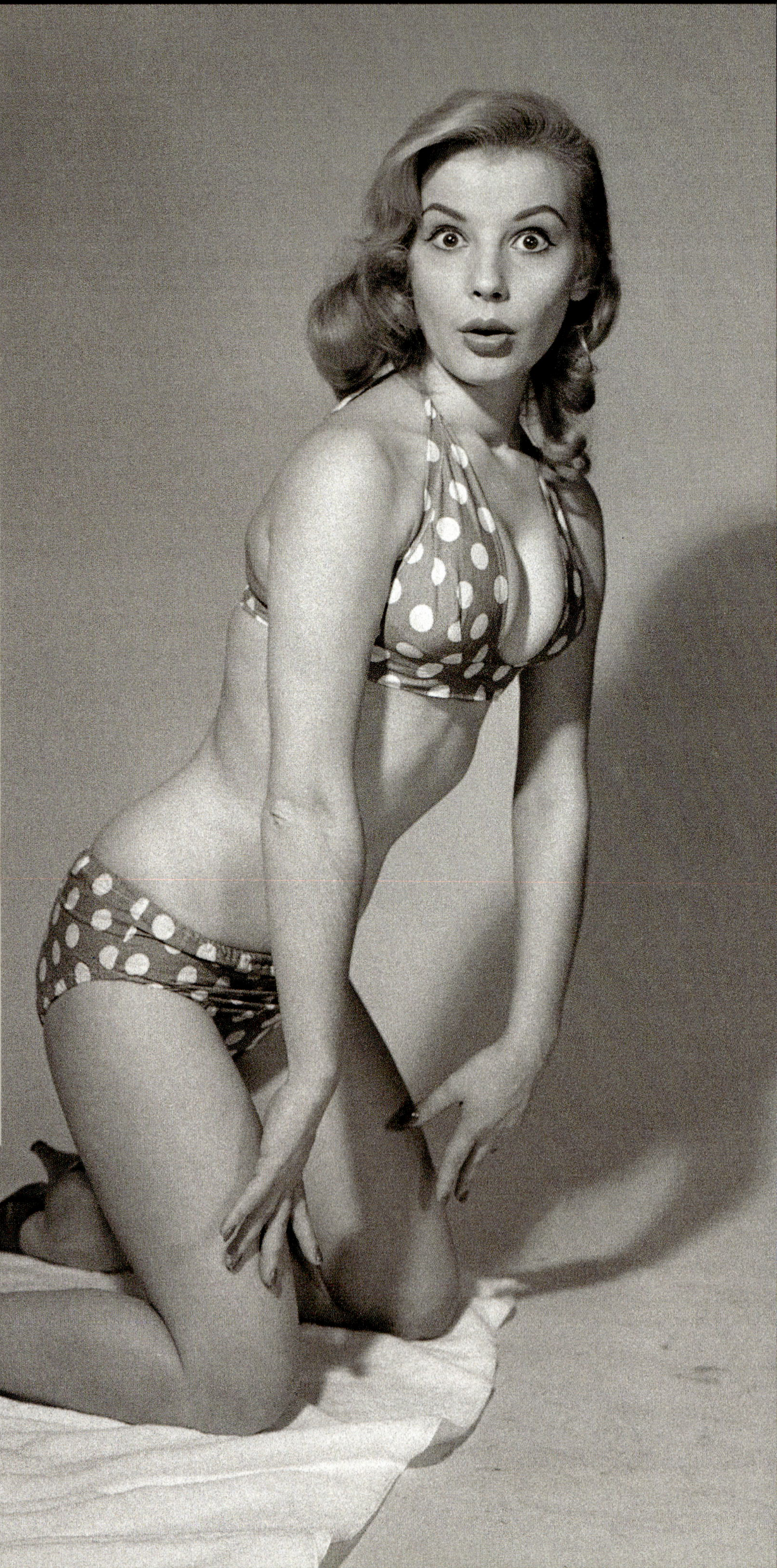

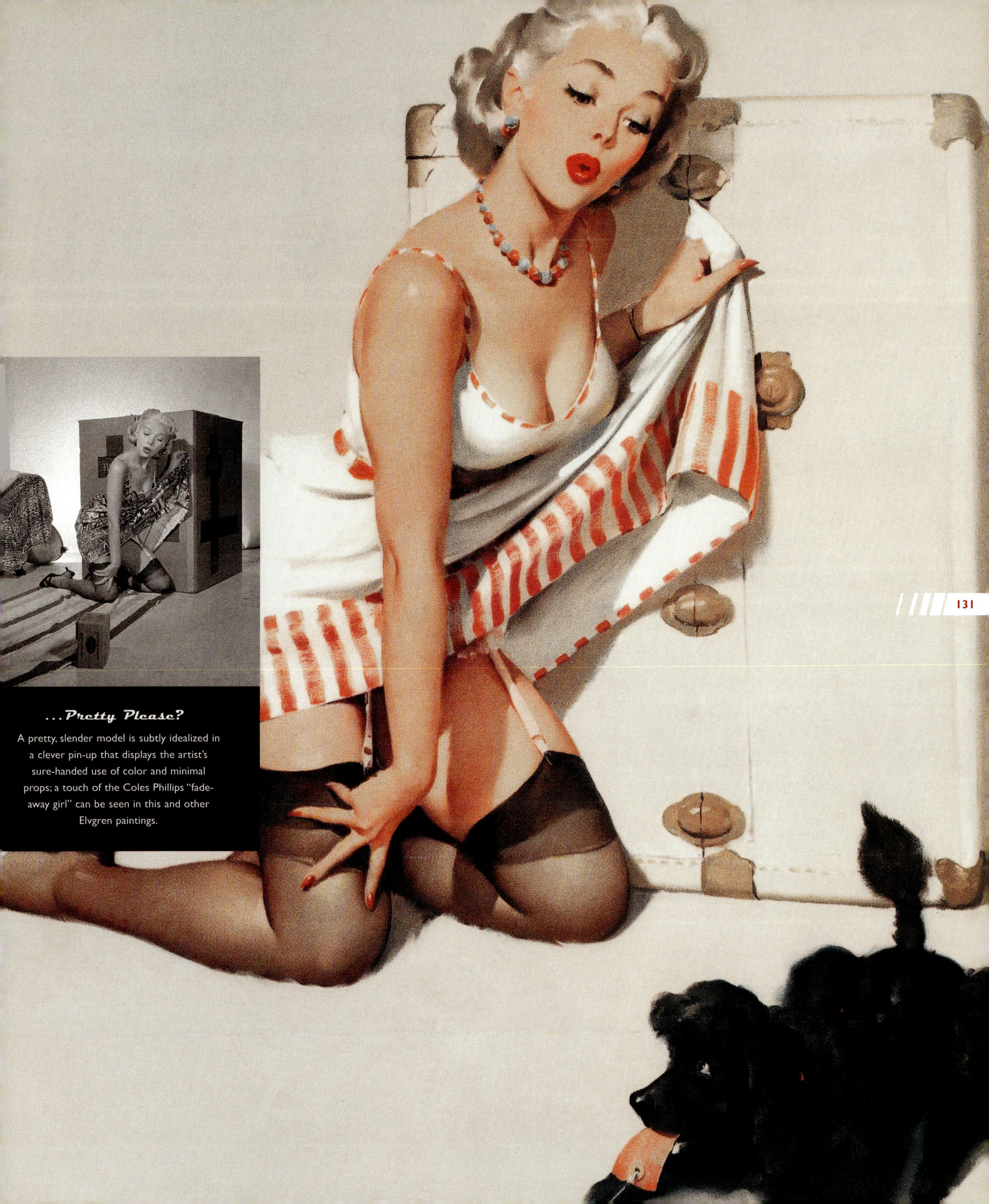

...Pretty Please?

A pretty, slender model is subtly idealized in a clever pin-up that displays the artist's sure-handed use of color and minimal props; a touch of the Coles Phillips "fade-away girl" can be seen in this and other Elvgren paintings.

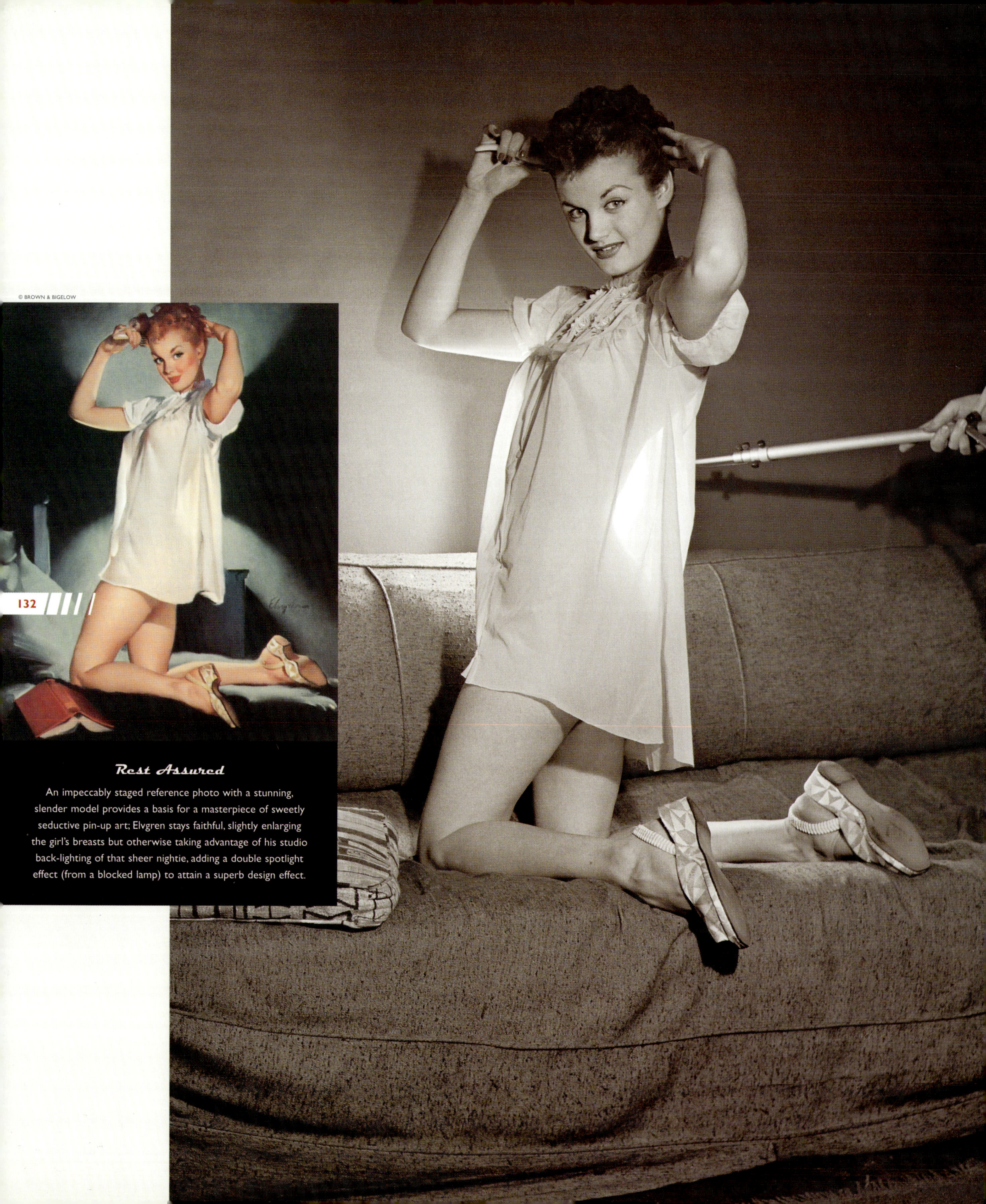

Rest Assured

An impeccably staged reference photo with a stunning, slender model provides a basis for a masterpiece of sweetly seductive pin-up art; Elvgren stays faithful, slightly enlarging the girl's breasts but otherwise taking advantage of his studio back-lighting of that sheer nightie, adding a double spotlight effect (from a blocked lamp) to attain a superb design effect.

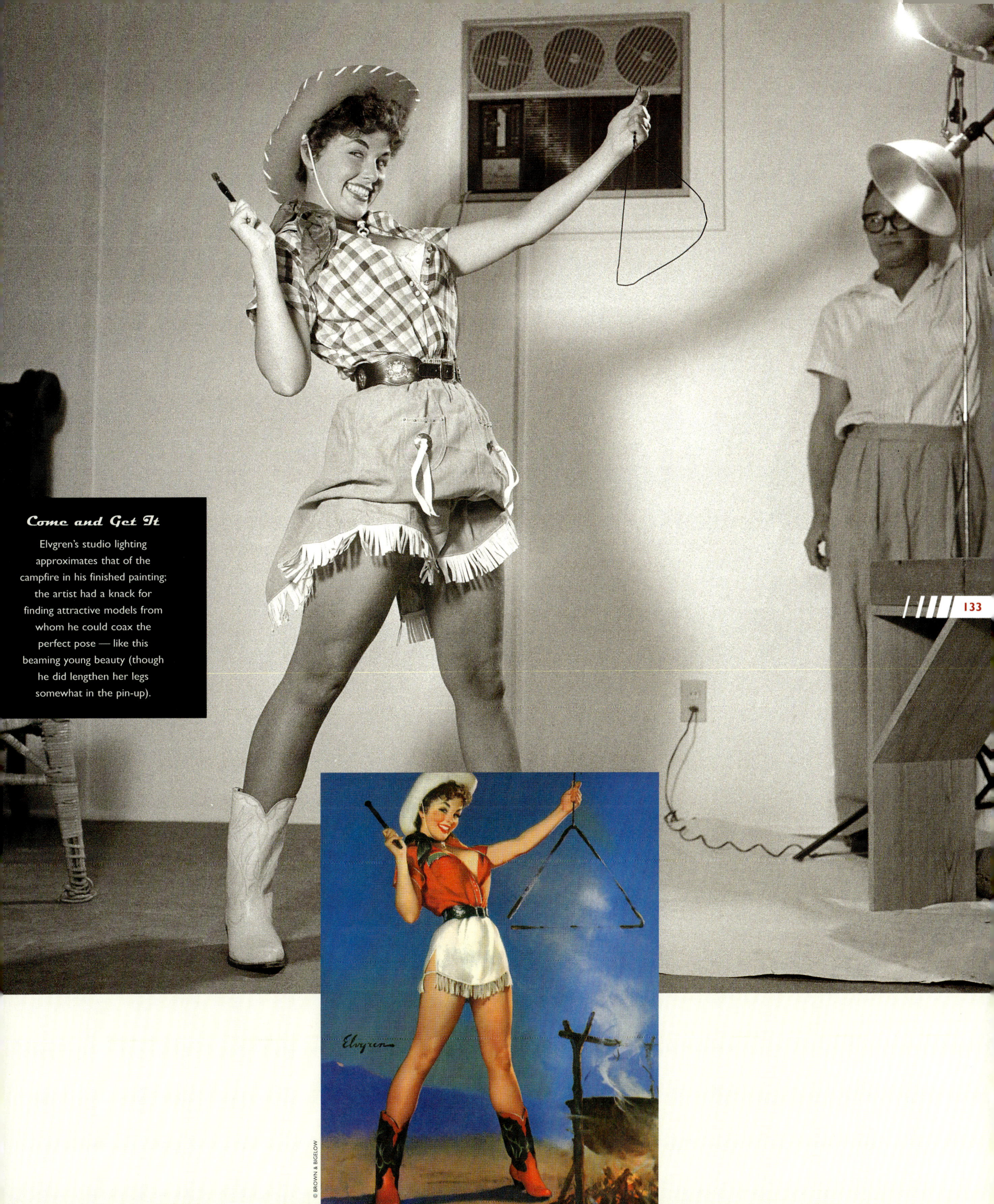

Come and Get It

Elvgren's studio lighting approximates that of the campfire in his finished painting; the artist had a knack for finding attractive models from whom he could coax the perfect pose — like this beaming young beauty (though he did lengthen her legs somewhat in the pin-up).

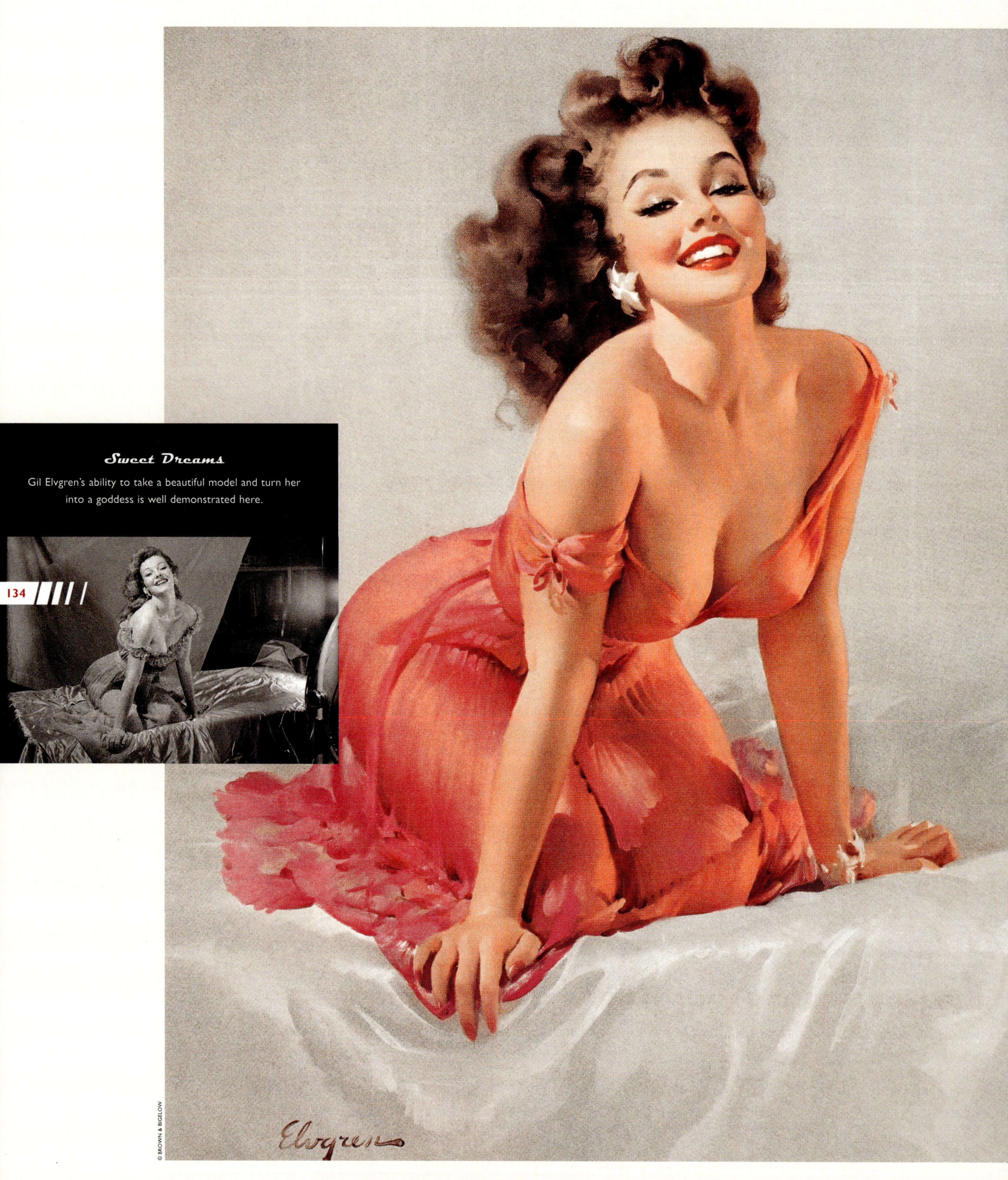

Sweet Dreams

Gil Elvgren's ability to take a beautiful model and turn her into a goddess is well demonstrated here.

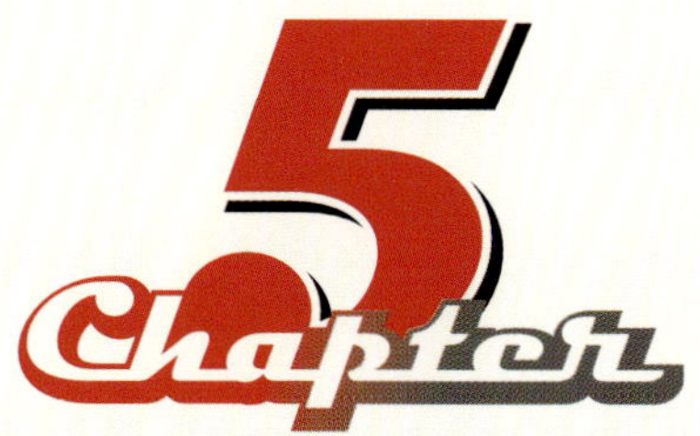

Brown & Bigelow Days

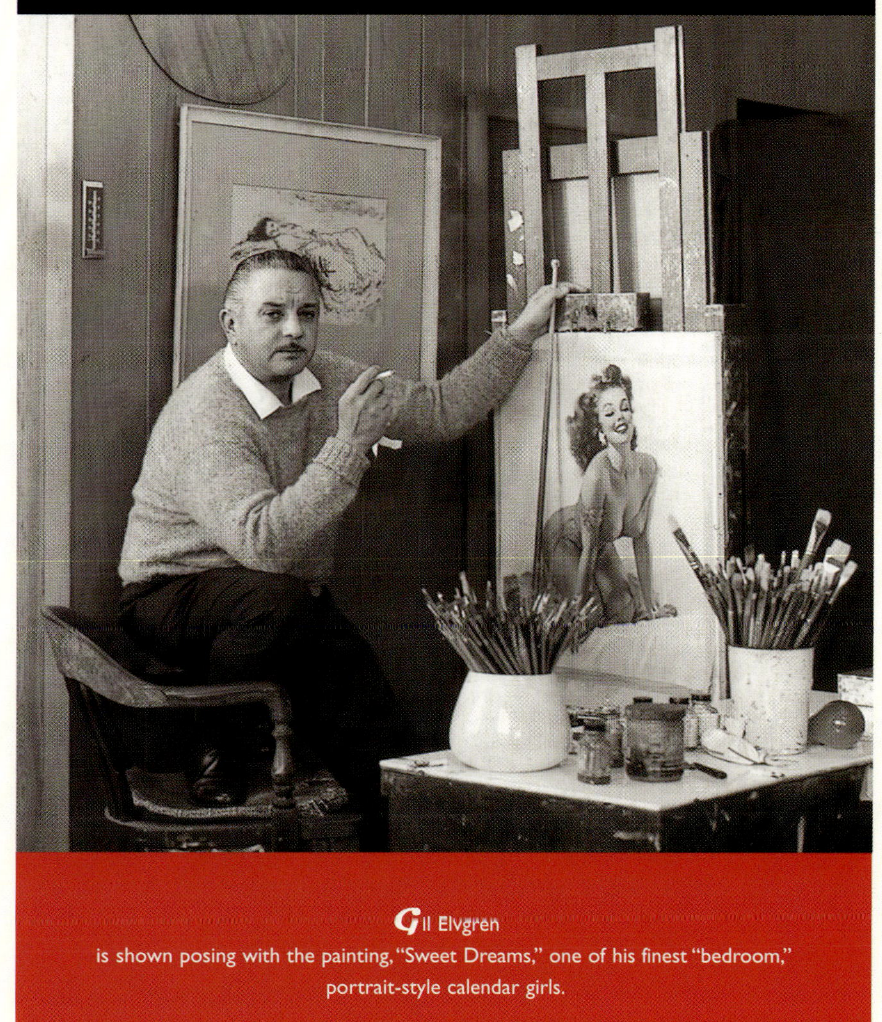

Gil Elvgren
is shown posing with the painting, "Sweet Dreams," one of his finest "bedroom," portrait-style calendar girls.

"I'm really a very lucky guy," Gil Elvgren was quoted as saying, at the height of his career. "I enjoy doing my paintings, and I think people like to see them. I can't think of anything I'd rather be doing." Gillette, Jr., playwright and distinguished educator, says his view of his father has always been "one of respect and admiration, with a dash of awe thrown in.... He had so many gifts." "Dad was not eccentric," he says, further reflecting on his father and his father's art. "He was practical. His artwork was commercial and essentially had a realistic patina about it... he never articulated his creations in terms of metaphor. A pretty, scantily clad girl standing on a scale — no abstractions here, no subtext, no theme — and the cultural statement often associated with his work, capturing the last gasps of an age of innocence, has been an interpretation made by others and only in hindsight. With Dad, what you see is what you get." To prove his point, Gil, Jr., mentions a portrait of a Eurasian girl, a partial nude, that received critical kudos in Chicago, early in his father's career. "The critics commented that the painting brought together the elements of East and West and so on and on. Dad's response, with a shake of his head, was 'all I did was paint what I saw.'" Whether Gil Elvgren had any intellectual grasp of what he created, however, is irrelevant, because what Gil Elvgren "saw" was sheer poetry. The romance of his idealized but not impossible "girls" wedded with an innate sense of design, color, and humorous storytelling elevates Elvgren to the first rank of American illustrators; and the nostalgia factor — that his calendars are associated with memories of barbershops, auto garages, and barracks, and with apple-cheeked Coca-Cola beauties beaming from billboards — assures him of a pop-cultural position not unlike that of, yes, Norman Rockwell. Elvgren, like Rockwell, is Americana; but it is Americana mixed lightly with erotica — an irresistible cocktail. Throughout his long career, Elvgren created many memorable images, and his relationships with several clients spanned decades — NAPA, the auto parts company, was a particularly dependable account, his "old reliable." His NAPA calendars, while featuring pretty girls, tended to have more detailed and specific backgrounds and thus hold a unique position in Elvgren's body of work. Another client of longstanding was Schmidt

On a visit to the Brown & Bigelow home office, Gil hunkers over a calendar image with art director Clair Fry.

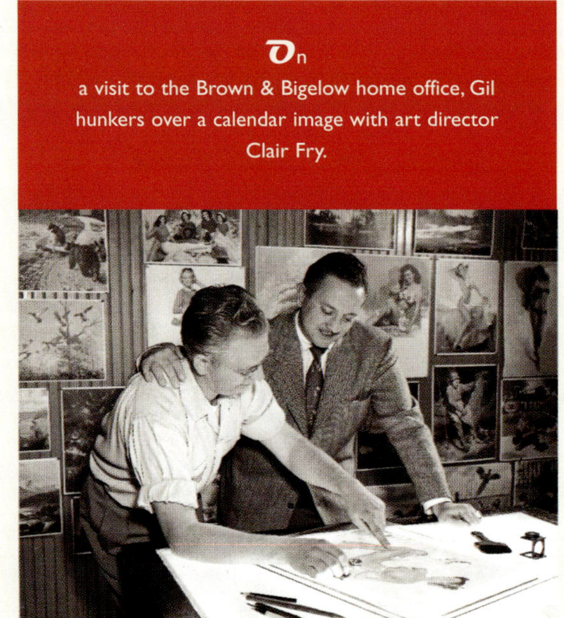

Lithograph, for whom he painted numerous "universal billboards" in the 1950s and 1960s. The printing firm, with major offices in Chicago and San Francisco, sold generic billboards, with a pretty Gil Elvgren girl (close-ups of faces for the most part) and a space for the advertiser to hawk its wares. Prolific as his work for these companies was, it is Elvgren's phenomenal output for Brown & Bigelow that represents his longest relationship with one company and his greatest contribution to pin-up art. In the mid-'40s, Brown & Bigelow, the giant among calendar companies, approached the artist on the basis of his Dow pin-ups, offering him a then-staggering $1,000 per painting. Elvgren began turning out around twenty calendar paintings a year, with specialized subjects—from nudes to cowgirls, from lingerie-wearing lovelies to prom queens—as Brown & Bigelow art director Clair Fry would direct him. (Elvgren only did a handful of nudes, because Brown & Bigelow eventually decided to back off from that subject matter, since they did so much business with church organizations.) "Gil had wit, not only with situations having a humorous turn," Fry told an interviewer, "but even more in the ingenuity and the inventiveness shown in his color schemes, poses, gestures, and all that goes into a lively, exciting statement that captures universal attention." Elvgren did have a wonderful, even wild imagination, and thought up many of the wry situations in his paintings. Nonetheless Elvgren would occasionally call on Fry to "get the gang up there" in St. Paul to help him come up with more scenarios for his "compromised cuties" paintings. And Elvgren rarely contributed to the various panel-cartoon-like, caption-style titles of the paintings; these came from Fry and the Brown & Bigelow staff. Fry—himself a talented illustrator, famed for his comical hobo paintings—considered Elvgren a cut above most commercial artists. "Gil's work was sincere and very honest," Fry told interviewer Larry Murphy. "The carefully thought-out gestures and expressions were done with such mastery that they conveyed the exact meaning Gil intended without the phony quality that exists in such a vast

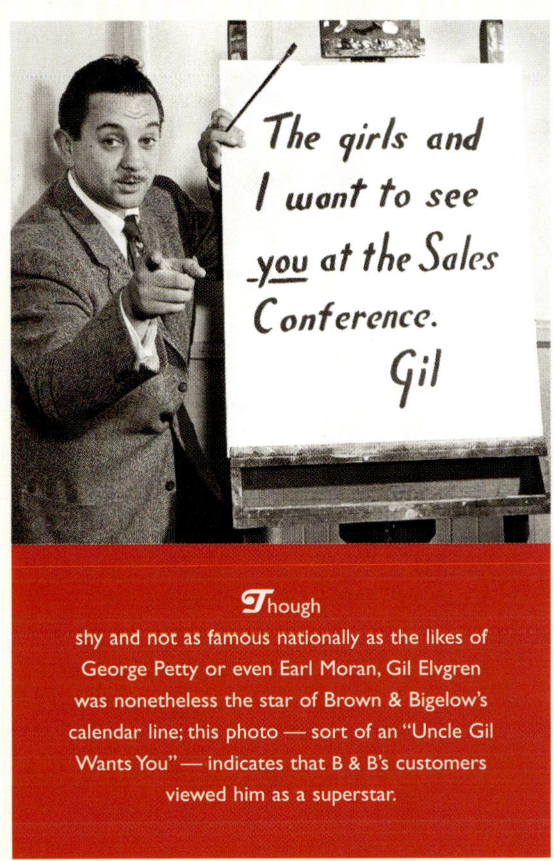

Though shy and not as famous nationally as the likes of George Petty or even Earl Moran, Gil Elvgren was nonetheless the star of Brown & Bigelow's calendar line; this photo — sort of an "Uncle Gil Wants You" — indicates that B & B's customers viewed him as a superstar.

percentage of commercial painting." Business letters to Elvgren from Fry—who was essentially his "boss"—read almost like fan letters (and most articles in national magazines on Elvgren, during his Brown & Bigelow days, include glowing testimonials from Fry referring to Elvgren's genius and surprisingly prescient opinions about the artist's secure position in mid-twentieth-century popular culture). In his letters to the artist, Fry frequently reported that "the Art Department" would gather around the latest batch of Elvgren paintings to "oooh and ahhh." "Much head shaking over how the hell a guy can be so good!" Fry told Elvgren in a 1946 letter.

But occasionally Elvgren would have to rework a painting, if it was too sexy, or not sexy enough. Now and then Fry would reluctantly forward letters of complaint about the sexier paintings. But as late as 1963, Fry was requesting that Elvgren make at least one painting per batch particularly sexy, depicting a subject "with bedroom eyes." "His relationship with Brown & Bigelow was tumultuous at times," Drake recalls, "but generally good, I think. Dad wasn't good at sticking to a schedule and was usually late with delivering paintings." Elvgren could be a procrastinator, particularly after he moved his studio to his home, and his correspondence with Fry shows the art director, however big a fan of Elvgren's he may have been, impatient with his star performer, and at times frantic, waiting for an overdue shipment of paintings.

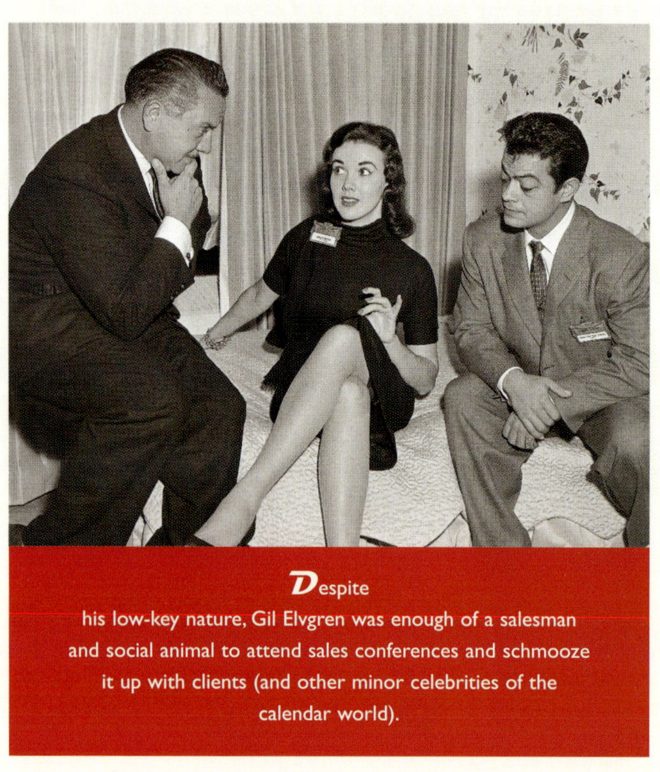

Despite his low-key nature, Gil Elvgren was enough of a salesman and social animal to attend sales conferences and schmooze it up with clients (and other minor celebrities of the calendar world).

"I remember one time, around 1954 or 1955," Drake says, "that Dad was very behind and worked really hard and finished about eight to ten paintings. He called Railway Express and told them to come by and pick up these four crates and deliver them to Brown & Bigelow in St. Paul. They asked if the paintings were to be insured and Dad replied, 'Yes—for $100,000.' Dad dreaded the idea of ever having to re-do a painting so he figured if they lost them, he might as well get paid well to re-do them." This was a huge sum in the mid-'50s and the next morning an armored truck arrived with two machine-gun-bearing guards, to pick up the crates of paintings. "We kids were very impressed," Drake says. Another bone of contention between Elvgren and his Brown & Bigelow bosses was their desire to show him off, to have him attend events and do publicity, which he abhorred. "Dad avoided these events," Drake says. "This was not the attitude that Brown & Bigelow wanted, but he was their golden boy of pin-ups and made them a lot of money, so they put up with it." Elvgren had a particularly good knack of creating a pin-up image that was at once a specific reference to a line of business inclined toward using calendars for advertising, and yet remained generic enough for any calendar customer's use. Often he would depict his sunny subjects in the midst of some do-it-yourself project, a beaming brunette with hammer in hand, a sweetly self-satisfied blonde building a birdhouse, images ideal for a hardware store calendar. Other Elvgren images depict nautical settings as wind-blown beauties attempt to climb a rope ladder from a boat onto a pier, perfect images for a calendar at a marine or boat shop. In "Cornered," a frustrated dream housewife — in an apron and a blue frock hiked over unhousewifely gartered nylons — has literally painted herself into a corner. Elvgren's use of red — on the partly painted floor, in the housewife's apron and her paint-spattered dress, on the paint can rim, and her lipstick and hair ribbon — is striking and bold and helps make "Cornered" the ideal image for a paint store calendar. And a paint store with an art department (like "Elvgren's" in St. Paul) might find the cherubic peasant-bloused blonde artist astride a make shift easel in "The Right Touch" just the right touch for the backroom wall. "Down Boy!" with its apple-cheeked brunette painting a pooch's portrait, would work equally well for that market. A vacuum cleaner shop would find appealing subject matter in the blonde of "What's Up?" who is hooked on a vacuum's phallic spout (despite his learned playwright son's speculation, Elvgren would seem at least loosely acquainted with metaphor). This distressed damsel is so pretty as to be nearly angelic and represents Elvgren's uncanny ability to take a

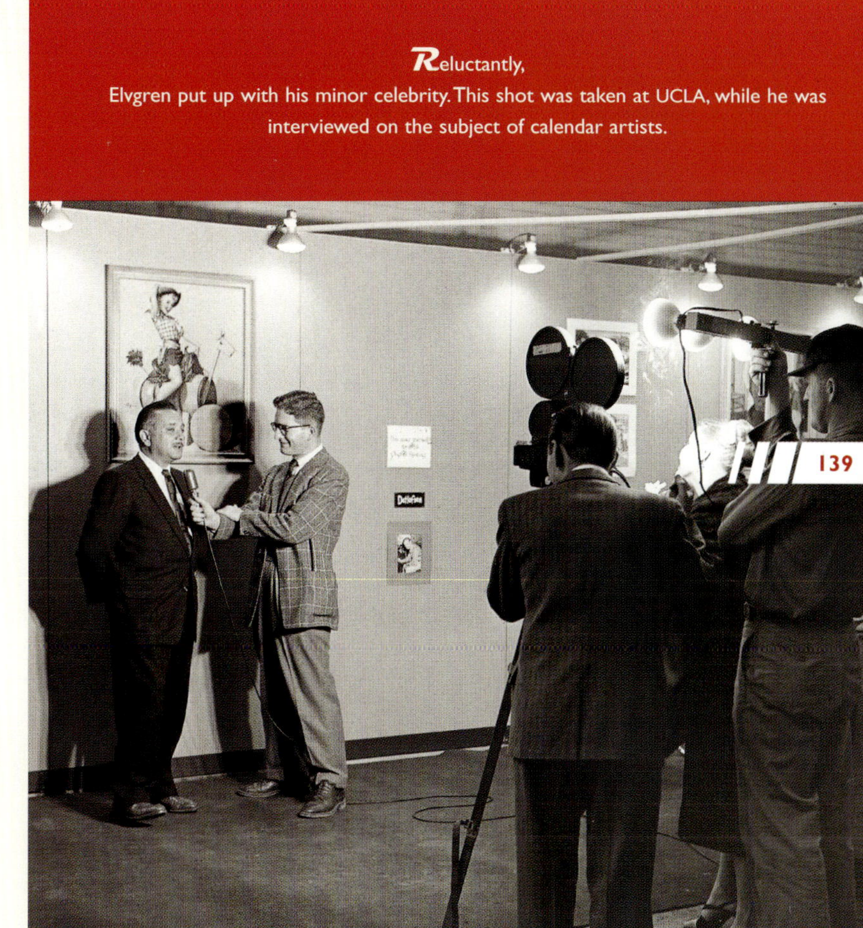

Reluctantly, Elvgren put up with his minor celebrity. This shot was taken at UCLA, while he was interviewed on the subject of calendar artists.

prosaic theme to unexpected lyrical heights. Elvgren (possibly with Clair Fry's guidance) cleverly chose subjects that tied into these various businesses and professions without making them so specific that the general public would lose interest. But the majority of Elvgren's calendar work had a more general feel and fell into two basic categories: cutely sexy and overtly sexy. Like many of the Dow paintings, the Brown & Bigelow images frequently depict an attractive young woman "in plight (oftentimes involving a piece of clothing)," as Gil, Jr., aptly puts it. "Pretty Please?" (also known as "Pretty Pleas") has a platinum blonde's dress caught in a locked steamer trunk, while her frisky pup keeps the key out of reach; the colorful touches of pinkish red on the girl's dress help draw the eye to her (as if the eye needed any help) in an image that, rather typically for Elvgren with his blondes, has an overall "blonde" look, with its tones of ivory highlighted by the gold clasps of the trunk. "A Shady Trick" finds a red-headed sweater girl mildly chagrined to discover her skirt has raised with the wicker shade she's been drawing; the almost shocking lime color of her sweater is echoed by the muted green of the phallic ferns in the background. Like many Elvgren girls, the redhead in "A Shady Trick" doesn't seem to mind, terribly, that her lovely legs have been exposed. One of the factors behind Elvgren's enduring appeal, it must be noted, is the fetishistic obsession with nylons and garters and frilly undergarments; the advent of pantyhose has added to the nostalgia value of many an Elvgren girl.

The redhead in "Partial Coverage" seems embarrassed to find that her red swimsuit is moth-eaten; but how embarrassed can she be, when she's already undressed for us? And in "Fit to be Tied," a redhead's sarong has either come undone or needs doing up — either way, she's neither embarrassed nor shy about seeking some off-camera volunteer's aid. As charming as the compromised-cuties paintings are, Elvgren seems at his best when he's being the least coy. "Enchanted," a rare full nude, combines Elvgren's love of the outdoors with his mastery of the female form; truly lyrical, this painting walks a narrow line between commercial and fine art. "Rest Assured," a softly lighted painting from the early '50s, depicts its lovely subject in a sheer nightie; this is straightforward, yet wholesome erotica, with nothing coquettish about full-bodied beauty. By the late '50s, Elvgren was bolder in depicting his lingerie-wearing subjects, and his subjects were equally bold in addressing the "camera" with unequivocal sexual invitation. The lights aren't down low in "Mona," and a woman like this — Mona isn't a "girl" exactly — is proud of her pulchritude, posing openly here. Yet even in these more straightforwardly sexual images, Elvgren seems to respect his subjects; whether they are innocent girls whose charms are betrayed by a naughty gust of wind, or worldly women who are pleased to display their attributes, they remain steadfastly "nice." "They do not," Elvgren insisted, "look like kept women."

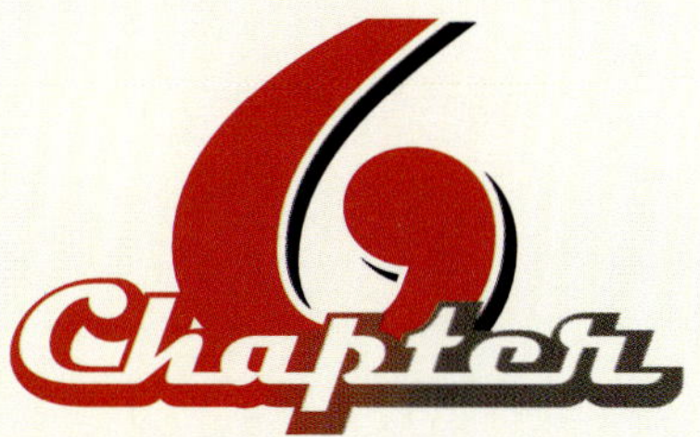

Friends and Rivals

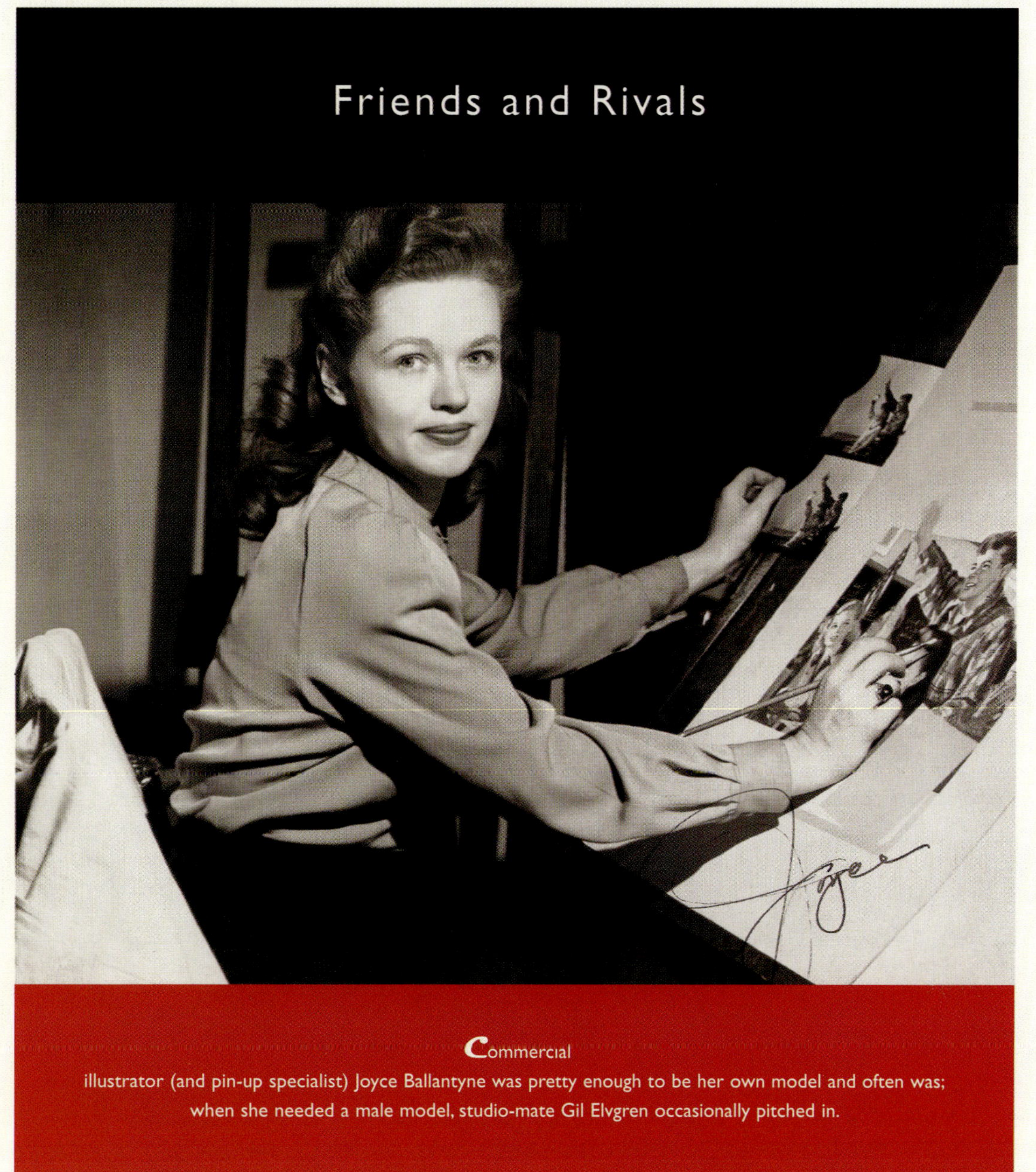

Commercial illustrator (and pin-up specialist) Joyce Ballantyne was pretty enough to be her own model and often was; when she needed a male model, studio-mate Gil Elvgren occasionally pitched in.

Working first in the Sundblom-dominated Stevens-Gross studio, and later for Brown & Bigelow, Gil Elvgren met (and sometimes worked with) a number of his contemporaries among pin-up artists. In addition, he influenced an entire school of pin-up artists who used similar technique and subject matter, as well as shared with Elvgren the medium of oils. At Brown & Bigelow, Elvgren's only real rival in popularity and significance was Earl Moran (1893–1984); however, Moran—who preceded Elvgren at Brown & Bigelow and was an established presence in the pin-up field prior even to Elvgren's Dow work—rarely worked in oil. Moran was a master of pastels, though he showed little if any influence of reigning Brown & Bigelow star Rolf Armstrong, whose domain he encroached upon in the '30s. Prolific Moran, Iowa-born, a Chicago Art Institute attendee, created lively, sexy girls whose relationship with the viewer was seldom a teasing one. If he outshines Elvgren in any way, it would be that Moran did not continually re-work a few types of situations, and his pin-ups have more variety than any other major contributor to the field. (He is also far more uneven than Elvgren, whose consistent quality amazed Brown & Bigelow art director Clair Fry.) Breaking in via advertising work for Sears, Roebuck & Company, Moran went on to magazine illustration (*Life*), movie posters (*Something for the Boys*, 1944) and even co-published an early "girlie" magazine, *Beauty Parade*, contributing covers (sometimes under his middle-name *nom de plume*, "Steffa"). His most enduring pin-ups feature his famous late '40s model, Marilyn Monroe. In his later career—perhaps influenced by Elvgren's dominance of the dying pin-up field—he turned to oils and, working from the late '50s until his death, created an outstanding series of sensual nudes for galleries and private individuals. In the early '40s, while still working for Dow, Elvgren began teaching at his alma mater. One of his best students at the American Academy of Art was Joyce Ballantyne, who later assisted him on paintings even while turning out some of the finest non-Elvgren Sundblom-school pin-ups herself. Elvgren's other apprentices include Harry Ekman and Bobby Toombs, both of whose work, at its best, approached Elvgren's. "Joyce Ballantyne worked at Stevens-Gross with Dad," Drake recalls. "She was also a pin-up artist and a beautiful redhead, and became a close friend of the family. Joyce often tells of the time when she was too sick to complete a commission on time. Dad painted it for her, duplicating her style, and no one ever was the wiser." Nebraska-born Ballantyne is a noteworthy member of the small "girl's club" among pin-up artists. Like pastel queen Zoë Mozert, another Brown & Bigelow star, Ballantyne captured a fresh, real sensuality in her subjects, and a palpable Elvgren-like sense of fun. Ballantyne's women were often depicted in a looser, more natural fashion than the studiously coy poses of her male counterparts, Elvgren included. She was (and probably still is) as attractive as a pin-up herself—strawberry blonde, green-eyed, and frequently barefoot. The vivid oils of advertising artist Ballantyne (Coppertone's little girl whose bathing suit is being tugged off by a playful puppy is hers) are among the very few that, at their best, rival Elvgren, and Drake's reminiscence partly confirms stories that Joyce at times assisted Elvgren when he was under the deadline gun. "Gil was a sincere, decent, warm, lovable man with a phenomenal talent," Ballantyne told an interviewer recently. "His paintings were relaxed and flowing—they had a timeless quality.... I loved Gil. We all did!" Just as Ballantyne occasionally posed for Elvgren, so did the artist pose for her, when a male figure was needed. "Harry Ekman was an apprentice to my father for a while in Winnetka," Drake says. "I remember him as a man with a quick, bright smile and a good sense of humor." Chicago artist Ekman worked side by side with fellow Sundblom shop veteran, Gil Elvgren, developing a lush style in oils that could be, at times, uncannily like that of his mentor. His own work appeared under both the Brown & Bigelow imprint and Shaw-Barton. Like Elvgren, Ekman specialized in calendars but also worked in advertising. Ekman's girls have the same fresh, wholesome glow as Elvgren's and are seen in such typical Elvgren-ish situations as bicycling, wading, and walking the dog. It has been speculated that Ekman may even have "ghosted" certain Elvgren-signed paintings, and while Drake adamantly asserts that no apprentice was ever allowed to touch his father's paintings, Eckman certainly was a gifted, if uneven, pupil. Bobby Toombs was living in Sarasota, Florida, doing large-head, small-body caricatures when Elvgren took him on as an apprentice. "I don't know if Dad came to him," Drake says, "or he came to Dad. But he wanted to be a real artist.... He had an easel in Dad's studio over the carport at our house. He would paint, and Dad would critique it." Elvgren was honest to a fault with his pupil, and Drake remembers Toombs sometimes taking the criticism badly and storming out. But Toombs always came back, after mulling over the master's words, and got back to work. "Bobby and his wife Rose were good friends to the family," Drake continues. "He learned well and became a very accomplished artist. Dad had seen his talent and knew that he had to be honest with him for him to learn. He did." Toombs, who did calendars for Louis Dow and Elvgren standby, NAPA, still produces extraordinary pin-ups from his Florida studio, and has evolved an Elvgren-influenced style that is nevertheless strikingly his own, a soft-focus, slightly more impressionistic approach than that of his teacher. Bill Medcalf has been assumed (by co-author Collins, among others) to be another Sundblom-shop graduate, and indeed his work is on occasion confused with Elvgren's. Medcalf did not study with Sundblom or assist Elvgren, however; instead, Elvgren was a role model, thus explaining the close resemblance. Though not as prolific (nor nearly as well-known) as Elvgren, Medcalf is perhaps the master's nearest equal, turning out lushly rendered oil paintings of gorgeous all-American girls, mostly for Brown & Bigelow, who seemed to view him as their "second" Elvgren. Medcalf's work turns up on calendars, both in girl next door tease situations and in the glamorous ball-gown genre, though he seems to have primarily devoted himself to providing pin-up girls to top advertising accounts, including Sylvania ("Miss Sylvania"—a one-time Elvgren client), Kelly Springfield Tires, and Elvgren's mainstay, NAPA. Walt Otto is another of the Elvgren-style pin-up artists, creating beaming American beauties in lushly painted oils on canvas. Despite a hyper-realistic, skillfully illustrational style typical of the Elvgren school, Otto's paintings contain cartoonier elements, particularly in the expressions of his winsome girls. An Otto girl—typically attired in short shorts or a swimming suit, occasionally tugged along by a cute mutt or two—stares unabashedly at the viewer. Petty-style line-drawing props and backgrounds further lend a cartoony feel to Otto's wonderful pin-ups. One of Elvgren's closest friends among his "rivals" was Albert Leslie Buell, who worked with Elvgren in the Sundblom shop in Chicago. His oils are among the best pin-ups in that medium, although existing originals (on board, not canvas) are much smaller than those of Elvgren, Ballantyne, and Ekman. Perhaps that explains a certain delicacy in his work; Buell's pretty girls really are "pretty." These girls next door are captured in typically girlish pursuits such as sewing, playing tennis, or swinging in a swing. Underclad as they are, Buell's girls have a wholesomeness, an ingenuousness, rare in the pin-up form. In some paintings (usually under his "Al Leslie" pseudonym, used when he was moonlighting from Brown & Bigelow), Buell strayed into the area of embarrassed coy cuties, often accompanied by cute puppies who inadvertently caused skirts to be raised. "Al Buell and his wife Ruth were longtime friends of the family," Drake reports. "Al used to paint pin-ups for Brown & Bigelow, but quit that when he became a Christian. He did magazine illustrations and later did mainly limited edition prints." Before an injury in 1993, Buell continued to paint commissions—portraits and landscapes. Edward Runci, like Medcalf, is an outstanding but unfortunately little-known or talked-about master of pin-ups in oil. His luxuriant brush strokes reveal a talent and skill comparable to Elvgren, though Runci apparently is not a graduate of the Sundblom shop. A World War II vet with combat experience, Runci was a portrait artist in Hollywood, California, when he was approached by a calendar company to do pin-ups. Runci's early '50s girls are rosy-cheeked, voluptuous, often blonde Marilyn Monroe types whose wholesome sensuality radiates off the canvas, even as they frequently get caught in Elvgren-ish compromising situations—climbing a fence to flee a bull, dress blowing up on a Ferris wheel ride. Another master technician in oils, versatile Art Frahm—yet another Chicago area artist and a likely Sundblom-shop graduate—can, at his best, compare favorably with Elvgren. But his significance comes out of his defining roles in two seemingly opposite pin-up categories. Frahm was known for his discreetly glamorous calendar girls, perfectly coifed, daringly décolletage-dressed, prom-date beauties aglow in the midst of romantic soft-focus settings, a pin-up sub-genre Elvgren himself occasionally dabbled in. But Frahm—whose commercial art ranged from magazine cover illustration to zany "hobo" calendar paintings—also excelled in (and perhaps created) the campily sexist "embarrassment" series for publisher A. Fox, in which a lovely girl is literally caught with her panties down, her lacy undies slipping to her ankles while she's in the process of bowling, walking the dog, or changing a tire. Gil Elvgren would never think of pushing taste to such limits, and Frahm's kitchsy paintings are virtual parodies of the master's cutely compromised beauties. Elvgren-style pin-up artist Edward D'Ancona worked out of Chicago and is probably yet another graduate of the influential Sundblom shop. Certainly his painterly style, with its lush brush strokes and warm colors, as well as the girl next door beauty of his subjects, suggests a close linkage to both Elvgren and Sundblom. A prolific contributor of calendar-girl art to numerous companies, D'Ancona's earliest works appear to have been for Elvgren alma mater, Louis F. Dow; these are stiff, even awkward pin-ups. Later, an improved D'Ancona landed advertising accounts, including several soft-drink firms that capitalized on his Sundblom-like style, so identified with Coca-Cola. By the early '50s, when he joined the ranks of Art Frahm and Edward Runci in painting glamour girls in gowns, he was among the handful of pin-up artists who could hold their own with Elvgren. Though by the mid-'50s Elvgren was clearly its star, Brown & Bigelow had an impressive stable of pin-up artists, many of them following not Elvgren's lead, but that of Earl MacPherson, who began the famous Brown & Bigelow "Sketchbook" series. These artists—Bill Randall, Ted Withers, K.O. Munson, and Freeman Eliot, among others—worked in media other than oil, for the most part pastel and/or gouache, and while they often followed Elvgren's pattern of compromised cuties, they worked more in the tradition of Moran and MacPherson. Only the final successor to MacPherson in the "Sketchbook" series borrowed from Elvgren's technique, and joined the short list of his true rivals: Fritz Willis, perhaps the last major pin-up artist of the Golden Age, and the only one truly reflecting the sexual revolution. Primarily known for depicting brazenly sensual '60s women in semi-nude array, Willis's work has a surface similarity to that of Elvgren, the sexy but innocent girls of the latter having little to do with the wanton women of the former. Oklahoma-born Willis had a distinguished career in magazine illustration—his clients including *Collier's*, *Redbook*, and *The Saturday Evening Post*—and his association with *Esquire* made him one of that magazine's earliest entries in its ultimately vain attempt to create a new Petty or Varga. From the beginning he combined a fashion-model look with the busty, long-legged pin-up queen, combining sophistication with sex appeal. While Elvgren worked until 1980, it is no mistake that his reputation is bound to the 1950s. The Rockwell of Cheesecake represented a more innocent time, and it took the more sophisticated women of Fritz Willis to temporarily bridge the generation gap. The swingin' '60s and free love (not to mention *Playboy* and *Penthouse*) were not compatible with the girls next door of Elvgren; and Willis represented the last, somewhat desperate gasp, of the classic pin-up.

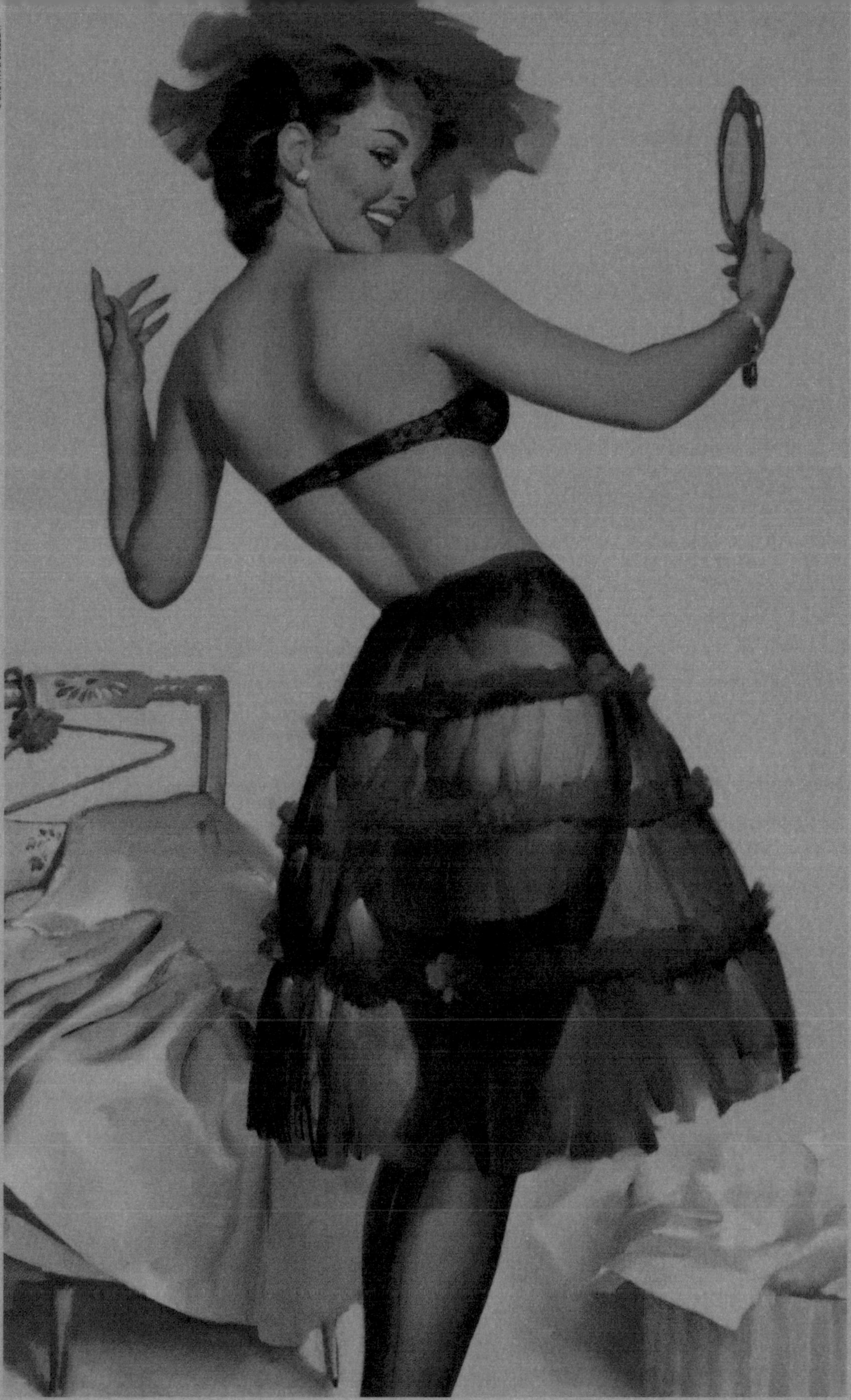

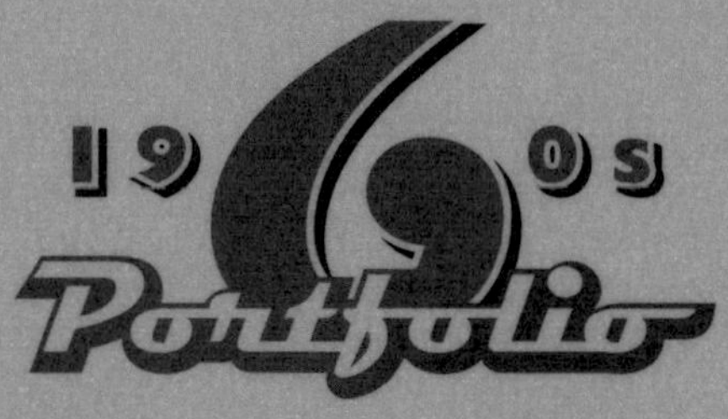
1960s
Portfolio

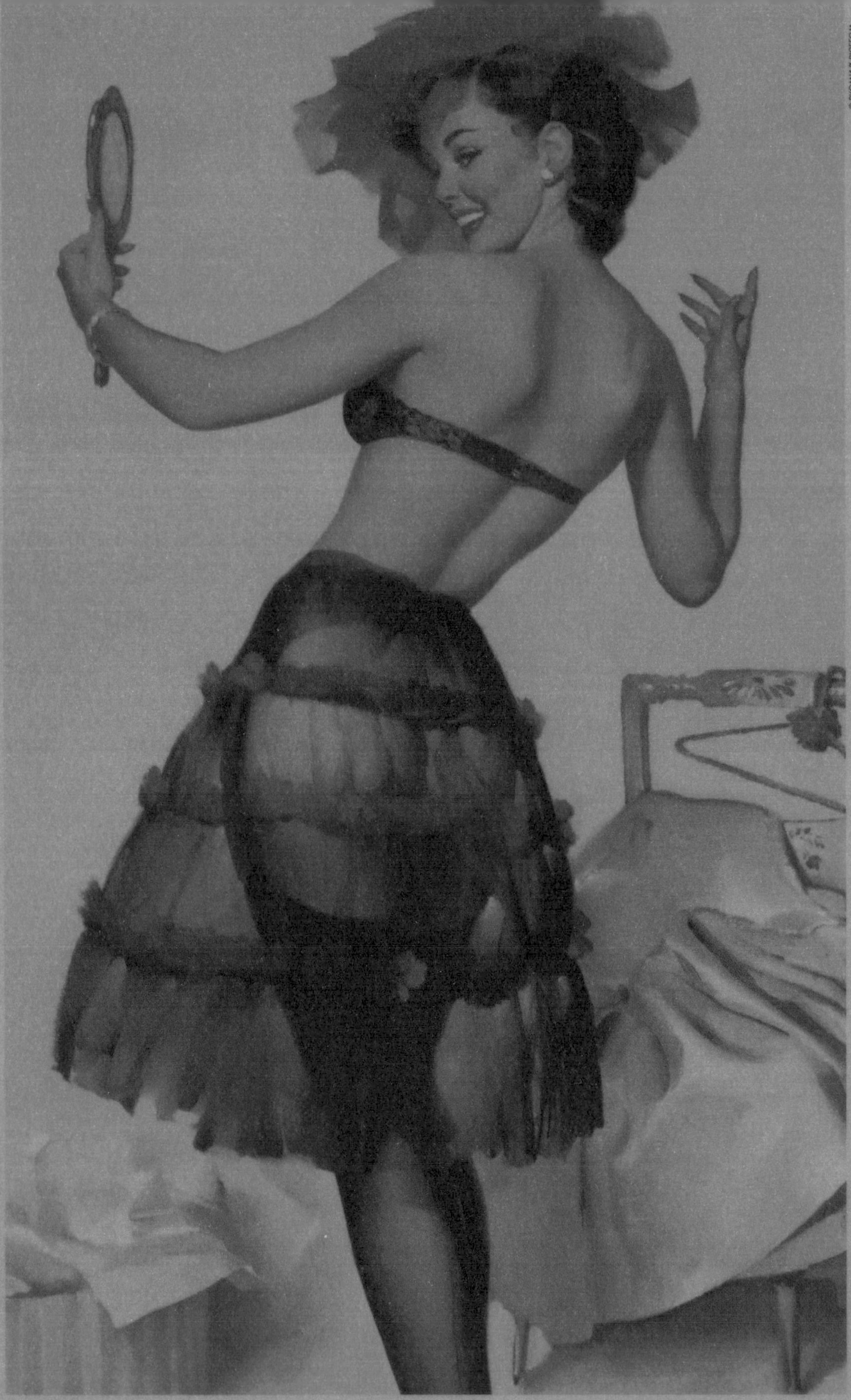

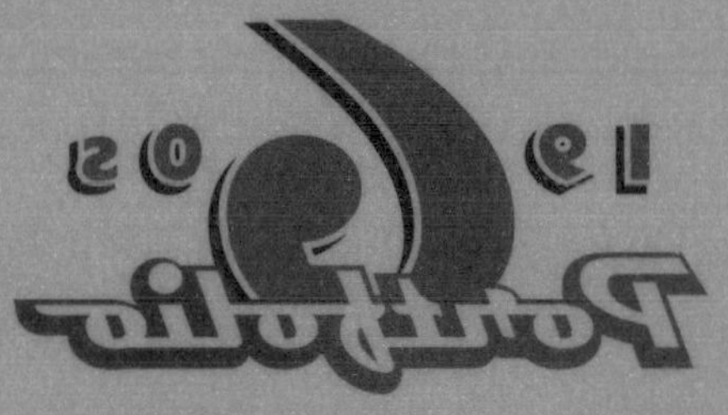
1950s
Portfolio

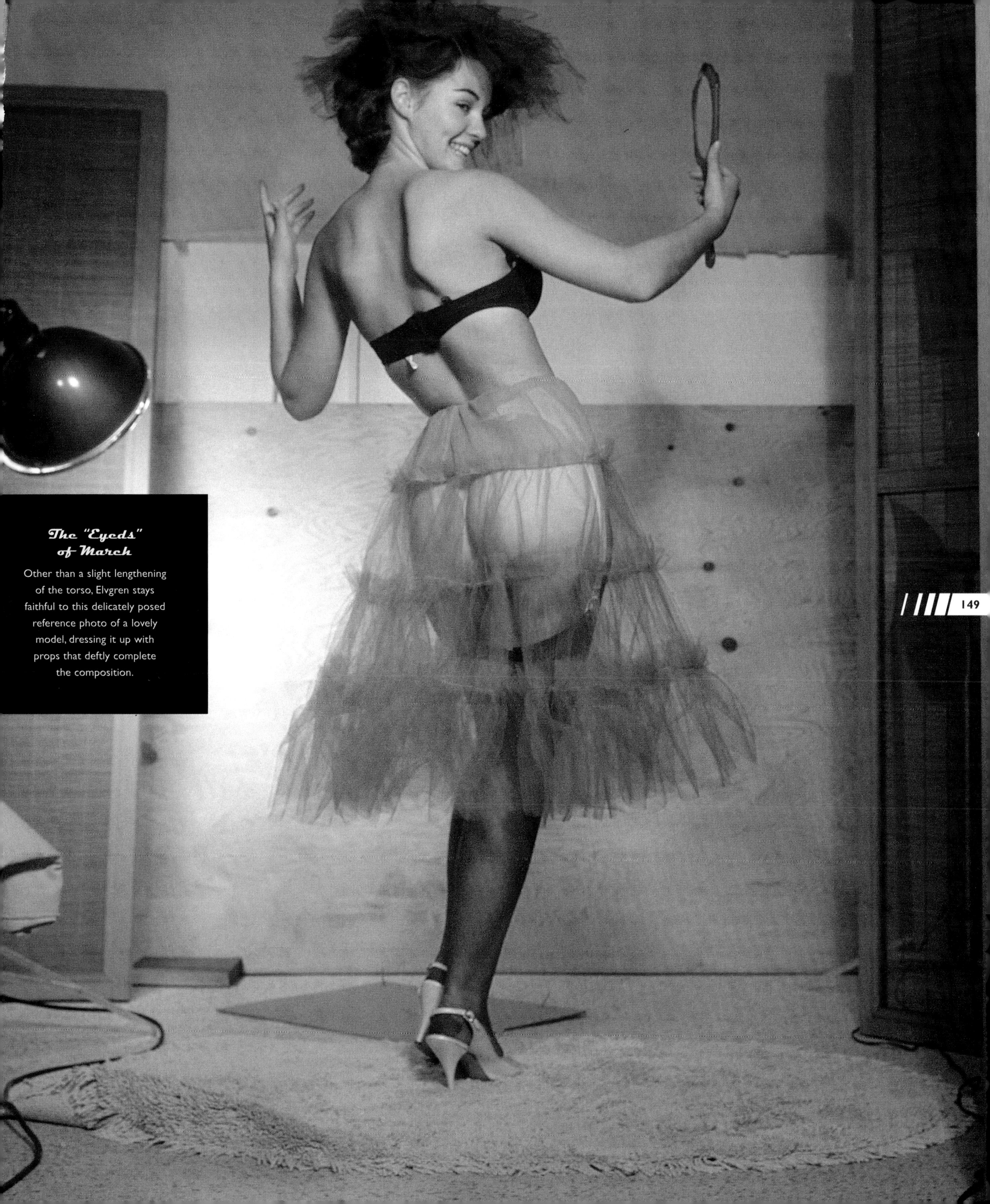

The "Eyeds" of March

Other than a slight lengthening of the torso, Elvgren stays faithful to this delicately posed reference photo of a lovely model, dressing it up with props that deftly complete the composition.

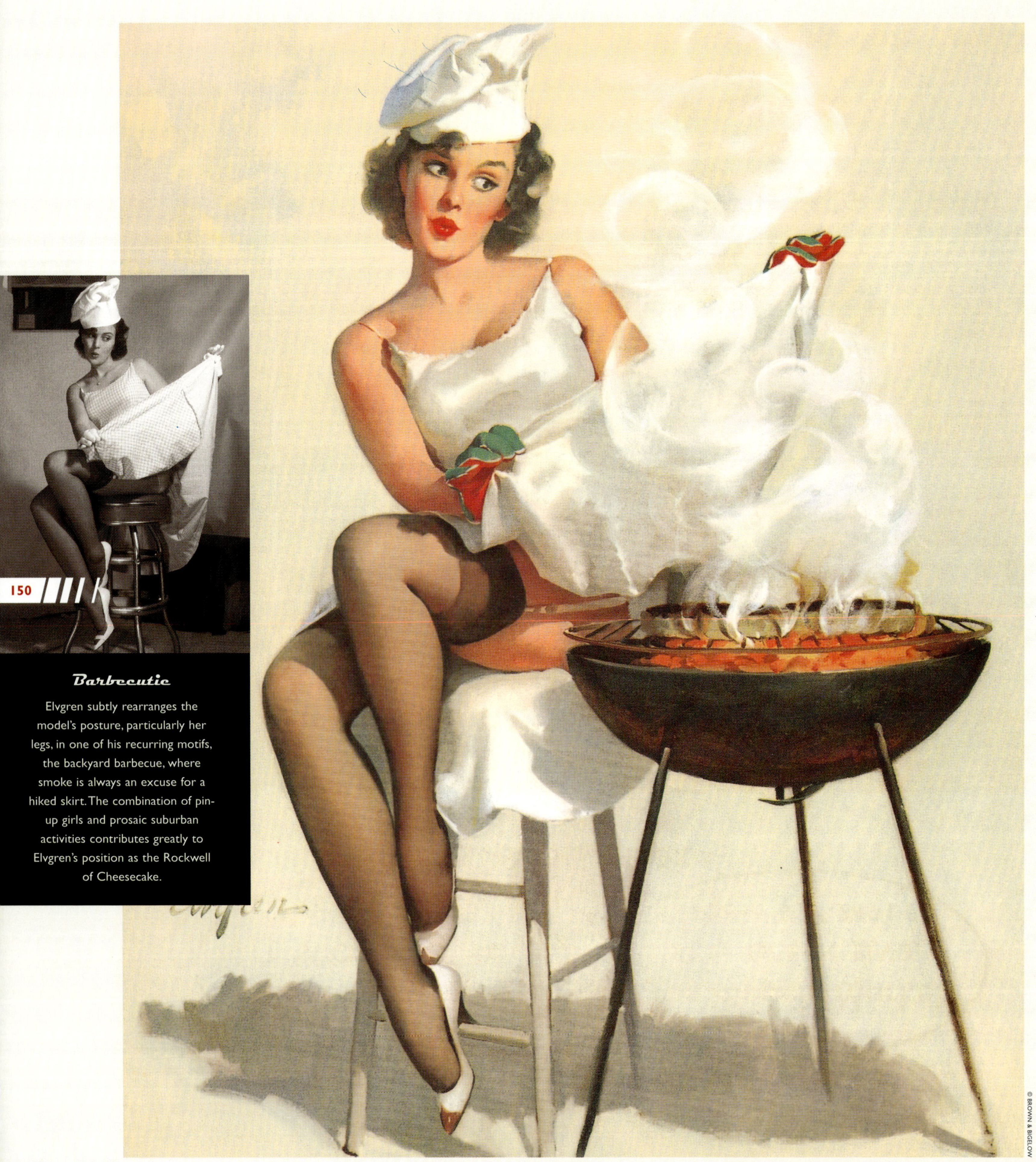

Barbecutie

Elvgren subtly rearranges the model's posture, particularly her legs, in one of his recurring motifs, the backyard barbecue, where smoke is always an excuse for a hiked skirt. The combination of pin-up girls and prosaic suburban activities contributes greatly to Elvgren's position as the Rockwell of Cheesecake.

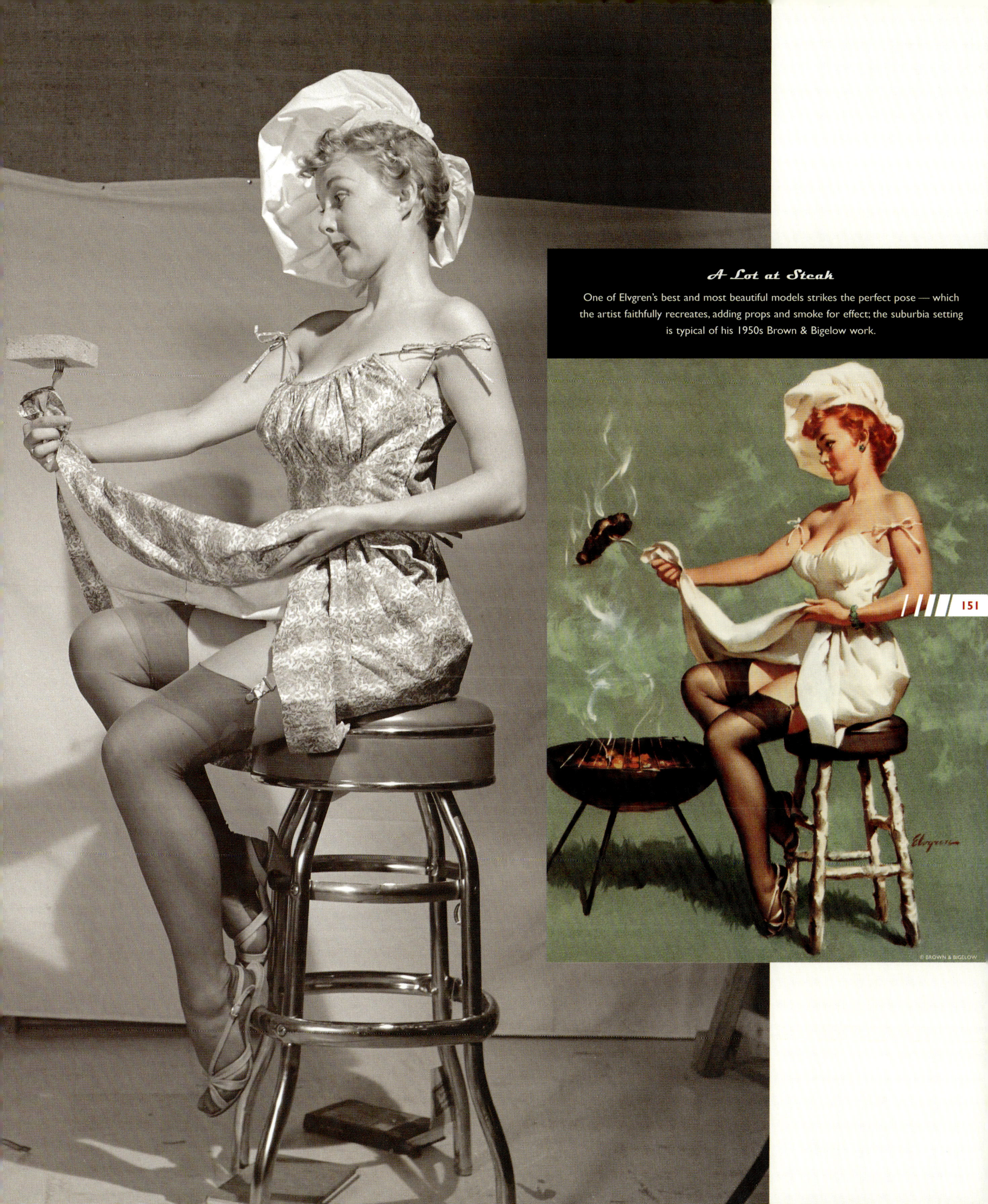

A Lot at Steak

One of Elvgren's best and most beautiful models strikes the perfect pose — which the artist faithfully recreates, adding props and smoke for effect; the suburbia setting is typical of his 1950s Brown & Bigelow work.

Keyed Up

The toy 'gator provides an outlandishly comic, even cartoon-like, touch to this late Brown & Bigelow image; for once the model (possibly, nude-magazine model Rusty Allen) is bustier than the pin-up version and truly seems an Elvgren girl come to life.

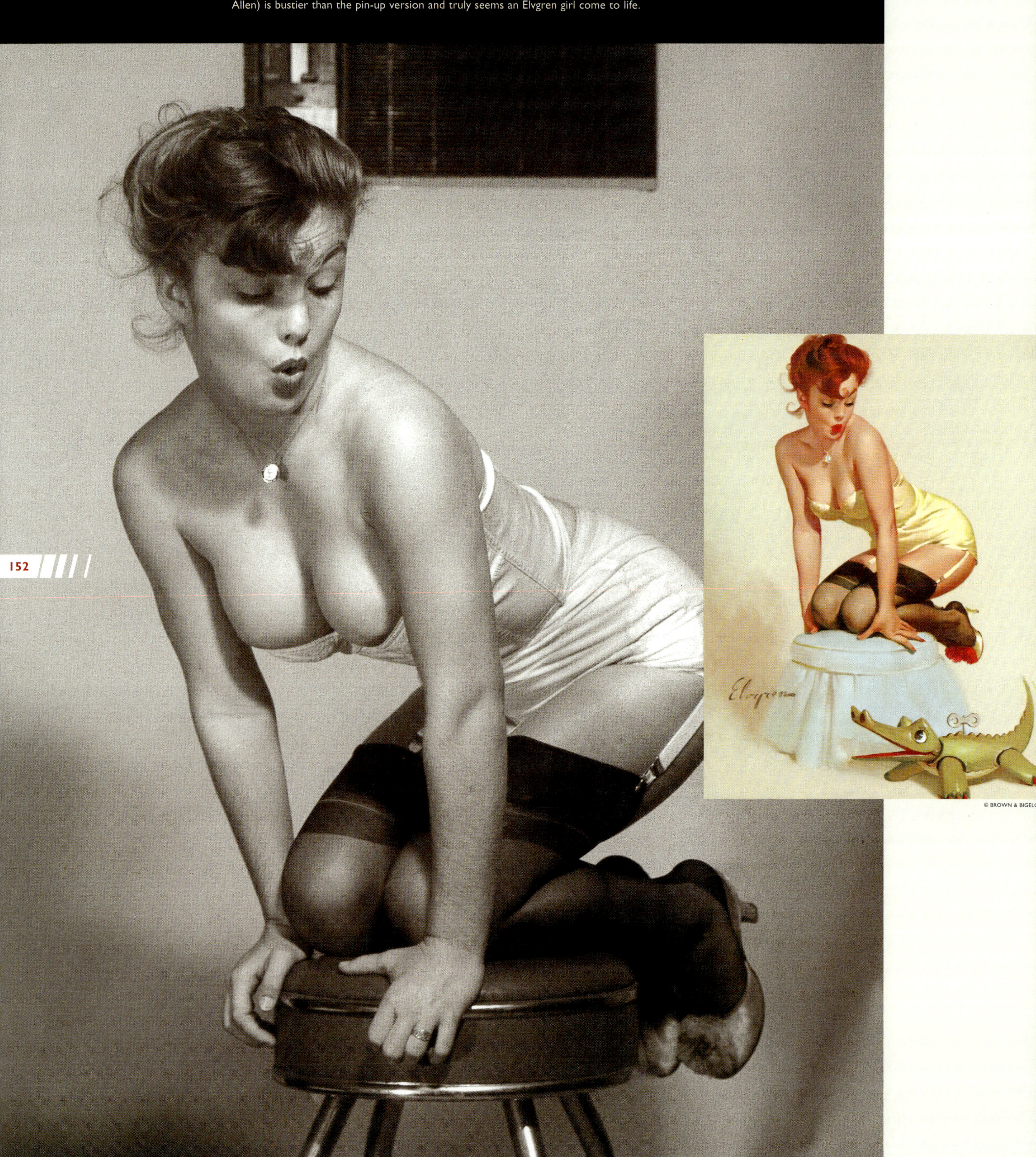

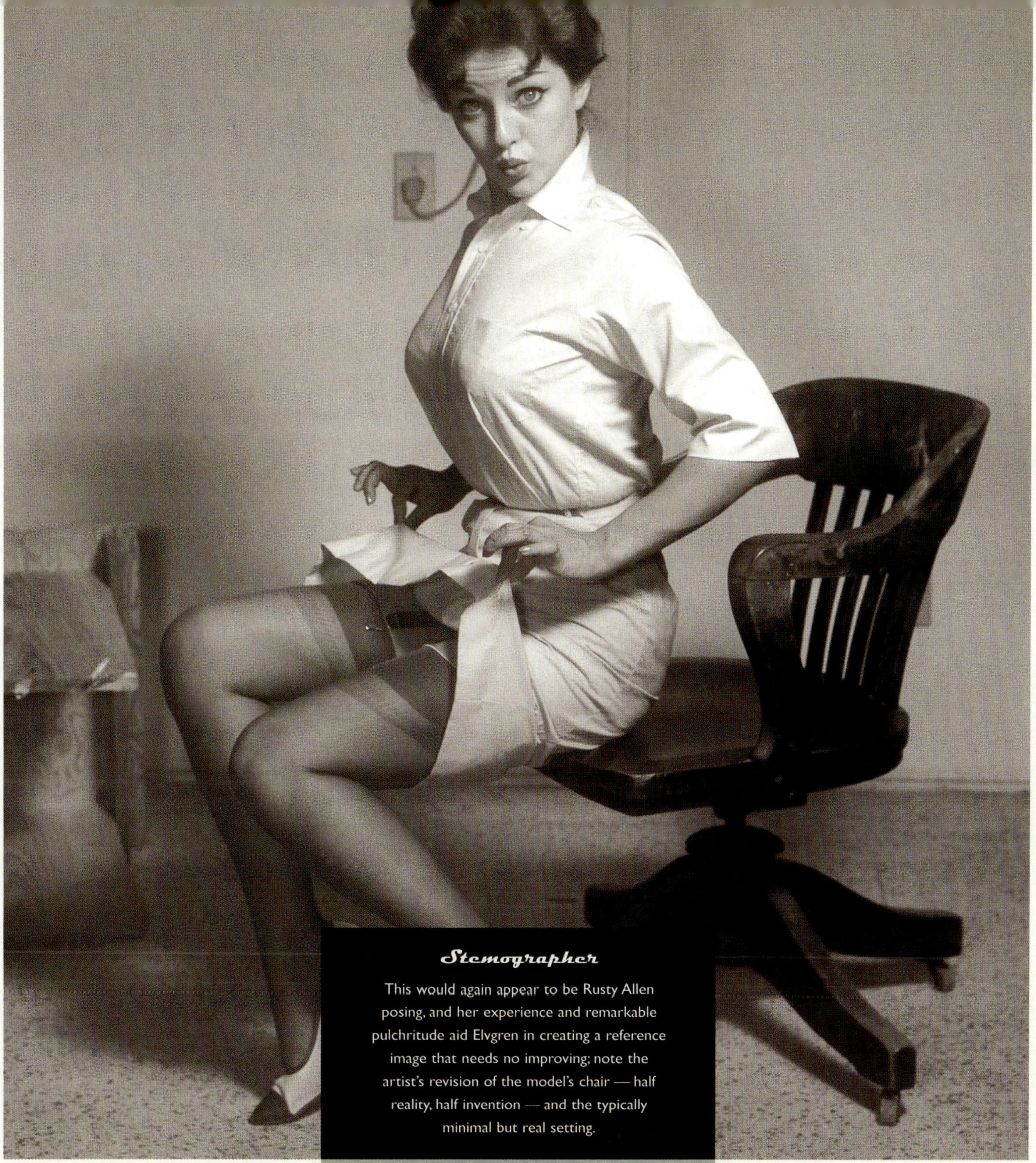

Stenographer

This would again appear to be Rusty Allen posing, and her experience and remarkable pulchritude aid Elvgren in creating a reference image that needs no improving; note the artist's revision of the model's chair — half reality, half invention — and the typically minimal but real setting.

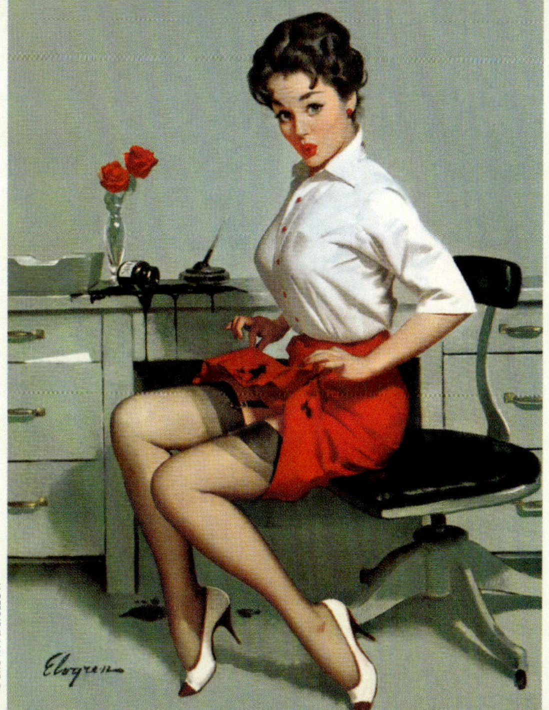

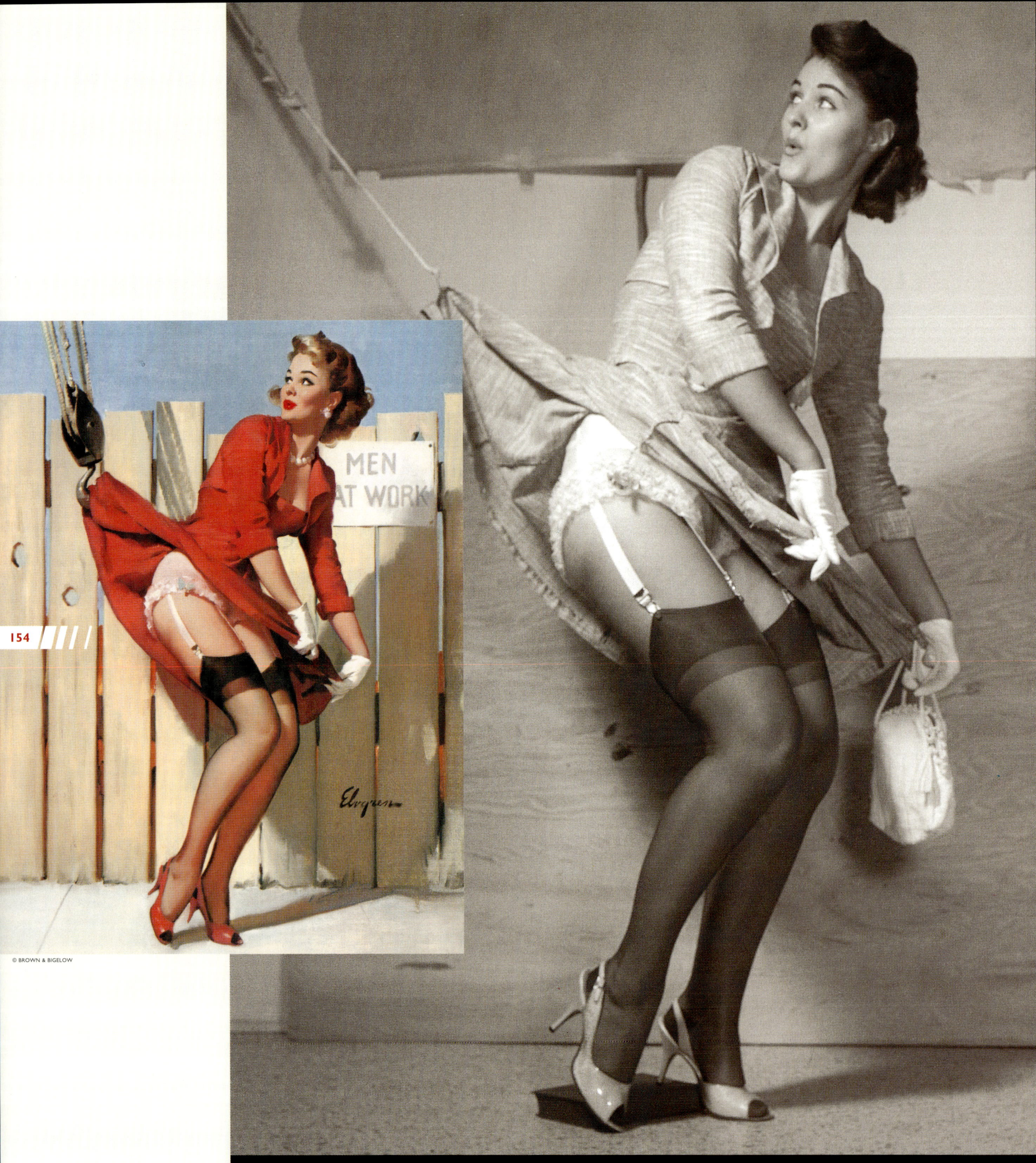

Unexpected Lift

The comical, almost cartoon-like compromising situation is an Elvgren staple; note how an attractive brunette model is transformed into a dazzling blonde.

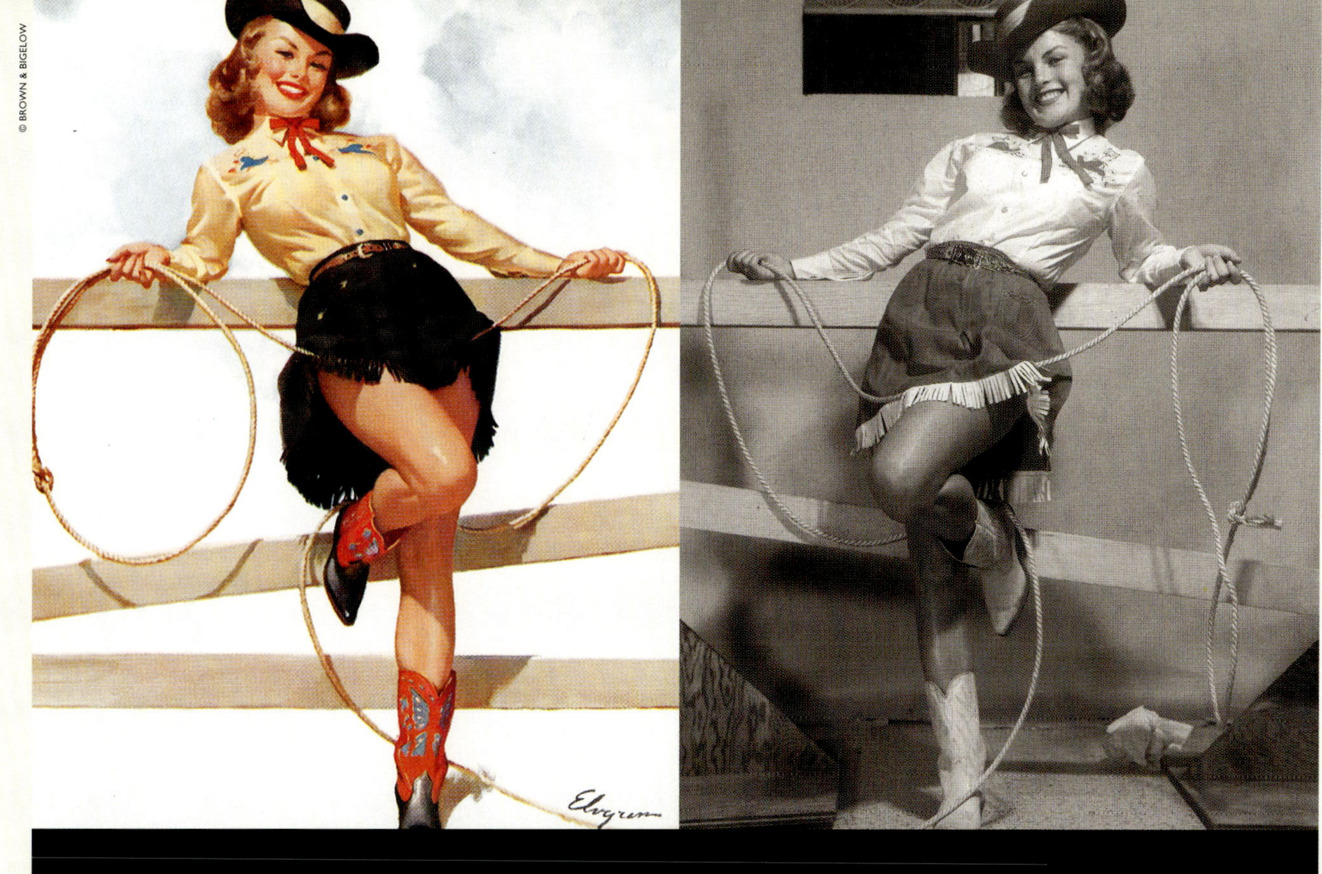

Ready for Roundup

Elvgren's cowgirls are probably his most popular pin-ups; design elements such as the circular lasso and the angular fence slats help center attention on the subject (not that she needs help).

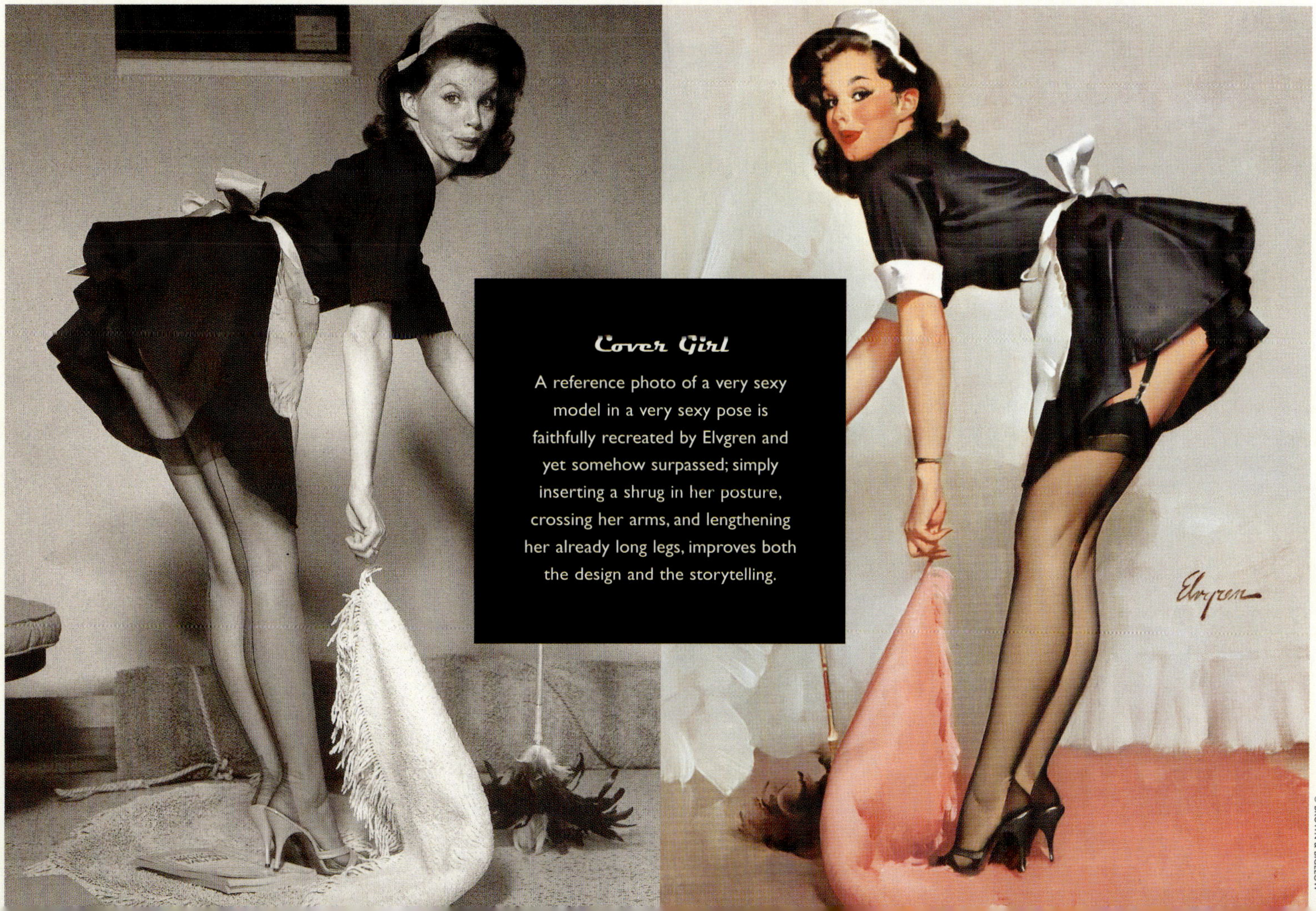

Cover Girl

A reference photo of a very sexy model in a very sexy pose is faithfully recreated by Elvgren and yet somehow surpassed; simply inserting a shrug in her posture, crossing her arms, and lengthening her already long legs, improves both the design and the storytelling.

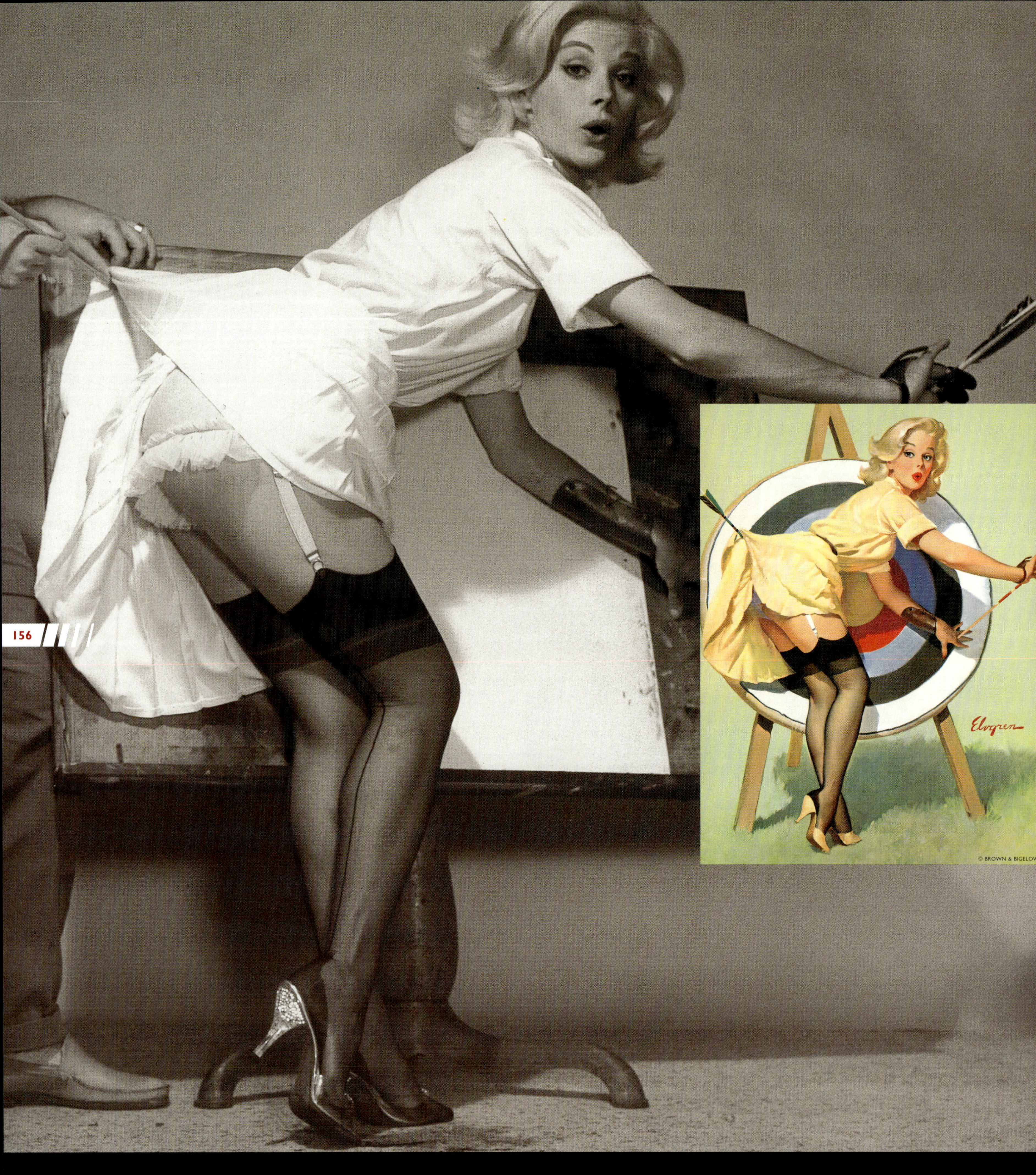

A Near Miss

Wish You Were Near

By the 1960s, his suburban fantasy slipping away, Elvgren frequently went for more straightforwardly erotic material; this very young model, as stunningly lovely as the pin-up itself, situated in bed, wishing her man were with her, would have been unthinkable a few years before.

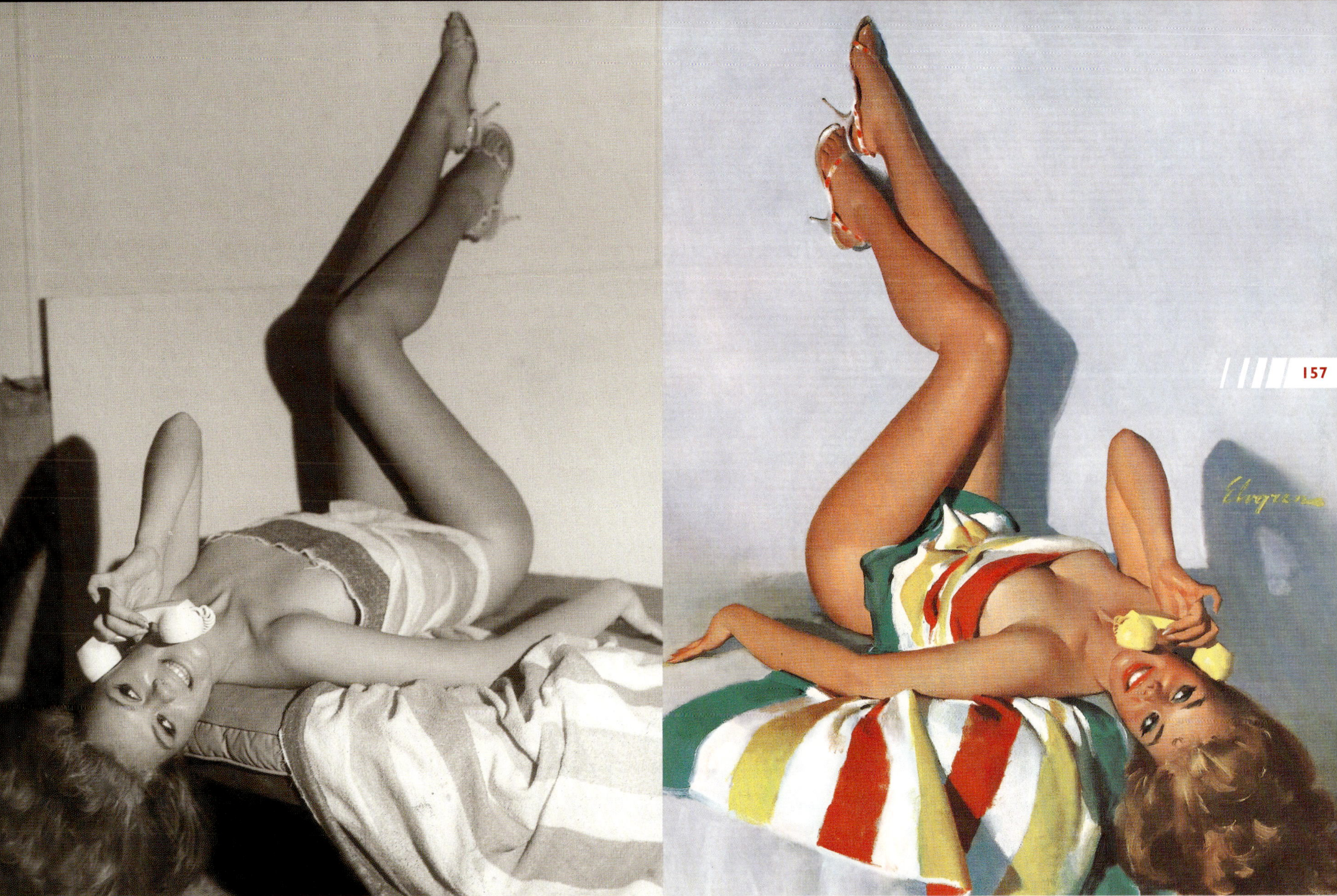

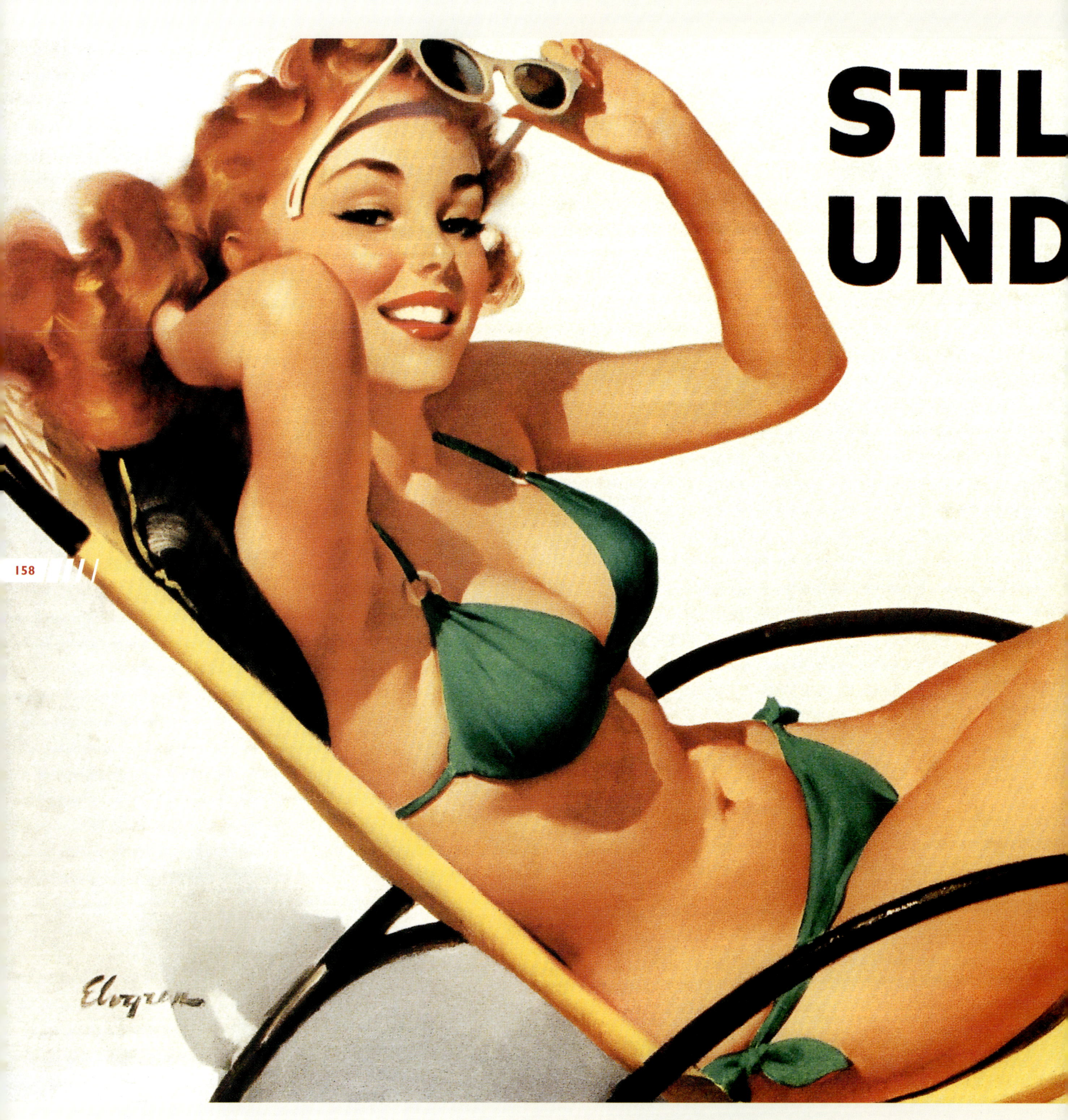

STIL
UND

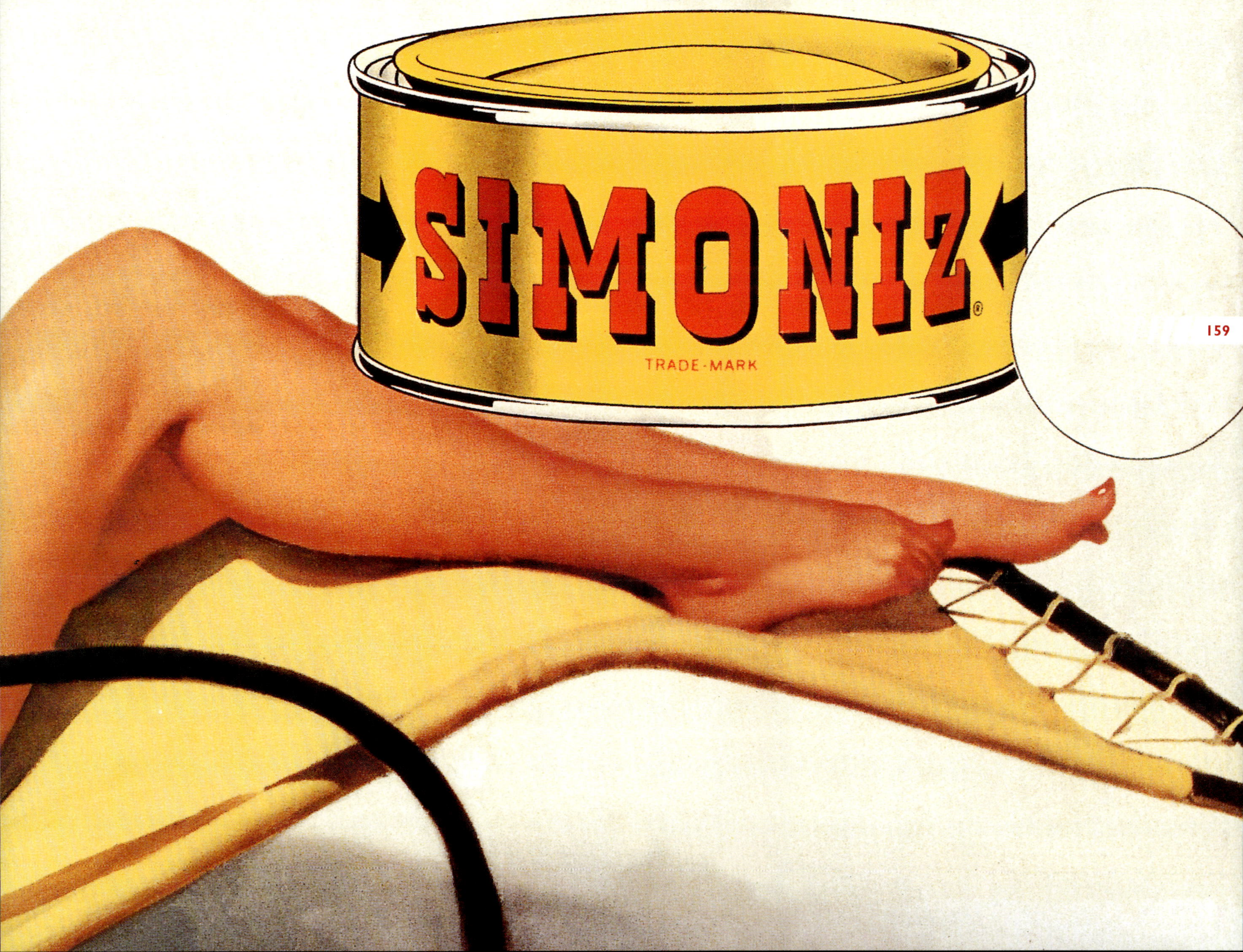

This is an outrageously sexy pin-up girl for a mainstream American ad; men all over America must have had the sudden urge to Simonize!

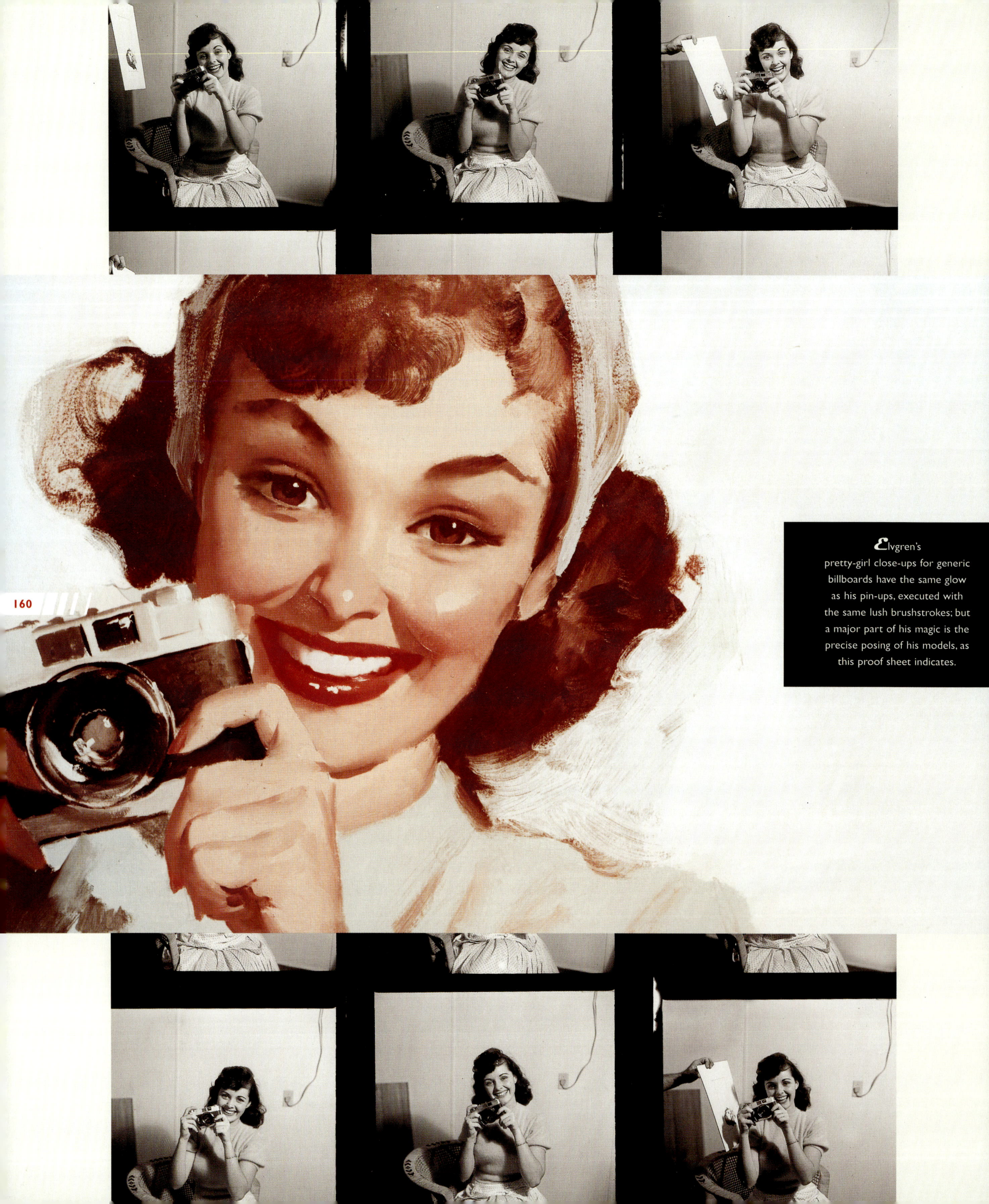

Elvgren's pretty-girl close-ups for generic billboards have the same glow as his pin-ups, executed with the same lush brushstrokes; but a major part of his magic is the precise posing of his models, as this proof sheet indicates.

Elvgren

seemed to work looser on many of his billboards, his brushwork emphasizing his Sundblom roots; this lovely housewife could moonlight as a pin-up girl any day. As usual, note Elvgren's search for the proper reference pose.

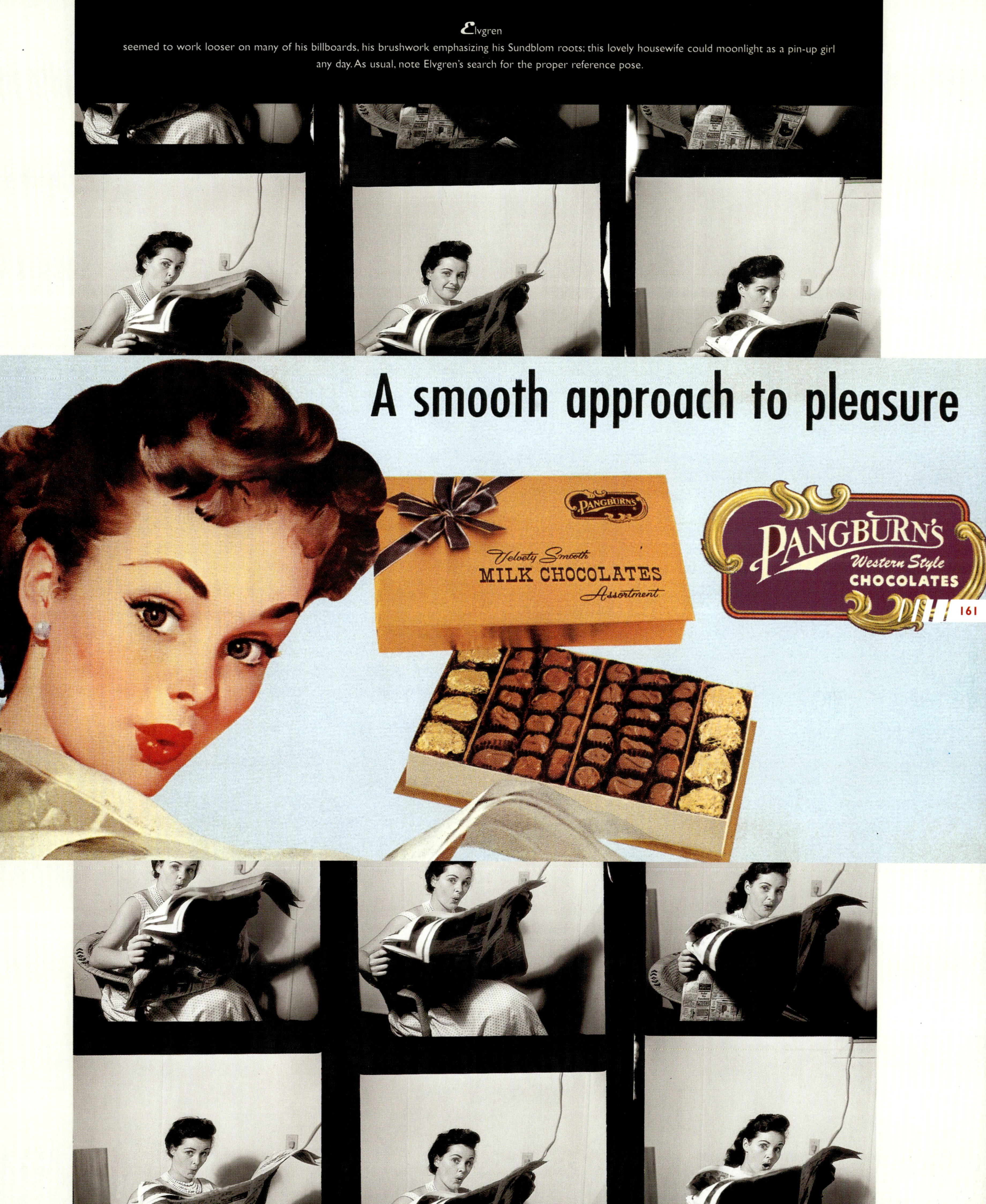

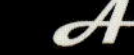

A particularly glowing backyard chefette again carries Elvgren's suburban fantasy, this time into a beer ad (the speared weenies send a mixed symbolic message at best); Gil's model here, like so many of the lovely girls he worked with, might have walked off one of his canvases.

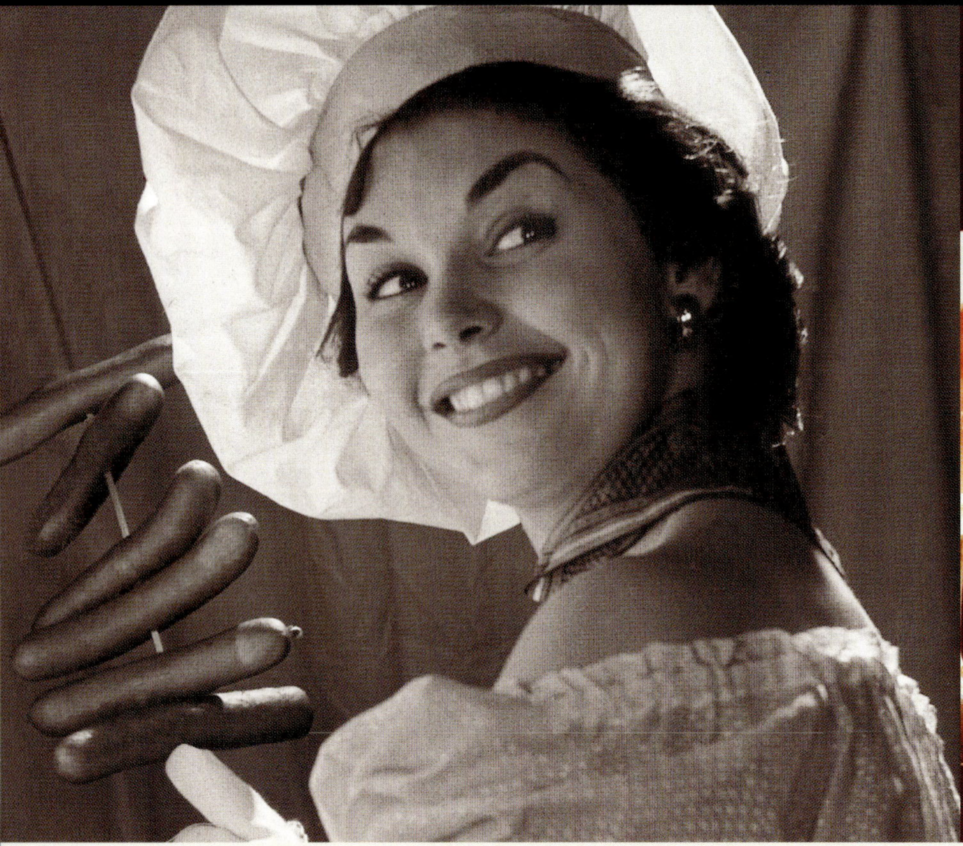

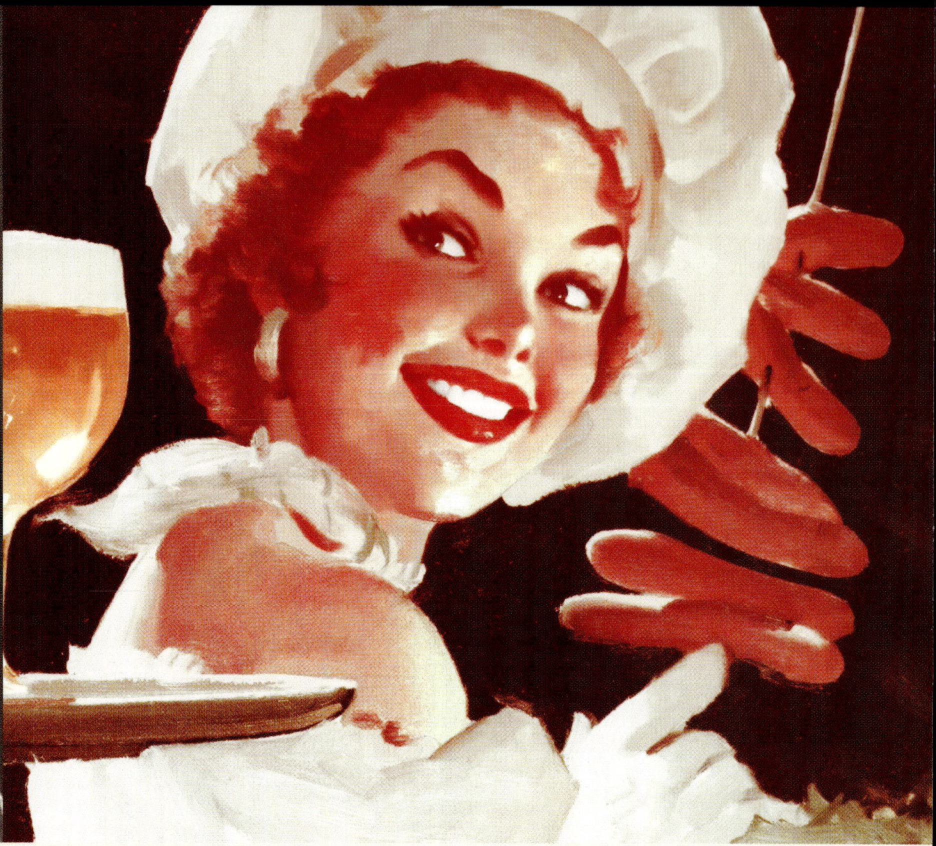

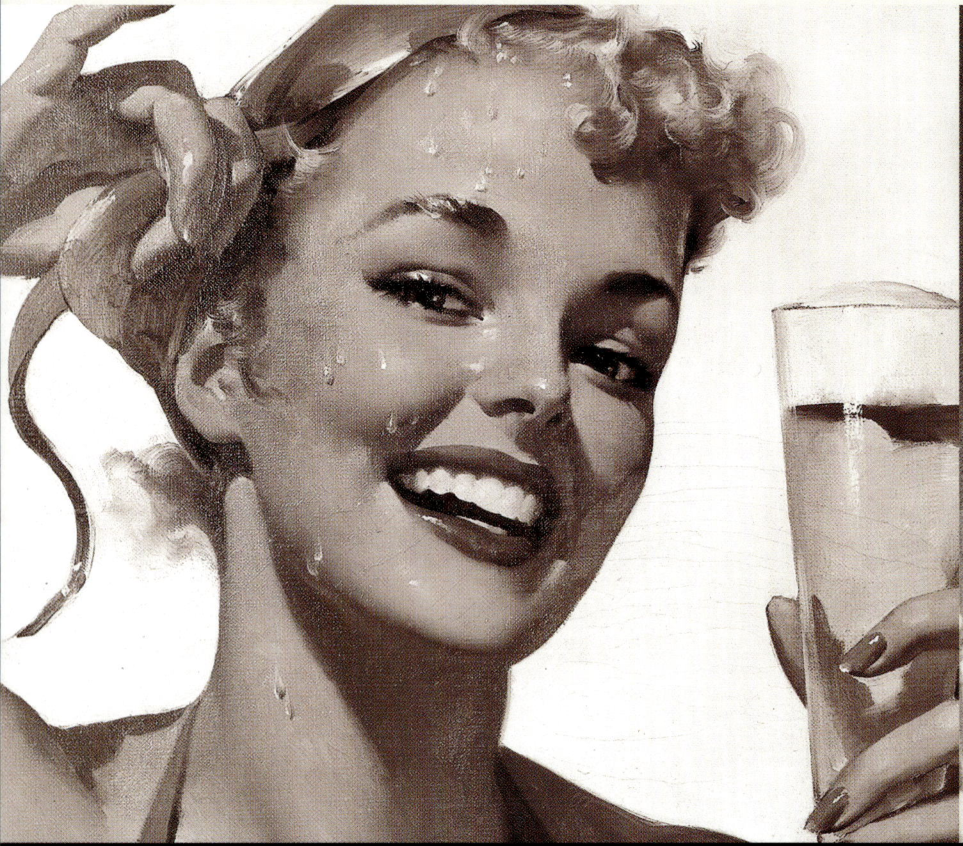

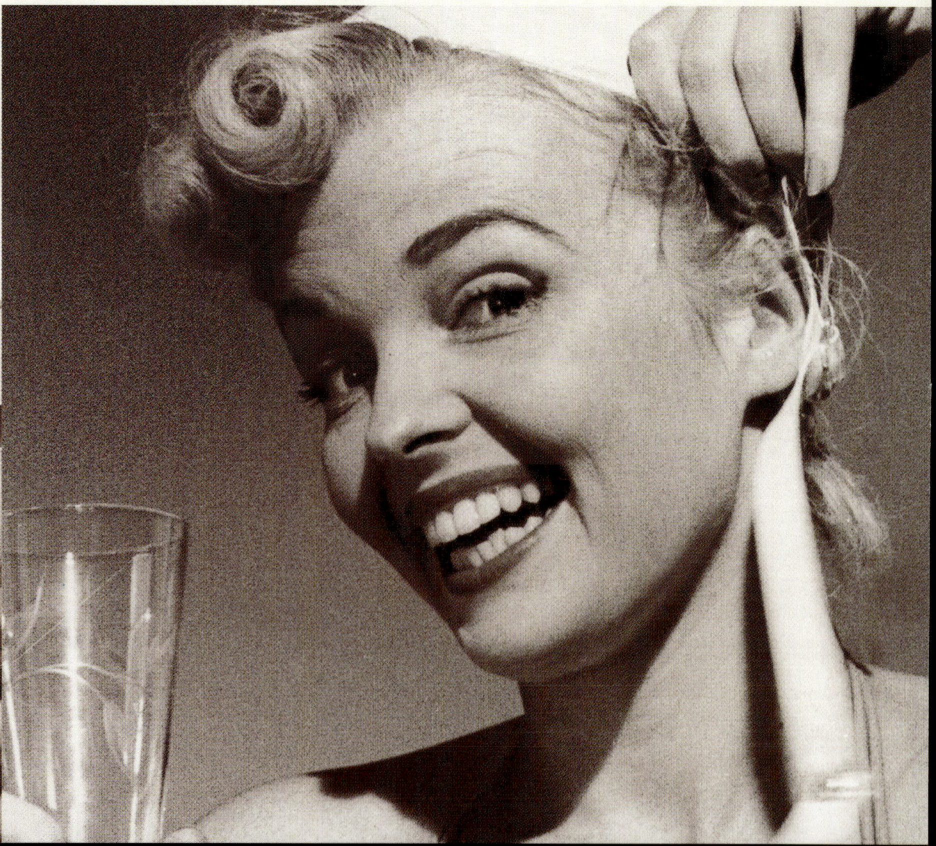

One of Elvgren's most radiant models provides perfect reference for another wholesome sales pitch for that favorite of swimmers everywhere — beer.

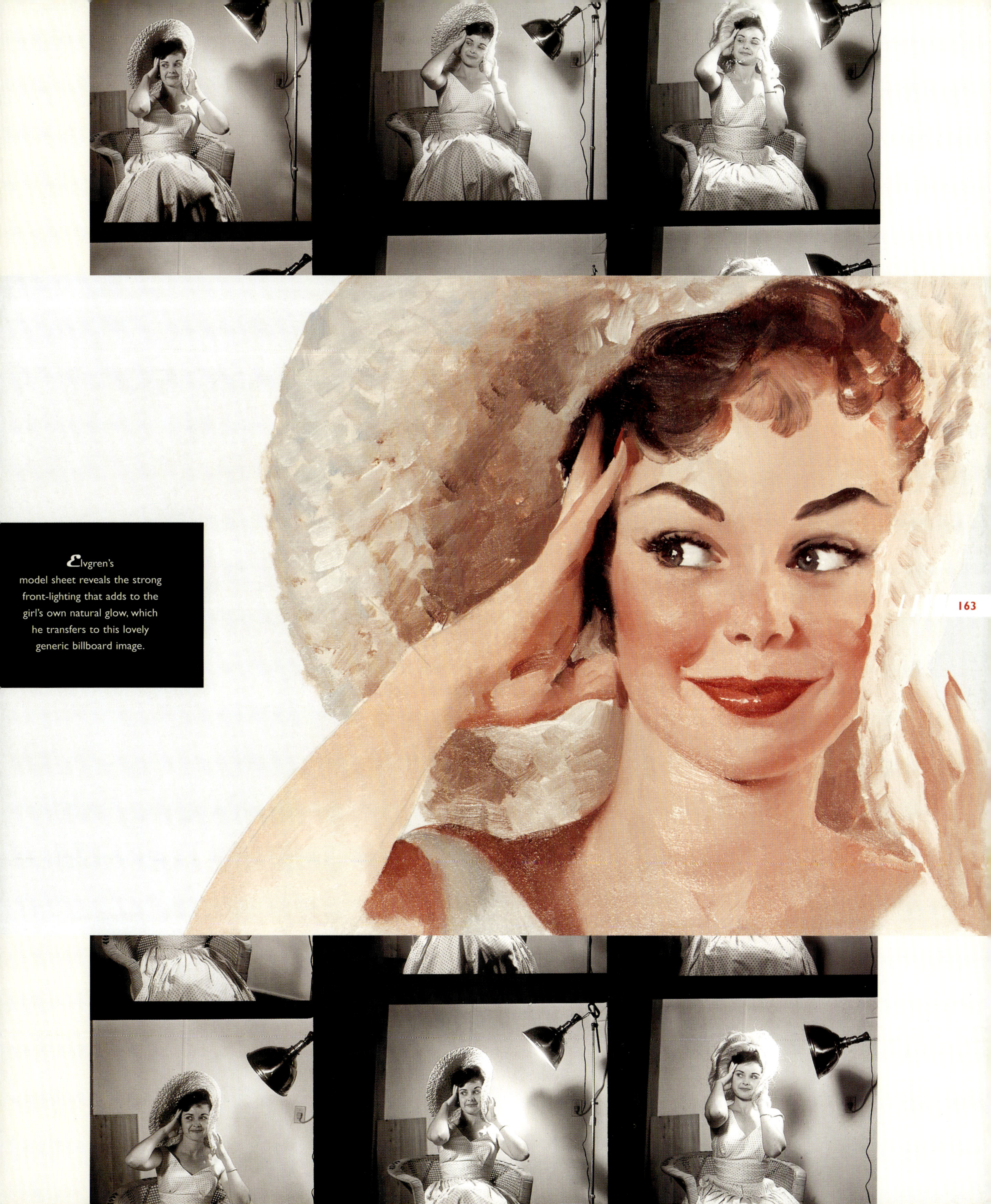

Elvgren's model sheet reveals the strong front-lighting that adds to the girl's own natural glow, which he transfers to this lovely generic billboard image.

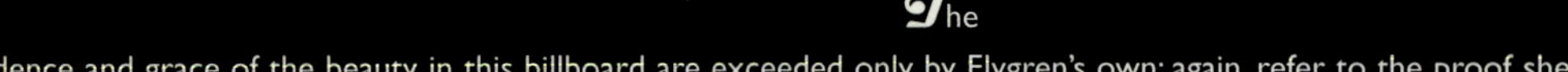

The confidence and grace of the beauty in this billboard are exceeded only by Elvgren's own; again, refer to the proof sheet to see the search for this "casual" moment.

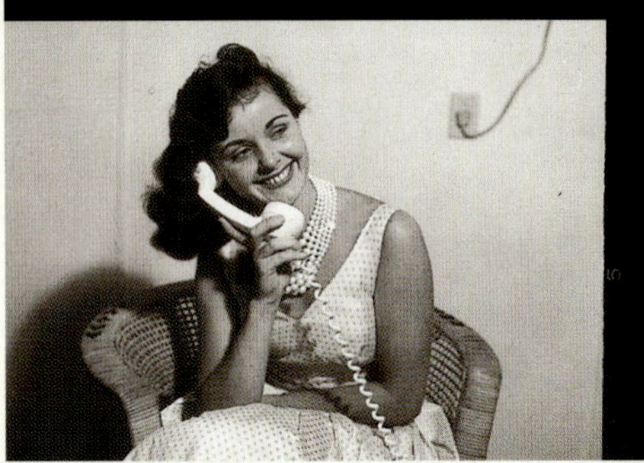

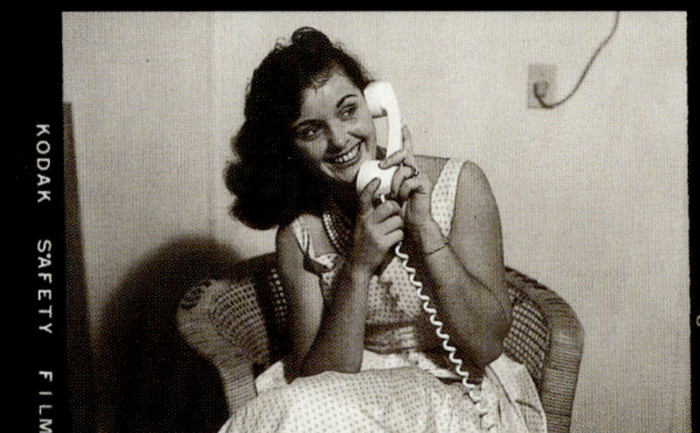

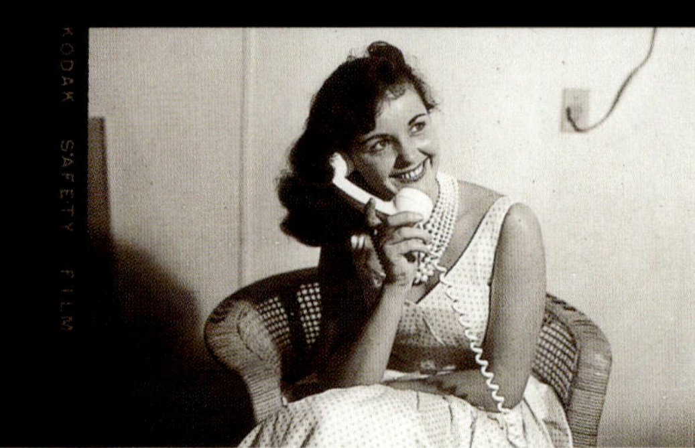

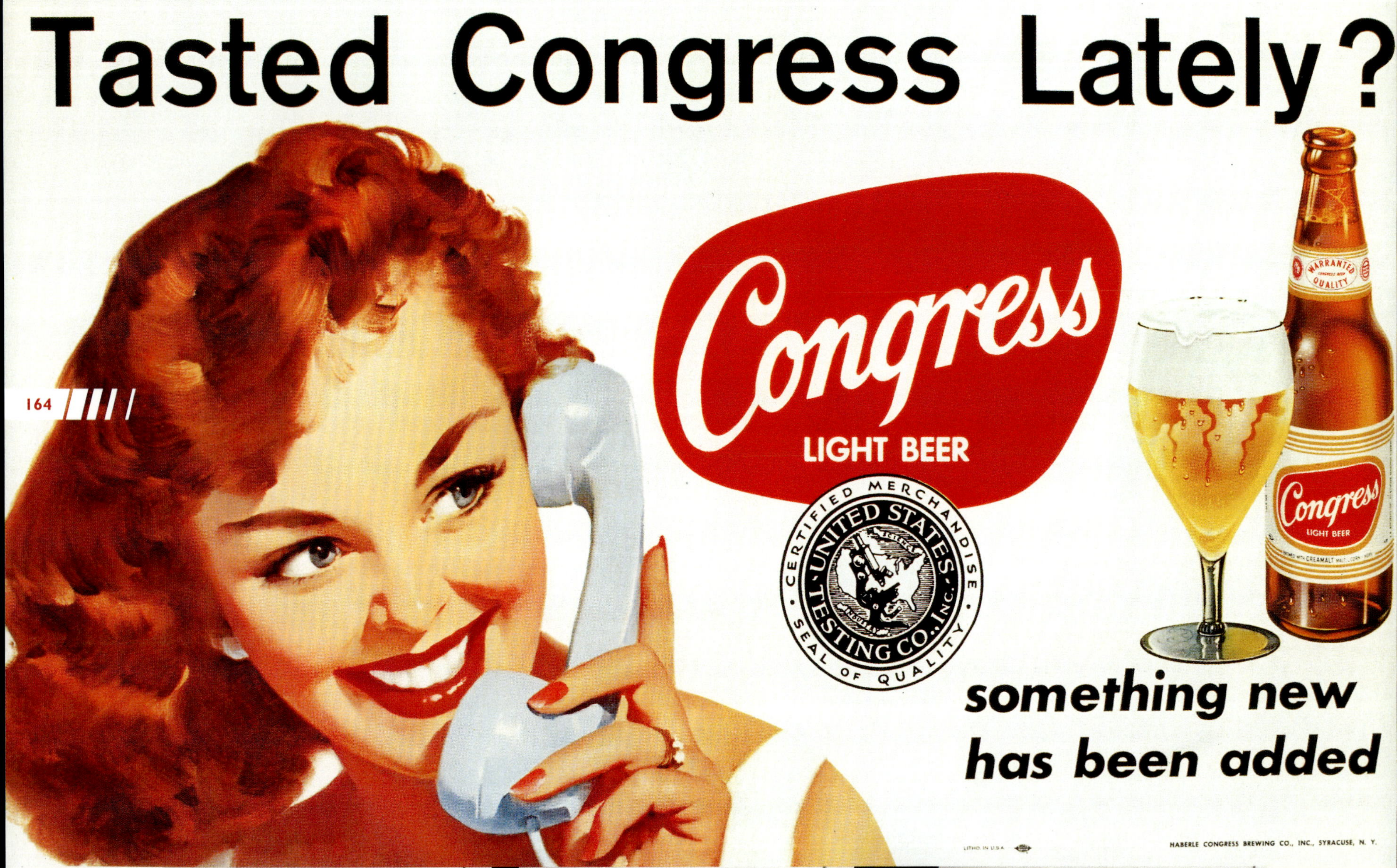

Tasted Congress Lately?

Congress
LIGHT BEER

CERTIFIED MERCHANDISE
UNITED STATES TESTING CO. INC.
SEAL OF QUALITY

WARRANTED QUALITY
Congress
LIGHT BEER

something new
has been added

LITHO IN U.S.A.

HABERLE CONGRESS BREWING CO., INC., SYRACUSE, N. Y.

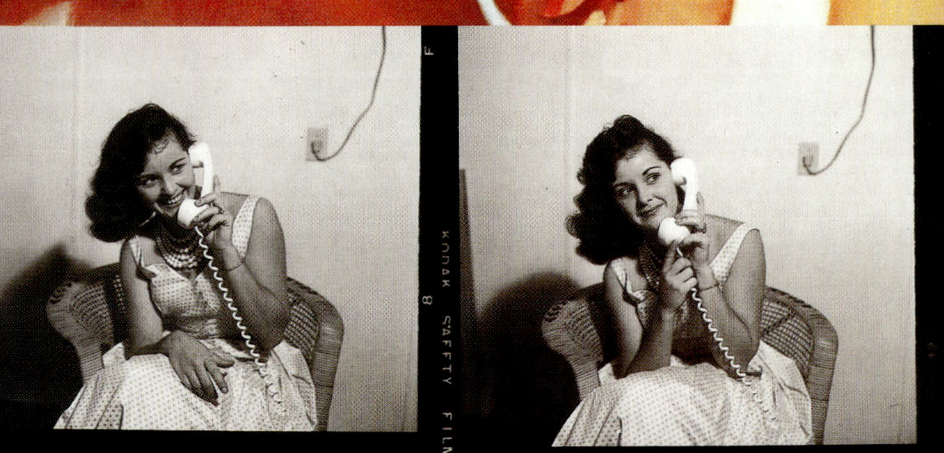

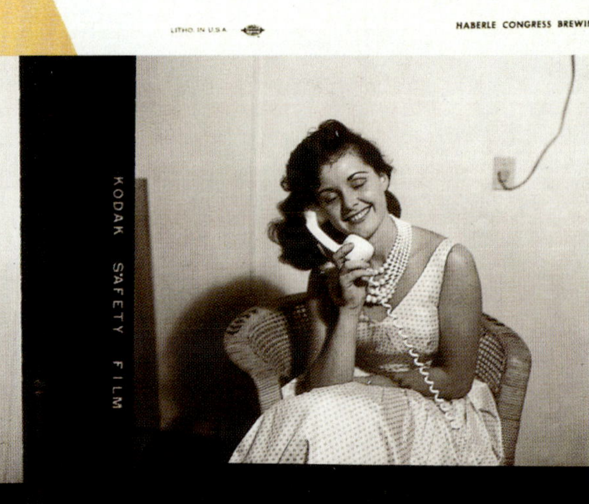

Elvgren's advertising and billboard girls are painted in a broader, more blatantly wholesome style, as this wide-eyed blonde and the cartoon-like floating "love" hearts indicate.

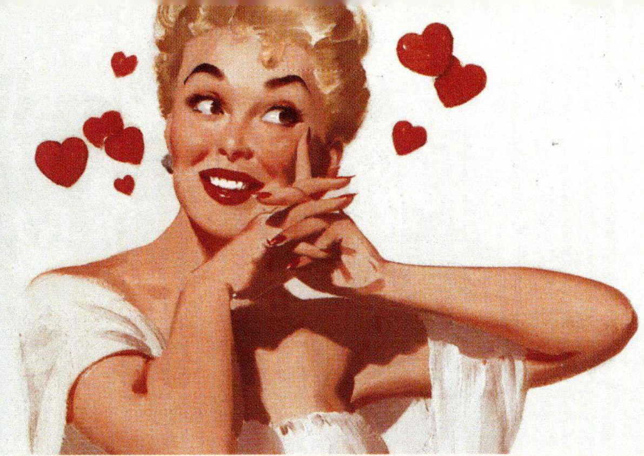

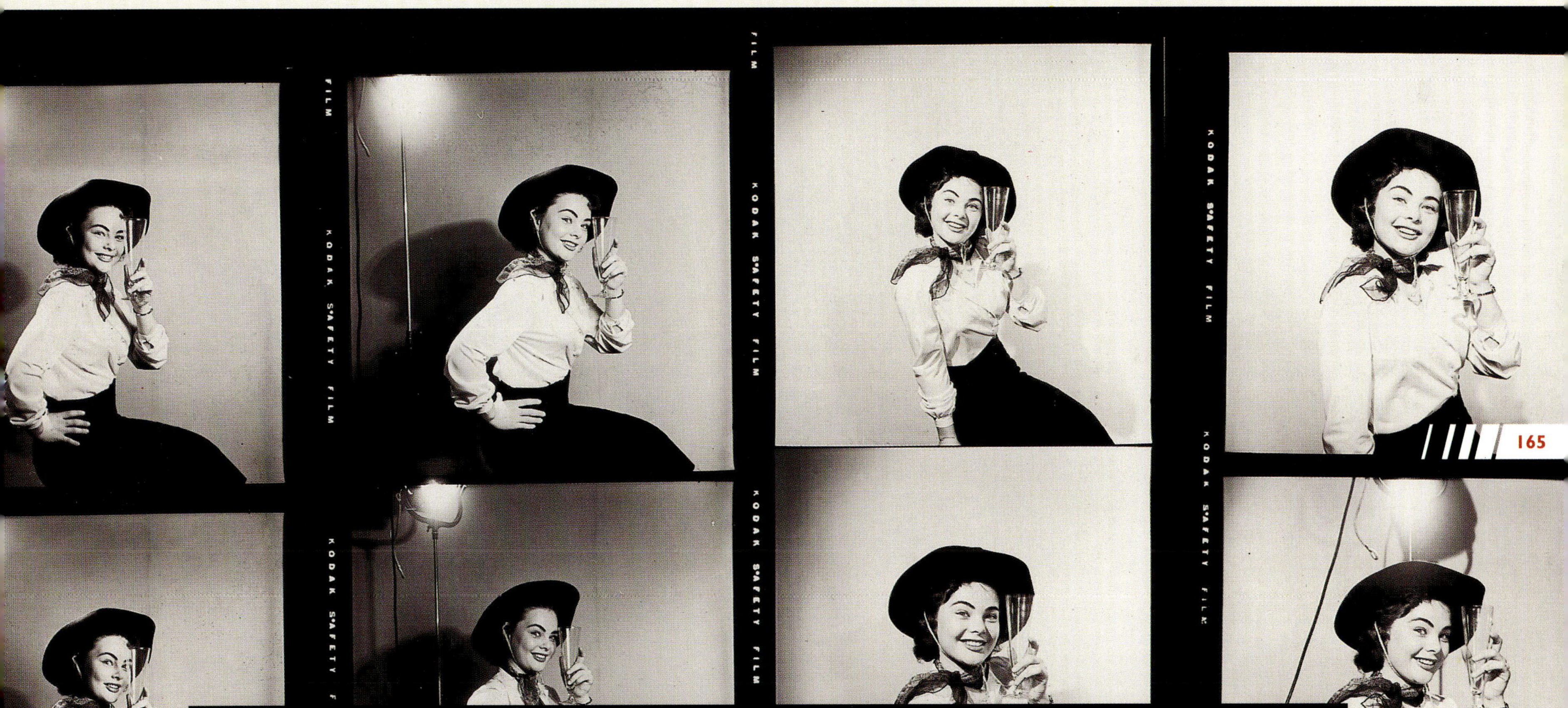

Posing a pretty girl holding a beer had to have been a difficult exercise for so deceptively simple an image; but an Elvgren cowgirl seems an inevitable salesgirl for a beer called Lone Star.

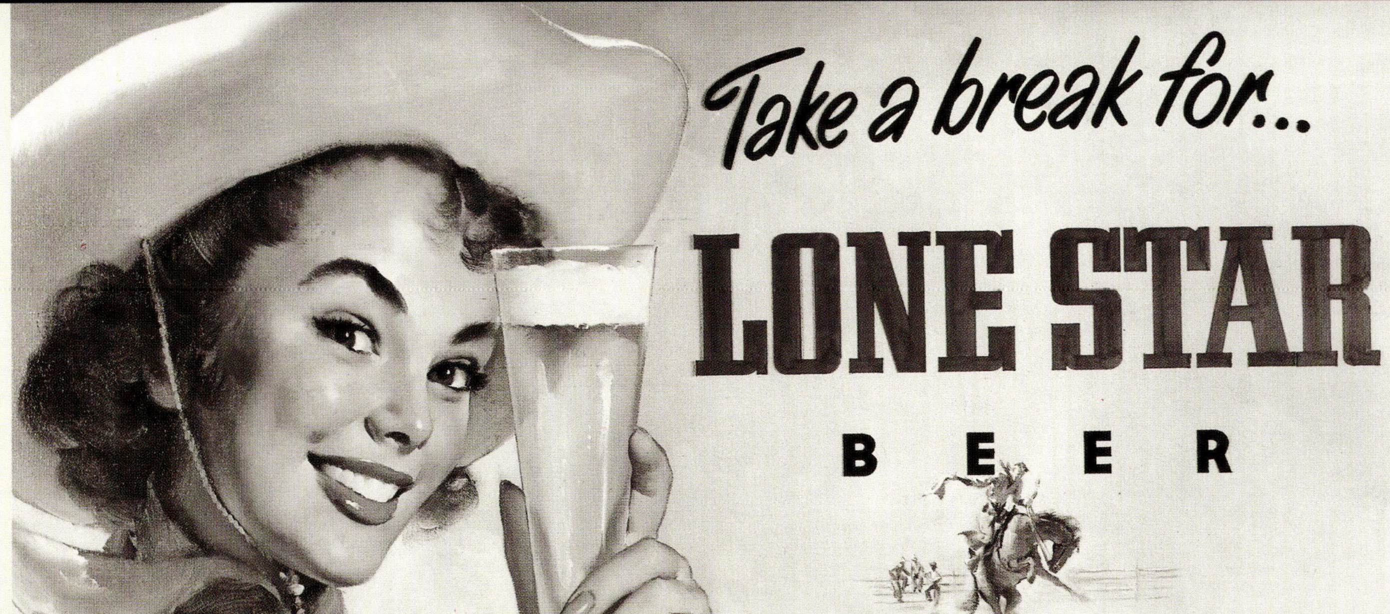

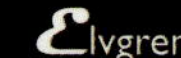

Elvgren strove hard to find a photo reference for this arrestingly designed beer ad; the artist worked for numerous beer accounts over the years, his lovely women giving allure and approval to the working-class, male beverage.

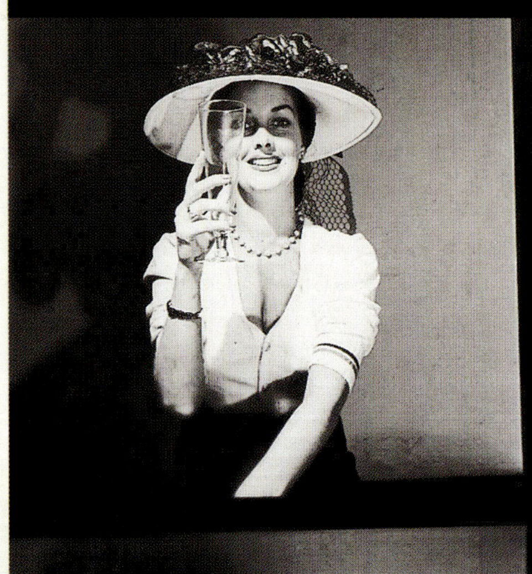

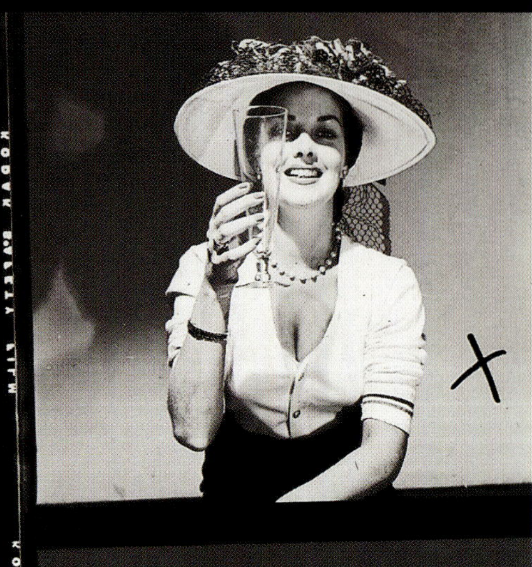

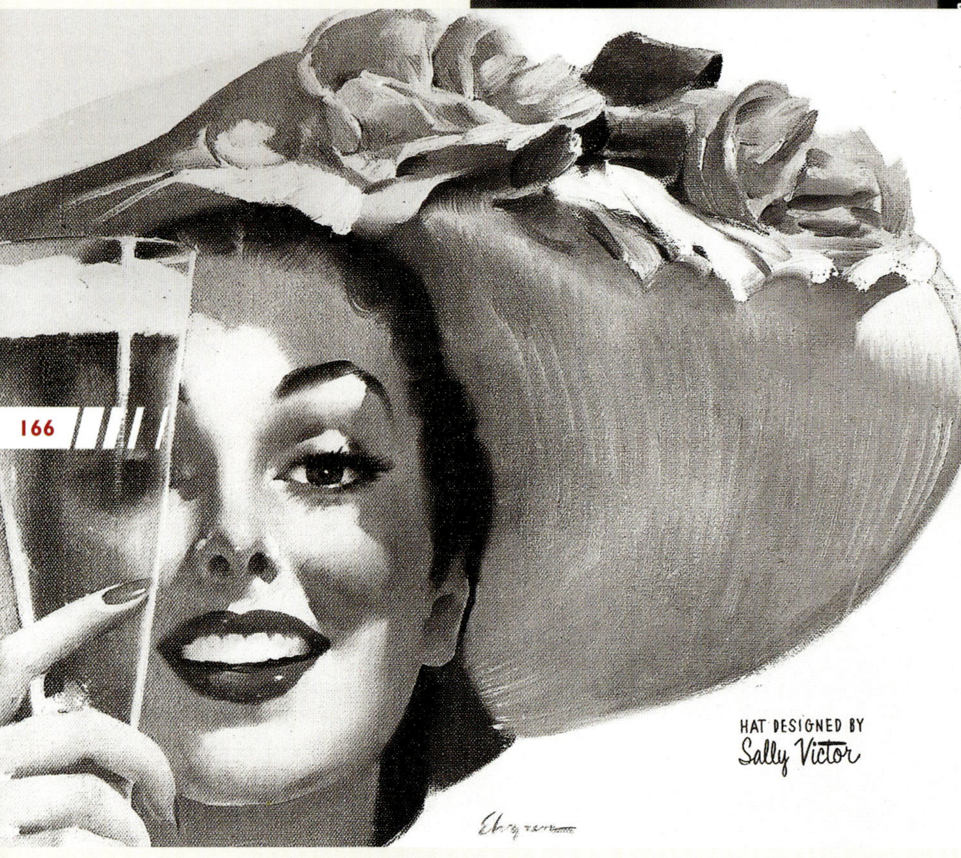

To you and me...

GENESEE

Light and Dry Beer & Ale to Satisfy

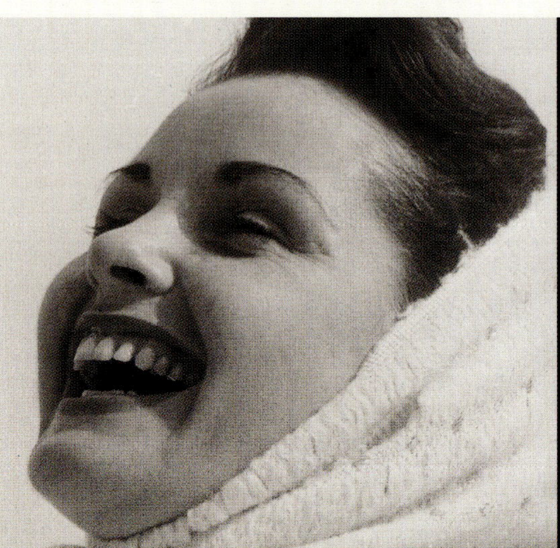

This lyrical, wintry billboard girl hints at Elvgren's skill as a portrait artist; typically, the artist begins with a pretty girl and gently idealizes her into a beauty.

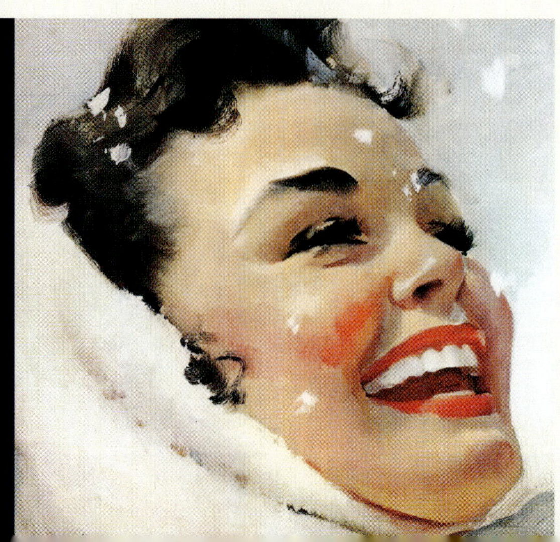

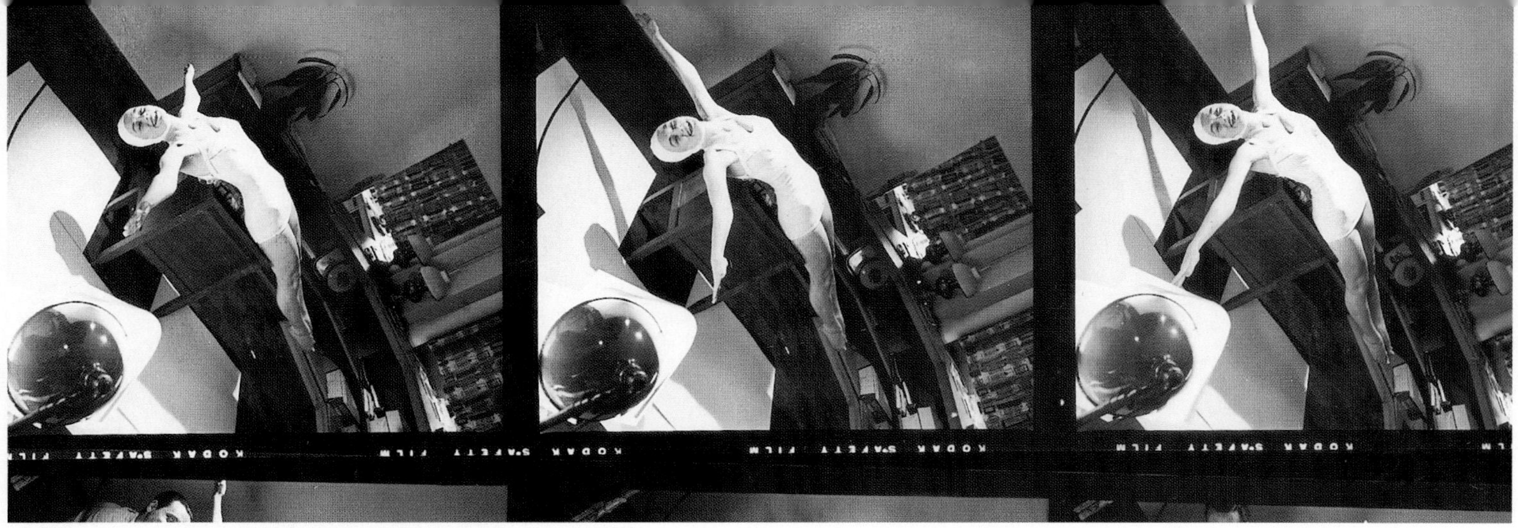

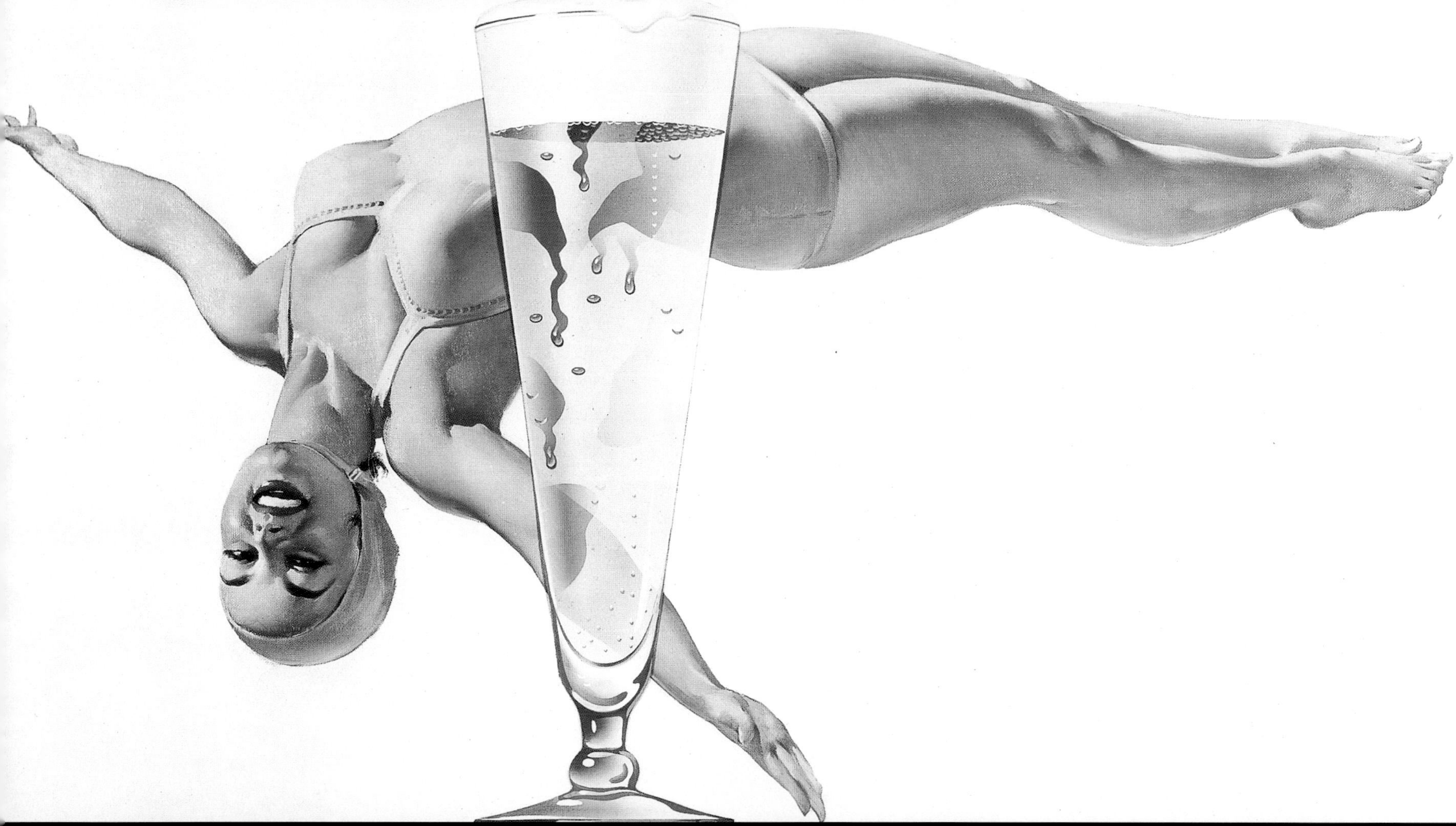

The sleekness of this diving beauty illustrates one of the few times Elvgren reveals the influence of George Petty; again, wholesome subject matter sells suds, the proof sheet indicating the elaborate lengths Elvgren takes to achieve the natural grace of this pose.

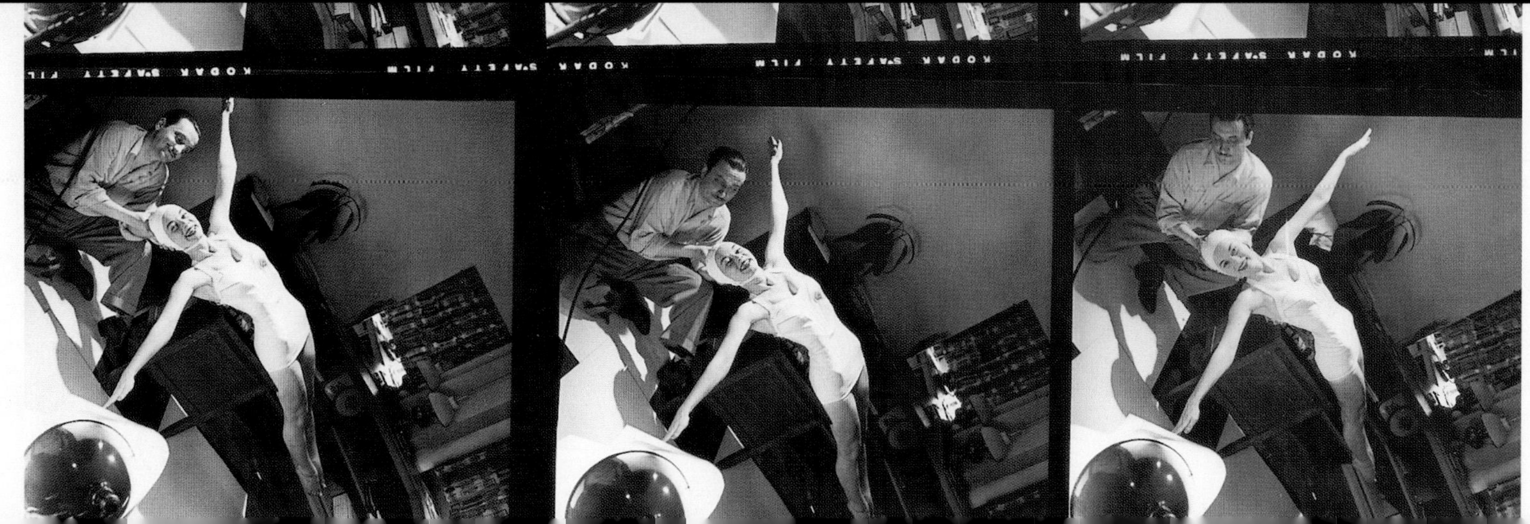

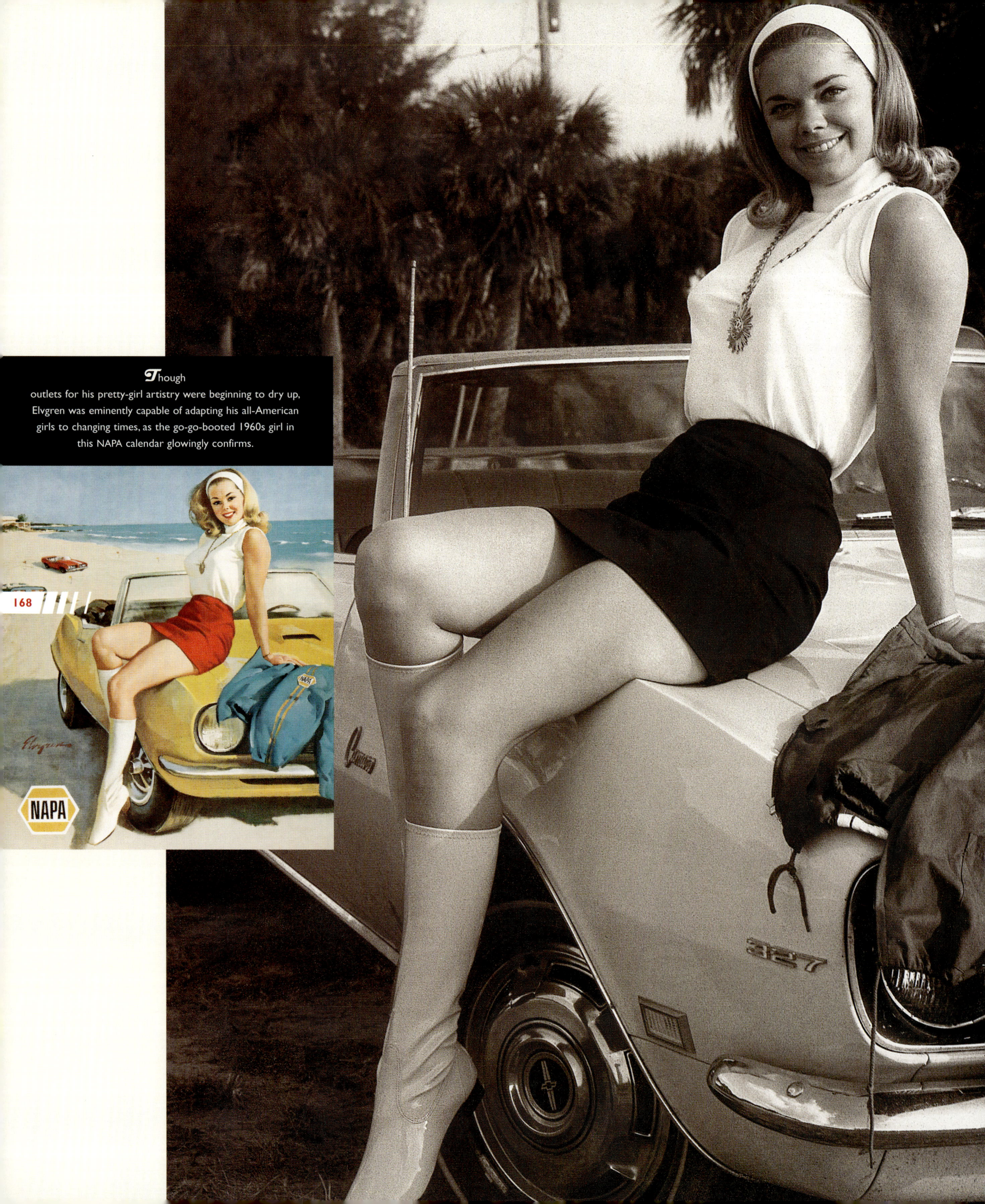

Though outlets for his pretty-girl artistry were beginning to dry up, Elvgren was eminently capable of adapting his all-American girls to changing times, as the go-go-booted 1960s girl in this NAPA calendar glowingly confirms.

Elvgren's love of outdoor sports frequently finds its way into his subject matter, witness this bathing beauty perched on a sailboat in one of Elvgren's later NAPA calendars.

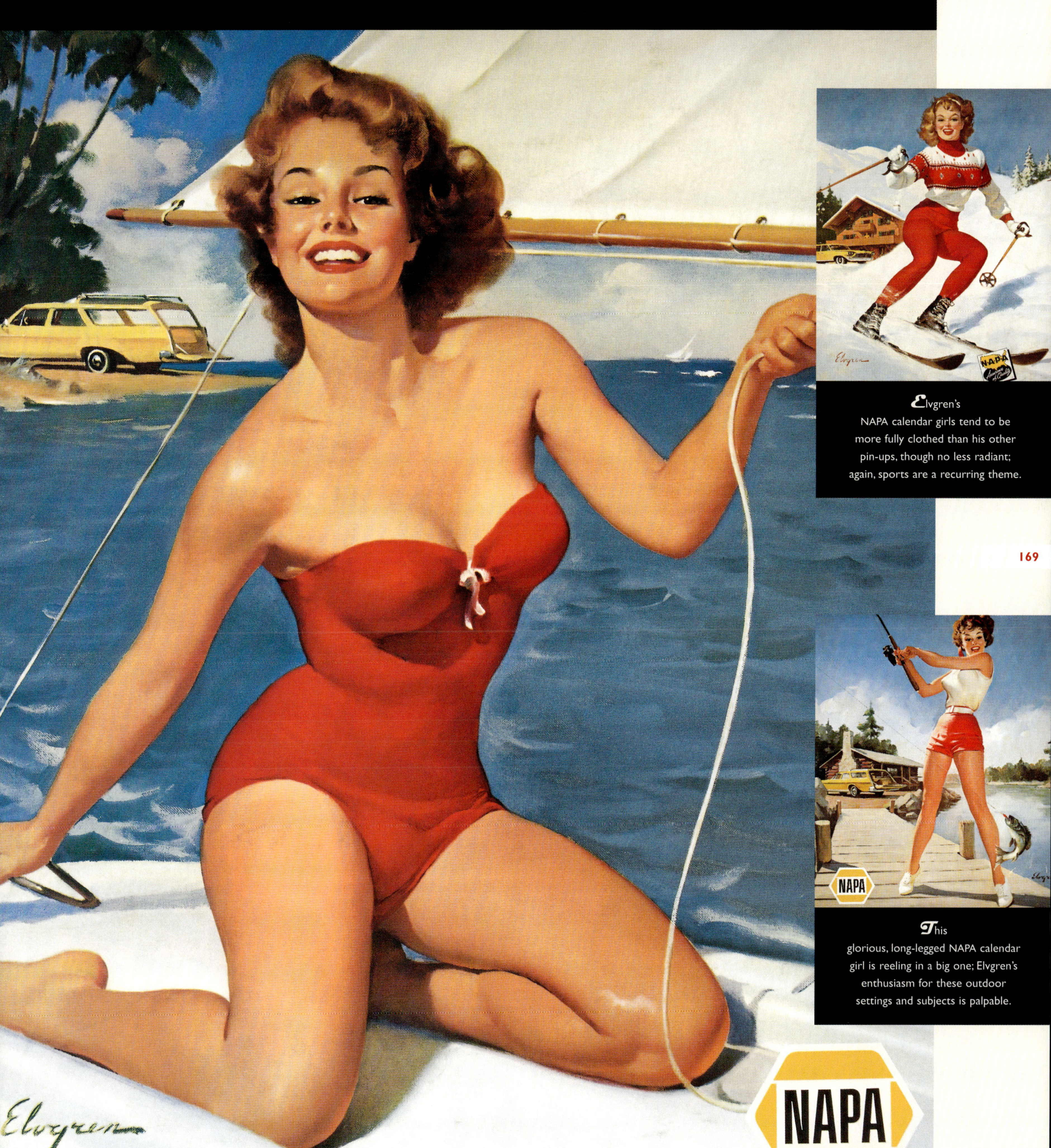

Elvgren's NAPA calendar girls tend to be more fully clothed than his other pin-ups, though no less radiant; again, sports are a recurring theme.

This glorious, long-legged NAPA calendar girl is reeling in a big one; Elvgren's enthusiasm for these outdoor settings and subjects is palpable.

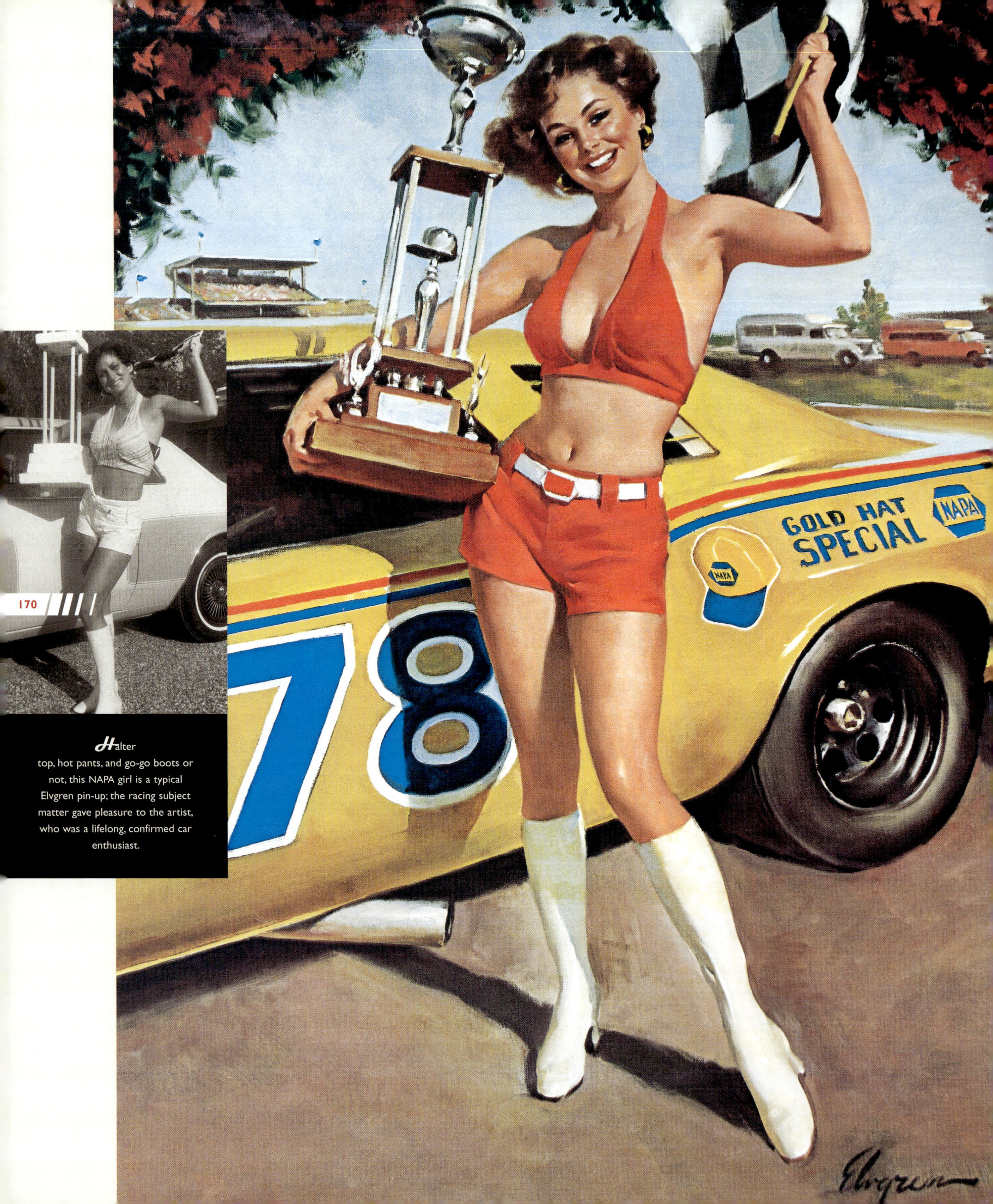

*H*alter top, hot pants, and go-go boots or not, this NAPA girl is a typical Elvgren pin-up; the racing subject matter gave pleasure to the artist, who was a lifelong, confirmed car enthusiast.

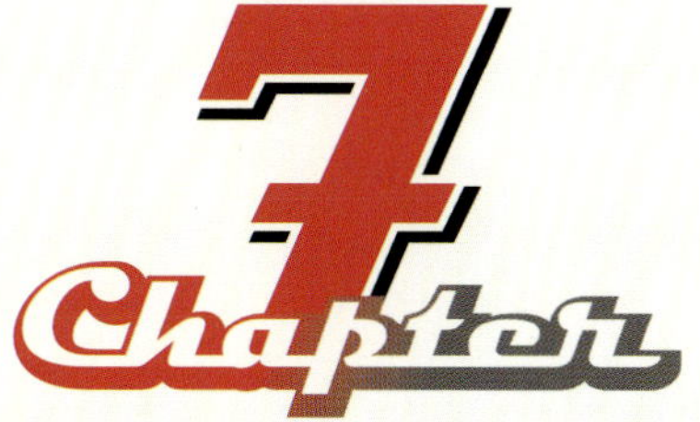

An Artist and His Models

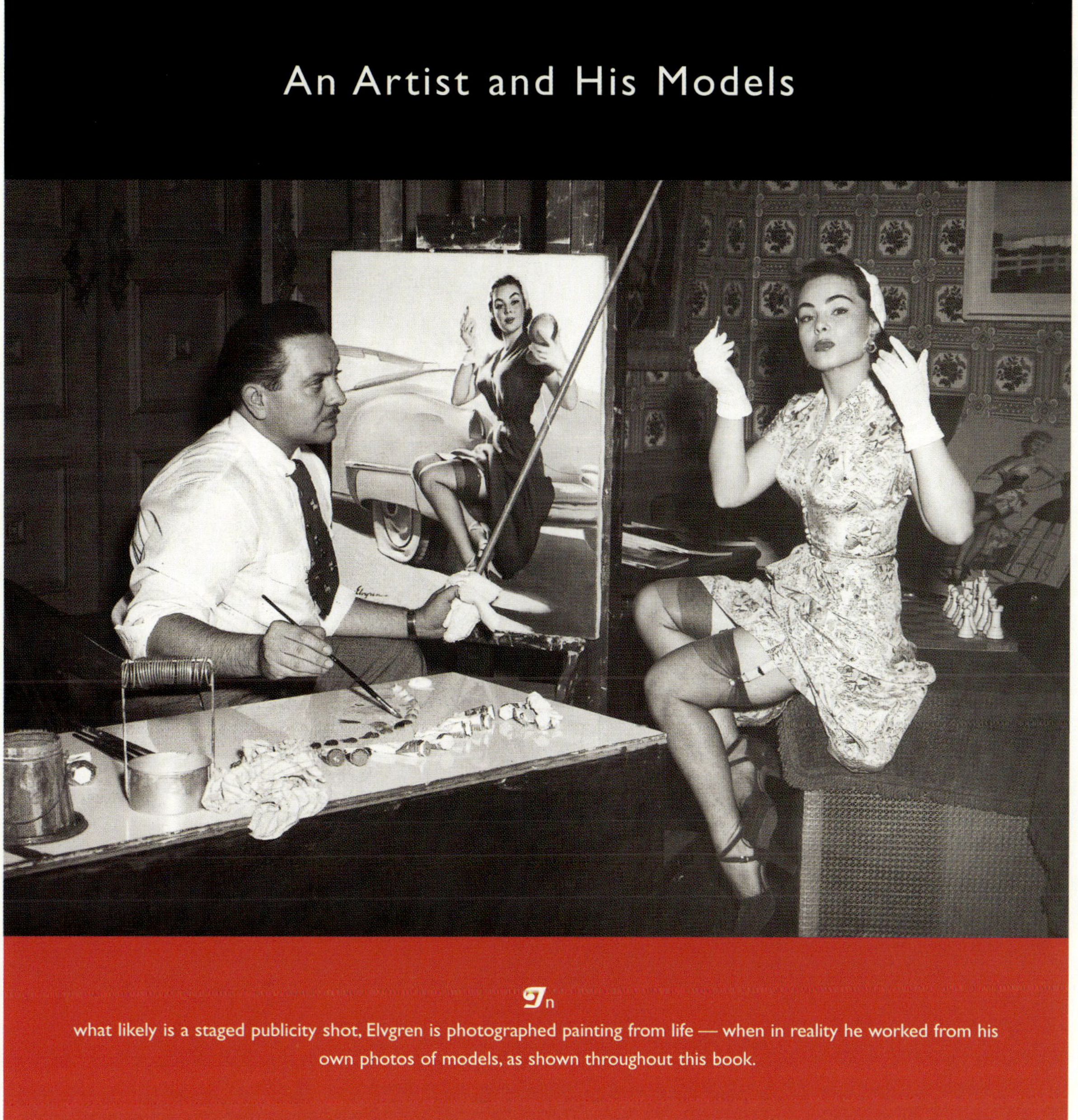

In what likely is a staged publicity shot, Elvgren is photographed painting from life — when in reality he worked from his own photos of models, as shown throughout this book.

In 1953 Gil Elvgren moved his family from a rented house on Foxdale Avenue in Winnetka, Illinois, to a beautiful French provincial house on Pine Street. This was the first home the Elvgrens owned, and Drake looks back on it fondly. "It was a huge house," he recalls, "and, once there, Dad decided to build his own studio at the house, which had a tremendous, high-ceilinged attic. He was suffering from a very severe case of gout, so he had his apprentice, Peter Darrow, go up into the attic and take every measurement he could think of, and make rough sketches." Elvgren took these measurements and designed a studio to his personal needs and specifications, even calculating the amount of lumber that would be needed. "It came out exactly as he had planned," Drake says. "From that point on, he usually had a studio at home." The artist was a stickler for painting in a studio bathed in north light; only under deadline emergencies would he work in artificial light, and rarely did he put in more than an eight-hour day. He did not like sunrise or sunset light. He mixed his own colors and kept his palette and brushes immaculate, with the help of son Drake, who cleaned them every night. "His studio always smelled of paint, mineral spirits, and cigarette smoke," Drake remembers. "I would scrape all but the base colors off his palette, and clean the area. The next morning, he would go up and mix all his colors anew, taking just a few minutes. It didn't seem to matter, a dab of this, a dab of that, some of this, and by golly it matched up yesterday's!" Elvgren positioned a mirror about ten feet behind him, and would stop and look at his painting in the mirror, to get a better perspective of what it would look like when reduced in the printing process. He used a Newel stick to rest his wrist on and used a white, glass-topped desk with numerous drawers for his equipment. (The glass top served as his palette.) He used a wide variety of brushes, every shape and size, but always the best. "He was very picky about his brushes," Drake says. The artist did not take frequent breaks, but when he reached a stopping place in a painting, or a costume break in a modeling session, he would

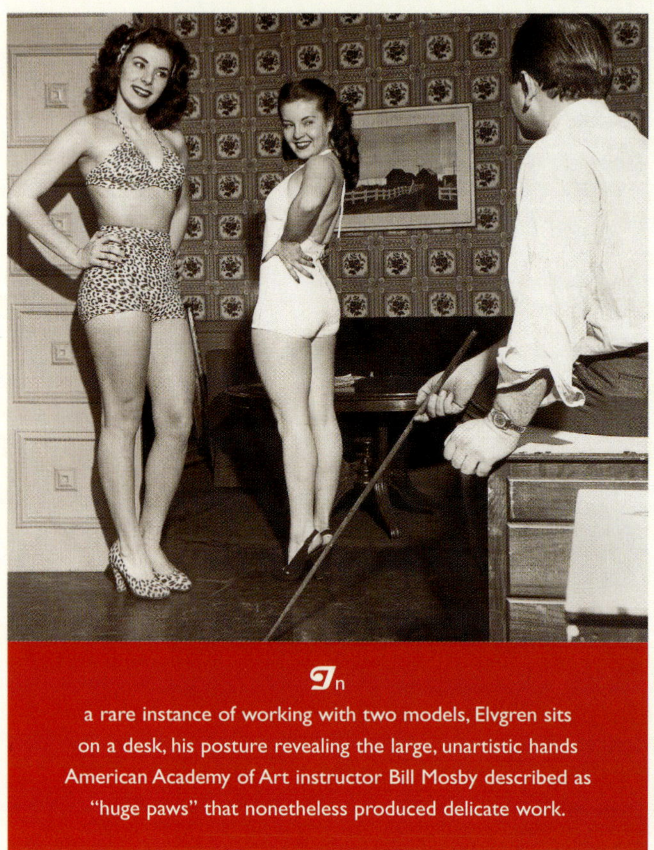

In a rare instance of working with two models, Elvgren sits on a desk, his posture revealing the large, unartistic hands American Academy of Art instructor Bill Mosby described as "huge paws" that nonetheless produced delicate work.

come down to have a cup of coffee with wife Janet; sometimes he would be accompanied by his current model, several of whom became like members of the family. While he didn't like interruptions, he was not one to turn away his children when they'd knock at his studio door. "It rarely took Dad more than three days to finish a painting," Drake says. "Occasionally, though very rarely, one would give him fits, and he would really have to struggle, maybe re-doing part of it." In interviews Elvgren said it took him five days to do a painting. Three days or five, his pin-ups are wonders of speedy hard work and skillful craftsmanship, quite apart from any claims of artistic merit. "I never saw Dad paint with anything other than oils," Drake remembers, "and on canvas. His charcoal portraits were on art paper and usually took him two to three hours." Elvgren would work up a sketch on the canvas itself, sometimes preceded by sketch-pad preliminary studies and then, in thick, masterful strokes, lay on primarily unmixed color, right from the tube. Thinner was reserved mostly for keeping his brushes moist and malleable. Despite numerous photos that depict Elvgren painting from live models, the artist worked chiefly from photographs he took himself. "He insisted on north light in his studio," Drake recalls, "and felt so confident of his color sense that he used only black-and-white photos to work from, because it captured light/dark contrast better than color shots." Elvgren also preferred black and white because he did not like to be influenced by the colors in the photo. "He would often just use the highlights," Drake says "He could make a model's hair, her skin tones, even her clothing, any color he wanted." Drake has been told by a number of renowned artists, including Ben Stahl, Thorton Utz, and Al Buell, that his father had one of the finest color senses of any artist. Despite this, some evidence suggests Elvgren may have on occasion used color film. An article in a 1954 Fawcett publication, *Photography Handbook*, shows the artist at work with sunny blonde

Another of the posed publicity photos that wrongly indicate Elvgren painted his models from life, this shot inadvertently suggests the casualness that must have been a part of the process, lovely girls in lingerie on a coffee, snack, or smoke break.

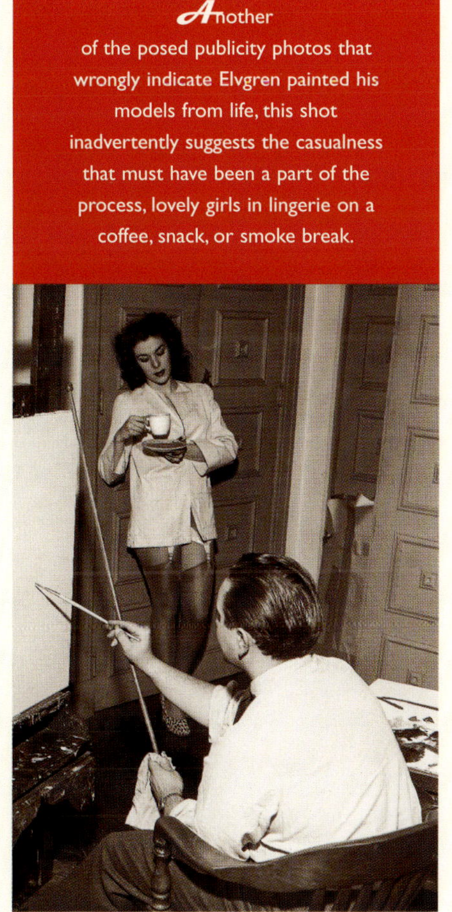

model Candy Montgomery. Author Ray Pinney reports that Elvgren shot the model in color with a Rolleiflex, and that the artist would take up to thirty-six shots to get a "thorough impression" of the model, the various photographs showing the stages of posing, lighting, and color testing.

"Although he uses one main photograph to paint from," Pinney reported, "he has a complete, correct visual picture of the model with which to work." The rest of Pinney's article supports Drake's memory, showing the artist at work as his own prop man and set construction carpenter, building backgrounds such as the fence Candy Montgomery sat upon in the pictures taken for a popular pin-up titled "Keeping Posted." Elvgren is seen trying out colored gelatin filters over white lights against a blue background and, when everything was properly positioned, rigging up a soft front floodlight to shoot his preliminary photos. This was typical of his painting technique, which as son Gil, Jr., has noted, "was often centered around a couple of props (a weight-loss machine, a scale, a saddle, a scrub brush, an animal) in a selective (noninclusive) background." The figure was almost always "in action," and — like a movie director — Elvgren positioned the model exactly in a planned pose. "The model is dressed with an eye to color, too," Pinney reported. "And as for the model, just any girl won't do." Elvgren required "a wholesome, typically American beauty, between seventeen and twenty... a smiling beauty." In fact, like Hitchcock storyboarding a film, Elvgren seemed to get his greatest satisfaction from this preliminary planning stage of his work, even developing his own photos. He took great care with the lighting of his subjects because it would dictate the tonal values of his painting; fussing with props, building his own scenery, was part of the storytelling process, and Elvgren was, with his illustrator's background, a storyteller at heart. "Most of my creative work is in front of the camera," Elvgren said in a 1951 interview with journalist Curtis Fuller. "I'm wringing wet by the time I get through taking a series of photographs of a model. I'm thinking of a thousand things at once — lights, camera, the model's pose, her attitude, my assignment. So it's no wonder I need a natural, good

In his studio, Gil and his model appraise a canvas in this posed publicity photo.

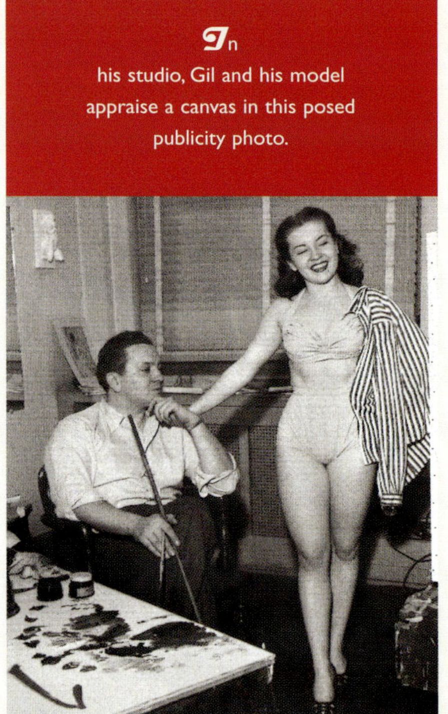

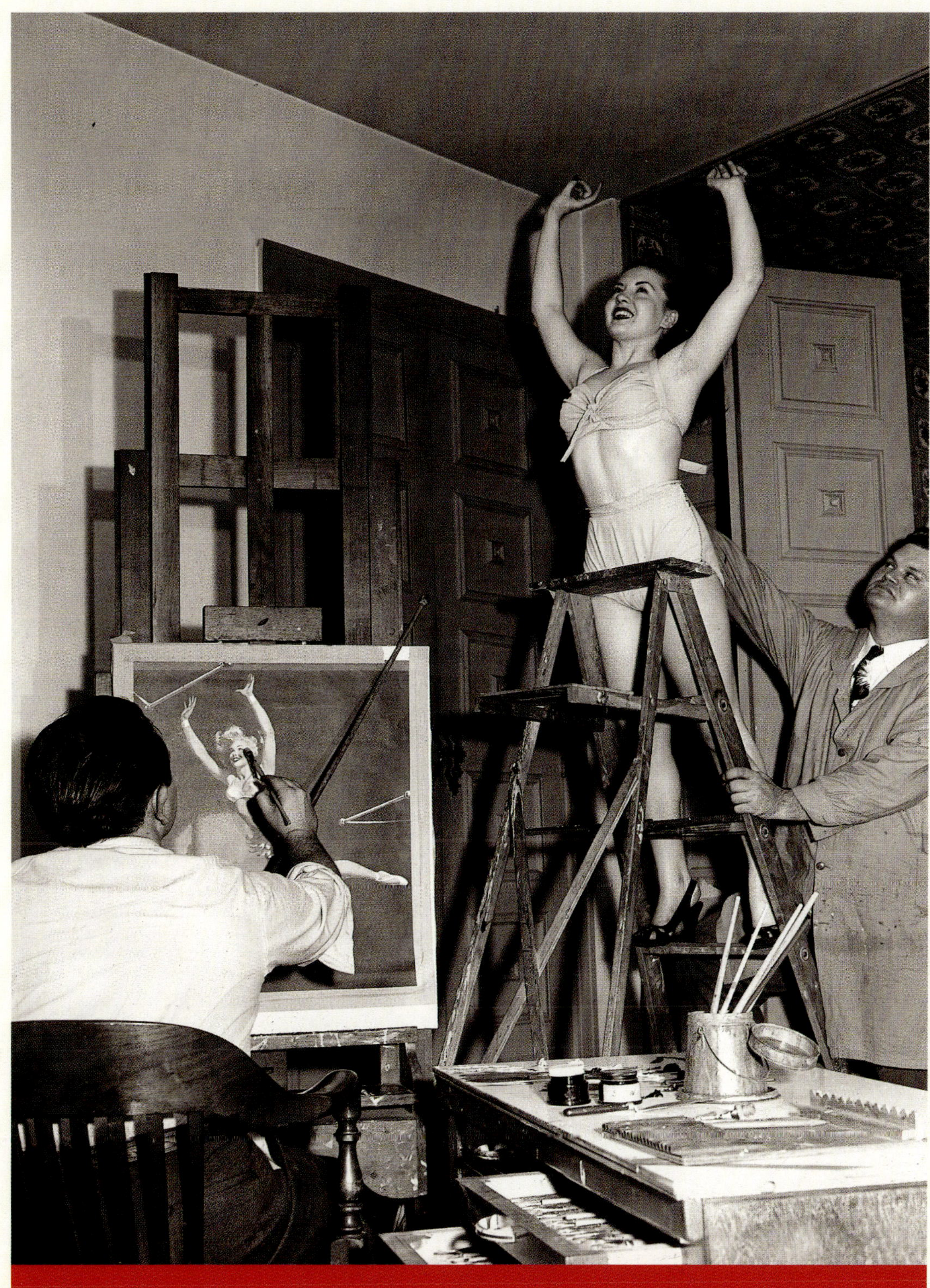

Though this photo clearly is staged for publicity purposes, it indicates Elvgren's use of assistants in the studio; were Elvgren wielding a camera and not a brush, this probably would be an accurate glimpse at the earliest stage of a pin-up.

model. The ideal model poses instinctively—sometimes even better than the artist can pose her." Nonetheless he was not a slave to his photo reference; in fact he compared himself to a plastic surgeon in plumping the lips, narrowing the hips, and lengthening the limbs of his girls. He looked for models who were poised and natural before the camera; they didn't have to be beautiful—he could stuff their bras with tissue paper and bob their noses with his paint brush, if necessary. To Elvgren, the perfect model had the face of a teenager and the body of a woman. "I'd rather work from a model who isn't the most beautiful girl in the world," Elvgren said, "because if she looks too beautiful, then I have too much of a tendency to copy from the photograph.... But if she has a few flaws, then I feel freer to make changes." When asked to define beauty, Elvgren hesitated, saying, "I could give you a lot of high-sounding words, but that would be the bunk." But the artist did admit "the head is very important," and that his models needed to have wide-set eyes, a high forehead, pert nose, full lips, and small ears; he also preferred longish necks ("short-necked girls look close-coupled"). Asked about a girl's chin, Elvgren betrayed a puckish sense of humor, saying, "I hope she has one." As for his models' figures, he said, "They should be full-busted but not overblown. Have nice arms and hands. Small waist." Elvgren told his son, Gil, Jr., that the most difficult part of the human anatomy were the hands and feet (and in one painting—"Pick of the Crop"—an Elvgren girl does appear with two left feet!). He also admitted that his girls could not likely exist in nature, that he depicted his models with smaller waists and longer legs than God had given them. "I have a certain concept, which may differ from other artists," Elvgren said. "Nevertheless, nearly any calendar artist will lengthen the legs and pinch in the waist." At times, finished paintings looked very much like their models; other times, they did not. Elvgren, though an accomplished portrait painter, was not attempting portraits of his models; the models were a means to his telling of a story of tongue-in-cheek romance. Elvgren occasionally used models from agencies, but professionally trained girls could present problems; on occasion he would take trips to Miami and Palm Springs for photo sessions with models. He did not like to be informed by a model what her "best side" was or be otherwise advised on how they would look their best. Elvgren often said that he wished to impress his personality on the painting, not the model's. "One model came down from New York to Sarasota," Drake recalls. "This was in the early '60s and she made $100 an hour. That was a fortune at that time, so Dad worked her over eight hours in one day, and took pictures for about six or eight paintings." More often the artist approached actresses. Candy Montgomery was appearing in the cast of the musical *High Button Shoes* when Elvgren approached her. Myrna Hansen, one of his favorite models, was an aspiring

Chicago actress who posed for at least twenty paintings, and often posed for his so-called "universal billboards" for Schmidt Lithograph. She began modeling for Elvgren at age seventeen and posed for him over a five-year period. Hansen went on to be a beauty-pageant winner and a Hollywood starlet. Hansen told an interviewer that Elvgren would arrange her in "contorted leg positions," in ill-fitting shoes that "hurt like mad." The model began using her own shoes after that, since "Mr. Elvgren wanted a certain look, and shoes were very important in a leggy pin-up pose." Stunning redhead Rusty Allen was a popular and well-known men's magazine model, with her many nude layouts including a centerfold appearance in *Rogue*, one of the better *Playboy* imitations of the era; she also appeared in "nudie cutie" movies, notably *Daughter of the Sun*, directed and produced, respectively, by exploitation pioneers Herschell Gordon Lewis and David F. Friedman. She was one of Elvgren's favorite models in the '60s and posed for at least fifteen paintings. Two of the most famous of Elvgren's model/actresses were Barbara Hale and Lola Albright. Hale, born in 1922, was an RKO starlet who achieved starring roles in the late '40s and early '50s, notably as Al Jolson's second wife in *Jolson Sings Again* (1949). The pretty brunette exuded a radiant wholesomeness that made her an ideal Elvgren model. Lola Albright, born in 1925, was a sultry, sophisticated blonde, perhaps a less likely candidate for Elvgren's brush but suitably beautiful; she played secondary roles in A pictures like the Sinatra vehicle, *The Tender Trap* (1956), and leads in B movies such as *The Monolith Monsters* (1957) and *Seven Guns to Mesa* (1960). Both actresses achieved more lasting fame in two of the 1950s seminal TV detective series, "Perry Mason," with Hale portraying Della Street to Raymond Burr's Mason, and Albright playing (and singing) the role of the nightclub thrush/girl friend Edie to Craig Stevens' character Peter Gunn. These major TV hits paved the way for both actresses to score better Hollywood roles, Albright in such respected films as *A Cold Wind in August* (1961) and *Lord Love a Duck* (1966), and Hale in the smash

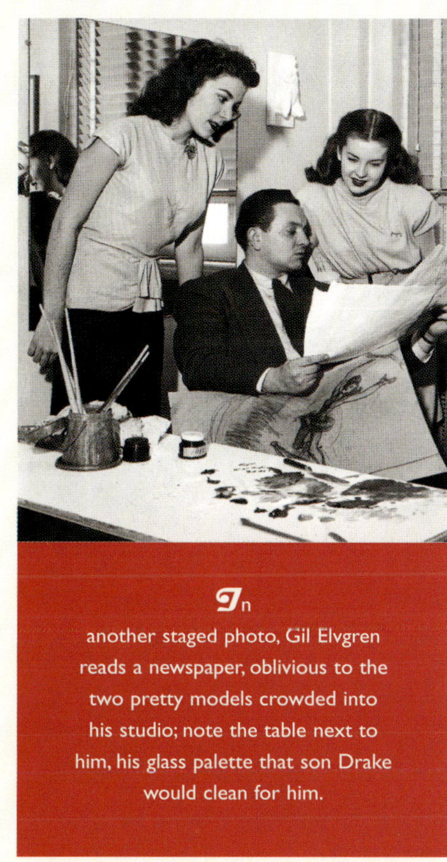

In another staged photo, Gil Elvgren reads a newspaper, oblivious to the two pretty models crowded into his studio; note the table next to him, his glass palette that son Drake would clean for him.

hit *Airport* (1969), as well as the long-running TV movie revival of the *Mason* series. Undoubtedly the most famous of the aspiring actresses who modeled for Elvgren is Kim Novak. Chicago girl Marilyn Novak, born in 1933, later changed her first name to avoid too close a comparison with Marilyn Monroe, even though she was hired to be Columbia Studios "answer" to the Twentieth Century Fox superstar. Novak, of course, became a major movie star and, though she was often criticized at the time as a "wooden" actress, her performances in such films as *Picnic* and *Vertigo* are now widely praised. Whatever her skills as an actress, Novak was a remarkably beautiful woman, and it's possible to pick out Elvgren paintings she may have modeled for. Looking at a Kim Novak motion picture of the '50s or early '60s—*Bell, Book and Candle*, for example—is to see a Gil Elvgren painting come to life. Elvgren, however, never worked with the actress he considered to be the embodiment of his perfect model: Novak's role model (and Earl Moran's favorite subject), Marilyn Monroe. Several Elvgren paintings indicate the artist may have used Monroe as a model, anyway, from published photos. Another Monroe rival, Sheree North, makes an apparent appearance wearing an over-stuffed bikini in "Rude Awakening," though there's no record of her ever modeling for the artist. Some sources list Myrna Loy, Donna Reed, Rosemarie Bowe (Mrs. Robert Stack), and Arlene Dahl among his actress models. Most of Elvgren's models did not go on to fame in other fields, however; they were either professional models or simply pretty "civilians" Elvgren approached. "Dad hated looking for models," Drake says. "And that's one reason once he found a good one, he used her over and over again. I've been with him when he would be driving along, see some cute girl walking or riding a bike, stop and ask her if she wanted to pose, give her a card, and drive on." Using amateurs allowed Elvgren to find subjects who had a certain naiveté and freshness. "There are a lot of pretty girls, but they have to be more than that," Elvgren told an interviewer. "Many times I see a pretty girl on the street who at first glance seems to have everything. Often I ask her if she would be willing to pose. But the minute she opens her mouth, I know that she doesn't have what I am looking for." Drake confirms this, saying, "Dad had a funny way of looking at

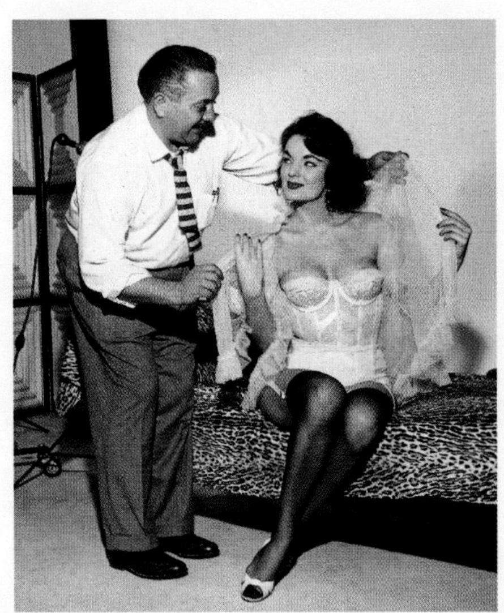

girls. He could spot a flaw in a second, even though no one else could. When he looked at a girl, he would examine her attributes to be a model, while most men might be examining something else entirely." Still, Elvgren wasn't after perfect beauty; he sought something more intangible in his models. He would often secretly test a model by the simple act of handing her a glass of Coca-Cola (what else?) to see if she would "seize the glass as though they were miners grabbing a shovel," or rather accept the glass and "hold it with elegance." If a model displayed, in this simple act, a certain natural grace, then she had what it took to model for Gil Elvgren. Elvgren was all business in his studio and high on his short list of pet peeves was a model who behaved too modestly before his camera. He felt that if a model were too concerned about how high her skirt was riding, or whether the picture she was posing for would come out too racy, that she would convey her discomfort in her posing, and this would be captured in his photographs. "One Hollywood model came complete with her mother to watch over her," Drake remembers. "Dad had the mother help with the posing, but it was one hectic session, for the mom wouldn't let more than just so much leg show or just so much cleavage." While Elvgren preferred the actresses and professional models, because, despite occasional vanity and fits of ego, they were professionals who knew what he wanted when he asked them, he did use a number of local amateurs. Son Drake even provided his father with a few in the later '60s. "I had been to a local nightclub," Drake recalls, "and had seen a really cute go-go dancer who might be good for Dad's work. He met her through me and actually did use her for a NAPA calendar. Another time when I was home on leave, I was dating a very cute girl named Mariann Pilot, and Dad asked her if she would pose for a NAPA calendar. She said yes, she did model for him, and he painted her!" Elvgren's most used model—posing for a

This photo and the one at left were apparently staged for publicity purposes (the calendar in the background matches the model's pose), but it does accurately suggest Elvgren's film-director-style control over his models and setting.

staggering seventy-five paintings — was Janet Rae, who sat for Elvgren from the late 1950s through the late 1960s. She was the daughter of Stu and Helene Rae, close Illinois friends of Gil and Janet, and Drake's godparents; the Raes had moved to Sarasota first, and the Elvgrens followed them there. "I love Janie Rae like a sister," Drake says. "I was raised with her around, and later babysat for her kids. She was almost family — Dad was her godfather." In her high-school days, brunette Janet Rae was a swimmer and diver and wore her hair very short; but wigs and Elvgren's imagination turned her into a long-haired blonde or brunette. Janet Rae recalled that Elvgren would often give her "free reign" to choose costumes, occasionally handing the girl a credit card, and despite a naturally shapely form, the model admitted that occasionally "falsies" or toilet paper were at times required to help fill out a bra beneath a dress. "When the lighting was exactly as he wanted it," she said, "Gil would show me how to pose, positioning my legs, feet arched . . . very important . . . hands just so, head turned this way or that." Another Janet — Elvgren's wife Janet — apparently modeled for him early on, but despite a lovely figure, her four-foot eleven-inch frame made her less than an ideal model. (Elvgren attempted several portraits of his wife but was never satisfied with the results, frustrated that he couldn't capture his wife's beauty.) Drake reports that his mother showed no apparent jealousy of the beautiful models who paraded through her husband's studio, outfitted though it was with a large collection of sexy dresses, filmy lingerie, and open-toed bedroom slippers; Janet trusted him implicitly. Elvgren always made sure an assistant or apprentice was present, rarely working alone with the young women. By all accounts, he was a faithful and devoted husband, deeply in love with his wife. Also petite but perfectly proportioned in the manner of a much taller woman, Anne McFadgen was another of Elvgren's favorite models and posed for him in the 1960s for at least eight paintings and a number of his "universal" billboards. She, too, became a close family friend. Other Elvgren models who posed for multiple (six or more) paintings include Lynn Davis, Mary Anne Rysdyh, Ginger Allison, Marlene Rielly, Lucy Balon, Sue Clarke, and Lorraine Rogers. Posing for less than six paintings were Betty Serrano, Gloria Mize, Marylyn Harold, Kay Lisa, and Pat Lucia. These are all models who posed for Brown & Bigelow paintings from the late '40s into the '60s. Marjorie Shuttleworth posed for several of Elvgren's paintings in the late '60s and early '70s. Older than most of his models — in her forties at the time — Marjorie also dated the artist, after the death of his beloved Janet. According to Drake, they "went together on and off for a long time." Published reports that he married one of his models (presumably Shuttleworth) after his wife's death are erroneous. In fact, after Janet's death, Elvgren confided in his son Gillette, Jr., that he didn't feel he could ever marry again. And he did not.

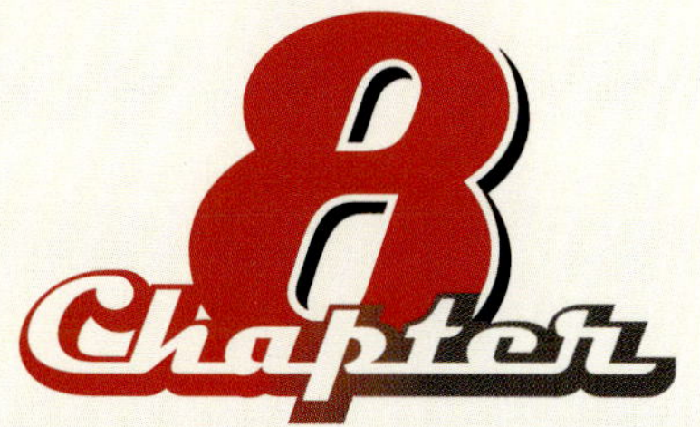

Family Man

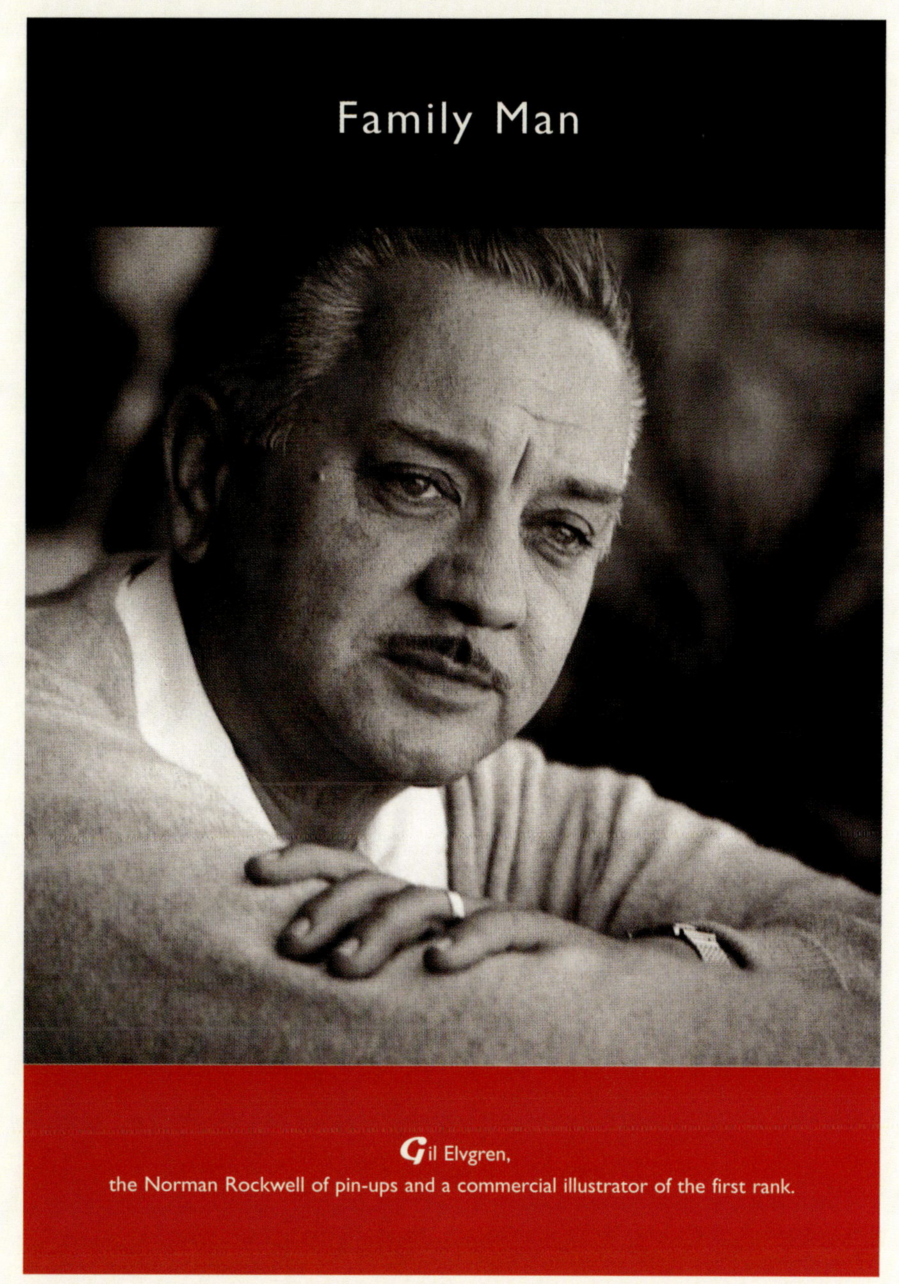

Gil Elvgren,
the Norman Rockwell of pin-ups and a commercial illustrator of the first rank.

By the early '50s, the Elvgrens were living the suburban life in Winnetka, Illinois, near Chicago — golf, church, fishing, family — an ideal, even idyllic existence right out of a Norman Rockwell *Saturday Evening Post* cover. Only a few years before, Gil Elvgren had been living a lifestyle more in line with that of an artist, particularly one whose racy work was frowned upon in more staid, respectable quarters. During the war years, he was something of a party animal, and he and Janet would go out almost every night, their rather affluent lifestyle including a live-in maid. Elvgren's friends on the party circuit included jazz musicians from Chicago nightclubs he frequented, and celebrities including such local luminaries as Dave Garroway, soon to be nationally famous as NBC's *Today Show*'s host, and Burr Tilstrom and Fran Allison, whose hip kid's show *Kukla, Fran and Ollie* was taking the airwaves by storm. How Elvgren's reactionary political views went over in these circles is not known, but perhaps the affable artist was cut some slack because of his considerable personal charm. While he could be opinionated and outspoken, even argumentative, Elvgren — his sweet, gentle shyness disappearing after a drink or two — was a story- and joke-teller of some renown. Though he was something of a minor celebrity during his lifetime, Elvgren was known to dislike public appearances such as panel television shows, where he could easily become tongue-tied; but, loosened up at a party, he could be something of a ham. "He couldn't speak without using his hands," Drake recalls, "and was very imaginative and animated. I never met anyone who didn't like him, even though they didn't agree with him." When the air at a party or cocktail lounge grew too hot with political opinions, Elvgren was known to retreat to the nearest piano. (He played by ear.) He loved music and was a Sinatra and, in later years, Streisand fan; but he also enjoyed classical music — Rachmaninoff, Berlioz, Mendelssohn. Celebrity was of no great import to Elvgren, though the local — and occasionally national — publicity he received did please him. As ill at ease as he was with public appearances, he didn't mind judging beauty contests; in Florida the pin-up artist was often a judge at Miss Sarasota and Miss Florida pageants. His tendency in these pageants was to ignore talent competition, as well as interviews designed to show an entrant's intelligence, and vote for the prettiest young woman, the one most nearly an "Elvgren girl." "Dad was making good money and meeting interesting people," Drake remembers, "but kids grow up, and around '47 my Mom felt Dad was neglecting his three children." When her demands for a change of lifestyle were ignored by her husband, Janet Elvgren moved out of the house on Foxdale Avenue, taking Karen, Drake, and Gil, Jr., with her, heading back to St. Paul. She refused to return until Elvgren changed his ways. He did. Gil Elvgren was deeply in love with Janet and, in his quiet way, adored his three children. "He became, I think, a very good father," Drake says. "He set up archery targets in the yard and taught us to shoot. Long vacations in the North Woods, and in Canada, too. He was a lot of fun with his children on vacations, teasing and playing tricks." The family enjoyed croquet, and Elvgren tossed the baseball with his boys and taught all three children how to shoot. (In the basement of one of their homes, Elvgren erected a fifty-foot gun range.) The kids received swimming and diving lessons, and Elvgren taught them to water-ski himself. He also insisted that his children receive music lessons, though he did not enjoy going to recitals, showing up only for the portions that involved his own kids. With the exception of following his son Gil, Jr.'s high-school football career, Elvgren ignored activities such as school days and class picnics. That minor lapse aside, Elvgren apparently satisfied Janet that he was a good father and family man, although religion was something of a bone of contention between husband and wife. In interviews Elvgren would describe himself as a "church goer," and son Drake feels his father believed in God, though apparently had trouble accepting the Bible as literal truth, particularly the Old Testament. "When my mother became a born-again Christian," Drake recalls, "it created a lot of tension in their relationship." Ironically it was another pin-up artist who brought Janet around to this new way of thinking about Christianity. Al Buell, who with his wife Ruth had long been friends of the family, quit doing pin-ups for Brown & Bigelow, upon becoming a born-again Christian, and moved strictly into magazine illustration and limited-edition prints. "Al and Ruth's faith greatly influenced my mother," Drake attests. Janet stopped drinking, though she did still attend parties with her husband, replacing cocktails with iced tea; this secretly irritated Elvgren. After Janet's death, however, Elvgren moved closer to his beloved wife's way of thinking — her children had come to share her faith — and Drake reports that six months before his father's death, Gil Elvgren "came to a saving knowledge of Jesus Christ." If Janet was bothered by her husband's mildly "sinful" way of making a living, it created few if any ripples in their Rockwell-esque family life. The Elvgrens would even sit at the breakfast or supper table, and Mom and the kids would pitch in ideas for how a girl's skirt might be lifted up (lawn mower? tree limb? bicycle?). Drake recalls, "He would say, 'Okay, I need some help,' and we would all start throwing ideas out. One of us would say something, and he would say something like, 'Done that twice before.'" Still, from these sessions, Elvgren would frequently come away with several workable ideas. "He would also skim through magazines for ads featuring women," Drake remembers. "Sometimes he would see something he thought he would like to paint, like a motorcycle or pelican or bubble pipe, and would then think of a way to somehow wrap a girl around that object. Occasionally he got an idea from television sitcoms, as TV began to be a part of our family life." Drake remembers his father having the kids go through magazines to help clip ads and illustrations by artists he admired, including Edwin Georgi, Harry Anderson, Mark Coomer, Ben Stahl, and his old mentor, Haddon "Sunny" Sundblom.

Gil, Jr., has a similar memory. "When desperate, Dad would offer me ten dollars an idea for every one he used in his paintings," he recalls. "I know it became especially hard for him to come up with a different cowgirl every year." Despite the creative demands, it was a good life for Gil Elvgren. Sometimes working only a few days a week, he enjoyed considerable leisure time, playing golf and pursuing other country-club activities with Janet and his friends. "Dad was always into the neighborhood," Drake remembers. "He liked people, knew all the neighbors and did things with them. . . . The only thing he didn't do was yard work. We always had someone come in for that once a week." Life continued on in much this fashion with a move to Sarasota, Florida, in 1956. Elvgren continued to enjoy "happy hour" at casual bars on Siesta Key in Sarasota, and his "buddies" (with whom he fished, played chess and partied) included bestselling mystery writer John D. MacDonald (only five hundred yards of water separated the Elvgren and MacDonald homes), noted author MacKinlay Kantor, and a number of artists, including Al Buell, Thorton Utz, Ben Stahl, and Stu Rae. On a California model hunt, he became friends with silent movie star Harold Lloyd. Kantor and MacDonald's books made it into at least one Elvgren painting, "Rare Edition," in which a blonde librarian perched precariously on a ladder drops a copy of Kantor's bestseller, *Spirit Lake*, while the spine of a MacDonald novel can be glimpsed near the girl's upraised dress. Screen legend Lloyd got Elvgren interested in 3-D still photography. Gil, Jr., remembers being shocked, at eight years of age, to shake the star's hand and realize Lloyd was missing two fingers. "It's funny, though," Drake recalls, "but Dad got as much pleasure being with anybody as he did with 'royalty.' He was never a snob, and if he liked you, he liked you, and it didn't matter if you were a garbage collector or the mayor." Gil Elvgren was making good money—sixty thousand a year, a considerable sum in 1960s terms—living in "show houses" and driving nice cars, a Cadillac and later a Jaguar and even a Mercedes Benz for himself, a Ford station wagon and later a four-door Dodge for Janet. Drake also recalls a "very fast" Dodge convertible that he borrowed for Saturday night drag racing! But Elvgren did not spoil his children. "Dad made sure his kids grew up with a healthy respect for the dollar," Drake says, "and we knew that nothing came free. There were no new cars, no extravagances for us." Drake once came home from a camping trip and mentioned to his father that he wanted to buy a custom-made knife that cost "a fortune." His father asked him why he didn't buy another, mass-produced knife that was "just as good and not nearly as expensive." Drake told his dad that he wanted "the best." "You can't always have the best," Elvgren told his son. "You always get the best," Drake reminded his dad. "Ah yes," Elvgren said, looking his son straight in the eye, "but I can afford the best." Drake considers this a valuable lesson and says he's used it throughout his life, adding, "It's too bad that Dad didn't listen to his own lessons and save a little. He died broke." Both Drake and Gil, Jr., have fond memories of their father but found him "hard to get close to at times." "He wasn't a 'hugger,'" Drake recalls, "and rarely expressed his love verbally." Gil, Jr., confirms this. "For being such a gracious and generous man, Dad was also shy and not terribly forthcoming with gestures or words of affection." When Drake was having trouble in his early college years, pursuing a party-animal lifestyle that may have seemed all too familiar to his father, Gil Elvgren came to his son and said, "Drake, you have three choices. One, go back to school and get passing grades, and I'll pay your way. Two, get out of the house. Three, join the service, and you'll be welcome here anytime." "Tough love works," Drake says. "I joined the Navy, learned electronics, went to Vietnam, came home, and went back to school, getting straight A's." Janet Elvgren died of pancreatic cancer in May 1966, while Drake was still in Vietnam. Gil Elvgren was devastated. Gil, Jr., says, "He so desperately loved that woman.... For the first time, I saw him as lost, adrift emotionally. When he lost Mother, he lost an anchor in his life. He withdrew from his friends socially, and he also lost something in his art, almost as if his work after this time strangely just stood still." "Dad was living alone," Drake recalls. "I came

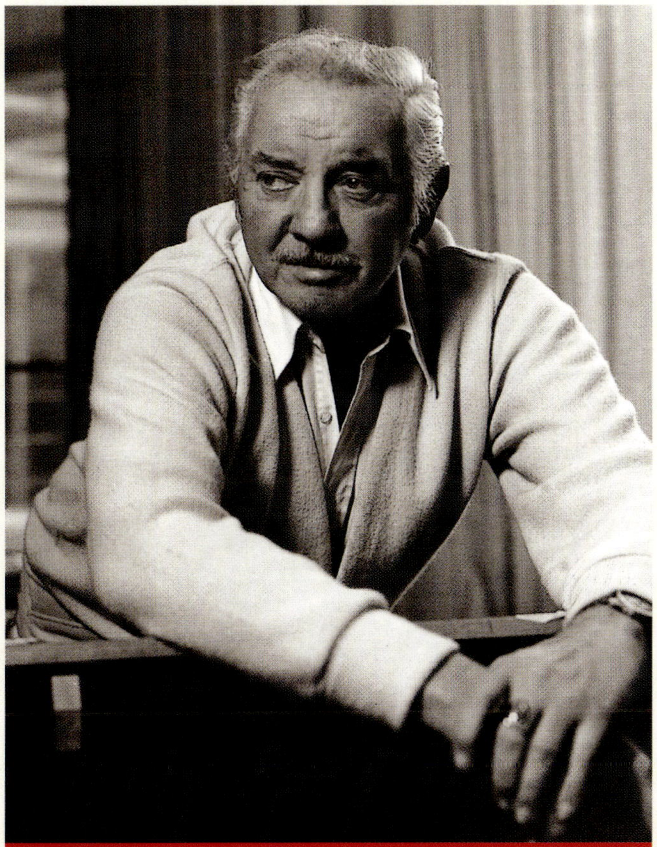

Distinguished, reserved, utterly professional, Gil Elvgren knew only that he had made a career out of his love for art; the beginnings of a revival of interest in his work, at his death in 1980, may have indicated to him the standing he would one day achieve as the Rockwell of the pin-up.

home and lived with him for a couple of years. We became very close friends. It was a very rewarding period in my life, getting to know him a lot better. We would often stay up late and just talk, maybe go down to the Beach Club for a few cool ones. We would share our deepest feelings." This period was also a tough one for Elvgren, the commercial artist. While the Norman Rockwell of Pin-up artists continued successfully painting calendar girls and doing pretty-girl advertising art, long past the glamour-art vogue, even such a star performer had to be affected by the dramatically changed market. By the mid-'70s his only major remaining client was his old reliable, NAPA, for whom he worked up to his death. Much of his time was given over to creating charcoal portraits and an occasional oil portrait. He was even given to swapping services with people, trading portraits or perhaps one of his precious guns for, say, TV or appliance repair. His two sons sent him money from time to time. "Dad just couldn't understand it when the pin-up business went away in the '70s," Drake says. "He was never really able to re-channel his career in other directions. He once said to my brother, probably in the late '70s, that maybe he had sold himself short by doing just pin-ups." But Gil Elvgren did live to see the beginnings of the new interest in pin-ups in general, and his work in particular. Fans began to contact him; in particular, Art Aimsie (whose Girl Whirl was the first gallery of pin-up art) was at the forefront of this renewed interest, with Charles Martignette (who co-authored the Tasachen coffee-table retrospective, *The Great American Pin-up* in 1996) coming up fast. At the same time, Elvgren attracted the attention of so-called comic book fandom. Comic book collectors were caught up in a 1970s revival of interest in "good girl comic book art," fueled by a fascination with fantasy artist Frank Frazetta, famous for his voluptuous girls (who carried a touch of Al Capp's Dogpatch damsels in their genes, as Frazetta was a longtime Capp assistant). Illustrator Elvgren, whose curvaceous cuties had influenced Frazetta in his own lushly painted oils-on-canvas, became a natural focus of fan attention and collecting. This attention must have pleased him, and given Elvgren at least an inkling that his work would survive him. True, his death in 1980 was noted by only a relative handful of pin-up enthusiasts; his last NAPA calendar appeared posthumously, in 1981. But in the intervening years, the resurgence of interest has swelled—as evidenced by Elvgren greeting cards, calendars, posters, trading cards, even wrist watches and cigarette lighters, as well as full-length books like this one. The wholesome, curvaceous, sunnily smiling calendar girls of the Norman Rockwell of Cheesecake—as all-American as Coca-Cola, and just as sweet—remain lively and very much alive, flirtatiously, insistently reminding generation after generation that Gil Elvgren will live forever.

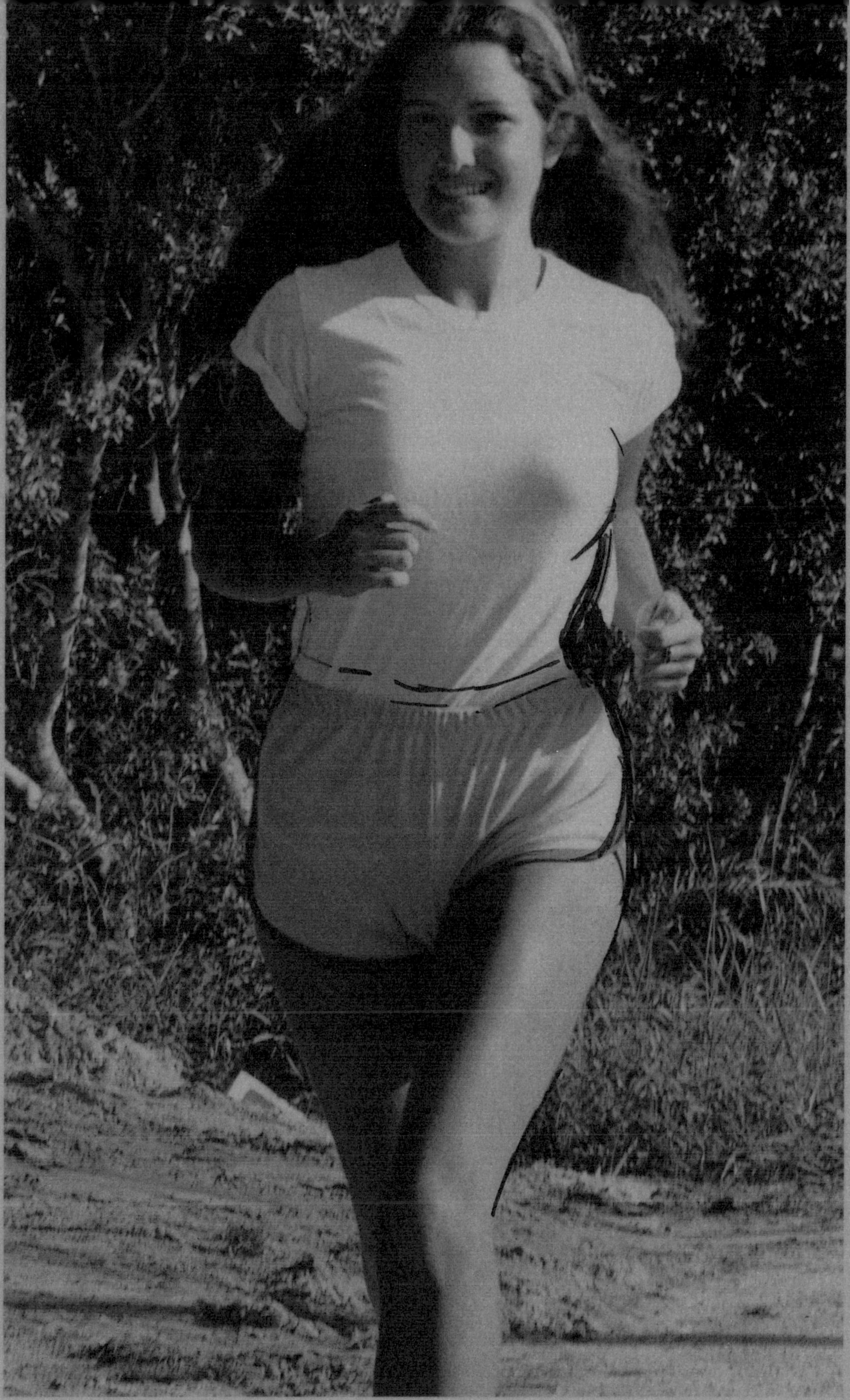

1970s Portfolio

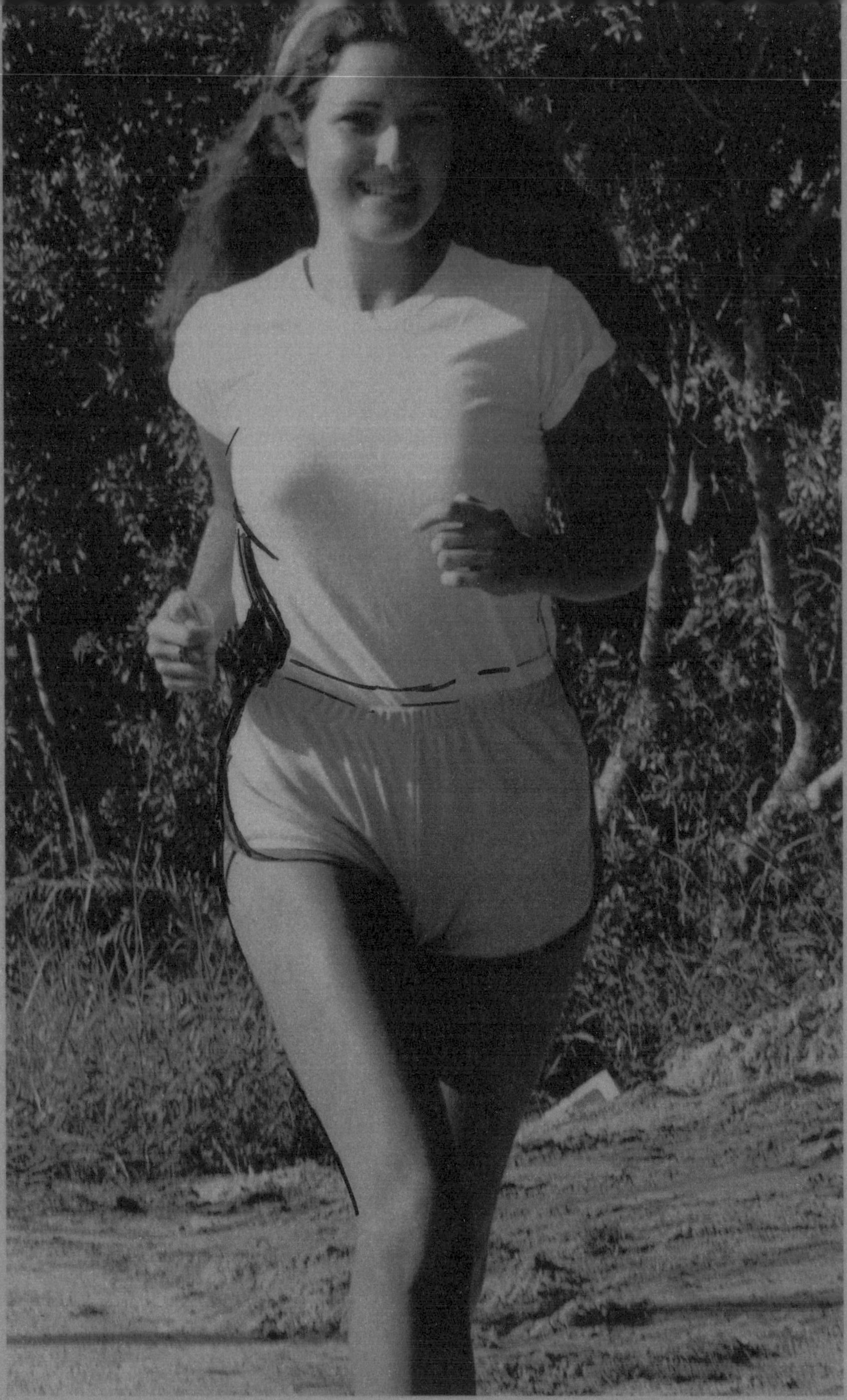

1970s Portfolio

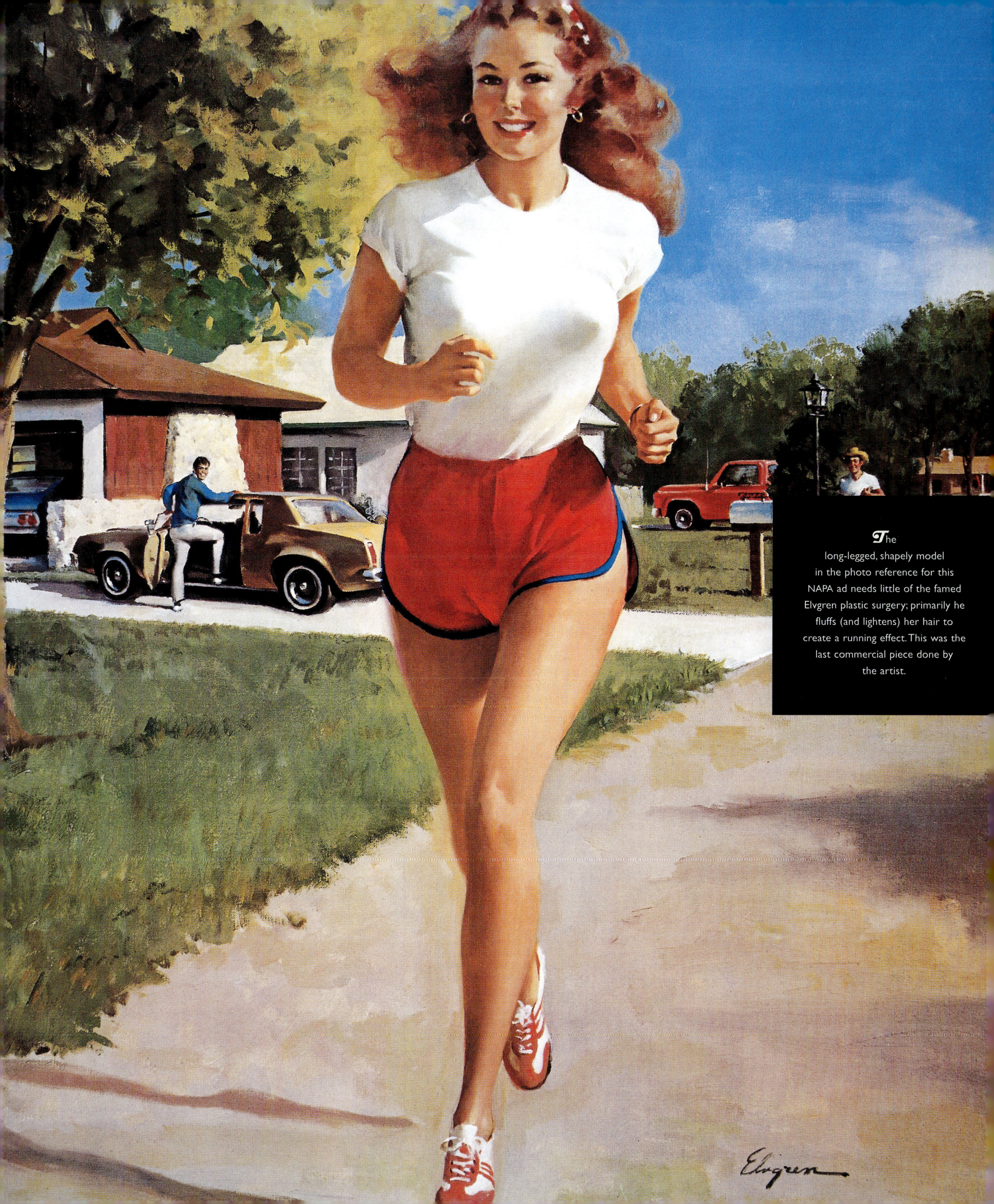

The long-legged, shapely model in the photo reference for this NAPA ad needs little of the famed Elvgren plastic surgery; primarily he fluffs (and lightens) her hair to create a running effect. This was the last commercial piece done by the artist.

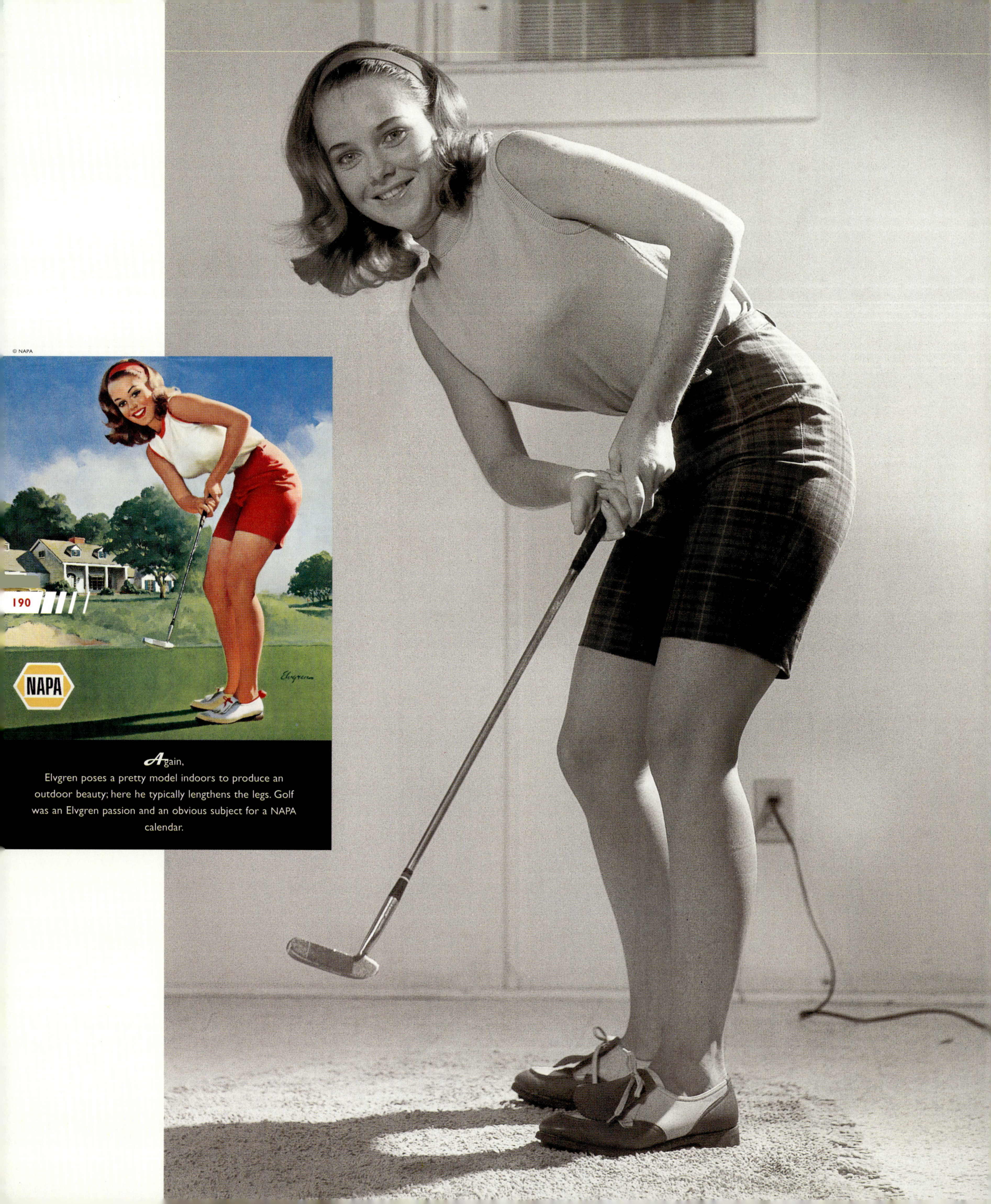

*A*gain, Elvgren poses a pretty model indoors to produce an outdoor beauty; here he typically lengthens the legs. Golf was an Elvgren passion and an obvious subject for a NAPA calendar.

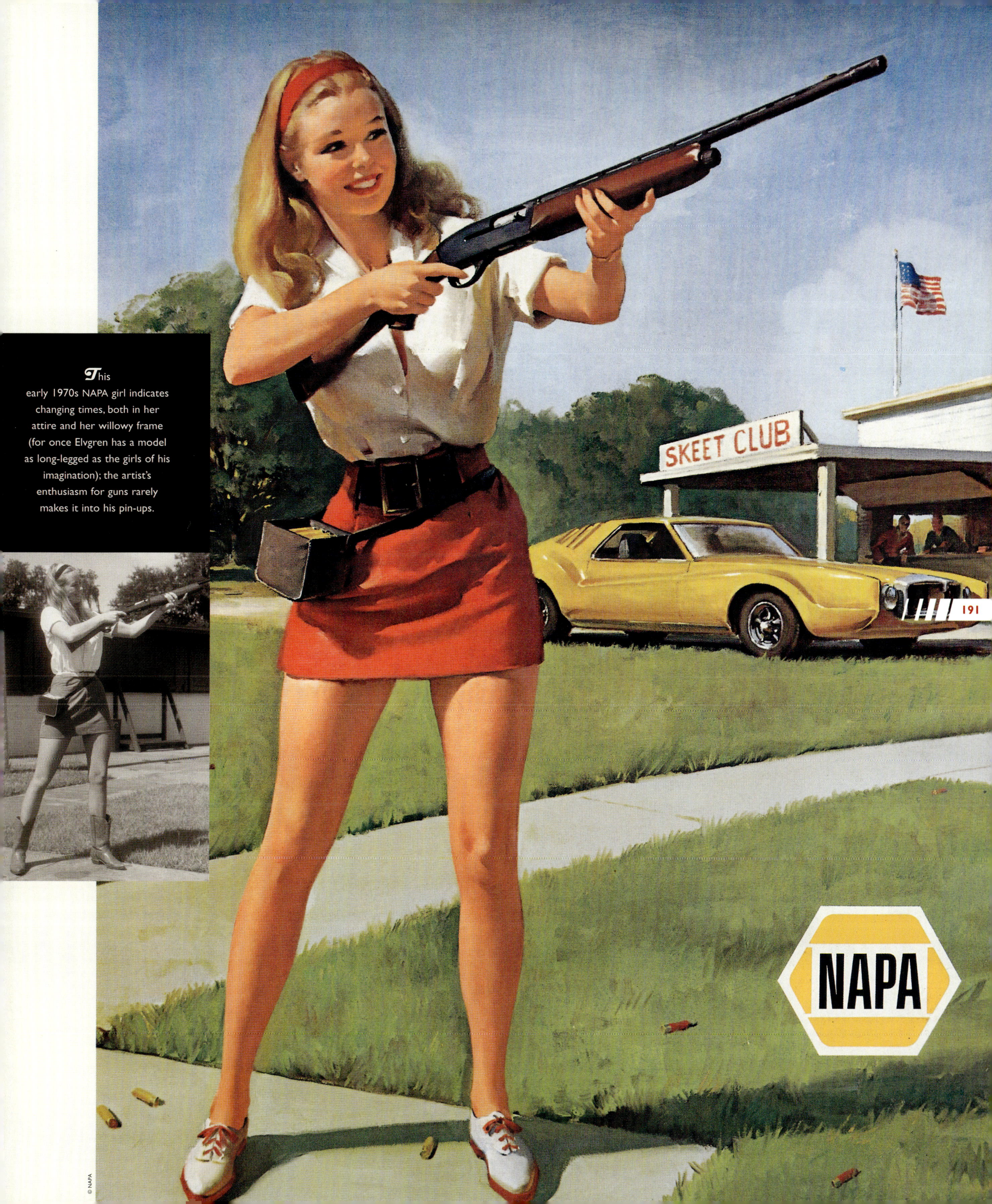

This early 1970s NAPA girl indicates changing times, both in her attire and her willowy frame (for once Elvgren has a model as long-legged as the girls of his imagination); the artist's enthusiasm for guns rarely makes it into his pin-ups.

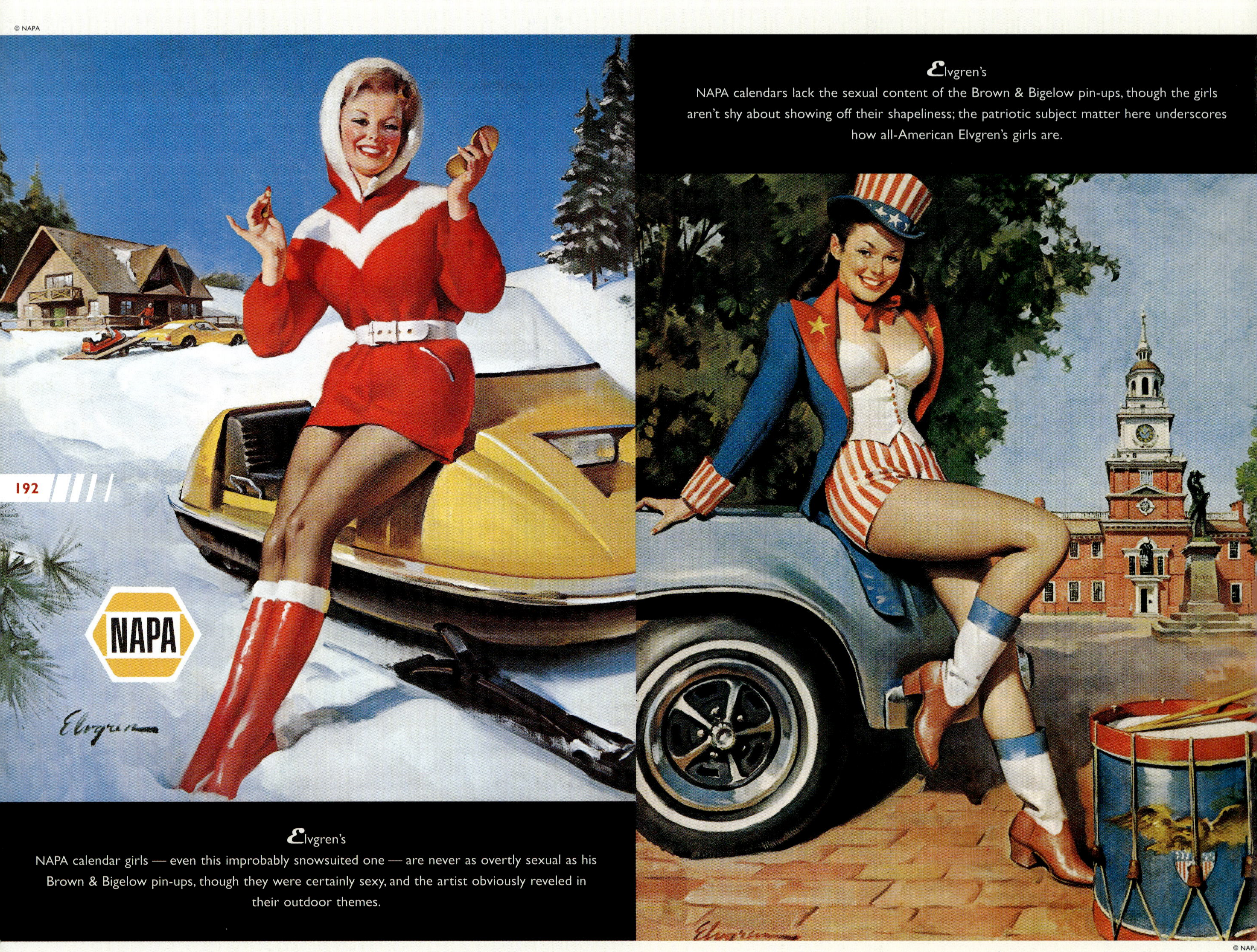

Elvgren's NAPA calendars lack the sexual content of the Brown & Bigelow pin-ups, though the girls aren't shy about showing off their shapeliness; the patriotic subject matter here underscores how all-American Elvgren's girls are.

Elvgren's NAPA calendar girls — even this improbably snowsuited one — are never as overtly sexual as his Brown & Bigelow pin-ups, though they were certainly sexy, and the artist obviously reveled in their outdoor themes.

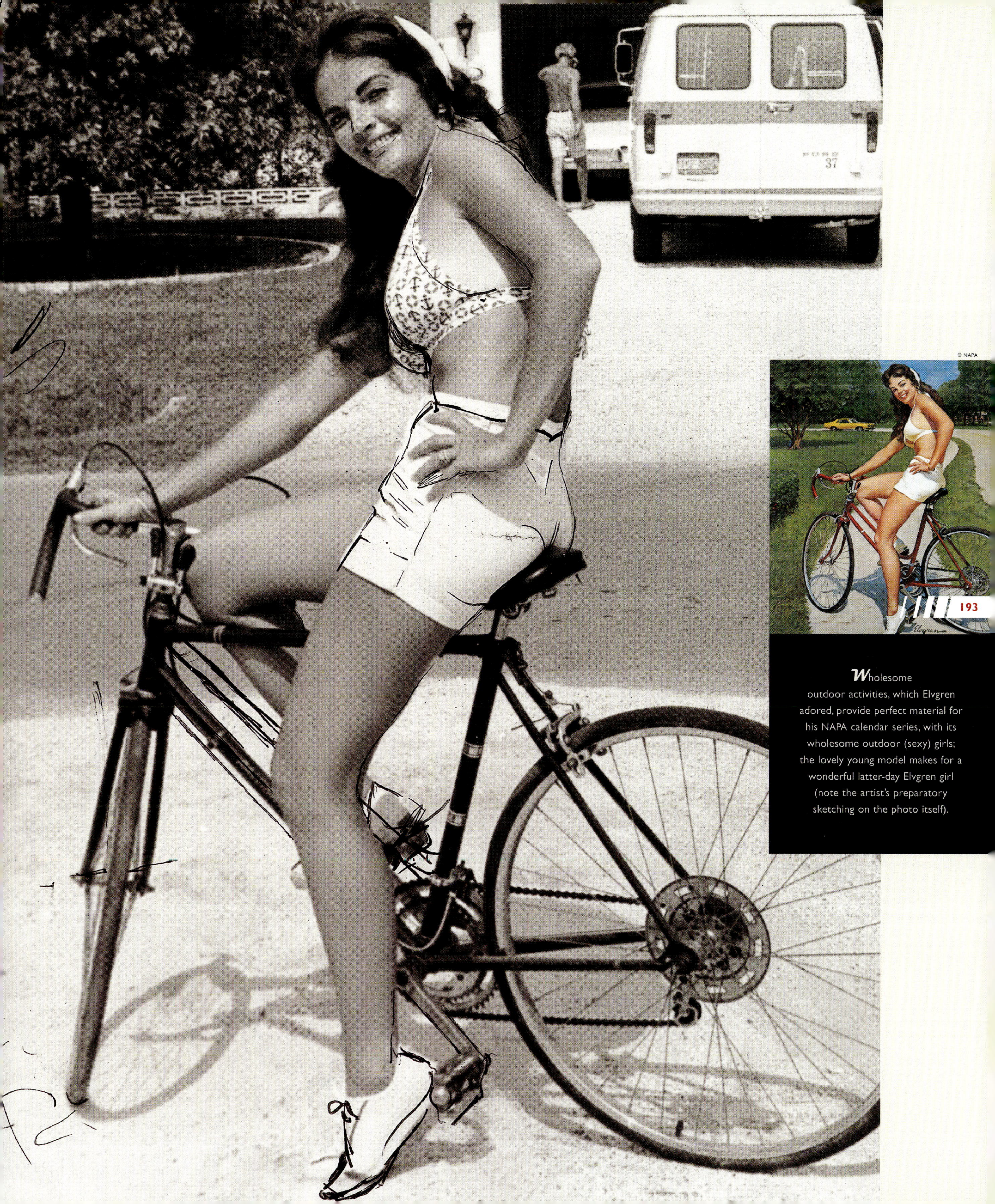

***W**holesome outdoor activities, which Elvgren adored, provide perfect material for his NAPA calendar series, with its wholesome outdoor (sexy) girls; the lovely young model makes for a wonderful latter-day Elvgren girl (note the artist's preparatory sketching on the photo itself).*

*G*il Elvgren, who had entertained servicemen during the war via his early pin-ups, chronicled the postwar world through his advertising accounts, such as NAPA; in this calendar piece, a wholesome lovely rollerskates down a suburban street — just what the American boys were fighting to preserve!

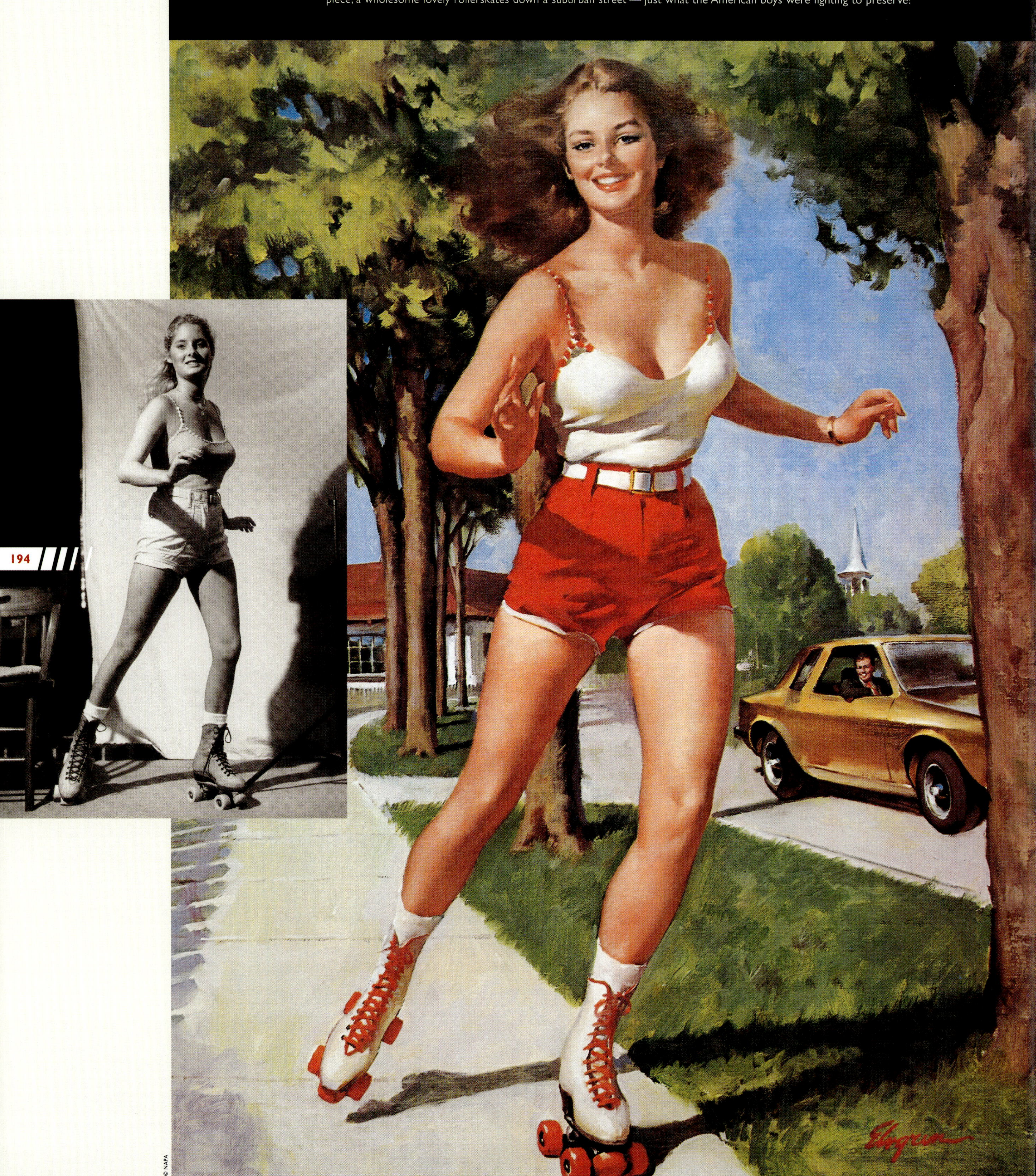

Index

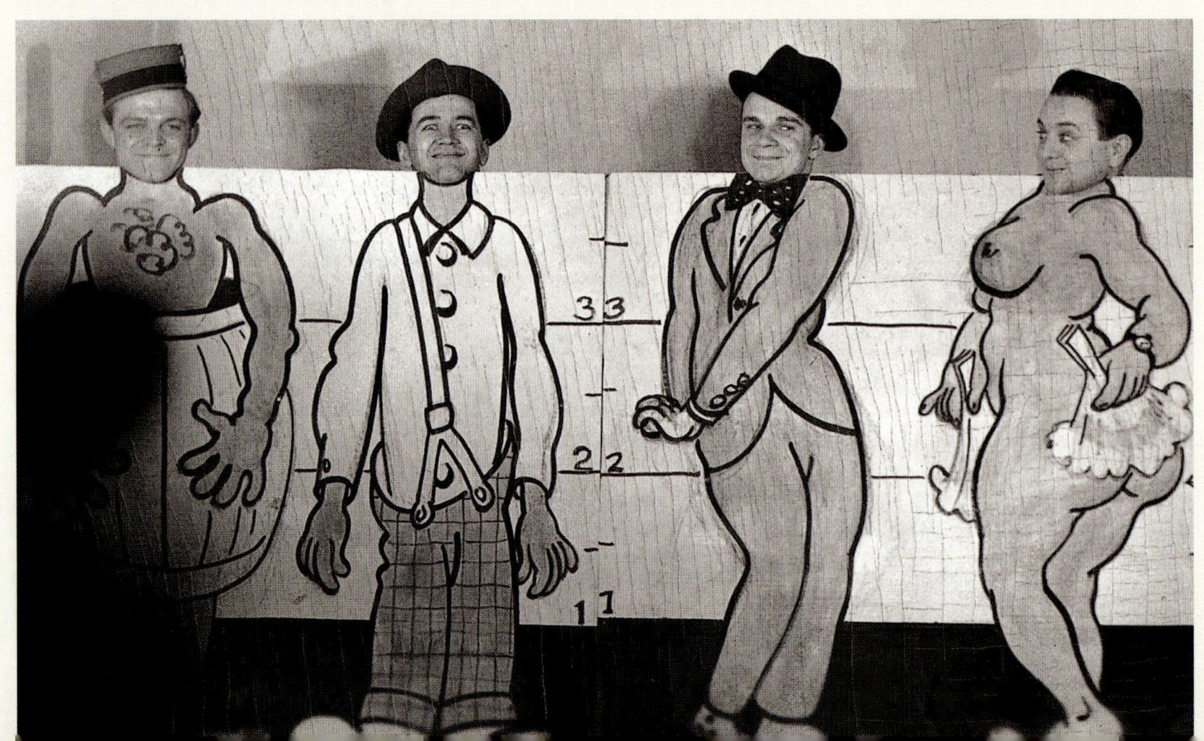
33
22
11

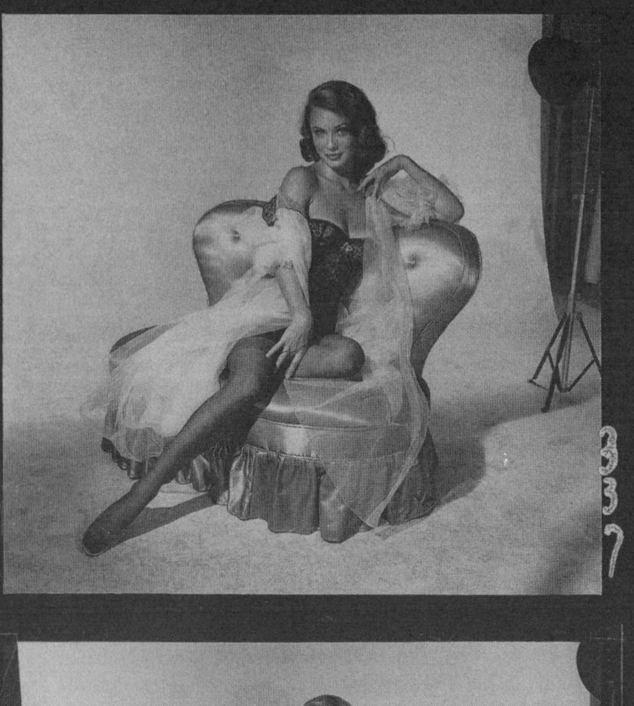
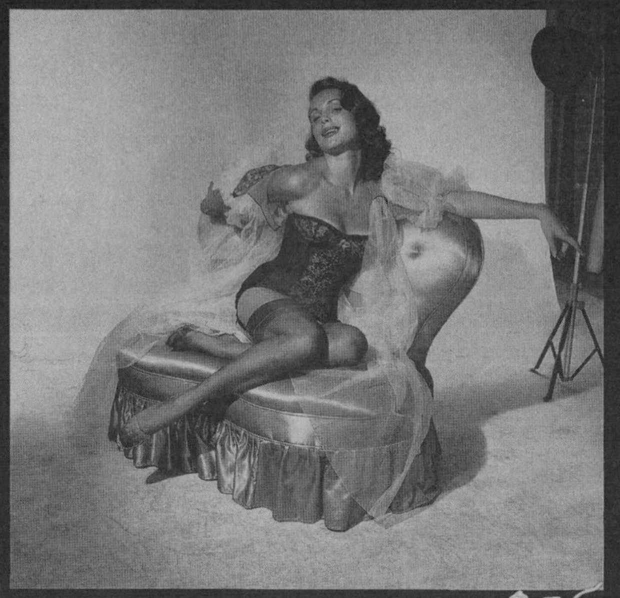
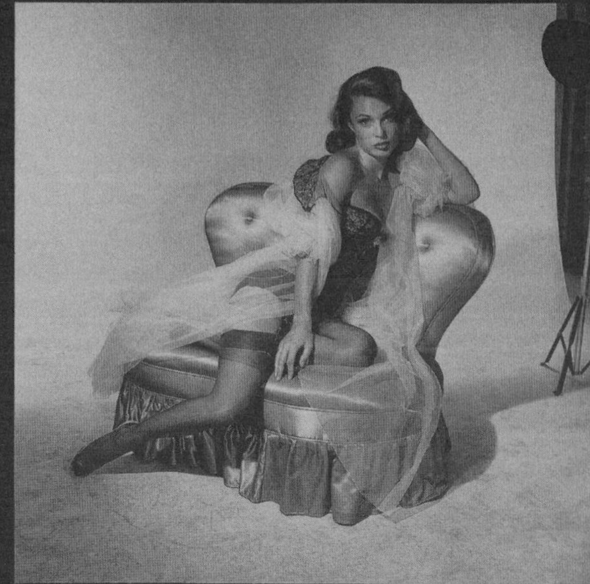
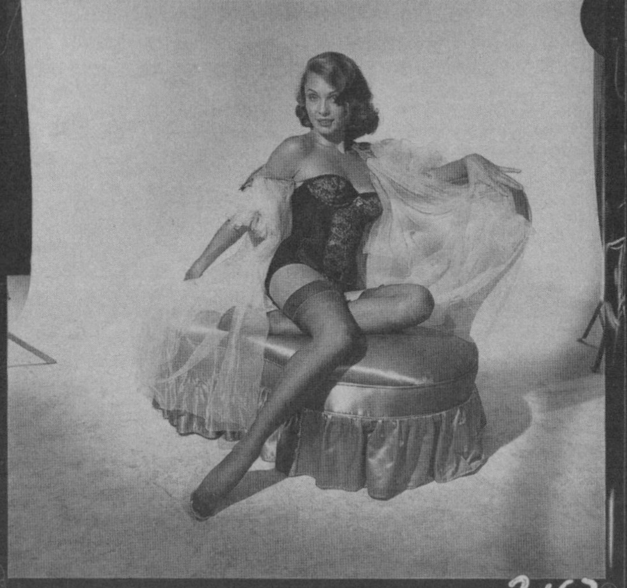
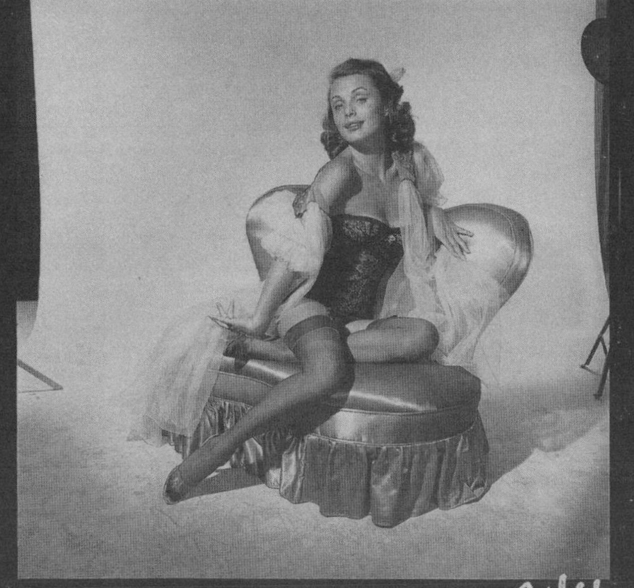
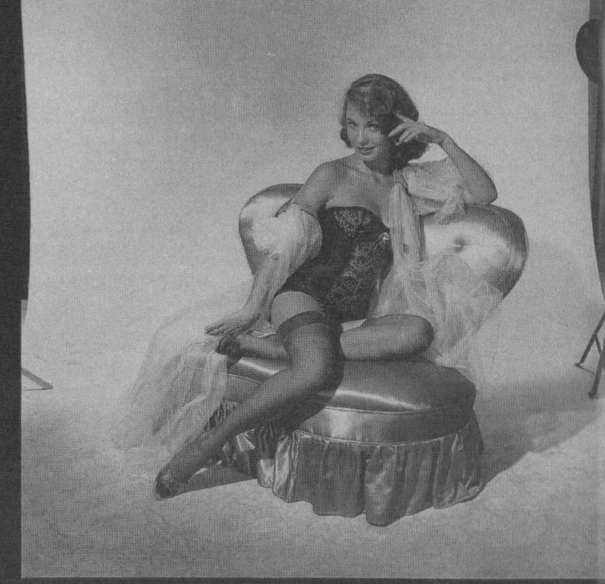
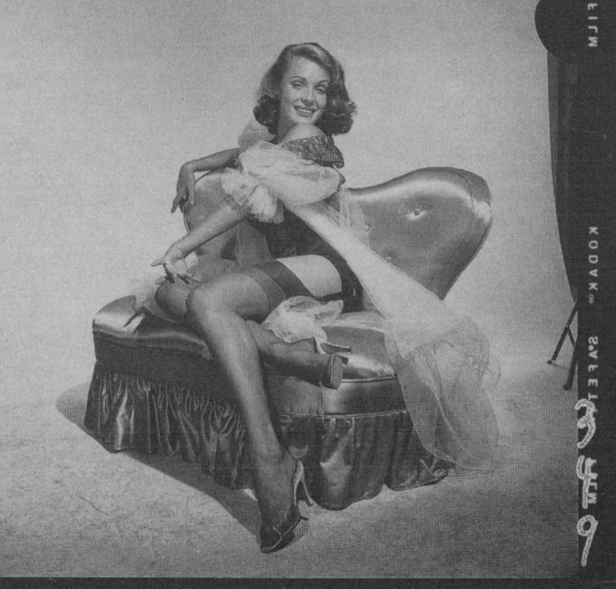
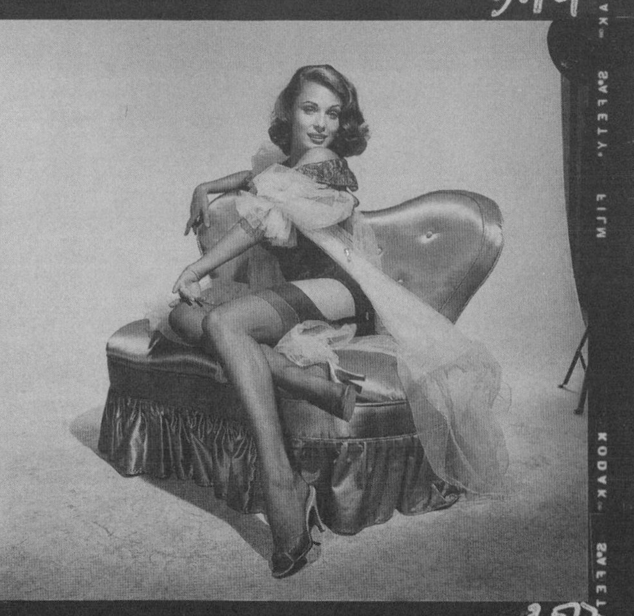
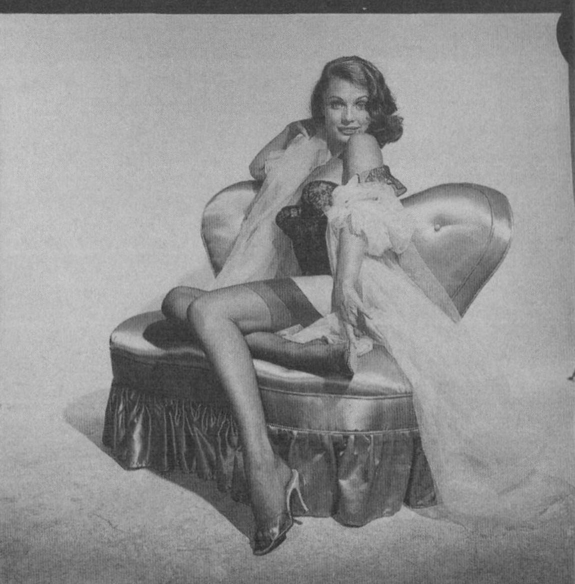